Bilingualism:
The Sociopragmatic-
Psycholinguistic Interface

Bilingualism:
The Sociopragmatic-
Psycholinguistic Interface

Joel Walters
Bar-Ilan University

Psychology Press
Taylor & Francis Group

New York   London

First published by

Lawrence Erlbaum Associates, Inc., Publishers
10 Industrial Avenue
Mahwah, New Jersey 07430

This edition published 2013 by Psychology Press

Psychology Press   Psychology Press
Taylor & Francis Group   Taylor & Francis Group
711 Third Avenue   27 Church Road, Hove
New York, NY 10017   East Sussex, BN3 2FA

*Psychology Press is an imprint of the Taylor & Francis Group,
an informa business*

Cover design by Sean Sciarrone

Library of Congress Cataloging-in-Publication Data

Walters, Joel.
    Bilinguailsm : the sociopragmatic-psycholinguistic interface /
Joel Walters.
        p. cm.

Includes bibliographical references and index.

ISBN 0-8058-4956-4 (cloth : alk. paper)
ISBN 0-8058-5269-7 (pbk. : alk. paper)
1. Bilinguilism.   I. Title.
P115.W35   2004
306.44'6—dc22   2004050606
                                              CIP

Table of Contents

4 Four Processing Mechanisms in Bilingual Production   149

5 Accounting for Bilingual Phenomena with the SPPL Model   199

6 Acquisition, Attrition, and Language Disturbances in Bilingualism   238

References   279

Author Index   306

Subject Index   312

Preface

Until recently, bilingualism was not an independent field of inquiry but was subsumed within other disciplinary studies. In sociology and anthropology, it was a tool for grouping differences and examining cultural uniqueness; in experimental psychology, it was a way to test the latest theory or hypothesis in memory; and, even in linguistics, the study of bilingualism was the exception to the rule in an academic field that promoted universals and ideal types. Today, the monolingual bias is fading, and bilingual inquiry is maturing as a science which needs an account of both its sociopragmatic and psycholinguistic parameters.

The present volume is a first attempt to do some of this interdisciplinary bridgework. The book grew out of the belief that language and linguistic research is the place to summon anthropologists, sociologists, and psychologists of all persuasions in a joint communicative effort. As a preview to the book's lack of orthodoxy, the following is a quotation from the last chapter:

> The distinctions pursued throughout, between structure and processing, between acquisition and use, and between sociopragmatics and psycholinguistics, have been aimed to contribute to a particular view of language. In that view, linguistic structure can never be more than a window to processing. Acquisition cannot be studied without a deep understanding of language use. And psycholinguistic processing is lifeless without sociopragmatic grounding.

In the ideal, the book will bring sociopragmatic aspects of bilingualism in from the field to the experimental labs of cognitive science, exposing the mental processes that lie beneath the social structures and functions of bilingualism. To get at the complex, somewhat elusive, interaction between structure and processing, I propose the Sociopragmatic-Psycholinguistic (SPPL) Model. It is hoped that this model will stimulate debate and research about some of the unstated claims and methods on the field sites and in the laboratories of bilingualism.

The book is structured as follows:

Chapter 1 asserts the uniqueness of bilingualism. It focuses on three phenomena to support this claim – codeswitching, fluency, and translation – and draws related support from bilingual behavior in counting/computing, cursing, and other areas of affect. The chapter situates the inter-disciplinary study of bilingualism as cutting across research in anthropology, sociology, psychology, and linguistics but as distinct from more purely linguistic work in second language acquisition and cross-linguistic studies. The main elements of the

SPPL approach are introduced, including modules for bilingual language choice and affect, and information components that account for social identity, context/genre, intentions, lexical and discourse formulation, and articulation. Four general processing mechanisms – imitation, variation, integration, and control – are also proposed to account for the flow of information among the modules and throughout the model. The SPPL Model is then related to three general issues in cognitive science—brain-behavior relations in neurolinguistics; the discrepancy between attitudes and behavior in social psychology; and the role of intentions in models of language behavior. These issues are framed in phenomenological, sociolinguistic, psycholinguistic, and neurolinguistic arguments for why the study of bilingualism needs yet another model of bilingual processing.

Chapter 2 presents ten models of bilingualism. There are more, but the ones selected come the closest to an opening for dialogue across the sociopragmatic-psycholinguistic divide. From the structural approaches of Carol Myers-Scotton, Michael Clyne, and Peter Auer in linguistics, processing claims that go beyond structure are identified. From the experimental laboratories of Anette de Groot and Judith Kroll, David Green, and Francois Grosjean, conceptual opportunities to incorporate sociopragmatics into experimental work are explored. The ethnographic, sociolinguistic voices of Ana Celia Zentella and Ben Rampton illustrate multiple levels of processing. The chapter ends with two approaches, Nanda Poulisse and Kees de Bot, chosen for review because of their grounding in monolingual models of speech production. In laying out common issues as well as the relevant differences, the chapter also describes the work of others which nourish the SPPL Model and its processing mechanisms.

Chapters 3 and 4, respectively, describe the structural elements and processing mechanisms of the SPPL Model of bilingualism, explaining how it differs from other models, and illustrating the kind of data that contributed to its development. Two modules, which organize and store information about *language choice* and *affect,* make it possible to look at the interplay between language choice and emotion at every stage of the game. The language choice module supports interconnected explanations of both sociopragmatically and psycholinguistically motivated codeswitching and other bilingual phenomena. The affective module offers an analogous framework for distinguishing socially and pragmatically-motivated slips of the tongue, and more phonetically and phonologically based tip-of-the-tongue and slips of the tongue phenomena.

The language choice and affect modules interact with a series of five other elements that map out the universe of bilingual speech from the most sociopragmatic grounding in elements like identity to psycholinguistic aspects of speech formulation. Each component is an attempt to illustrate something about language production in general and bilingual processing in particular. The SPPL Model assumes that L1 and L2 information is grounded in the social world, and language choices are presumed to be possible at every stage of production from intention to articulation.

Shaped like a ladder and closely interrelated, the SPPL Model creates a structure through which is possible to map out the way four processing engines interact with structure through every stage of bilingual speech production. The four mechanisms that drive the flow of information in the SPPL Model are: *imitation, variation, integration,* and *control.* Chapters 3 and 4 try to methodically track the interrelationship between structure and process in bilingual speech production, illustrating each stage with concrete examples.

The SPPL Model inherits much from its sociopragmatic origins and bases. Chapters 3 and 4 try to spell out in detail how this heritage is enriched by integrating psycholinguistic approaches. Other key elements that differentiate this model from others are the genre component that discriminates between conversations and scripts, and the centrality of the notion of intentions. As one follows the model, another assertion emerges, an assertion that stretches beyond the strict boundaries of bilingual research: that bilingual lemmas are not universal, invariant representations of lexical knowledge.

Chapter 5 returns to the phenomena that are central to bilingual processing: codeswitching, fluency/interference, and translation. SPPL and its processing mechanisms are used to account for: (a) sociopragmatic and psycholinguistic differences in these three bilingual phenomena; (b) the import of identity, contextual, and discourse functions in sociopragmatic CS; (c) directionality and triggering in psycholinguistic CS; and (d) differences among fluency, automaticity, and completeness in bilingual processing.

This chapter shows how sociopragmatic codeswitching is distinguished from structural-psycholinguistic codeswitching in terms of intentionality and directionality. Sociopragmatic CS is goal-driven and motivated by external, contextual factors. Structural-psycholinguistic CS stems from individual linguistic and mental factors: in particular, lexicalization differences between two languages and disturbances in word retrieval. Sociopragmatic factors easily prompt CS to both L1 and L2, while word finding and fluency are more likely to lead the bilingual to the safe haven of the preferred or primary language. Interference, when CS does not work perfectly, is a useful starting point for a discussion about fluency, automaticity, and completeness in bilingual processing.

The remaining topics in Chapter 5, translation and interpretation, counting and computing, and cursing, are treated more selectively. The study of simultaneous interpretation will find more relevance in the sociopragmatics of SPPL--in particular the respective identities of the speaker and interpreter, context, and genre--while written translation will benefit more from its psycholinguistic aspects for formulation and articulation in examining questions about lexical gaps, fuzzy categories, and word retrieval. The chapter ends by making the book's methodological subtext explicit, offering a set of guidelines for research on bilingual processing.

Chapter 6 applies the SPPL Model to the everyday problems of bilingual child language acquisition, attrition and loss, and language disorders. The section on acquisition focuses on questions of lexical differentiation and translation equivalents among child bilinguals. It suggests that the basic processes of discrimination and classification and the variation mechanism are critical to a fuller understanding of acquisition in bilingualism. The section also argues that translation equivalents in early bilingual lexical acquisition are not a purely lexical phenomenon but can be seen to conform to Eve Clark's pragmatic 'principle of contrast.' This section also raises the somewhat unorthodox idea that codeswitching and translation may be useful in teaching second languages.

The investigation of loss and attrition in bilingualism presents an unresolved problem regarding how to distinguish language structures that have been lost from those which were never acquired. The chapter suggests that attrition research begin to address this problem by looking more closely at processing issues. This chapter also demonstrates how three components in SPPL – the language choice module, the intentional component, and the formulator – can be used to integrate social and psycholinguistic information in studies which have heretofore focused almost exclusively on the lexicon. SPPL's imitation and variation processing mechanisms are suggested as potentially useful for getting at some of the common variance between attrition in language pathology and language loss due to social factors such as immigration.

The chapter ends with an application of the model to the study of language disturbances in bilingual children. The interface between the fields of language disorders and bilingualism poses special problems, both ethical and technical, which have made scientific progress especially difficult. In laying out some of these difficulties, I juxtapose the idea that bilingualism leads to cognitive advantages against a consensus that language disorders are cognitively debilitating. These competing concerns raise a possibility that bilingualism might be cognitively stimulating for children whose language does not develop normally. The more conventional position, that bilingualism and language disorders both have enervating effects on the child's limited cognitive resources, raises serious questions for the line of research that argues for the cognitive advantages of bilingualism. Leaving these questions to horse racing fans, the remainder of the section is devoted to outlining issues and creating a framework for examining bilingualism and language disorders as an integral element of social and psycholinguistic phenomena. SPPL is offered as a starting point for an assessment framework for studying and diagnosing bilingual children with language disorders. The approach is illustrated with examples from social identity, speech acts, and basic level processes of classification.

I gratefully acknowledge my intellectual roots in sociology at Dartmouth College and in sociopragmatics in the first years of the Program in Applied

Psycholinguistics at Boston University. Bruce Fraser was an advisor and mentor then and has remained one throughout my academic life. Paula Menyuk's influence will be evident. My colleagues and friends at Bar-Ilan University deserve special thanks--in particular, Jonathan Fine who read the manuscript at various stages of its life. My students and former students--in particular David Hanauer, Shimon Baumel, Zhanna Burstein-Feldman, Julia Festman, and Inbal Regev, contributed encouragement, data, and challenges to the reasonable as well as outrageous claims. But most of all my thanks go to my friend Yuval Wolf, with whom I share most of what I know about philosophy of science and cognitive psychology, and lots more about the important things in life.

Last, but by no stretch of the imagination least, I want to express my appreciation to my colleagues at Lawrence Erlbaum Associates: To Bill Webber who early on passed the baton to Cathleen Petree. Cathleen, whose professional eyes and ears made my sociopragmatic voice clearer and set a high standard for the written quality of the manuscript. She indirectly guided me to my writing tutor, Mike Eilan, who was a lot more than an editor on this book.

My wife Lora and my children are my personal bilingual legacies. They share with me in dedicating this book to the blessed memories of my parents, Mitchell G. and Natalie N. Walters, and to their antecedent American monolingualism.

1 Bilingual Phenomena

FROM PSYCHOLINGUISTICS TO SOCIAL COGNITION: TOWARD A COGNITIVE SOCIOLINGUISTICS

For a bilingual, speaking in two languages and flipping between them is as easy and as natural as breathing. It's harder, however, to describe the phenomena of bilingualism than it is to come up with a scientifically reasonable way of talking about breath. Bilingualism is a complex facility, and any attempt to describe it, of necessity calls on distinctly different perspectives.

Within a sentence, across speaking turns, from topic to topic, setting to setting, listener to listener, bilinguals of all kinds weave their two languages in ways that mesmerize the untutored observer, not unlike a piano-violin duet. The child of a two language home, the native-born child of immigrant parents, the hearing impaired user of ASL and spoken English, the hotel desk clerk, the hospital intake nurse, the fruit vendor in the open market, the airport control tower operator, and the student on a study abroad program all play the tune in clearly different ways. There are both sociopragmatic and psycholinguistic factors involved in this duet, and it seems a matter of which–or both–perspectives one chooses. The tremendous progress in bilingualism research during the past five years, with two new journals and a variety of annual international conferences devoted solely to the topic, has created the need to adjust perspectives with a model that accounts for the breadth of progress being made.

The focus here is on bilingualism, but the center of gravity is language itself, and as such, this work chooses a linguistics that incorporates sociopragmatic as well as psycholinguistic schemata and structural as well as processing constructs to account for the variety of influences that are part of the bilingual experience and essential to explain bilingual phenomena.[1]

This is not, however, the only level of complexity. When a bilingual speaks, even in the most extravagantly codeswitched sentence, words come out in an ordered, linear sequence. The factors that make this take place are densely layered and largely non-sequential. A bilingual might decide to choose a word or phrase based on participants in the conversation, the memory of similar previous interactions, the inability to match tenses, a stutter brought upon by the genre called for in the particular time or place, and the tools and impediments of routine and inclination she uses to stay focused on target while hearing and talking in two languages.

The dynamic nature of the various influences which created that linear codeswitched sentence make it intuitively obvious that structure alone will do a poor job of accounting for this dense interactive layering, and we need to go beyond the structure-function divide and incorporate the notions of both structure and processing into a sociopragmatic-psycholinguistic model. Things start to get complicated before we have even started the first sketch of the model that makes up this book.

To make navigation through this multidimensional construct easier and more productive, I have adopted a matrix-oriented approach that specifies how information flows through the model in a process of constant interaction with non-linear elements of consciousness, language and surroundings. The matrix with its granular foundations creates order, and may also be useful to identify areas of scientific interest worthy of future research or dialogue.

The methodological goals of the present work also aim for broad scope—including variety in data gathering settings and techniques. Research on social aspects of bilingualism is typically based on ethnographic field research or on 'reported language use' from interviews or questionnaires. Psycholinguistic studies, on the other hand, are generally conducted in laboratory settings, and tend to ignore social aspects of bilingualism. Both orientations tend to make assumptions based on aggregated data from anonymous individuals or groups, even when the real interest is individual bilingualism. Another purpose is to bring together a range of research settings and methodological approaches, while trying to make the methodology an integral part of substantive theory (e.g. Anderson, 1996).

Professional translators know that the act of converting complex thoughts and images into another language often exposes problems that are superficially imperceptible to the native reader because semantic differences in concepts across languages tend to test the chains of argumentation. Those acts of translation go beyond the words and grammar of a particular sentence or paragraph, beyond the structure of the source text. They depend on whatever we choose to call meaning—a kind of substance that the act of translation moves from one context with its places, people and language to another.

Analogously, a model of bilingual processing must by default test the robustness and resilience of monolingual models and concepts, not because it sets out to do so, but because the transposition of assumptions, models and theoretical constructs to a two language situation can expose cracks in seemingly solid foundations. We must not forget that bilingualism is not a 'special case' with unique phenomena. Many hundreds of millions of people are bilingual and language models have to take this into account. This book does not intend to enter the labyrinth of monolingual processing, but if that does happen to the reader, it will be fortuitously interesting.

The book is structured as follows: Chapter 1 describes the issues, delineates some borders and raises the big questions it is hoped this book will have some part in answering. Chapter 2 describes the depth of work and context created by those researchers in the field whose work is most relevant to this investigation.

Chapters 3 and 4 are the heart of the book, with Chapter 3 describing the structure of the Sociopragmatic Psycholinguistic (SPPL) Model and Chapter 4 specifying the processing mechanisms in the model. In Chapter 5 we return to use the SPPL Model to explain unique bilingual phenomena, and in Chapter 6 to look at applications–to language acquisition, language loss, and language disturbances.

The rest of this chapter proceeds as follows: After situating the study of bilingualism in a range of disciplines that deal with language contact and doing some simple fence work, I lay out some issues in cognitive science this work relates to. Then I introduce the SPPL Model along with the phenomena the model intends to account for. Finally, I present four arguments motivating the need for the model.

To summarize, an integrated framework to study bilingualism is intended:
- ❏ to show that language is essentially a social phenomenon
- ❏ to delineate the interaction between structures and processes in bilingualism
- ❏ to create a clearinghouse for examining data from the various disciplines involved in researching bilingualism
- ❏ to show that methodology does not have to be compromised to accommodate sociopragmatic as well as psycholinguistic phenomena

SITUATING BILINGUALISM: CONSTRAINTS, BORDERS AND LIMITS

The limits of this book are indicative of its biases, and implicitly indicative of those with whom we wish to engage in dialogue. Some of the biases have already been referred to. There are several others that need to be made more explicit, with reasons given for the roads not taken.

Three related (but relatively independent) lines of research have addressed some of the issues in this book: second language acquisition, cross-linguistic studies, and bilingualism.

Second language acquisition (SLA) studies have been concerned with the course of development as well as with processes and strategies at various stages of language learning. Data collection in SLA studies tends to be motivated recently by linguistic theory, focused on structural or functional aspects of spoken language and based on natural language speech samples. Generally, this line of research has been less interested in social and pragmatic aspects of language use, be it language use in social contexts or language use and processing in laboratory experiments. On the other hand, language use is the primary focus of this work. (For exceptions to this trend in SLA, see the work in inter-language pragmatics, Bardovi-Harlig, 1999; Kasper, 2001 and studies on age and critical period, Birdsong, 1999.)

Cross-linguistic studies take language structure and language acquisition as primary concerns. They are usually conducted in the framework of generative linguistic theory, following the lead of first language acquisition research. The present work is interested in structure and generative theory only as much as it can tell us something about bilingual processing and bilingual individuals.

Studies in bilingualism have proliferated so widely and rapidly in recent years that most scholars will now find it difficult even to keep up with the reading. A great deal of bilingual research has roots in both sociolinguistic and psycholinguistic approaches, but by and large bilingual studies have followed disciplinary tracks. My focus on structural as well as functional aspects of bilingualism is an attempt to integrate methods and findings in a model of bilingual processing.[2]

To attempt this synthesis, I had to sacrifice comprehensive coverage of the wealth of bilingualism research published recently. In choosing to enter into dialogue with a particular researcher, I have sought those works that address questions of processing as well as representation, the sociopragmatic as well as the psycholinguistic. In doing so, primarily syntactic/structural approaches to the study of second language acquisition (e.g. Epstein, Flynn, & Martohardjono, 1996), bilingual codeswitching (e.g. MacSwan, 2000; Poplack, 1997), and contact linguistics (e.g. Winford, 2002) are largely ignored. Poplack's goals and assumptions will help clarify why. Her main interest is to address questions in linguistic theory, which focus on language and its structure, rather than on use and processing. In Poplack's words: "A primary goal of any study of language mixture is to determine the properties of internal grammars of bilinguals" (1997:199). Her assumption is that structural analysis should precede and guide sociolinguistic investigation (1997:178).

Poplack's approach is specifically concerned with grammatical constraints on codeswitching. In this tradition, the grammar is autonomous while the speaker is subservient to the syntax. This orientation fits well with interests in language as an autonomous system, but not with a focus on integrating social and psycholinguistic aspects of processing, where the speaker's intentions and behavior may be more important than the grammar.

The present work also slights developmental issues, focusing on processing in language use. Thus, Pienemann's (1998) contributions to the role of processing in second language acquisition and developmental studies of bilingualism (e.g. Bialystok, 2001; Dopke, 1992; Muller & Hulk, 2001) are not treated here. In the same vein, research that examines correlations between bilingualism and cognitive development is not referred to explicitly (e.g. Cummins, 1991).

Beyond the ten models and approaches reviewed here explicitly (see Chapter 2), there are others potentially relevant for their interactive and processing perspectives, e.g. Dijkstra's Bilingual Interactive Activation (BIA) Model (Van Heuven, Dijkstra, & Grainger, 1998), Emmorey's (2003) studies of bilingual signers, and Herdina and Jessner's (2001) Dynamic Model of trilingualism. Although this work is not examined in detail, due to limitations of space and in the interests of simplicity, it is referred to when relevant, for example, when issues such as language tags and interactivity come up.

Beyond the domestic concerns of these three disciplines spawned by an interest in the study of bilingualism, there are general issues in cognitive science that bear on the work that follows. Three such issues are introduced in the following section.

BETWEEN MIND AND METHOD: THE COGNITIVE PRISM OF BILINGUALISM

The attempt to create an integrated framework for the study of social and psychological aspects of bilingualism raises several issues: one substantive, another methodological, and a third which is as yet unresolvable, but is becoming so important that it deserves serious consideration by anyone conducting research in the field.

- ❏ The substantive issue is how to get at the hinges that link structure and processing. The position here is that those hinges are in fact the intentions of the individual bilingual speaker manifested through various stages of speech production. Language data, from codeswitching in spontaneous speech to latencies in bilingual lexical decision tasks, need to be evaluated in terms of the roles that intentionality, will, and purpose play in human behavior. The idea of a stimulus as the beginning of a linear chain that causes a response is very different from the notion of a stimulus in a human being who should give himself some credit for intentional behavior if he chooses to write about the subject.

- ❏ A problem that has haunted social psychologists and has only recently begun to raise its specter in the study of bilingualism is the discrepancy between attitudes and behavior. Voters don't always respond in pre-election surveys in the same ways they vote; and bilinguals don't always speak straight about codeswitching even though they codeswitch fluently and frequently. This problem is important for integrating data about language attitudes with findings about language behavior, in laboratory tasks as well as in field-based investigations. Even a tentative resolution of this question is needed to assess the kind of data that would be both relevant and desirable in the integrated study of sociopragmatic and psycholinguistic information in bilingual processing.

- ❏ A third issue, not addressed expressly in this book, but which is likely to increase in importance as new technologies expose more and more detail about the anatomy and physiology of the brain, is the language-brain connection. In neurolinguistics, this issue revolves around 'localization of function,' but it goes beyond, touching on the extent to which structure (of the brain) and processing (of language) are mapped one onto the other. In second language acquisition, one question that follows from this one is whether cognitive activity, for example, when a monolingual learns a second language, might bring about changes in human neurobiology. An affirmative response to this question helps make an argument for a bilingual processing model that is more than just a monolingual clone. For studies of bilingualism, this question is reversed, and monolingual processing is seen as a subset of plurilingual processing. The question then becomes: How does the human brain, eminently capable of multi-tasking, function in a situation of reduced cognitive demand such as monolingual processing?

These three issues, addressed briefly here, form different parts of the book which follows, the first as a core part of the argument, the second as methodological subtext, and the third as something for the reader to keep in the back of his/her mind.

CONSISTENT ENDS BY VARIABLE MEANS: A ROLE FOR INTENTION AND VARIATION

Two constructs that have yet to come under close scrutiny in bilingual research are intention and variation. Often, in what's considered the 'best' of experimental psychology, the only place that intention finds expression is in the instructions dictated to the subject by the experimenter. In many, perhaps most, studies of human behavior, the human subject is more often *object* than *subject*. In this tradition, intentions are considered external, manipulable, and in general an experimental nuisance to the core interest of the study. This view of human information processing affords exaggerated importance to external stimuli as the starting point and basis for behavior while ignoring the internal origin and nature of intentions. That which cannot be manipulated may still exist, even and especially for those most ostensibly free of the behaviorist tar brush. Or in simple terms, every day bilinguals deliberately and intentionally choose, many times, which of their two languages to use, so we cannot ignore intentions.

In this experimental tradition, variation is also considered a disturbance, and an obstruction to the proverbial quest for statistical significance. The theoretical bias underlying the present work is that intentions and variation need grounding in the design and method of any study of bilingualism, whatever its orientation.

The road to intentions, said to be found at the conceptualizing stage of language production (e.g. Levelt, Roelofs, & Meyer, 1999), has been the one less traveled in cognitive science, being left largely to philosophers (e.g. Searle, 1969; Bratman, 1987) and linguists (Bach & Harnish, 1979; Morgan, 1978). The research of Duranti (1993) in anthropological linguistics, Gibbs (1999) in experimental psycholinguistics, and my own work in micro-sociolinguistics (Walters, 1980, 1981, 2001) are attempts to change this imbalance. Curiously, early on in sociolinguistics, Hymes (1974) identified 'intent' in his "ethnography of speaking" taxonomy, but this construct was not picked up to the same extent that contextual and textual factors such as setting, participants, and genre were. Part of the reason for the neglect of intentions in empirical study has been that it is so difficult to create operational terms and procedures to deal with this most internal and intimate construct. Another reason may be residual methodological influences of behaviorist psychology, which restricted research to observables. The shift of cognitive science to mentalism may not have extended to methods, and methods have their way of coloring the allowable universe of discourse.

In the proposed model of bilingual production (see below and Chapter 3), intentions are a central concern: in the model's information components, in the modules proposed to handle language choice and affective information, in the review and discussion of the mechanisms proposed to handle bilingual processing (Chapter 4), and in the account of uniquely bilingual phenomena such as codeswitching, interference, and translation (Chapter 5). One of the major issues addressed in that fifth chapter is the distinction between intentional and putatively 'non-intentional' codeswitching.

Methodological issues related to a speaker's intentions, from data gathering to analysis and interpretation, are also pursued in this volume, and there are two suggestions to attain veridical data about intentions. One is to collect and compare across multiple data sources, including but not limited to interviews, behavioral measures, role playing, and metalinguistic judgment tasks. Another is to make use of the testing procedures of Perceptual Control Theory (PCT), a paradigm grounded in the psychology of William James, in which intentions are built into the constructs of the model as well as the methods derived from it. PCT rejects a linear, stimulus-organism-response (S-O-R) approach in favor of circular causality and negative feedback, where behavior is not the terminal response in a linear chain but a variable means to control perception.

As an illustration, using PCT would be like installing a virtual camcorder on the conceptual joystick used by a bilingual speaking in his or her less favored language (L2) while trying to discuss an intimately familiar concept in L1. The bilingual will try to zoom in on the subject again and again until he or she gets it right. Examination of the feedback cycle provides a measurable means of gauging something to do with intentions because the cycle occurs when intentions are *not* fulfilled to the desired effect.

Variation is a construct that has been interpreted in many ways, and one of the purposes of this work is to clarify some of the resulting fuzziness. Another aim is to offer a processing role for the variation construct in the study of bilingualism. In language production, Levelt et al.'s (1999) notion of perspective taking is grounded in lexical variation. Levelt defines this as the "verbalization problem," which can be paraphrased as the inherent variation in mapping intentions to form. De Bot and Schreuder (1993) speak about "considerable variation" in the sound production of bilinguals, offering activation and temporal/attentional factors as explanations for the phenomenon. Waugh (1976) tells us that Jakobson observed two types of creativity in his notion of the dynamic nature of language, and that both types rest on variation, one sociolinguistic and one more pragmatic/stylistic. Perspective taking for Levelt, sound variation for De Bot, and sociolinguistic/stylistic variation for Jakobson all relate to variation in linguistic structure. In Chapter 4, I review three notions of variation in addition to three of my own. One, like those cited here, is grounded in language structure. A second, from work in micro-sociolinguistics, focuses on functional-pragmatic variation. The third, variation in behavior, is an attempt to offer a processing dimension to the construct.

ATTITUDES AND BEHAVIOR: A RELATIONSHIP OF UNCERTAINTY

Attitudes and behavior are not the same thing, neither for voting surveys and voting behavior nor for language attitudes and language use. The relationship between attitudes and behavior is not simple, and may not even be linear or curvilinear. Data about language use cannot necessarily be inferred from data on language attitudes. Both need careful scrutiny to see what each kind of data accounts for and does not account for. The discrepancies between attitudinal and behavioral data, a major issue in social psychology for some time (see Petty, Wegener & Fabrigar, 1997 for a review), have only recently made their way into the field of bilingualism. Using both attitudinal and behavioral measures of codeswitching, including the matched-guise procedure, language diaries, and actual conversations involving codeswitching, Lawson and Sachdev (2000) document discrepancies between attitudinal and behavioral data. To foreshadow methodological arguments that will follow: The authors found that the bias bilinguals had about mixing their languages tilted their reports about codeswitching. Bilinguals who think it is "bad" to codeswitch still did it but were not very accurate when asked to report on what they were doing.

One way to approach this issue is to ask whether behavioral data from recordings and observations of actual language use offer better insight into bilingual phenomena than attitudinal data from questionnaires, self-reports, and language diaries. The differences in methodology have led to possibly more disputation than the actual substance might justify. In fact, methodological disputes may be the primary impediment to advancement in the science of bilingualism. I would approach these methodological differences by following the lead of Lawson and Sachdev, making use of both attitudinal and behavioral measures in a single study. Attitudinal measures are particularly lacking in laboratory studies of bilingual processing. Behavioral measures of language use are labor intensive and, as such, often give way to questionnaires, self-report, and other less arduous methods of data collection and analysis in studies of social and pragmatic aspects of bilingualism. In the same way that intention, meaning, and sound are integrated in language production, both laboratory and field research have methods that need not necessarily be adversarial. In the chapters that follow, I try to examine some of this complexity, in particular in methodological notes and in suggestions for future research.

BRAIN AND LANGUAGE: STRUCTURAL BASES FOR BEHAVIORAL DIFFERENCES

Long before PET scans and fMRI techniques opened a window to the brain, clinical evidence from aphasias and experimental techniques involving dichotic listening and tachistoscopic presentation were used to examine the relationship between brain and behavior in bilingualism. Most, if not all, of this work is predicated on a notion of localization of function: a specific area of the brain is said to be responsible for performance on a particular linguistic task. Albert and Obler (1978) were among the first to argue that there was more right hemisphere brain activity in the language processing of bilinguals (with no clear statement about which language was more represented in that hemisphere). While a detailed mapping of structural evidence for the uniqueness of a bilingual brain may still be out of reach, both laboratory and field-based bilingual research over the last two decades do allow us to talk about processing differences in bilinguals (e.g., Abutalebi, Cappa & Perani, 2001; Klein, et al. 1994; Price, Green, & von Studnitz, 1999)

Ullman (2001) takes the localization issue even further, connecting it to a distinction between declarative and procedural knowledge and adding a developmental dimension to account for second language processing. Declarative knowledge is claimed to underlie lexical processing (both semantic and episodic memory) and to be used in "learning arbitrarily related information." This kind of learning is assumed to involve associations and contextual information, to be more explicit, and "not informationally encapsulated." Procedural knowledge is said to underlie grammatical abilities as well as other motor and cognitive functions. Information of this type is processed as "skills and habits" and is considered to be modular. Regarding localization of these functions, temporal lobe areas are claimed to be the neuroanatomical substrates of lexical-declarative processing, while frontal basal ganglia of the left hemisphere are presumed responsible for grammatical-procedural knowledge.

Drawing on critical period data (e.g. Birdsong, 1999), Ullman (2001) proposes an age-related shift from use of more automatic, procedural knowledge in L1 to more explicit, lexically-based processing in L2. Ullman acknowledges the similarity of his model to Paradis' (1995) distinction between L1 and L2, based on more automatic and implicit processing in the native tongue. Ullman's approach, while still essentially localizationist in nature (e.g. when he states that

"Aspects of grammatical processing are less dependent upon left frontal and basal ganglia structures in L2 than in L1," p. 118), does, however, make use of data indicating a much broader range of anatomical structures and does refer to the relationship between linguistic processing and other motor and cognitive activity. The broader perspective on localization and reliance on processing notions that go beyond one-to-one language-brain mappings open the door to speculation about the role of cerebral plasticity in linguistic functioning and conceivable connections between language and motor functions.[3]

Localizationist arguments cannot account for all of the complexity in the interaction between brain and language. This is especially the case when one notes the possibility that cognitive activity (in this case, bilingualism) may lead to structural changes in neurobiology, though this does not necessarily mean that the subsequent structural changes will make any cognitive difference. This argument leaves open the possibility that bilingual brains may be structured differently, but that bilinguals still process language similarly to monolinguals.

Questions regarding the relationship between structure and processing are systems questions in Perceptual Control Theory (PCT) terms (Powers, 1978; Cziko, 1995). In that framework, structure and process may be two levels in a hierarchy of control loops. Alternatively, they may operate at the same level. If so, structural features in the neurobiology of bilingualism may influence cognitive processing in bilingualism. And that relationship may be governed by a linear, feedforward mechanism. But it seems just as likely that structure and process are bi-directional, in which case characteristics in the cognitive processing of fluent bilinguals may not show up as structural changes. If, however, the mechanism which relates cognitive and biological systems in bilingualism is a negative feedback loop, then cognitive activity, especially repeated cognitive activity, should lead to changes in neurobiological structure, which will in turn influence the nature of cognitive processing, perhaps making it more efficient and leading to increased fluency. This paragraph foreshadows the sections on PCT in Chapters 4 and 5.

SUMMARY

A cognitive science approach to bilingualism is heavily influenced by all three of the above issues, and the model I offer to account for bilingual phenomena attempts to address each of them (in different ways). The constructs of intention and variation will be most visible in the information sources and processing mechanisms of the model. The model includes a central information component where intentions are the link between sociopragmatic and psycholinguistic information. In addition, the model distinguishes between structural and processing aspects of variation. In the functional architecture of the model, variation takes the form of multiple sources of information and multiple links between those sources. In terms of processing, variation is a mechanism for alternating between and among various sources of information, the most salient being first and second language information. Perceptual Control Theory is offered as one way to explain some of the complexity in these processes and to account for some of the processing aspects of language contact phenomena such as codeswitching, interference, and translation.

The attitude-behavior discrepancy, taken from social psychology and applied to sociolinguistic aspects of bilingualism here, finds expression in the sociopragmatic components of the model. Throughout this work, this incongruity is used as a methodological conscience for examining the work of others as well as for assessing appropriateness of methodological techniques to investigate various aspects of the model and its processing mechanisms.

Finally, mapping of language-brain relationships in bilingualism, while beyond the scope of the structural components and processing mechanisms of the present work, is mentioned here as a biological alternative to the computational metaphor, perhaps the next dichotomy in need of a merger in a cognitive science of bilingualism.

THE SPPL MODEL AND ITS PROCESSING CLAIMS

The Sociopragmatic Psycholinguistic (SPPL) processing Model[4] is intended as an inclusive framework. The functional architecture of the model specifies the structural components (its architecture) and their main functions. The processing mechanisms describe how information flows between the various components of the model.

The SPPL Model contains seven sources of information, represented by the rectangles in Figure 1.1. The two modules that run vertically along the sides show that **language choice** and **affective** information are available at every stage of language production. The **language choice** module and its interaction with the other information components are the central foci of this work. In the left-to-right direction of the two-headed arrows, it indicates (moving down the internal components of the model) that it is responsible for making L1 and L2 information available to the bilingual speaker (1) in the construction of identity, (2) in the choice of where to speak, and in preferences for interlocutors and genres, (3) in the formulation of an intention, (4) in the retrieval of concepts and words, and, finally, (5) in the articulation of an utterance. In the right-to-left direction of the arrows, the language choice component is responsible for selecting, regulating, and retrieving information from those internal components and integrating them with the speaker's linguistic choices. The **language choice module** in Figure 1.1 is useful primarily to account for a range of language contact phenomena, including a distinction between sociopragmatically and psycholinguistically motivated codeswitching.

Figure 1.1 Functional architecture of the Sociopragmatic-Psycholinguistic (SPPL) Model of bilingualism

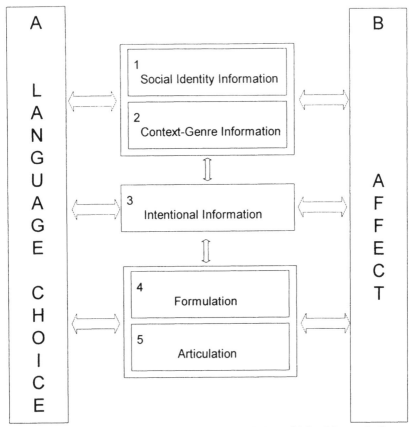

The **affective module**, about which less will be said in this work (but see Walters, 2002, ms), has an analogous framework for distinguishing socially and pragmatically-motivated pragmatic markers and those which are used to convey fluency and other discourse formulation functions. This module is also useful for characterizing differences between more affectively motivated slips of the tongue (of the Freudian type) and more phonetically and phonologically-based tip-of-the-tongue phenomena.

The five internal components of the model characterize stages in language production. They take us from the most intimate chambers of personal and social identity to the articulatory output of an utterance. Each component is an attempt to illustrate something about language production in general and bilingual processing in particular. The SPPL Model assumes that information about language choice is grounded in the social world, and language choices are possible at every stage of production (from identity through intention to articulation). Thus, this approach opts for parsimony, favoring a single language choice regulator to interact with each source of information.

Social identity is the lead component. It shows that language production in general and bilingualism in particular are grounded in the social world of the speaker. My view here is that social identity is multidimensional and dynamic, changing as the bilingual makes new friends, switches jobs, and integrates language choices regarding accent, names, and greetings with these elements of social life.

The *contextual/genre component*, which specifies setting and participants, genre and topic information in conversational interaction addresses the classical question in micro-sociolinguistics of 'who speaks which language to whom, where, and about which topic.' It accounts for code alternation between immigrant parents and their native-born children as well as the public-private distinction in literature and polemics on bilingual education. The genre subcomponent tries to show that scripted language like the interactions in doctor-patient exchanges does not have the same patterns of use as spontaneous conversation.

The central component of the model is responsible for identifying the *speaker's intentions* and their bilingual features. Originating in speech act theory and elaborated to include pragmatic markers (e.g. well, ya' know, kind of), greetings, and lexical choice, this component bridges the upper sociopragmatic sources of information with lower psycholinguistic sources. A speaker's intention (to request, to promise, to deceive, to blame) is peppered with bilingual information, from subtle indicators of the speaker's identity hidden in the pragmatic markers or prosodic shape of the utterance to lexical preferences influenced by psycholinguistic factors such as interference and lexical gaps.

The bilingual *formulator*, the locus of the bulk of psycholinguistic research on bilingual processing, gets at the heart of lexical representation or how words are stored in the brain. Monolingual models of lexical processing posit a universal, dictionary-like lemma containing syntactic and semantic information that maps into a morphophonological lexeme. The SPPL Model is based on a different concept. Lexical formulation in the SPPL Model contains pragmatic information as well as structural features. The formulator also specifies discourse patterns to handle relevance, cohesion, and sequencing of information.

The principle advantage of the SPPL approach to formulation is that it accounts for incompleteness in the bilingual's knowledge. All bilinguals, and in fact even monolinguals, experience lexical near-misses, which the listener perceives as malapropisms. The model attempts to characterize this variability by incorporating pragmatic and discourse information in the formulator and by making bilingual information available from the language choice module.

The fifth component, the bilingual *articulator,* accounts for the fact that bilinguals, even those without a trace of an accent, show evidence (sometimes only via precise acoustical measurements) of a merged system of sounds. The

Spanish-English bilingual produces neither the sounds of Spanish nor the sounds of English. Again, the SPPL Model and its bilingual articulator attempt to characterize this uniqueness as well as variability within and across speakers.

Two levels of **processing** characterize the interaction between and among the modules and components of the SPPL Model. Basic level cognitive processes (attention, discrimination, recognition, identification/recall, classification, and categorization) are distinguished from the four mechanisms that drive the flow of information in the model. The mechanisms–*imitation*, *variation*, *integration*, and *control*–are critical to an understanding of bilingual processing, and are shown (in Chapter 4) to be grounded conceptually in linguistics and in the other social sciences. Here relevant empirical evidence, from a broad range of research as well as my own studies of bilingualism, forms the crux of the argument on behalf of the processing constructs. Another, no less important aim in making explicit processing claims is to introduce two general-purpose theories of processing, Anderson's Functional Theory of Cognition and Powers' Perceptual Control Theory, to the field of bilingualism.

Chapter 4 includes a detailed mapping of how each of these four mechanisms interacts with each of the components of the model effectively creating a structured multi-dimensional matrix that I believe is essential to accommodate the many factors that come into play in bilingual speech.

The information components and processing mechanisms of the SPPL Model can be used to account for codeswitching, interference, translation and interpretation, computation, and cursing. Structurally, the model's architecture positions these phenomena in bilingual production, while the four processing mechanisms are intended to show how these phenomena are carried out.

Sociopragmatic *codeswitching* is distinguished here from structural-psycho-linguistic codeswitching in terms of intentionality and directionality. For example, a Russian immigrant biologist to Israel would codeswitch into Hebrew to show how much he understood about his new job but would codeswitch back to Russian to describe a particular kind of existential frustration because Hebrew just doesn't have that kind of terminology with all of its Soviet associations. Similarly, a Cordovan-born ivy-league professor would feign a non-native accent in English in order to project her minority identity and status in faculty meetings at an American university, but would converse in accentless, idiomatic English with her native English-speaking graduate students.

Sociopragmatic codeswitching is goal-driven and motivated by identity as well as external, contextual factors; structural-psycholinguistic codeswitching (CS) stems from individual linguistic and mental factors, in particular difficulties in finding words and lack of structural equivalence between languages. As in the previous examples, social factors easily prompt codeswitching to the less preferred language, while familiarity would suggest the safe haven of the preferred or primary language when the bilingual is confronted with word finding and fluency issues. In processing terms, codeswitching is particularly characterized as involving the mechanisms of imitation and variation.

Interference, or the point in which codeswitching gives way to traces of the unintended language, serves as a useful point to start a discussion about fluency, automaticity, and completeness in bilingual processing. I define *completeness* as a structural property of language, while *fluency* and *automaticity* are discussed in processing terms. These constructs are used to sort out a number of issues related to interference, in particular, the size of vocabulary, rate of speech, and cross-language transfer.

This train of thought leads to a discussion of **translation** and **interpretation** under the terms of the major information components of the SPPL Model. The sociopragmatic aspects of the model, in other words, the identities of the speaker and interpreter, and the context, are shown to be more useful in researching simultaneous interpretation, while the psycholinguistic components of the model (formulation and articulation) are of greater interest in examining translation.

Computation and **cursing**, although not essentially bilingual in their nature, bring to light some unique phenomena among bilinguals. Most bilinguals have a preference for counting in a single, original language, even if they are highly fluent in both languages. This could be the soft, monolingual underbelly of bilingualism. Sociopragmatic aspects of the model offer insight to the learning contexts of bilingual computation, while psycholinguistic processing aspects of the model may help reach a better understanding of automaticity in computation.

The model's structural and processing components also offer a theoretical framework to investigate cursing among bilinguals. For example, when a bilingual prefers to curse in a non-native language, one can examine sociopragmatic issues such as the relationship between language and affect, and psycholinguistic issues related to directionality and triggering of codeswitching.

The SPPL Model and its processing features are not intended as an ivory tower of Babel. I am also interested in bilingual acquisition, language attrition among immigrants, and application of the model to the study of language disturbances in bilingual children. The interface between the fields of language disorders and bilingualism poses special problems, both ethical and technical, which have made scientific progress especially difficult.

The idea that bilingualism may lead to cognitive advantages competes with the generally accepted view in clinical and educational settings that language disorders are cognitively debilitating. This raises the unorthodox possibility that bilingualism might be cognitively stimulating for children whose language does not develop normally. The more conventional position, that bilingualism and language disorders both have enervating effects on the child's limited cognitive resources, raises serious problems for the line of research that argues for the cognitive advantages of bilingualism.

The SPPL Model and its processing mechanisms are based on assumptions that look at a very broad world of influences and factors that affect production of bilingual speech. As such, it might be helpful as a starting point for an assessment framework for studying and diagnosing bilingual children with language disorders.

BILINGUAL PHENOMENA AND PHENOMENA IN BILINGUALISM

Codeswitching, interference, and translation are uniquely bilingual phenomena. Certain kinds of cursing, calculating, and dreaming can also be uniquely bilingual. The first three are related to *language structure* as well as to *language use*. At this level, one could say that codeswitching, interference, and translation each has a somewhat equivalent monolingual[5] counterpart. For bilingual codeswitching (CS), the monolingual counterpart is register or style shifting, including the ability to modify one's speech as a function of changes in setting, topic, or listener. But, bilingual CS requires all components of the SPPL for a reasonable account; register shifting can be restricted to phonetic and lexical levels of processing and characterized sensibly by contextual factors of the interaction alone. The putative counterpart of interference in the monolingual domain is the problem of lexical access. Bilingual interference, in contrast, involves a range of structural and processing issues that cannot be handled by models designed to account for monolingual word retrieval. Finally, paraphrase, the monolingual notion closest to translation, is primarily lexical and syntactic. It is missing the sociopragmatic elements argued for here.

When we look more closely at language use, and especially at its sociopragmatic and psycholinguistic dimensions, then the bilingual character of these phenomena becomes much clearer. Sociopragmatic aspects of codeswitching draw from a person's identity and from the relevant parameters of "context of situation[6]," in particular setting, topic, and participants (incorporated in components 1 and 2 in the SPPL Model, Figure 1.1). For the bilingual person, identity and context are essential to an understanding of his or her bilingualism.

Psycholinguistic aspects of codeswitching include thinking up, devising, and working out an intention, formulating that intention, and articulating it. These components of language production entail lexical storage, lexical choice, and lexical access. When the speaker is bilingual, even in an extremely sheltered monolingual environment and even when operating in a single language, bilingual lexical processing is an ever-present fact of life. One assumption in this work is that these phenomena–codeswitching, interference, and translation–are unique to bilinguals. Their alleged parallels in monolingual language are as yet undocumented claims. The proposal here is to argue for the uniqueness of bilingualism as a linguistic, psycholinguistic, and sociolinguistic phenomenon.

FUZZY BORDERS BETWEEN SOCIOLINGUISTICS AND PSYCHOLINGUISTICS

This section tries to give a feel for some of the crossing between disciplinary lines. Recently, linguists of all varieties, from hardcore generativists to sociolinguists (ethnographers as well as orthodox variationists) and psycholinguists (whether naturalists or passionate experimentalists) appear to have converging interests. The lowest common denominator that links these interests is agreement on descriptions of common phenomena and assumptions. The maximum level of cooperation would be in a unified model and a shared set of methods.

Among those in the best position to offer a unified approach to the study of bilingualism is Myers-Scotton, whose research on codeswitching has dealt with social motivations (1993), structural constraints (1993/1997), and lexical organization (1995). Her roots in sociolinguistics and collaborative work with a generative grammarian give broad scope to her studies. Her most recent model indicates a strong interest in processing, taking her into the heart of cognitive psychology. In this model, she uses structural phenomena (constraints on codeswitching) as explanations for processing. As yet, the sociolinguistic aspects of her work have not been integrated fully with the processing portions of her model, but the crossing of disciplinary boundaries is clear and present. (See Chapter 2 for a detailed discussion of this work.)

Sociolinguistics is no longer the monolithic fortress it was in the heyday of Labovian variationism. As variationist research struggles to hold its own with the flood of ethnographies on bilingual identity, both structural insights and processing issues tend to get lost in the sectarian battles between quantitative and qualitative methodologies. I argue here for an end to these battles. Bilingual ethnographies offer incisive perceptions of bilingual language use that might never be achieved by a hypothetico-deductive approach involving variables and quantification. Ethnography and interactional sociolinguistics also provide a framework for examining multiple sources of information, looking at language scaffolded within individual, interpersonal, and institutional contexts. The insights of ethnography are, however, the bane of their appeal, with their rich interpretive frameworks shackled in the proverbial observer's paradox.

The variationist framework remains relevant here because of what it may tell us about processing (see Chapter 4). Poplack and Meechan (1997:199) begin from an interest in structure, but move quickly to a notion of language grounded in processing notions such as activation: "...what grammar is utilized at the point where languages meet? Do speakers operate with a single base grammar which is on occasion overlaid with lexical items from another language or are different grammars activated at different times...what structural principles govern their juxtaposition?"

The merger of sociopragmatic and psycholinguistic perspectives offered in this work nevertheless challenges the assumptions of the variationist model of codeswitching (Sankoff, 1998). First, the bilingual is not necessarily assumed to be fully competent in one language, let alone two (see the discussion of incompleteness, especially regarding representation and lemmas, in Chapter 5). Second, evidence is shown for linguistic convergence at every single level of linguistic analysis, from phonetics to pragmatics (see the discussion of Myers-Scotton on compromise forms and Clyne on fusion forms in the next chapter). And third, the existence of translation equivalents for any reasonable number of sentences is not at all inevitable for just about every notion of translation, especially those that rely on computational methods (again, see Chapter 5).

What I've tried to do in this brief section is to give a taste for potential dialogue among a variety of sub-disciplines in linguistics and to carve out an area where the common interest lies. The next sections map out the territory.

BILINGUALS AND BILINGUALISM

Much of the history of bilingual research reads more like a scratch sheet in horse racing or a scorecard for a baseball game. In the senseless debate over whether bilinguals are more intelligent or more cognitively flexible than monolinguals, the bilinguals always come out losers. Not because they always perform worse than monolinguals. In fact, from 1962 (Peal & Lambert) onwards there are more reports of bilinguals outperforming monolinguals on cognitive tasks. Rather, bilinguals are the losers because they are forced to march to the beat of the monolingual drummer.

In an effort to focus more directly on bilinguals, Lambert patented a distinction first introduced by Weinreich between compound and coordinate bilinguals, which in effect moved the center of interest to questions of definition and classification. This distinction was intended originally as an abstract theoretical construct and did not aim to make any claims about brain organization. Lambert came from social psychology and knew his limits with Donald Hebb, many years his senior, not far down the hall in the Psychology Department at McGill.

The compound-coordinate partition was instantiated in terms of the age and context in which the second language was acquired. Compound bilinguals were defined as those who had acquired both languages before the age of six in the same contexts (for example at home). Coordinate bilinguals were those who had acquired one of their languages after that age and in a different context (for example at school). This distinction generated the lion's share of research for more than two decades, and even a scathing attack on dichotomies in general and this one in particular (Diller, 1970) could not eliminate the mark it has made on the study of bilingualism. On the contrary, it has reappeared persistently in the investigation of bilingual memory under the competing hypotheses labeled separate vs. shared and interdependent vs. independent representations.

Another attempt to define and classify bilinguals, one which has become more prevalent recently especially in developmental and neurolinguistic studies (see, for example, Genesee, 2001 and Abutalebi, Cappa & Perani, 2001, respectively), was McLaughlin's (1987) distinction between early and late acquisition. These labels attribute more importance to age than to social factors such as context of acquisition. The category 'early bilinguals' may mask a range of differences. For example, when the bilingual child's primary caretaker (usually the mother) speaks the same language as that of their immediate neighborhood and the dominant language of society, one pattern of bilingualism may develop. But when the primary caretaker is monolingual in a language other than those of the immediate or wider context, a different kind of bilingualism might develop (note, for example, the languages and genders of the parents in Genesee, 2001). Similarly, a first-born child does not develop language along the same trajectory as a second, third, or fourth born, whose input is influenced more by older siblings than by adults. Further refinement of the early-late distinction probably should take into account birth order, gender of both parents and children, and societal bilingualism.

Societal bilingualism, termed diglossia[7] in the sociolinguistics literature, concerns the prevalence of bilinguals in a particular community, city, or region. It has been made relevant to problems of definition and classification of individual bilinguals in the distinction between additive and subtractive bilinguals (Lambert, 1977; Lambert & Taylor, 1991). Anglophones acquiring French in Quebec or Spanish in immersion programs in California have been considered additive bilinguals. Spanish-speakers in North America, minority language groups in just about every Western country (e.g. Punjabi speakers in the UK, Turks in Germany, Maghreb Arabic speakers in the Netherlands) are regarded as 'at risk' for loss of their native language, and labeled 'subtractive' bilinguals. It is clear how these terms and definitions overlap with the social prestige and ethnolinguistic vitality associated with the languages in question.

At present, there is no research group studying second and third generation bilinguals like the Salk Institute does for congenitally deaf children. Perhaps there should be. But this book is not about kinds of bilingualism. The focus here is on bilingual phenomena–codeswitching, interference, translation–and how they are represented and processed in a more general account of bilingualism. These phenomena exist in all kinds of bilinguals, compound and coordinate, early and late, additive and subtractive, immigrant and indigenous, fluent and less proficient. They may lend themselves to clearer observation in some bilinguals than in others, but that is beside the point in a study that attempts to clarify the nature of bilingual phenomena within a framework useful for creating an overall picture.

SUBSTANTIVE ISSUES UNDERLYING TERMINOLOGICAL BATTLES

A review of the terminology of bilingualism will probably be of some use here for two reasons. First, such a review allows readers to make sense of research in a mushrooming field that has generated scores of new books, workshops, conferences, and symposia in the past several years. Second, the act of classifying bilingual terminology will offer further insight into my biases and assumptions.

Two distinctions can be made, one substantive and one more interpretive, both grounded in the philosophy of linguistic science. Substantively, there is a difference between bilingual phenomena and phenomena in bilingualism. Philosophically, there is a distinction between observations and explanations (Chomsky, 1965), between facts and constructs. Codeswitching, interference, and translation/interpretation are taken to be phenomena unique to bilingualism. These are bilingual phenomena. They can be distinguished from other phenomena, such as cursing and calculating (adding, subtracting, multiplying, and dividing), which are not unique to bilingualism but have aspects that interact with bilingualism in novel ways. Both observable facts and abstract constructs are tools necessary for describing mental processes.

The speed at which words are produced (somewhere between two and five per second) is a fact. The number of words produced in a segment of speech is a fact. The production of a string of native language speech in an English utterance is a fact. Notions such as code alternation, code mixing, fusion forms, language tags, language cues, activation, inhibition, and subsets are not facts. They are abstract, metaphoric constructs, used as labels either to account for facts, or to make other constructs easier to understand.

The following paragraphs attempt to give a feel for the density of terminology that has developed during the search for explanations of bilingual phenomena. Here, as throughout the book, I link the work in bilingualism to its relevant structural, functional, and processing dimensions. The untutored reader is asked to be patient until the next chapter, where the most relevant terms are introduced with appropriate background information.[8]

Bilingual speech and the linguistics of codeswitching. In the study of codeswitching, codemixing, and interference, most of the terminology is relatively transparently used to characterize *structural phenomena*. Auer's insertional, alternational, and turn-initial categories are examples. Muysken (2000) also uses the terms insertional and alternational, adding as well the construct 'congruent lexicalization' to describe what he calls *processes* to distinguish patterns of code-mixing. His notion of process centers on representation and the relationships of structural elements, apparently in the generative tradition (cf. Jackendoff, 2002) which considers processing a metaphor for the derivation of structural descriptions.

Somewhat nearer to the *processing* orientation in the present work, but still fairly close to observable phenomena are De Bot's, Grosjean's and Leuenberger's notions of 'codeswitching density.' Sometimes the labels become more interpretive, as can be seen in terms such as 'sustained divergence' and 'ritualistic' and 'formulaic' codeswitching. Clyne's 'triggers' and Poplack's 'flags,' both intended to describe the kinds of lexical items which precede and mark codeswitching, are more interpretive when these same authors speak about triggering and flagging. The latter terms are no longer restricted to structure, and their gerundive form may imply an interest in processing phenomena such as fluency and planning. Similarly, terms such as 'fusion words' (Clyne) and 'compromise forms' (Poulisse, Myers-Scotton), used to describe codeswitching within word boundaries simultaneously imply access of language information from more than one language and at more than one level of processing, clearly beyond a surface level of description.

Memory in bilinguals and the languages of processing. General descriptions of bilinguals and bilingualism as 'compound,' 'coordinate,' and 'subordinate' are attempts to capture some of the complexity in the relationship between an individual bilingual's two languages. This line of research began in structural linguistics (Haugen, 1953; Weinreich, 1953), continued in the early days of psycholinguistics (e.g. Ervin-Tripp & Osgood, 1954), and has been current in the psychology of bilingualism in the distinction between shared and separate representation (e.g. Francis, 1999). Bilingual studies have not yet explicitly addressed other fundamental constructs in memory research, e.g. between semantic and episodic memory, between storage and retrieval. Conceptual and semantic memory are often conflated in this tradition. Elsewhere, terms such as 'matrix language' (Myers-Scotton) and 'base language' (Grosjean) are also intended to describe L1-L2 relationships, sometimes focused on languages and sometimes on speakers. And the names which De Groot and Kroll have adopted for their evolving model–'word association,' 'concept mediated,' and 'revised hierarchical'–imply different levels of processing. Paradis' Three-Store Model evokes similar notions.

Abstract constructs such as 'language tags,' 'activation,' and 'selection' are attempts to describe processes and processing, the less observable aspects of bilingual language. In their conventional use, language tags are language labels attached to lexemes in order to distinguish lexical entries in a single storage bilingual system, or to facilitate retrieval in tasks involving cross-language processing. In various theories of bilingual formulation, *language tags* indicate information about which language(s) a speaker has activated; they are usually found at low levels of lexical production, closer to articulation than to conceptual, syntactic, and semantic aspects of formulation.

In the SPPL Model, a language choice module that has more general availability of information from two languages in effect makes language tags available at the conceptual, lemma, and lexemic levels of representation (see Albert & Obler, 1978 for earlier usage of the term; and Green, 1998, Li & Farkas, 2002 for more recent treatment). *Activation* is a term adopted when referring to individual lexical items or sets of them, but this construct has also been used to refer to an entire language system, as in Grosjean's monolingual and bilingual modes and Green's selected-activated-dormant distinction. These latter uses are primarily psycholinguistic, but the authors do make mention of social factors in various ways (see Green, 1986, and Grosjean's, 1997, notion of language modes).

Social processes and processing of social information. Even when Ferguson (1959) introduced the term 'diglossia' to describe the use of "two or more varieties of the same language...under different conditions," he admitted that the word for 'bilingualism' carried a similar meaning in some European languages. Macro-sociolinguistic studies in this tradition were directed at identifying social features (e.g. functions, prestige, standardization, stability) and structural elements (grammar, lexicon, phonology) to classify language use in speech communities and in wider societal contexts. Micro-sociolinguistics addresses social processes between individuals and in small groups, where setting, topic, and speech act function are key terms. Li Wei's (2000) introduction to the eight sociolinguistic papers in his *Bilingualism Reader* adds conversation analysis and social networks to these frameworks, the latter noted for its combining of macro and micro-level bilingualism. The next chapter discusses two of the most prominent ethnographies of bilingualism (Rampton and Zentella) in a field which is tirelessly expanding. Among the terms likely to confuse an outsider (and a fair share of insiders) are: context, situation, language choice, domain, and function. Even the addition of a modifier (e.g. linguistic context, social context, speech act function, pragmatic function) doesn't always help clarify the full intent, and the critical reader needs to rely on further contextual information, including the nature of the publication and the author's intellectual roots.

A small sample of the terminology describing social *processes* relevant to bilingualism includes immigration, urbanization, secularization, assimilation, acculturation, and enclaving. At the micro-level we read about micro-processes of talk, verbal interaction, discourse processes, and more specifically about negotiating, positioning, the speaker-voice distinction, and constructing identity. Processing terms of a more abstract nature include Goffman's notion of footing, formulaicness, and Turner's liminality.

Structure and function in bilingual processing. While the structural elements in linguistics (e.g. NPs, clauses, deictics, discourse markers) may be abstract constructs, within the discipline they have accepted meanings. In psycholinguistics, the labels given to stimulus items may not be transparent to an outsider, but within the discipline the tasks and procedures are relatively conventional ways of defining the phenomenon of interest (e.g. priming, pro-active interference). In sociolinguistics, traditional structural constructs related to societal bilingualism, e.g. ethnicity, role, status, have solid roots in sociology. Across disciplines, however, the notion of structure is not the same. Linguistic rules to describe relationships between elements within and across sentences are not the same as social rules to describe interpersonal relationships, constraints on behavior or "rule governed activity of a symbolic character."[9] Similarly, the *functions* of NPs in a sentence, speech act *functions*, the *functional* architecture of a psycholinguistic processing model, and the *functions* of bilingual codeswitching do not share a common meaning. The polysemy in the *function* construct is context-dependent, and it is the discipline which defines the context. To achieve the kind of cross-disciplinary dialogue we are after, we need to try to understand both the theory-internal terms and to go beyond those terms to get at common interests.

A more penetrating look at some of the terminology does, however, reveal we can get to some of the shared meaning across the structural-social divide. For example, compare: lexical relations and social relations; 'ambiguity' in structural linguistics vs. liminality in anthropology; word order, interaction order, and social order, and violation of word order vs. upheaval in social order.

Behind the terminological mask. One of the issues which go beyond terminological differences is the notion of levels of processing. For the classical linguist, these levels are phonology, morphology, syntax, semantics, and hopefully pragmatics. For the psychologist, levels of processing can be seen in distinctions between deep and shallow orthography in reading research, in semantic vs. episodic memory, and more fundamentally in the differences among sensation, perception, and cognition. In sociolinguistics and symbolic interactionism, we can pull macro, medial, and micro levels of processing out of the notion of scaffolding. National and regional attitudes to race and religion, institutional role, interpersonal relationships, and ethnic identity are integrated in a speaker's binguality; they all contribute to a composite, bilingual identity, which is then expressed in language use. Rampton's study of 'out-group' language crossing and Zentella's anthropolitical linguistic investigations of codeswitching illustrate the scaffolding of race, ethnicity, setting, topic, speaker/listener, and a host of individual features of identity on a full range of linguistic features, from intentions to lexis, from discourse to articulation.

By looking at levels of linguistic representation, levels of processing in psycholinguistics, and scaffolding of social and linguistic processes, we go beyond differences between speaker/listener in pragmatics and sociolinguistics and animator/author/principal in Bakhtinian criticism. We go beyond terminological differences between speaker and voice, situation and context, and between codeswitching, codemixing, code blending, and code crossing.

Methods in bilingualism. Two relatively rare phenomena in aphasia (*paradoxical translation* and *alternate antagonism*) are relevant, more for the insight they offer in methodology than for the substantive issues they raise. The first of these two conditions describes a bilingual aphasic patient who was able to translate into a language he could not use spontaneously, but could not translate into the language he was able to use spontaneously (Paradis, Goldblum & Abidi, 1982). A patient with alternate antagonism was able to produce only one of his two languages spontaneously on one day and the other of his two languages the following day, but was not able to speak both languages spontaneously on the same day.

Both of these phenomena raise important questions about the nature of those elements of the language processing system that remain intact following trauma to the brain. For example, is there a separate area of the brain or a particular configuration of neural circuitry responsible for translation? To what extent did the patient with alternate antagonism respond to changes in setting, topic, and interlocutor on the day in which one language was intact and the other impaired or inoperative? These questions are further challenged by an analogy William Brewer once made, claiming that studying aphasia to find out how language is processed is tantamount to investigating the hardware of a computer after treating it with a sledge hammer.[10]

Methodologically, the question is whether a model of bilingual processing should take into account highly idiosyncratic behavior to understand general principles. The short answer to this question is yes, since ultimately we are interested in the individual person using language. To be sure, we conduct experiments, run surveys, administer questionnaires, and record details of case studies, sometimes on large numbers of subjects. After calculating means and standard deviations and running analyses of variance and post hoc comparisons, our real interest (at least in this work) is the performance of the individual bilingual. We would like to be able to explain and predict one individual person's behavior with language. And lest we think this methodological issue is unique to clinical situations, we can turn around the issue of non-native accent, and see the importance of studying exceptional, but numbered, adult language learners who, despite an advanced age of acquisition, are able to produce fluent, accentless speech in a second language. Here, too, the interest is the behavior of individual people, with or without foreign accents and everywhere in between.

My goal here is to bring clarity. As Francis (1999) articulates so clearly, researchers in bilingualism are post-Tower of Babel victims, in need of interpreters of our scientific idiom. We do not yet have the same terminological conventions of physics, where an atom is an atom and a proton is a proton. This brief inventory of terminology and issues from the field of bilingualism can be summarized as follows: In some cases, we encounter terms that are labels for observable facts or claims that can be verified. These are phenomena. Some are unique to bilingualism, and some interact uniquely with bilingualism. We also run into terminology that is more metaphoric. The less transparent terms are more likely to be found in sociolinguistic studies of bilingualism, while interpretive notions are more common in psycholinguistic investigations, possibly in an attempt to capture notions of processing which do not lend themselves to direct observation.

FOUR ARGUMENTS FOR ANOTHER MODEL OF BILINGUAL PROCESSING

The brief taste of the terminological/definitional problems above provides a very partial indication of the somewhat fragmented approach to bilingualism and why a comprehensive model would be useful.

The background for the arguments to be presented here comes in part from Cook's (1992) position that bilinguals are 'multicompetent' and process language in ways that differ essentially from those of monolinguals. These arguments echo an earlier question raised in the literature on second language acquisition about whether first and second language acquisition represent different processes and entail different strategies (Macnamara, 1976; Ervin-Tripp, 1974). Of the four arguments for a model of bilingual processing I offer here, perhaps none is sufficient in and of itself or in combination with one of the others. Together, however, they do offer an alternative to what Cook, Grosjean and others have called a 'monolingual bias' in bilingual research.

A PHENOMENOLOGICAL ARGUMENT

One argument in favor of a distinct model of bilingual processing is the need to account for the unique aspects of bilingualism. It was demonstrated above that in bilingualism, sociopragmatic and psycholinguistic aspects of language processing come together in ways that they do not exhibit in monolingual language use. Codeswitching involves uniquely bilingual aspects of identity and context as well as formulation and articulation. Style and register shifting do not cross these lines. Translation does; paraphrase does not.

One does not have to go as far as Lawson and Sachdev (2000) who claim that codeswitching is an independent variety of language to make the argument for uniqueness. It would be easier to flip the question. Creating a framework that could argue both in the psycholinguistic and sociopragmatic arenas that codeswitching was *not* unique would be laborious, far from elegant and constantly begging the question of its existence. Add to this the notion that existing models of monolingual language cannot provide a satisfactory account of codeswitching, and you have more than enough icing on the cake of uniqueness. As far as tools are concerned, monolingual investigations of style and register shifting, paraphrase, and word finding difficulties leave unanswered questions about codeswitching, interference, and translation. The integrative model proposed in this book will address these issues and hopefully answer them productively.

A SOCIOLINGUISTIC ARGUMENT

Staats' (1999) comments about the need for "unifying infrastructure" in psychology is no less applicable to sociolinguistic studies of bilingualism. As research paradigms investigating social aspects of bilingualism have proliferated (e.g. ethnography, conversational analysis, symbolic interactionism, Labovian variation, ethnolinguistic vitality), each body of knowledge has made finer and finer distinctions about the phenomenon. Thus, scientists know more and more about tinier and tinier bits of the whole story. This fact about the history of our science makes scholars feel bad, partly because of pressure from society and partly due to intellectual integrity. The tiny 'bits' are essential parts of the larger picture, but that picture does not always project clearly when the focus is on the details. Staats calls for joining these many bits together, to build what he calls unified, "overarching" frameworks.

Sociolinguists find it difficult to sleep in other scientific beds, probably more due to methodological differences of opinion than to substantive dispute. The integrated model of bilingual processing proposed in this work is an attempt to create an arena for dialogue, to widen the scope of sociolinguistic research, adding micro-level phenomena and processing issues to the bilingual agenda. And, besides casting the sociolinguistic net wider, the approach suggested here also offers a means to validate group trends by grounding them in data about individual bilinguals.

In order to get us beyond our differences, the model needs two axes. It needs to operate at a level of abstraction and it needs to maintain a reasonable level of complexity. In the SPPL Model, the abstraction is found in the constructs, both the information components and the processing mechanisms. Complexity is found in the number and kinds of allowable interactions among the processing mechanisms, laid out in detail in Chapter 4.

Complex problems need complex models. It wouldn't surprise me if bilingualism were not the only area of linguistic interest which could benefit from an integration of sociopragmatic and psycholinguistic information and a merger of structural and processing phenomena.

Lest the reader think that my interest here is strictly theoretical, it is important to mention that this book has a strong empirical and practical concerns. Some of the SPPL Model's empirical expression is found in the course of the exposition in Chapter 3 and in the description of ways to address processing in Chapter 4. Practical concerns are the focus of Chapter 6, where I explain how the model and the processing mechanisms set up a framework for understanding some of the tough questions in bilingual language acquisition, language loss, and language disorders.

Finally, many scholars in sociolinguistics bring with them a social conscience, along with preferences for language diversity and native language maintenance. Those preferences are sometimes motivated by a researcher's own language background, ethnicity, or political orientation. The monolingual, majority culture, conservative sociolinguist may be as rare a species as a first generation native speaker of Esperanto. Social conscience and similar motives may compromise objectivity, especially in the selection of subjects and materials, in construction of the design, and in the interpretation of data. But that objectivity need not necessarily be an impediment to good science. As long as the methods can be internally and externally validated, the study will contribute to the science.

A NEUROLINGUISTIC ARGUMENT

Three positions regarding bilingualism and cerebral organization can be identified in the literature. One maintains that bilingualism and monolingualism are represented identically, i.e. by the same cortical structures. Another position is that bilingualism just misses the full force of Brewer's sledge hammer, placing heavy cognitive demands on a limited capacity processor and causing deleterious effects in fluency and cognitive processing. A third position opts for differences, claiming that the 'bilingual brain' looks and behaves in unique ways. The first position leads to approaches and frameworks where bilingualism is cloned onto a monolingual model. The second approach comes out the mouths of speech clinicians and teachers who marginalize parents of bilingual children by telling them to stick to one language, usually the language of the school.

The third stance is the one argued for here. It follows Albert and Obler's (1978) early view (derived from findings in bilingual aphasia and experiments in laterality) that the 'bilingual brain' may be lateralized differently than the monolingual one. Recent support for this position comes from electro-physiological and functional imaging studies (e.g. Damasio et al., 1996). The authors describe the nature of the neurobiological microstructures underlying retrieval of names for people, animals, and tools as follows:

> ...We do not envisage them [the neurobiological microstructures] as rigid 'modules' or hard-edged 'centres', because we see their structure and operation as being acquired and modified by learning. An individual's learning experience of concepts of a similar kind (such as manipulable tools), and their corresponding words, leads to the recruitment, within the available neural architecture, of a critical set of spatially proximate microcircuits...We presume that the number of microcircuits recruited to operate as intermediaries for a certain range of concepts and words varies with the learning experience (pp. 504-505).

Following this line, cognitive activity, in particular specialized, repetitive cognitive activity such as the use of a second language, should lead to structural and processing changes in human neurobiology. This would mean that the brain of a bilingual individual, specialized for two languages, might differ structurally (e.g. in mass, density, shape) and process language differently than the brain of a monolingual person.

Storage and retrieval, comprehension and production, and other aspects of language processing are the kind of cognitive activities that can be expected to generate changes in the structure of the 'bilingual brain.' Whether these changes involve an increase in density or shape of the cerebral cortex, more electrical activity across the synapses, or increased bloodflow in the arteries in particular areas of the brain is not the issue here. Rather, the prima facie possibility that bilingual brains may be structurally (anatomically or neurophysiologically) different than monolingual brains is reason enough to begin work on a model of bilingual processing, distinct from those that attempt to account for monolingual language processing. Hopefully we will be much wiser one day with regard to brain and language relationships in bilingual speech. To reach that point however, we need a better map of bilingual production to pinpoint exactly those elements that would yield the clearest results from physical investigations.

A PSYCHOLINGUISTIC ARGUMENT

Facts about bilingual processing and studies confirming them (or at least not rejecting them) offer another kind of argument for an independent model of bilingualism. Just about every published journal article comparing bilinguals and monolinguals has, not surprisingly, reported group differences. In strictly lexical terms, these differences show up as faster response times and fewer errors for monolinguals than for bilinguals, an effect (perhaps the most robust effect) documented across a wide variety of recognition, naming and lexical decision tasks (e.g. de Groot & Kroll, 1997). In addition to data from the lexical level of processing, some researchers (e.g. Magiste, 1982) have claimed that bilinguals produce language slower than monolinguals. Other relevant evidence includes differences between monolinguals and bilinguals on almost every task, from phoneme-monitoring (Azuma, 1991) and word recognition (Grosjean & Frauenfelder, 1997) to reading comprehension (Segalowitz, 1986) and divergent thinking/originality, intelligence, and attitude surveys (see Cook, 1997 for a review of cognitive aspects of this work). Summarizing those group studies, four areas can be noted:

- ❑ Rate of speech may differ across the two languages, even in the most balanced bilinguals (Magiste, 1982)
- ❑ Voice onset times for a bilingual's two languages differ from each other as well as from those of monolinguals (Caramazza et al., 1973; Flege, 1993; Obler, 1982; Zampini & Green, 2001)
- ❑ Vocabularies differ in level (Lambert & Tucker, 1972; Pearson, Fernandez & Oller, 1993) as well as content/domain
- ❑ Speech acts are encoded differently across a bilingual's two languages (Walters, 1979, 2001)

It is noteworthy that the first two of these differences are sound-based and the latter two are meaning-based. These are the poles of the linguistic spectrum: phonetics and pragmatics. The first two are central to an understanding of fluency and articulation in bilingualism, while vocabularies and speech acts offer essential insight into the processes of formulating meaning and constructing identity. These poles also represent the core content of sociolinguistic inquiry, where phonetic and lexical variation serve as the main sources of data. This parallel is not idiosyncratic, and points to issues that require explanation. A model of bilingualism should incorporate processing issues and sociolinguistic phenomena in a unified framework, which is what the SPPL Model aspires to do.

CHAPTER CODA

The four arguments presented here cover a range of sociolinguistic and psycholinguistic research. They also draw on methodologies not usually found in the same array. Phenomenology and sociolinguistics make strange bedfellows with neurolinguistics and psycholinguistics, not only because their questions are not the same, but also because of the way they choose to address these questions. These disciplines, however, all have direct bearing on the central questions of bilingualism, and even if their perspectives are somewhat disparate, we must not dismiss the opportunity to examine them together for reasons of intellectual convenience. The challenge is then to find a framework broad enough to accommodate the range of different perspectives, and knit tightly enough to provide coherent, systematic accounts of the main questions in the field.

This is the challenge the SPPL Model sets out to meet. It tries to do so by referring constantly and systematically to the interplay between structural features and processing mechanisms. The structure is spelled out in Chapter 3 and the processing mechanisms in Chapter 4. To understand why it has to be pulled together we need to look first at the wisdom, insight, and depth that stand behind the range of perspectives the SPPL Model aims to pull together. That's what Chapter 2, which follows, is all about.

NOTES

---

[1] Tabouret-Keller (1995) reissued a call by Ludi (1990) following the third European Science Foundation workshop on codeswitching for the kind of interdisciplinary conversation that this volume attempts.

[2] Francis (2000:14) cuts up the pie differently. In her response to Pavlenko (1999), she distinguishes within-subject studies of bilinguals from cross-linguistic/cross-cultural studies of monolinguals and studies that compare bilinguals with monolinguals of L1 and L2.

[3] See, for example, Sieratzki & Woll's (1998) work on spinal muscular atrophy children.

[4] Some of the issues and parts of the model presented in this work were introduced at the 1999 Veldhoven Conference on Language Maintenance and Loss, at the International Conference on Linguistics in Athens (2001), and in the proceedings published following those meetings (Walters, 2001, in press).

[5] For most of this work, I use the more conventional (Greek-Latin) codeswitched forms 'monolingual' and 'bilingual.' Exceptions to this convention are cases where I cite work that has adopted the more purist term, 'unilingual.'

[6] The term and idea behind it is from Malinowski and Firth, introduced to American sociolinguistics by Hymes (1974).

[7] It should be noted that this use of diglossia extends the meaning originally intended by Ferguson (1959) and exemplified in the differences between classical and colloquial Arabic.

[8] The tutored reader is referred to Francis (1999) for an eye-opening critique of the terminological morass on the cognitive-psycholinguistic end of bilingualism.

[9] This quotation is taken from Rampton (1995); for a discussion of the substantive issues, see Chapter 2.

[10] Personal communication (circa 1979).

2 Ten Perspectives on Bilingualism

Ten models or approaches with explicit claims about the nature of bilingualism are reviewed here. They are classified, somewhat arbitrarily, as linguistic/structural, sociolinguistic, psycholinguistic, and monolingual-based. The division is arbitrary because each of the approaches contains structural elements, and each one makes verifiable claims about processing, although sometimes those claims are not focused on the same phenomenon and sometimes are not transparent to the reader. It is the purpose of this chapter to make some of these claims explicit.

The models selected here have much to recommend them. Some (Myers-Scotton and Poulisse) are notable for their overall assessment of what kind of phenomena a bilingual model must account for; others (Myers-Scotton, Clyne, Auer, Rampton, Zentella and Green) are most valuable for making explicit and refutable claims about codeswitching; still others (De Groot & Kroll, Green, Grosjean, and De Bot) are of great interest for their focus on underlying psychological mechanisms. All together, the most outstanding feature of these ten approaches is not necessarily their conceptual orientation, but the kind of data they count as evidence. Myers-Scotton (1992, 2002) pulls from sociolinguistics and generative theory and makes use of frequency data. Clyne (1967, 2003) engages in traditional linguistic argumentation, using examples and counter-examples to support his claims. Auer (1998) applies the techniques of conversational analysis, inferring process from discourse structure. Rampton's (1995) work draws from a broad spectrum of ethnographic, discourse analysis, and symbolic interactionist techniques to explain both micro (individual, interpersonal) and macro (institutional, societal) aspects of verbal interaction. Zentella (1997) is in some ways more classically anthropological in the wide net she casts, and in other ways unorthodox in the quantitative and qualitative detail she provides about the Puerto Rican children and adults in her study. Grosjean (1997) and Green (1986, 1998) conduct laboratory experiments. And de Bot (1992; de Bot & Schreuder, 1993) and Poulisse (1997) are eclectic and integrative in their methodological approaches, relying on both laboratory and field-based data.

The ten approaches will be reviewed in light of my intent to merge sociopragmatic and psycholinguistic phenomena in a unified framework. After a brief outline of the traditions I have engaged, I will treat each approach by first summarizing its major tenets and then discussing those aspects of the models most relevant to the proposals in this book. As we proceed, there are suggestions for research to help create a more integrated sociopragmatic and psycholinguistic approach to the study of bilingual processing.

INTELLECTUAL ROOTS: A PURPOSEFUL AND SELECTIVE OUTLINE

The present work owes a large debt to a variety of approaches in sociology, linguistics and psychology. They are a selective function of my own intellectual history, which began in sociological theory, made its way from the <u>Aspects</u> Model of generative linguistics to psycholinguistics and micro-sociolinguistics, and later added training in experimental cognitive psychology.

Sociological theory, as developed by Parsons (1967) and extended to the sociology of language by Fishman (1964) and to sociolinguistics by Williams (1995), was helpful in identifying relevant domains of social structure. This translated into the identity component of the SPPL Model (Figure 1.1). Hymes' (1967) taxonomy for the ethnography of speaking was a starting point for identifying relevant sources of information. It is most obvious in the contextual component of the model (component 2 in Figure 1.1). Gee (1990) provided a direction to link social constructs and linguistic data. More indirectly, the tradition of Durkheim and Weber also contributed. Durkheim's influence came principally from his detailed structural analysis in *The Elementary Forms of Religious Life* and Weber's from his 19th century sociology of the world's major religions. This thread will be seen most clearly in the tradition which Rampton (see below) takes from Durkheim to Goffman, in particular the latter's work on 'interaction ritual.' Weber also contributed the construct of ideal types, which along with Chomsky's notion of an ideal speaker-hearer, is rejected here in favor of real speakers and individual analyses.

From linguistics, Fraser (1987, 1996) and Blakemore (1987) provide substantive insight into pragmatic and discourse markers, and Schiffrin's (1987) work offers a methodology for how they are structured in oral discourse. This work is most relevant to the genre and intentional elements of the SPPL Model (components 2 and 3 in Figure 1.1). Waugh's (1976) summary and review of Jakobson's life's work helped bring me to some of the insights in the present book, especially regarding the relationship between imitation and variation, two processing mechanisms discussed in Chapter 4.

Among the comprehensive models in a functionalist tradition in psychology that have contributed to this work are Norman H. Anderson's Information Integration Theory and Functional Measurement and William Powers' Perceptual Control Theory. For the processing aspects of the present work, Anderson (1981, 1982, 1996) and Powers (1973, 1978) are challenges to one-dimensional, linear models prevalent in psychology. Anderson's Functional Measurement approach gave me a framework and a methodology for handling more both L1 and L2 information and incentive to aspire to a unified model.

Powers taught me about the notion of control and, based on the psychology of James (1890), offers a role for will, volition, and intent in cognitive science.

In my first attempts to integrate sociological, social psychological, and linguistic phenomena in a unified framework (Dittmar, Spolsky & Walters, 1997, 1998), Bourhis' (1979) model of micro-sociolinguistic, social psychological and macro-sociolinguistic determinants of codeswitching was particularly helpful. A more recent attempt at an integrative model (Landry & Bourhis, 1997), this one to account for additive and subtractive bilingualism, includes sociological, socio-psychological and psychological factors, all of which influence language behavior in contact situations. The present work draws on his proposals to link social and psychological, macro and micro phenomena in bilingual language use. It tries to go beyond disciplinary traditions in an attempt to account for various phenomena in bilingual production and to incorporate processing and processing mechanisms into this framework.

SQUEEZING PROCESSING OUT OF STRUCTURE: LINGUISTIC APPROACHES TO BILINGUALISM

I chose three models of bilingualism to start this discussion. All three are distinctly structural. This means that their focus is on the building blocks of language, the nouns and the verbs of syntax, the locatives and temporals of semantics, and the turns and repairs of discourse. Nevertheless, these models do make claims about processing, sometimes explicit and sometimes subtle or even implicit in their data analyses. Myers-Scotton's work on codeswitching (CS), originally sociolinguistic in orientation, has gravitated towards the terminology and constructs of generative theory, and more recently to interests in lexical organization and bilingual processing. Her model is reviewed more thoroughly than some of the other approaches, partly to introduce some of the constructs needed in the rest of the chapter and partly for its explicit claims about bilingual processing. One of the things which makes Myers-Scotton's model and research unique is that it tries to combine macro-social factors with linguistic phenomena in a single framework. Following a review of this attempt at integration, her view of lemmas, intentions, and activation is examined. With the backdrop of this work, I review Clyne's recent and not so recent work on triggering. In this work, the structural aspects of triggering are said to activate codeswitching. Finally, Auer's research takes bilingual production beyond the lexical and sentence level of processing, focusing on interactive aspects of codeswitching.

MYERS-SCOTTON: FROM MATRIX LANGUAGE FRAMES TO ABSTRACT LEVEL
PROCESSING

Among researchers of codeswitching (CS), Myers-Scotton's work has the
widest scope. Her studies include research centered mainly, but not exclusively,
on social motivations (e.g. Scotton, 1986; Myers-Scotton, 1993a); on structural
constraints (e.g. Scotton, 1988; Myers-Scotton, 1992, 1993b); and more
recently, on lexical organization and bilingual production (Myers-Scotton, 1992;
Myers-Scotton, 1995; Myers-Scotton & Jake, 1995; Jake & Myers-Scotton,
1997). Her most recent effort (Myers-Scotton, 2002) includes a modification of
her Matrix Language Frame (MLF) Model, elaborating some of the terms and
postulates of the original proposal and offering a new sub-model that
distinguishes among three levels of processing: conceptual, functional, and
positional. The conceptual level is said to "bundle" intentions "into semantic and
pragmatic features associated with lexemes" (Myers-Scotton & Jake, 1995: 981-
2). The functional level is said to activate predicate-argument structure. The
positional level is responsible for giving lexemes their morpho-phonological realization.

The new research program introduces a distinction between classical and
non-classical CS. Classical CS presupposes sufficient proficiency to produce
monolingual utterances in each language and when codeswitching, a single,
clearly distinguishable Matrix Language which determines the grammatical
frame (Jake & Myers-Scotton, 2000:2; Myers-Scotton, 2002:8). The new model
also offers the possibility of a Composite Matrix Language, accounting for
codeswitching data that the original MLF Model could not handle. These data
are said to occur in situations when the bilingual does not have "full" access to
both grammars, where the "abstract morphosyntactic frame [is] derived from
more than one source language" (Myers-Scotton, 2002:105). The composite
matrix language involves convergence at one or more levels of the MLF Model,
and is said to occur for both sociopolitical and psycholinguistic reasons when
there is language shift and attrition. With a somewhat broader and more
integrative outlook, I think the mechanisms involved in composite CS and
convergence could be more generally applicable to the kind of stable
bilingualism, for example, in the Puerto Rican and Chicano communities in the
US. The idea here of not having full access to both grammars is comparable to
the notion of 'incompleteness' in Poulisse's work, which is discussed below, and
to proposals in the following chapters to incorporate a more dynamic, modifiable
conception of representation into models of bilingualism.

Regarding the relative importance of social and structural information,
Myers-Scotton (1993) states: "…that both sets of factors have a role in shaping
CS utterances, but with a division of labor which gives structural factors the role
of prime mover: First, grammatical processes designate permissible forms of
CS; then social processes regulate selection among the range of permissible
forms." This strong claim is balanced by an 'apology' to her sociolinguistic
origins:

Social factors have their own contribution. Most important, because
they impinge upon choice from a set of structural options, they can
become central in language change. Socially motivated choices may
suppress other options over time (Myers-Scotton, 1993:476).

Based on this work, her 'stated' position can be summarized as structuralist for
individual language use and as sociolinguistic for macro-phenomena such as
language change. But, when it comes to an explanation of how the model
operates, individual bilingual processing does involve both social and
psychological information. In Jake and Myers-Scotton (1997), the authors state:
"The choice of the ML [Matrix Language] is largely based on sociolinguistic
and psycholinguistic considerations, even though it is the structural
consequences of its choice which are of interest here" (p. 26).

Thus, despite statements that the purpose of the MLF Model is "to explain
structural constraints on code-switching" (Myers-Scotton, 1992), the model, its
assumptions, and the arguments that support it go well beyond its structural
features, encompassing sociolinguistic as well as psycholinguistic issues. For
example, the following assumptions are made:

CS is not qualitatively different from other naturally-occurring
language data...it differs only in being subject to the added constraints
of the...MLF Model (1992:102).

The MLF Model takes a 'principles and parameters' approach...It does not
espouse any current syntactic theory...While the model borrows some labels and
definitions from GB [Government and Binding] theory, it uses them only as
heuristic devices...it is compatible with a more lexically-based syntactic theory
such as LFG [Lexical Functional Grammar] and GPSG [General Phrase
Structure Grammar].

The languages of CS are not "equal partners in determining CS
structure" (1992:103; 1995:982)

The first of these assumptions may be questioned on both empirical and
conceptual grounds. No speech analysis studies have been reported to date that
compare rate of speech, pauses, and intonation contours for monolingual and CS
utterances and for different kinds of CS. Conceptually, this assumption might
lead to the (perhaps erroneous) conclusion that the same processes that underlie
monolingual processes can be used to account for bilingual processing. It also
gives the impression that the author believes in a unified processing mechanism
for handling unilingual as well as bilingual data. This inference would not fit the
ML-EL (Matrix Language-Embedded Language) distinction, which implies that
the two languages of a bilingual are psychologically separable. Finally, this
assumption might be motivated by a generative bias, as can be seen from its
juxtaposition with the second assumption, which positions the model in terms of
linguistic theory. Thus, I would propose that the first assumption was included to
place the research program squarely in the structural camp. The third assumption
makes strong claims regarding bilingual processing, implying that the two

languages of a bilingual are separate and distinguishable. This assumption and its instantiation in the model disregard a meaningful subset of CS data, considered non-classical CS by the author and labeled convergence and attrition phenomena by other researchers. These findings apparently led Myers-Scotton to modify her model. This last assumption also ignores a set of experimental findings from lexical decision tasks that are claimed as evidence for single or shared storage (e.g. Costa & Caramazza, 1999; Caramazza & Brones, 1980).

Social elements and structural features in the MLF Model. The primary goal of Myers-Scotton's research program, from her introduction of the Matrix Language Frame (MLF) Model to her recent extension and elaboration of that model, has been to "demonstrate that the structure of classic codeswitching (CS) between two languages is principled and therefore can be predicted" (Myers-Scotton, 1993, 1997, 1999). At the structural core of the original model are two distinctions, one unique to bilingualism and the other adopted from linguistic research that goes beyond the study of bilingualism. The former is the ML-EL (Matrix Language-Embedded Language) distinction, which claims that one language, the Matrix Language, determines the grammatical frame into which the other language is inserted. The second distinction, between content and system morphemes (cf., other distinctions: thematic-functional, open-closed class, and open-stop words) is the basis of a claim that system morphemes in general come from the matrix language.[1]

In successive presentations of the original model, Myers-Scotton (1992, 1993, 1995) discusses the need for independent (non-structural) criteria to decide which language is the matrix frame. In Myers-Scotton (1992) she prefers to determine the matrix language by using a sociolinguistic criterion (viz. the most widely used language in the community as measured by "the number of types of interactions in which it is the more socially unmarked choice") over psycholinguistic factors (first language, level of proficiency). In that same work, for an operational definition to classify CS data, both of these criteria are thrown out in favor of a frequency standard: "The ML can be defined as the language providing relatively more morphemes for the relevant interaction than the other languages used in the same conversation" (1992:105).[2] This definition is qualified by two conditions: that it excludes cultural borrowings and that the discourse is not restricted to a single sentence. Myers-Scotton acknowledges two sociolinguistic factors, community language shift and changes in situational factors or topic, as important in determining the ML, but leaves the operational definition as cited here.

In Myers-Scotton (1995), the following criteria are said to combine to determine the ML: a. the unmarked language, i.e. the one used for 'solidarity-building'; b. speakers' reports or judgments, i.e. what speakers say is the ML; c. relative frequency of morphemes: the ML has more than the EL. In that paper, Myers-Scotton describes the process of identifying the ML as dynamic, stating that the ML can change within an interaction as a function of situational shifts (i.e. topic, participants) and 'over time' as a result of shifts in values. While this 'dynamic' notion is developed only later (2002:64-65, 99), it leaves open the possibility that sociopragmatic knowledge may play a role beyond the conceptual level of processing. The MLF Model assumes that after conceptualization, structural constraints kick in and take over responsibility for on-line processing. If one could show that sociopragmatic considerations contribute at these levels of processing, and I think they can, then the model will need to incorporate such phenomena into its assertions and methodology. But the role of the ML and its distinction from the EL take a back seat in Myers Scotton's more recent attempts to explain situations in which neither of the two languages can be fully identified by the MLF Model.

Lemmas, intentions, and activation in a model of bilingual production. Myers-Scotton proposed two new sub-models as additions to the MLF Model (Myers-Scotton, 1999, 2002; Jake & Myers-Scotton, 2000; Myers-Scotton & Jake, 2000). These sub-models were apparently introduced to handle examples of CS that cannot be accounted for by the original MLF Model, and to "show what happens structurally when speakers do not have access to the grammatical structure of the desired Matrix Language, or when–for social reasons–the Matrix Language is turning over to a new Matrix Language (i.e., language shift)." These sub-models include elaboration of the content-system morpheme distinction and a 'levels of processing' approach. The former (labeled the 4-M sub-model) distinguishes among content morphemes, early system morphemes and two kinds of late system morphemes. The other sub-model, which is of greater interest here, is called the Abstract Level Model. It distinguishes among three levels of processing, as mentioned above: a lexical-conceptual level, a predicate-argument structure level, and morphological realization patterns. The predicate-argument level may itself split into a lemma level and a functional level (see Figure 2.1). The lemma level represents content morphemes and early system morphemes, which serve as input to the functional level of processing, where morphosyntactic and morphophonological formulation take place and late system morphemes are incorporated. This sub-model tries to explain how a bilingual, when generating a codeswitched utterance, selects lexical-conceptual information from one code and predicate-argument structure from the other, creating a composite matrix language. I would argue that this same explanation can be applied to Clyne's transference 'errors,' to DeWaele's (1998) lexical innovations, and to a large body of morpho-syntactic interlanguage phenomena.

Figure 2.1 Myers-Scotton & Jake's Abstract Level Model (from Myers-Scotton & Jake, 2000, Figure 1)

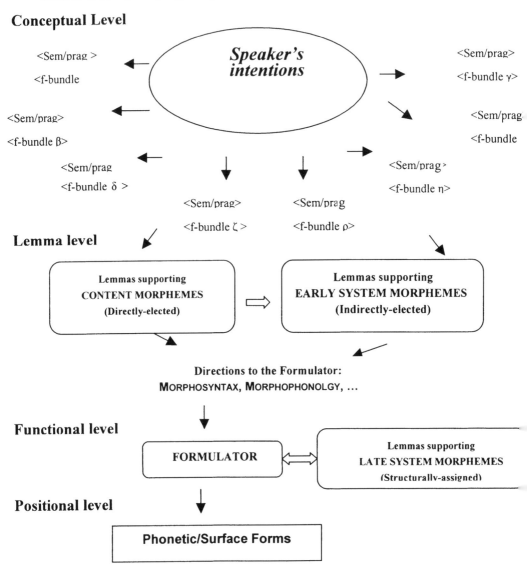

Myers-Scotton's recent interests in bilingual production (Myers-Scotton, 1995, 2002; Myers-Scotton & Jake, 1995, 2000), which she herself would classify as structural, are focused on congruence-checking of the two languages at each of the levels of processing in the Abstract Level Model. Her proposed bilingual production model advances a design that makes detailed (and refutable) claims, supported with a wide range of data across different language pairs. Some of the assumptions and constructs in that model, however, raise several important questions. They can be summarized as follows:

- ❑ Bilinguals have a single mental lexicon with language-specific entries (lemmas).
- ❑ Lemmas are abstract representations of pragmatic, semantic, syntactic, and morphological information.
- ❑ Incongruence of lemmas in two languages "motivates mixed constituents in code-switching."
- ❑ The conceptualizer converts universally-available semantic and pragmatic information to language-specific semantic/pragmatic feature bundles.

(from Myers-Scotton & Jake, 1995: 986-7)

The first premise clarifies an ambiguity in the earlier MLF Model that implied separate, or at least separable, processors for each of the two languages through its division of utterances into matrix and embedded languages. But the original model restricted itself to classical CS. The current version not only purports to handle mixed constituents (see Figure 2), but also focuses more closely on the lexicon. As I will claim in later chapters, a single mental lexicon may be a more elegant way of accounting for a variety of language contact phenomena, including interference, codeswitching, and some of the normal processes involved in translation and simultaneous interpretation.

At this stage, I would, however, question the viability of language-specific *lemmas*. The conventional definition of a lemma is of an abstract representation of semantic, syntactic, and morphological information. This notion follows Levelt (1989), who defines the construct as an abstract entity containing all non-phonological information. Activation of a lemma is also said to involve "decisions made at the most abstract level of production, the conceptual level" (Levelt, p. 236). Applying these constructs to CS, Myers-Scotton (1995) indicates that both "informational aspects of the message" and "pragmatic and socio-pragmatic considerations" contribute to a decision about which of a bilingual's two languages will be the source of the lemma. In discussing the EL [embedded language] island trigger hypothesis, Myers-Scotton (1995) states: "...decisions resulting in CS (i.e. decisions away from a monolingual discourse in the ML or the EL) would seem to be largely pragmatically or socio-pragmatically based. That is, the act of CS conveys some type of intentionality in addition to referential information" (1995: 249). This is not an abstract picture in which the lemma is an ideal entity and activation takes place at one or more structural level of processing. Rather, lemmas here are language-specific, and activation is situation-specific, depending on sociopragmatic con-siderations derived from the setting, topic, participants, and a speaker's intentions.

So how can lemmas be both abstract and language-specific? Moreover, how can pragmatic information, which by definition is situation- or context-specific, be abstract? Either, one has to give up the language-specific notion of a lemma and perhaps also its pragmatic elements, or abandon its abstract nature. To give up language- and situation-specificity means that language tags as well as pragmatic information have to be inserted or encoded at some other stage of production. To abandon the abstract notion of a lemma is equivalent to giving up the lemma-lexeme distinction. The latter choice might be preferred in a more statistically-based model of bilingual production, but for a symbolic model like the one reviewed here, the only viable alternative is to modify the claims regarding language-specific lemmas. Data presented by Myers-Scotton as well as by Clyne (2003) indicate that language contact phenomena have been documented at every linguistic level of processing. So, for the sake of parsimony and arguments to be made later, I will propose that language-specific information needs to be available at every stage of language production. I will also argue that lemmas are not universal, dictionary-like representations, but that they differ between speakers as well as across time for individual speakers.

Regarding processing, in distinguishing between the ML and EL, Myers-Scotton (1995:238-9) claims that "one language is more activated than the other(s)". She bases this claim in part on Green's (1986) model and Grosjean's (1988) word recognition data. In describing the *activation* process in the EL Island Trigger Hypothesis, she once claimed: "Activating EL lemmas triggers the formulator in the production process to inhibit all ML morphosyntactic procedures and to activate EL procedures so that the current constituent surfaces as an EL island" (Myers-Scotton, 1993:491). Most references to inhibition have been taken out of the recent description of the model (Myers-Scotton, 2002), being relegated to the point at which EL islands are generated. In the current model, a notion of varying levels of activation of ML and EL prevails. There are several problems with this account. There are no data that one of the two languages of a bilingual is deliberately 'inhibited' or suppressed. Slower perhaps, or less salient, but available and accessible nonetheless.

Another problem is that this account relates only to a subset of Myers-Scotton's own data, namely, those utterances described as ML + EL, ML islands and EL islands. It cannot handle what she now calls composite matrix language utterances or what Poulisse and Bongaerts (1994) call 'blends' and what Clyne (2003) calls fusion forms, e.g. *noce* 'no want' for no (Eng) + roce (Heb 'want'); *muzi* 'move' fem. imp. for move (Eng) + zuzi (Heb move).[3] A third reason to look for another account is to have a more unified framework to handle CS data. Clyne (2003) identifies language contact phenomena at every level of linguistic processing (see below). A unified framework that could handle all of these phenomena would certainly be more economical. Thus, it is not surprising that Myers-Scotton abandoned the original MLF account of CS data in favor of a model that is more differentiated vis-à-vis the kind of content and system morphemes it can handle, and more inclusive with respect to the kind of CS data it can account for.

In the new approach, specifically in their presentation of the 4-M Model, Myers-Scotton and Jake (2000) no longer speak about overall activation of the matrix language. Activation in the ML is defined in terms of system morphemes. And, in the 4-M Model four kinds of morphemes (content morphemes and three types of system morphemes) are specified in terms of whether they assign a thematic role, whether or not they are activated, and whether they refer to grammatical information outside their maximal projection. Content morphemes (e.g. nouns, verbs, adjectives) and early system morphemes (e.g. definiteness, gender, and number in Spanish definite articles) are said to be activated at the lemma level of analysis. In this framework information about a lemma's abstract lexical structure (its constituent structure and how it fits into a larger constituent) is "projected and provides input to the formulator to spell out surface forms" (p. 13). Late system morphemes have two varieties, "bridges" and "outsiders." Bridges are said to combine morphemes into larger units (e.g. chew+up, p. 4). Outsiders indicate "coindexical relationships across maximal projections" (e.g. the+toy). Late system morphemes are not activated until formulation. In this view, languages need not be activated. Words are activated, morphemes are activated, syllables and phonemes are activated. But languages, in toto, are not necessarily activated. The activation notion here has been differentiated and incorporated into many of the terms of model. It does not, however, make reference to speaker intentions and sociopragmatic information, two crucial components for any reasonable account of bilingual codeswitching.

Notes on data and method. The sources of data in Myers-Scotton's research program are in one sense broad-based and diverse. The research makes use of sociolinguistic distinctions in data analyses, e.g. first vs. second generation bilinguals. The model handles examples of classical codeswitching, namely, ML+EL, ML islands, and EL islands, as well as mixed utterances from a wide variety of language contact phenomena of a syntactic, semantic and to some extent pragmatic nature.[4] The model treats these data by classical linguistic argumentation, the claims being supported by attested examples and reinforced by the absence of contrasting cases (Myers-Scotton, Chapter 4; Myers-Scotton & Jake, 1995: 1003, example 14a).

The model also draws on frequency data, i.e. the number and proportion of instances of CS as a function of monolingual vs. bilingual vs. composite utterances, as a function of mixed constituents vs. EL islands, and as a function of syntactic category (Jake & Myers-Scotton, 2000). In fact, approximately four percent of the corpus could not be accounted for in terms of the ML-EL distinction, and this may have been what led to modification and elaboration of the original model.

Despite the breadth and diversity in the treatment of the data, the sociolinguistic motivations for CS are not fully integrated with the data analyses.

For example, when arguing that CS is a "tool in social negotiations," Myers-Scotton provides a lengthy description of national and regional (Western Kenya) language use patterns (for English, Swahili and local dialects) and the conversational setting (rural bar), details of the participants' mother tongue dialect (Lwidakho), local norms for making refusals, and previous linguistic context (pp. 476-477). However, little or no sociopragmatic background is provided when it comes to presenting examples to support the MLF Model and its hypotheses.

Moreover, neither the examples nor the quantitative data are ever broken down to give a portrait of an individual language user. The utterance is the object of study. The speaker is anonymous. This shortcoming is somewhat less problematic for the theoretical value of the model, but is a serious drawback to its empirical foundation. For example, one might want to know something about the informant's language learning history in order to answer the authors' question about the prevalence of English IP/EL[4] islands (Myers-Scotton & Jake, 2000, p. 11, example 12). The data may be partly the result of language learning strategies that stress imitation and mimesis; they could also be due to first language learning experiences in traditional frameworks that value memorization and quotation. Moreover, when the authors mention the importance of the large number (20%) of long IPs in the Arabic/English corpus, if they are concentrated among a small number of speakers, or even a single speaker, their conclusions might not be the same. The reader, unfortunately, is not privy to this information.

Summary and conclusions. In effect, the MLF research program is at a crossroads. Currently sociolinguistic factors in CS remain on the outside. They are a way to divide informants (first vs. second generation) and, to some extent in earlier work, a way to decide which language is the ML. But sociolinguistic and pragmatic information is also important for individual production. A bilingual's identity plays a role in whether, when, and how to codeswitch. Generational identity is only part of the story. Thus there is a need to incorporate sociolinguistic and pragmatic knowledge more directly in the constructs and methodology of the model.

Another issue worthy of future research on this model concerns the distinction between classical and non-classical CS. The model proposes one set of criteria to handle classical CS, i.e. those utterances for which bilinguals have access to the grammars of both languages, and another set of criteria to handle those utterances for which the two grammars are not congruent. The initial MLF Model, which distinguished between the Matrix Language, implies a two-track processor for bilingual production. The elaborated model, including its 4-M and abstract level components, states explicitly that bilinguals have a single lexicon, which includes procedures for checking congruence of conceptual, functional, and morphophonological information. The new model offers so much in the way of explanation for different kinds of CS that I'm not sure why the ML-EL distinction needs to be maintained. In suggesting that this separation might be unnecessary, I assume that both languages are considered activated and available. Lexical processing can be accomplished by a single architecture and a single set of mechanisms. Classical CS can be handled by the constructs of the 4-M and abstract level components the same way they handle non-congruent pragmatic, semantic, and syntactic features. In this way, the bilingual saves a major processing decision.

TRANSFERENCE AND CONVERGENCE, TRIGGERING AND TRANSVERSION: CLYNE'S PERSPECTIVE ON LANGUAGE CONTACT PHENOMENA
   Clyne, in research dating back to 1967, offers a terminology, a taxonomy and more recently (Clyne, 2003), a model to account for both structural and processing aspects of language contact. Transference (a term he prefers to CS in order to avoid different connotations of the latter expression) and convergence are structural constructs, while triggering and transversion relate more to processing issues.
   Clyne formulates two questions relevant to processing in general and articulatory planning in particular. He asks how "plurilinguals utilize the resources of their two or more languages when they switch" and how "they control the activation" of those languages. He offers three options for the activation question: separation, adaptation, and mixing. Separation is accomplished by a process he calls *transversion*, which is defined as the activation of one language and deactivation of the other. Adaptation involves lexical and semantic *transference*, where both languages participate in production, but only a single language surfaces lexically. Mixing is defined as "phonologically unintegrated transference." For separation and adaptation, the two languages of a bilingual are kept apart; for mixing they are not. Clyne also mentions that the two former processes may be intentional, but that mixing is "less conscious" (Clyne, 1967:196-7).
   While fleshing out these three options, Clyne discusses a wide range of structural linguistic strategies for "juxtaposing material from two or more languages." These include: lexical facilitation, tonal facilitation, syntactic convergence, and phonological and prosodic compromise. The main constructs in these strategies are transference and convergence, facilitation, and transversion. *Transference* is the term Clyne uses to describe language contact phenomena at all linguistic levels, including lexical, semantic, phonetic, phonological, prosodic, tonemic, graphemic, morphological, syntactic, pragmatic, and combinations thereof (e.g. lexicosyntactic, semantosyntactic). *Convergence* is defined in Clyne (2003) as "moving toward the other language" and said to be "due to perceptual identification between items in the two languages in contact as a potential facilitator of lexical transference.". From this statement, it appears that convergence has both structural and processing elements. The process is 'perceptual identification,' and the result is convergence of the two languages.

Facilitation-triggering (cf. Clyne, 1967, 1969, 1972, 1980, 2003) also has both structural and processing dimensions. "Transversion is facilitated by trigger-words–words at the intersection of two or more language systems which, consequently, may cause speakers to lose their linguistic bearings and continue in another language" (Clyne, ms:12). Four sources of facilitation are discussed. First, *lexical triggers* are specified as phonologically unintegrated transfers, bilingual homophones (i.e. cognates between the two languages), proper nouns, and compromise forms. *Tonal facilitation* is similar in that the speaker equates the pitch and stress of the items in the two languages. Clyne cites two studies conducted in Australia as evidence. In Ho-Dac (1997) 85 percent of the instances of CS from Vietnamese-English bilinguals were found on high- and mid-pitched tones. The addition of emphatic particles with high tones serves as further evidence of facilitation. Zheng (1997) found that 98 percent of the instances of CS among Mandarin-English bilinguals occurred after falling (high or neutral) tones (i.e. those perceived as cross-linguistically most similar). A third way of triggering transversion (or more technically, activation of one language and deactivation of the other) is *syntactic convergence*, which is comparable to Myers-Scotton's notion of a composite matrix language, Muysken's (1997) congruent lexicalization, and Poplack's (1980) equivalence constraint. While the latter are primarily structural treatments of CS, it is here that Clyne is most explicit regarding processing, claiming that it is "perceptual identification" between the two languages which serves as the facilitator of CS. Finally, *phonological and prosodic compromise forms* are mentioned as a fourth source of convergence.

In facilitation, lexical, tonal, syntactic and sound-based structural elements seem to drive the system and 'trigger' CS. In contrast, Clyne (2003) introduces a strong role for articulatory planning and attitudes in his latest work on this subject. He says that language users 'plan ahead' when they use language, and subconsciously might anticipate the trigger-word when they transverse. "Their language planning in relation to transference and transversion is attitudinally driven. They also decide what degree of convergence is acceptable to them" (2000:2). Looking at the relative contribution of intentions and attitudes in the structural and psycholinguistic aspects of CS, one might say that intentions and attitudes get the system moving, but structural and psycholinguistic aspects of CS then acquire autonomy of their own. If this is the intention, then Clyne's short statements about the background of the speaker before presenting his examples may be a start towards combining sociopragmatic and psycholinguistic information in a single framework. Nevertheless, when it comes down to the final reckoning from an operational and interpretive point of view, the structural phenomena clearly have an upper hand in his view.

Clyne addresses issues that have not yet reached the forefront of CS literature. His idea of 'trigger-words' as anticipatory is not addressed in any of the other models of bilingual production. His notions of integrating linguistic material from two languages with consciousness and intentionality in CS, while only mentioned briefly throughout these writings, are ideas that demand rigorous treatment, both conceptually and empirically, in order to further advance the study of CS and bilingualism.

A note on method. Clyne's work is clearly structural in approach. It is also broad, touching on most linguistic domains, from phonetic to pragmatic. In my opinion, the import of the work lies in the uniqueness of the data, in its distinctive classification, and in the rich interpretive framework he offers. Clyne does not hesitate to invoke notions of process (e.g. perceptual identification). Nor does he hesitate to declare a need for more data. Of particular note in this regard is his reference to data on pauses in his discussion of tonal facilitation; this line of research would contribute meaningfully to an understanding of fluency in codeswitching. Also noteworthy is his call "to collect large amounts of data from a very small number of plurilinguals to ascertain the probability of specific lexical items facilitating transversion." This focus on the data of individuals, even in sociopragmatic research, is advanced throughout the remainder of the present work.

NEGOTIATING LANGUAGE CHOICE VIA STRUCTURAL SEQUENCING: AUER'S CONVERSATIONAL ANALYSIS

Auer's (1984, 1995) approach derives from the tradition of conversational analysis (Gumperz, 1982, 1992), which goes beyond the work discussed so far in several ways. First, it expands the level of analysis, investigating CS within, as well as across, speaker turns. Conversational analysis also entails social aspects of language use. Auer (1995:115) declares that the purpose of this approach is "to reconstruct the social processes of displaying and ascribing bilingualism." Third, Auer intends his theory of conversational code-alternation to be relevant to language choice and transferable to CS and to cut across a variety of bilingual situations and settings.

Auer sides with the camp that sees bilingualism as distinctive in that it affords the bilingual speaker "resources not available to monolingual speakers for the constitution of socially meaningful verbal activities" (115-116). Although some of the tools and methods he uses were developed for studying monolingual situations and speakers, their grounding in sociopragmatic aspects of language use make them readily applicable to the study of bilingualism. From the start, his view of CS as a *contextualization cue* and his claim that monolinguals would use prosody and gesture in situations where bilinguals use CS (p. 123) might give the impression that bilinguals are being judged by a monolingual standard. But his methodological approach is subtler than that. Further along (p. 130) while discussing the negotiation of language choice in a Canadian example (from Heller, 1982), Auer cites monolingual norms of interaction (i.e. reformulation, a change of intensity, elaboration) in order to show that in the same situation a bilingual is likely to be negotiating language choice. Thus, CS is a contextual-ization cue available only to bilinguals. And one of its social functions, the negotiation of language choice, is also unique to bilingual situations.

Although the model is socially-based and linguistically-oriented, one of Auer's (1995) observations does have significant implications for processing. This observation comes when he reviews other "pragmatic theories of code-alternation." In that review, Auer criticizes Fishman's (Fishman, Cooper & Ma, 1971) search for correlations between speech events and language choice, noting that speech event and speakers cannot be unambiguously tied to a particular language. Furthermore, he maintains, I believe correctly, that situational factors "underspecify language choice." (See also Heller's, 1988, notion of "strategic ambiguity" in this light.) This observation in the interpersonal domain can be applied to language processing at other levels. For example, if the bilingual speaker leaves language choice 'underspecified' and open to negotiation, perhaps certain aspects of lexical processing may also be left underspecified. In the model presented in the next chapter, I raise the possibility that lemmas in bilinguals are not universal representations of linguistic knowledge, but rather differ between speakers and even differ within a speaker, as linguistic knowledge is added or attrited.

Auer also criticizes taxonomies of "loci" or "functions" of CS (e.g. reported speech and quotation, change of participants in a conversation, role and topic shift, topicalization, language play, reiterations, and side comments) as empirically deficient. In rejecting correlational and taxonomic approaches, Auer opts for viewing CS as a "contextualization cue" in order to explain "sequential patterns of language choice" (p. 124). He delineates four major patterns of code alternation (several of them involving more than one variant).

Pattern I, labeled 'discourse-related' CS, is said to mark a shift in *participants*, *events*, or *topic*. This is what is meant by contextualization of a particular conversational feature. *Pattern Ia* describes what happens when a speaker begins speaking one language, which has already been used by another speaker. Later in the conversation the first speaker switches to another code, which is adopted by the other speaker. Here the switch occurs between speaking turns. *Pattern Ib* is said to occur when Speaker 1 begins speaking one language and switches within a speaking turn to a second code. As in the first pattern, Speaker 2 responds in the code of Speaker 1. In this case, however, the switch occurs within the speaking turn of Speaker 1.

Pattern II, which Auer calls both 'language negotiation' and 'preference-related switching,' is known in the CS literature as 'one speaker, one language.' Two variants are offered: *Pattern IIa* describes what happens when Speaker 1 uses one language exclusively, while Speaker 2 uses a different code. *Pattern IIb* is used to characterize the following situation: After several exchanges where speakers are using different codes, one of them adopts the language of the interlocutor. Although Auer claims that this pattern is more "usual" (1995:125), it would seem to be an open question, given the number of immigrants and their children who use Pattern IIa as the primary mode for communicating.

Pattern III is typified by turn-internal CS, which Auer claims may serve more than a single function. He points out that turn-internal CS can serve a discourse function, e.g. for emphasis, topic/comment shift as well as an interpersonal function, where CS within a speaking turn allows language choice to remain open, i.e. as a part of the conversation to be negotiated. This pattern is claimed to be evidence that no 'base language' has been selected. This challenges Myers-Scotton's original MLF Model but is in tune with her later Composite Matrix Model. Two variants are proposed for Pattern III, one where both speakers continue within-turn CS for several exchanges, the other where Speaker 1 codeswitches, and Speaker 2 responds in a single language.

Finally, Pattern IV is labeled transfer or insertion in order to distinguish it from CS. Not much is said about this pattern other than that it can be "discourse- or participant- related" (Auer, 1995:126).

The patterns and their variants summarized here are the structural basis for a conversation analytic perspective on bilingual interaction. Auer's approach to bilingualism is grounded in the idea that language is a social phenomenon, even though his methodology is distinctly structural. The patterns are rooted in structural units. Notions of 'first pair part' and 'second pair part' are structural constructs from conversational analysis (e.g. Sacks, Schegloff, & Jefferson, 1977). In fact, the whole idea of a speaking turn is fundamentally structural. But in Auer's framework, structure is used in the service of functional categories and social constructs, in particular, the negotiation of language choice in bilingual interaction. Thus, while the model offers no explicit statement about individual bilingual processing, its merger of social and structural aspects of language use is important for a more comprehensive, inclusive view of bilingual production.

More recent work by Auer expands the domain of his typology of bilingualism as well as the data it accounts for. Auer (1999) distinguishes three types of bilingual language behavior, which he labels codeswitching (CS), language mixing (LM), and fused lects (FLS). These phenomena are said to range along a continuum from pragmatics and discourse to a more grammaticalized system. Along another dimension, Auer distinguishes between alternational and insertional switching/mixing. Alternational switching refers to bilingual situations "in which a return after the switch into the previous language is not predictable" (1998:313). Insertional switching is more grammatically integrated, mainly involving incorporation of content words into another language environment. CS and LM show evidence of both alternational and in-sertional switching, but switching in a fused lect is said to be solely insertional.

In this framework, CS is characterized primarily in sociolinguistic terms as: preference for one language at a time. It indicates "otherness" and involves negotiation, functional alternation, rhetorical/stylistic devices. It is found primarily at clausal junctures. Language Mixing, defined in contrast to CS, is described as: a "group style." Not functionally distinct and more grammatically restricted, it generally occurs within clausal boundaries, and if insertional, involves a matrix language. The language contact phenomena in a Fused Lect are said to be even more grammatically constrained and to involve more stable form-function relationships.

Auer's approach goes beyond the structuralism of Myers-Scotton and Clyne, both in the scope of analysis and in terms of the speaker's motivations. Auer is still a structuralist in his typology of patterns, which draw on the tools of conversational analysis. He is also a structuralist in his distinctions among CS, LM, and FLS and between alternational and insertional switching/mixing. But he is a card-carrying functionalist when he defines his four patterns in terms of notions such as participants, events, and topic, and when he draws on constructs such as negotiation and group style to distinguish CS from LM. This is a conventional division between linguistic and social categories. Processing is not one of Auer's primary interests, but his notion of negotiation may have implications for processing, even at the level of lexical representation and retrieval.

ETHNOGRAPHIES OF BILINGUALISM: MULTIPLE LEVELS AND RICH INTERPRETATION

In the main, sociolinguistics and the sociology of language are not supposed to be interested in cognitive aspects of bilingualism and bilingual individuals. Thus, on the surface there wouldn't appear to be much room for dialogue or even contact over the issues raised in this book. Fortunately, recent scholarship has gifted us with discourse analysis and cognitive anthropology to treat some of the disciplinary sectarianism that has plagued the field of bilingualism. The two approaches discussed in this section stand out for their differences as well as their similarities. Rampton casts his net widely, theoretically as well as empirically; Zentella's generality emerges from the details of her fine tuned analyses and the way she assembles them. Rampton eschews numbers; Zentella doesn't hesitate to use quantitative evidence to support her arguments. Rampton is ethnic outsider, adult and middle class in a multilingual, multi-ethnic adolescent working class culture; Zentella is an in-group 'member of the tribe,' more a part of the Puerto Rican community she studies than her education and status would aver. Both approaches make extensive use of ethnographic observation and discourse analysis. Both scaffold societal issues on intermediate social roles and micro level language data. And both, in their own ways, get at structure as well as processing.

The following section, on language crossing, begins by identifying the phenomenon of interest, by distinguishing it from codeswitching, and by situating it in its disciplinary frameworks. Next the primary theoretical constructs in Rampton's approach are described. On this background, I attempt to characterize his notion of processing, with a particular focus on his explanation of liminality in language crossing, a construct potentiality related to variation in the SPPL Model. The section ends with methodological comments on the fit between theory and data and the kind of data it would take to make his work more accessible for other disciplinary approaches to bilingualism.

Zentella's approach to bilingualism is first situated across a range of disciplines which have contributed to the expanding domain of linguistics. Next, the scaffolding of ethnicity and educational policy issues on data from individuals shows another way to approach levels of structure. For processing, code switching is the center of attention, in particular Zentella's focus on parity across languages and directionality of switching. The section ends with some comments on methodology.

CODESWITCHING AND CROSSING: RAMPTON IN THE SOUTH MIDLANDS

'Language crossing' is the phenomenon which occurs when a speaker uses a language or dialect he or she is not expected to use, viz. one "which isn't generally thought not to 'belong' to the speaker." It is said to involve "movement across quite sharply felt social or ethnic boundaries" (Rampton, 1999:291). Crossing is the phenomenon which occurs when an anglo-Canadian uses Canadian French, when a Bengali or other South Asian speaks Caribbean Creole, or when a native Creole speaker switches to Panjabi. Code crossing is a notion grounded in societal and interactional sociolinguistics. Unlike code-switching and codemixing, which can be identified by reference to linguistic form alone, language crossing requires knowledge and expectations at the societal level, an interactional context, and a degree of facility with multiple codes.

Rampton (1995) identifies his view of *codeswitching* in part with Auer's code 'alternation' construct, citing its roots in Gumperz' notion of CS as a 'contextualization cue' and mentioning Auer's discourse-related (addressee, topic, event) and participant-related (speaker) code alternation as most relevant. Rampton finds a need to go beyond these distinctions, labeling them 'situational' in the more classic sense of Gumperz' distinction between situational and metaphorical codeswitching. *Language crossing*, however, due to its occurrence at "interstitial and ambiguous moments" (Rampton, 1995:196) and 'partial violation of co-occurrence expectations' (Gumperz, 1982:98), is considered more metaphorical. It focuses centrally on 'disruption' and 'suspension' of expectations or norms and a recognition by both speaker and listener that they are not involved in "business quite as usual, that things are not quite what they seem, and that there are reasons for going beyond a literal interpretation of the situation" (Rampton, 1995:299, footnote 2). For this reason and to avoid terminological confusion (a refreshing admission), Rampton prefers the term figurative code-switching. In Rampton's words, "language crossing was intimately connected to moments (and/or themes) where the normal social order was loosened, and it either responded to these, or indeed produced or enhanced them" (1995: 219).

Despite his wide range of interests, Rampton in no way sacrifices depth for breadth in his explanatory approach to language crossing. The journey through the South Midlands takes us from the sociology of race and ethnicity and the sociolinguistics of language, register, and variety to discourse analysis and ethnography. It begins in the streets and on the playgrounds and comes full circle to the politics and policy of second language learning. The depth of the approach is both empirical and theoretical. The data range from the finest grain analyses of phonetics and prosody to the abstract constructs of pragmatics and sociology. Beyond the linguistics of codeswitching (e.g. Gumperz and Auer), Rampton challenges the British sociology of race stratification (Hewitt and Gilroy) and engages the anthropology and ethnography of Turner and the Hills. His theory reaches its peak in his dialogue with Bakhtin.

Rampton's framework includes four major dimensions of linguistic and socio-cultural organization: (1) language use, (2) interaction structure and processes, (3) institutional organisation, and (4) participants' knowledge about ethnic groups. The most relevant of these dimensions for the present work is his notion of interaction structure and processes. Prior to a discussion of structure and process, I briefly review the other three constructs.

In language use, he includes speech act functions, communicative intents, speech events, and sequential analysis (all of which find expression in different places in the SPPL Model). Rampton's third construct, institutional organization, includes situation, setting, purpose, participants, and activity types (e.g. buying, selling, chatting, negotiating). He declares this analytic component as less relevant to his study, since all of the participants come from roughly the same institutional frameworks. With regard to ethnicity (housed in the social identity component of the SPPL Model), Rampton includes "ideas and feelings about ethnic groups, their attributes, their positions in society, their prestige, their interrelationships..." (Rampton, 1995:15). Although he states unequivocally that ethnicity is not a "socio-cognitive" construct (p. 349), he makes very clear his view that behavior and experience influence knowledge and attitudes towards ethnic groups and ethnicity. Perhaps this is Rampton setting his limits, perhaps his philosophical position. In either case, this is one point with which the approach I am arguing for here would take issue, claiming ethnicity to be both social and cognitive.

Among 'interaction structures,' Rampton begins with the traditional distinction between speaker and listener. Then, citing the work of Goffman and Levinson, breaks down the notion of speaker into animator, author, and principal. Among the processes said to be involved in interaction are: the way participants arrange themselves, the 'moral ground rules' they apply in a given situation, expectations regarding 'situational propriety,' respect and facework (Rampton, 1995:347). The distinction between structure and process is further elaborated in the next section, since it is here that sociolinguistic approaches to bilingualism differ most critically.

Structure, function, and processing in Rampton's sociolinguistics. In a descriptive, sociolinguistic approach to crossing, Rampton lists six 'functions' of language crossing, under the general heading of 'negotiating the distribution of goods and services.' On the surface, these functions all answer the classic question about 'who speaks which language to whom, where, when, and why' and most of them fit relatively neatly into Hymes' (1974) taxonomy for the interaction of language and social life (setting, participants, event, etc.).

1. to mark the initials stages of certain events, e.g. detention, basketball
2. to respond to a teacher's request
3. to mark a high level of concentration at the request of the researcher
4. as a way of concluding and summarizing an interactive event
5. to signal potentially 'valuable' information
6. to indicate "when adults were gaining unratified access to information about pupil activities that they might subsequently use against them"

Example 2.1 *Extract II.4 from Rampton (1995:75)*

1	Asif:	lay's getting a bit suspicious man
2	Kazim:	mm
3	:	(what's wrong with) (8.0)
4	Kazim:	( )
5	:	( )
6	:	( )
7	:	( ) (4.0)
8	Kazim:	nice ennit
9	:	([football)
10	Asif:	[mm (5.0)
11	Jagdish:	I am 'wat'ching,you: ((others laugh))
12	Salim:	I am 'vat 'ching, you::
13	Jagdish:	((light laugh))
14	Jagdish:	Conrad (comes and leans) there man
15	:	( )
16	Salim:	CONRAD (.) CONRAD (.)
17	Conrad:	what?
18	Salim:	((quietly)): come on (1.0)

The last of these functions, which gets into perceptions and intentions not accessible to all conversational participants equally, goes beyond the former five descriptive categories. It is illustrated in the segment reproduced here (from Extract II.4, Rampton, 1995:75), in which Jagdish, a 15-year-old of Indian descent 'crosses' to SAE to indicate to his compatriots that they are being watched by a white adult cafeteria worker and that their 'business scheme' for 'taking' extra lunch to be sold later is about to be laid bare. The excerpt is used to explain Goffman's notion of 'interactional boundaries' and its usefulness for an understanding of the symbolic meaning of SAE as occurring "when Asian youngsters were negotiating participation in an interactional enclosure in which a white adult would have some control or influence over them."

But Rampton's analysis does not stop at the descriptive and structural. At the heart of his notion of language crossing is the distinction between speaker and voice (pp. 218-224; p. 278). The language crosser is conventionally a 'speaker' of one language (e.g. English vernacular), but in language crossing uses the language (e.g. SAE), the idiom (e.g. lexis), and the discourse (interaction order) to express a different voice. Rampton's summary of the findings on adolescent crossing illustrates the speaker-voice disjunction for SAE, Creole, and Panjabi. Language crossing into SAE was used as a voice distinct from the speaker's personal identity, for example, in order to convey the voice/identity of a wrongdoer or offender. It was also used as a way to elicit deference, but avoided in the company of native Asians, especially Panjabis, where SAE crossing might be perceived as derogatory. Creole, on the other hand, was found overall to be more 'integrated' with local vernacular English, perhaps making the speaker-voice distinction somewhat less noticeable. Rampton notes that Creole elicited limited deference and would be perceived as 'pretentious' if used among native Afro-Caribbeans. As an emerging language of wider communication among British adolescents, Creole was also described as an object of language learning, "a well-defined destination that motivated many young people" (p. 221). The speaker-voice distinction finds expression here in some of the constraints on Creole language learning, since acquisition of Creole in natural environments was 'inhibited' by the presence of native speakers. Thus, anglos' or Asians' use of Creole requires that they distinguish their speaker identity from their language learner voice in some very subtle ways. In further contrast, Panjabi crossing on the playground required the presence of Indian and Pakistani adolescents. That language was also characterized, according to Rampton, as reflective of language and status 'indeterminacy,' since non-Panjabis crossing into Panjabi did not allow themselves to assume subordinate roles, thus contravening some of the expected social norms for this language. In effect, their voice (Panjabi) is not the same as either their own social identity nor that of Panjabi. Rampton describes this as a sociolinguistic "no-man's land" (p. 221).

Rampton's views on processing also cover broad scope. He refers throughout his work to the "micro-processes of talk" and to discourse processes, like those described in Jagdish's crossing into SAE in the excerpt above and the speaker-voice distinctions among SAE, Creole, and Panjabi. Rampton also makes reference to institutional processes and devotes meaningful space to political processes, which involve negotiation of the value of different ethnicities and languages. At the micro, interactional level, processing involves expectations, feelings, and avoidance of a particular code; at the macro level, processing means the politics of ethnicity, class, and gender as adolescents negotiate their identities. Rampton argues that language crossing, as an out-group phenomenon, is more constrained and ritualized than in-group codeswitching, and as such "is likely to be a more consistently fruitful site for examination of the intersection of macro and micro social processes" (p. 284).

Rampton's most explicit statement related to mental processing comes prior to his introduction to the notions of ritual and symbol. He states:

> When we process an ordinary utterance in everyday communication, we analyse its propositions and integrate this with relevant pieces of world knowledge that we have brought to bear. In contrast, symbolic statements present a problem for routine propositional interpretation: they are often paradoxical and fairly immune to empirical contradiction. It is much harder to reconcile them with the bits of encyclopaedic knowledge that we first invoke, and this sets off the more extended process of memory search... (Rampton, 1995:83).

The psycholinguistic claim implicit here is that symbolic meaning is processed in a bottom-up fashion and that it involves additional mental effort. These claims stand in stark opposition to the top-down approach argued for in the SPPL Model. There, and in the next chapters, I maintain that language processing begins from the point of a speaker's social identity. Well before propositional analysis and memory search, the language user brings to bear demographic, ethnic, political, and other aspects of identity and integrates them with contextual and genre features of the interaction, intentions, and a range of micro level discourse, lexical, and articulatory aspects of formulation. I would also argue that the same underlying psycholinguistic processes used to understand ordinary utterances (if there is such an animal) are invoked to understand the presumed complexity of "symbolic statements." This is economical in ways not unlike the parsimony proposed in SPPL's single 'Language Choice Module' to handle both sociopragmatic and psycholinguistic codeswitching. I'm not sure Rampton would disagree. He doesn't seem to be particularly vested in the ordinary/symbolic distinction, since he devotes considerable space in one of his concluding chapters to showing similarities between crossing and codeswitching as well as the generality of the crossing phenomenon (pp. 276-280, 284-289).

Ritualization and liminality as ways to get at processing. Another entry point to Rampton's (1995, 1999) notion of processing comes from his discussion of language crossing as ritualized and what he calls its liminality. He draws on Bloch's (1985) view of ritual as a "means of communication...to refer and connote only in the vaguest of ways" (p. 699) and contrasts it with that of Lukes, who defines ritual as "rule governed activity of a symbolic character which draws the attention of its participants to objects of thought and feeling [objects, relationships, situations, ideas, etc.] that they hold to be of special significance" (Lukes, 1975:291).

Going beyond this openly cognitive perspective on ritual, Rampton shows three ways from his Creole data that "...acts and events...differ in the extent to which they are ritualised" (p. 205). At the sociopragmatic level (of speech events, setting and participants, and genre), he shows how games, cross-sex interaction and joking abuse exchanges involve a "relatively major suspension of the norms of ordinary conduct." At the level of speech acts, requests, suggestions, and disagreements were "more fleeting" and involved only "minor uncertainty." And, finally, the use of Creole by white adolescents was claimed to be even less direct. Rampton defines this continuum of ritualization in terms of their liminality, symbolism, and formulaicness. The construct of greatest interest here is liminality. Grounded in the anthropology of Victor Turner, who studied initiation rites in tribal and agrarian cultures, liminality is the term used to describe periods of transition between 'separation' and 'incorporation.' Turner, as quoted by Rampton, describes liminality as

- ❑ "a period and area of ambiguity"
- ❑ "a sort of social limbo"
- ❑ cessation or postponement of social relations
- ❑ moratorium of rights and obligations
- ❑ upheaval in the social order   (Turner, 1974:24, 27)

Rampton (1995:193-4), in choosing this construct to understand adolescence and transitions in racial identities, characterizes liminality as follows:

- ❑ "the ordered flow of life [is] loosened"
- ❑ "normal social relations could not be taken for granted"
- ❑ "boundary phases around interactional engagement are occasions of relative uncertainty"
- ❑ "breach [of] normative expectations of conduct"
- ❑ "weak points in the 'interaction order'"
- ❑ "an agreed relaxation of the rules and constraints of ordinary behavior"
- ❑ "interaction is...unusually vested with both risk and promise"

He goes on to discuss Turner's distinction between liminal and liminoid cultures. Liminoid interaction is said to be more individual than collective; more related to leisure events such as art, sport and games than to the "cyclical calendrical, biological, social structural rhythms" in churches, clubs, and the workplace; more marginal, fragmentary, and experimental and less "centrally integrated into the total social process"; more idiosyncratic, particular, and creative; and more likely to "contain social critiques, expose wrongs in mainstream structures and organisation; seeds of cultural transformation, discontent with the ways things are culturally..." (Turner, 1974:54-5) .

Rampton rejects a rigid distinction between the liminal and the liminoid, arguing that crossing displays elements of both kinds of societies. In micro level interaction, it occurs "at interstitial and ambiguous moments" and is found in particular in Panjabi crossing, e.g. in abusive joking and games and in self-directed utterances. In abusive joking, crossing was said to involve a "competitive orientation"; in self-directed utterances it expressed "uncertainty about personal entitlement to an out-group language" (p. 196). In all cases, language crossing represented a departure from the language behavior patterns of the dominant culture (p. 197).

These functions of language crossing are more subtle and complex than the one-to-one mappings of descriptive sociolinguistics between language and setting or language and participants. They assume that adolescents have incisive psychological knowledge about ethnicity, language, and social interaction. When whites and blacks cross into Panjabi in games and in joking abuse, there is a process more subtle than a simple link between language and speech event. There is an intention to "provoke remedial action." When SAE is used for emphasis, it is more than a direct tie of language to pragmatic function. There is an attempt to "restore orderliness."

Levels of processing. And in all of these examples among Rampton's 400 or more instances of language crossing, the micro level processes are a reflection of institutional and political processes played out at higher levels of social analysis. Theoretically, Rampton uses Lukes to take us from the mental activities of thoughts, feelings, and beliefs to these macro level processes. For Lukes, political ritual is the 'mobilisation of bias'... which includes "values, beliefs, rituals...and constitutional procedures ('rules of the game') that operate systematically and consistently to the benefit of certain persons and groups at the expense of others" (Lukes, 1975:302, 305). According to Rampton, at the level of interpersonal interaction, code crossing is intended to "disrupt smooth transition" and to camouflage the speaker's identity (p. 84). And, at the societal level of processing, code crossing into SAE, as a 'mobilisation of bias,' can be ascribed one or more of the following interpretations:

❑   as evidence for Anglo-Asian racial conflict
❑   as showing that "knowledge [and recognition] of ethnic stratification was not problematic for adolescents in multicultural urban Britain"
❑   as giving a sense of "legitimacy...[to] institutional relations and ultimately...affect the user's willingness to participate in them" (p. 86)

Rampton's intellectual candor in leaving his findings on SAE code crossing open to such broad interpretation are claimed here to add to the strength of the 'variation' notion which emerges from his work. In fact, with regard to SAE, Rampton states explicitly that the symbolic meaning(s) of code crossing are "open to variation and negotiation." This vagueness, openness, loosening, and variation is what Rampton claims allow us to make the connections between the verbal, interactional level of processing and institutional, societal issues such as race and ethnicity.

Some notes on method. The most important methodological characteristic of Rampton's work is the almost perfect fit between the principal phenomenon he studied and one of its central methodological features. Language crossing is defined as out-group language behavior, and Rampton is the unparalleled out-group researcher. Even the most perceptive in-group researcher would not have attained the same insights that Rampton, the adult, middle-class, white teacher did with his multi-racial, working class, adolescent participants. The very construct of language crossing is an outsider's take on a phenomenon which had been the exclusive domain of bilingual communities.

One characteristic which distinguishes Rampton's empirical approach from the linguistic approaches in the previous section is that language crossing cannot be identified simplified by looking for occurrences of SAE, Panjabi and Creole words and phrases embedded in stretches of English vernacular speech. From the phonetic and prosodic detail of his transcripts of verbal interaction, it is clear that great pains have been taken in analyzing and evaluating data. For SAE alone, Rampton lists no less than a dozen distinguishing features ranging from non-nuclear stress and abrupt pitch changes to retroflexion, aspiration, glottalisation, and nasalisation. On the other hand, this fine-grained detail is hidden in the richly interpretive exposition and the broad theoretical framework. The phonetic and syntactic details would make his analyses more transparent, especially in articulating the connections between macro and micro levels of processing. More details about the backgrounds of the participants, especially their language repertoires and preferences, would also contribute in this regard.

Another thing conspicuously missing from Rampton's work is quantitative data to support his proposals and arguments. It is clear that quantitative analyses have been conducted, since he does report the overall numbers for hours of recording, transcription, and instances of crossing for each of the three languages investigated. Moreover, Rampton is not principally opposed to numbers, since he even calls for such analysis in order to attain "a really robust characterisation" of the symbolic differences among the three languages he worked with.

The intent here is not to discredit the decisions Rampton made in presenting his work to the scientific community. These are choices and decisions every researcher makes, even those who strive for wide-scope and integration. Rather, my purpose here is to say what it would take to make that work more adaptable to the dialogic function of the present volume: my attempt to find ways of accommodating ethnographic, discourse, and experimental approaches to bilingualism in a single framework.

Rampton's work is relevant to the issues raised in the final chapter, in particular for its contribution to the field of second language acquisition and teaching. At present, I turn to an in-group ethnography of another bilingual minority community, Zentella's studies of Puerto Rican bilingualism.

HOME, SCHOOL AND BLOQUE: ZENTELLA'S ANTHROPOLITICAL LINGUISTICS

Zentella's studies involved 37 children, from 20 households, 4 patterns of care giving, and 6 age-based social networks. Most of these lives were lived in one of two tenements on a single street known fondly to in-group members as *el bloque*. The language varieties of *el bloque* included seven distinct linguistic repertoires and six degrees of bilingualism. Zentella's language data focused in particular on five of the children, recorded over an 18-month period, during which time they produced 1685 instances of codeswitching.

As an exemplar of qualitative research, it cuts across a wide spectrum of linguistics, sociology, and anthropology. It is more structural than Rampton's approach, but no less functional. It is linguistically documented in different ways, providing detailed quantitative accounts of the syntactic points at which codeswitching occurs and constraints on where it does not. Zentella's work draws from and contributes to four sub-disciplines in linguistics. Her investigation of the functions and strategies of "Spanglish" and her analysis of attrition across generations are sociolinguistic, more quantitative than discourse-oriented. Her case studies of Isabel and Maria advance the fields of child and adolescent language from a socialization perspective. The research on cross-generational Spanish attrition contributes to the field of socio-historical linguistics. And the work in its entirety is a model for educational linguistics, especially with regard to bilingual education.

Scaffolding social structure onto language. The structuralism of Zentella's research goes beyond the syntactic points and directionality of codeswitching. The ethnographic description and analysis take the reader from issues such as race and ethnicity to the streets and hallways of el bloque. The social networks among children, teens, 'young dudes,' young mothers and male and female adults along with the seven linguistic repertoires (e.g. Puerto Rican English, Non-Standard Puerto Rican Spanish, African American Vernacular English, Hispanic English) formed the diverse array of data points which constituted one level of sociolinguistic structure of el bloque. At another level (within the household), it took six different patterns of language use to account for the relationship between language and dyadic communication in the 20 families. The most prevalent of these patterns (i. Spanish among caregivers; ii. Spanish from caregivers to children; iii. Spanish from children to adults; and iv. English from children to caregivers) were found in six households. Another five households revealed Spanish when caregivers spoke and English when children spoke, regardless of interlocutor. But a full nine households did not fit either of these patterns. The variation in household patterns is yet another example of bilingual diversity. But, the center of interest for Zentella's work is focused on the individuals and their language use and how they fit into the homes and social networks of el bloque. It is via the five focal children and their language use that Zentella crafts the relationships among the different levels of social structure.

The approach to bilingual processing is less explicit in Zentella's work than it was in Rampton's. In that sense, she is more linguist than sociologist. In both approaches we had to dig deeply to find precise reference to processing. The tradition in linguistics is more structural, where questions of representation have taken precedence over questions of language use and language processing. In Zentella's research, two entry points to an understanding of how bilinguals process language can be inferred from her analysis of Spanglish communication strategies in terms of parity and directionality.

Beginning with her structural analyses of codeswitching, Zentella argues for parity between English and Spanish in the speech of her focal participants. In a comparison of her work on codeswitching (Zentella, 1997) with that of Poplack (1980) and Lipski (1985), roughly the same syntactic hierarchy emerged, with switching occurring more at sentence boundaries (.23 of the cases), somewhat less on nouns (.14) and clause boundaries (.12), and relatively infrequently on object NPs and conjunctions (.06). In terms of constituents, Zentella reports a preference for codeswitching to English on tags, adjectives, and predicate adjectives and to Spanish for determiners, fillers, prepositions, conjunctions, and pronouns. A more conservative, structurally-based interpretation of these data would state that English favors switching on major constituents and open class items, whereas Spanish switching is relegated to closed class items. English is for pragmatics (tags) and content (adjectives), Spanish is for grammar. But Zentella does not choose this path. Instead, she goes on to point out that these instances of codeswitching, favoring one language or the other, were short segments "inserted into a longer stretch of discourse in the other language" (p. 120). And then she interprets: "...the frequent embedding of small constituents had the effect of continually reasserting and recreating children's dual New York-Puerto Rican identity." Because they had a "foot in both worlds, they never spoke in one for very long without acknowledging and incorporating the other, especially in informal speech." This is what she means by parity.

Turning now to Zentella's sociolinguistic analyses, let me preface my remarks by stating that the short exposition to follow cannot do justice to the depth and complexity of her approach. She begins by distinguishing between "on the spot" and "in the head" codeswitching. The former can be attributed to "observables" i.e. the conversational setting, linguistic and social identities of the participants, and the language of the utterances which preceded the switch. "In the head" codeswitching involves speaker's knowledge about "how to manage conversations, how to achieve intentions in verbal interaction, and how to show respect for the social values of the community, the status of the interactants, and the symbolic value of the languages" (pp. 82-83). For analysis, the 803 instances of codeswitching were broken down into three groups of strategies, "footing, clarification and/or emphasis, and crutch-like code mixing."[5] Actually, the complexity is even more acute: The category 'footing' is split into realignment (itself with eight different types) and appeal/control (itself with three types); clarification/ emphasis is subdivided into four categories; and crutch-like code mixing has six sub-strategies of its own. Zentella's data include multiple examples for each of the 21 strategies as well as distributional evidence documenting the frequency of each one in the corpus.

A further level analysis looks at the individual differences in codeswitching, comparing codeswitching into English and Spanish across the five children in terms of their language dominance and age. Here again Zentella argues for parity between English and Spanish, the proportion of switches into each language hovering around 50 percent (ranging from 45-52% for English and 48-55% for Spanish across the five children). The parity notion is supported by the fact that 12 of 21 conversational strategies were used at the same relative frequencies in both languages. The nine codeswitching strategies which did show differences between English and Spanish cut across all linguistic domains for both languages. Spanish-biased strategies included discourse and pragmatic techniques (narrative frame breaks, quotations, and appositions) as well as lower level 'crutches' (parallelisms and fillers/hesitations). Codeswitching to English was marked by a preference for a range of footing strategies (e.g. to mitigate and aggravate requests, checking) as well as 'crutches' like triggering.

Zentella's dialectic in explaining how English, the language of power, could show a preference for both 'mitigating' and 'aggravating' requests illustrates the complex relationship between social identity and micro-level, interactive aspects of the situation. It also clarifies a difference between the language and direction of codeswitching and the very presence of codeswitching. Zentella assumes a high-low, power-solidarity distinction between English and Spanish in the New York Puerto Rican community, and in fact, that distinction is reasonable, given the economic and political domination of this ethnolinguistic minority group. But such a one-dimensional distinction would map language use directly onto social identity without taking into account interpersonal, communicative, and psycholinguistic factors in codeswitching. Zentella offers three possible explanations for the apparent anomaly that English was used for both low-status (mitigating) as well as power-oriented (aggravating) functions. One possibility raised was that communication took precedence over social identity, and in making requests, the Puerto Rican caregivers wanted to make sure their child interlocutors understood them. For this explanation, codeswitching is a pragmatic, communicative marker; it prevails over social identity. Another explanation was that codeswitching was a feature of speaker intentions, used to intensify the pragmatic function, i.e. mitigation or aggravation, and was not related to either identity or to the speaker's evaluation of the listener's linguistic abilities.

A third, more abstract, explanation suggests it was "the fact of switching" that was important, not the language of the switch or its directionality. Zentella does not deny the symbolic importance of the direction of codeswitching, stating explicitly that directionality can "play upon the symbolic values linked to the languages in the repertoire, and these might also be employed to advantage, such as to add social meaning" (p. 111). But, in the analysis described here, she is painting the broader picture, a portrait of complexity, where codeswitching can take on a range of functions. In doing so, she assembles further evidence for the more abstract function of the third possibility by reminding the reader that codeswitching was found at all grammatical levels and for all conversational strategies. Bilingualism, at this subtle, abstract level of processing takes us beyond the linguistic constituents, the conversational strategies, and the particular language and direction of codeswitching. Bilingualism is the goal, and codeswitching is one means to that goal. In terms of identity, codeswitching is a way that the Puerto Rican children in Zentella's study show they "lived on the border" and that they were "unwilling to relinquish a foothold in either" [of their two worlds]. "'Spanglish' moved them to the center of their bilingual world, which they continued to create and define in every interaction" (Zentella, 1997:114).

Methodological notes. At the outset of this book, in the sociolinguistic argument for the SPPL Model, I mentioned that having a social conscience is an apparent prerequisite to membership in the club. As an in-group ethnic studying her own linguistic community, Zentella makes explicit, at several junctures, the way she handles the Observer's Paradox. She also makes explicit her political, activist, and rigorously sophisticated advocacy of bilingualism. Sophisticated because her convictions on behalf of bilingualism are grounded empirically and embedded in the multi-layered complexity of identity, interaction, and linguistic structure. In arguing her case for anthropolitical linguistics, Zentella strikes an unconventional balance between the empathy she expresses for Isabel (and her struggle with a ruthless education system) and the tireless detail of her data analyses.

As an insider, Zentella's best insights came because she knew how and when to pose the question. She presents the fruits of this labor in the first lines of her book: "One day in El Barrio...I asked a nine year old of Puerto Rican background what language she spoke with her sisters and brothers. 'Hablamos los dos. We speak both...' " This response gave the ethnographer-linguist both the content and form of codeswitching. In discourse analysis, especially when conducted by an outsider, the verbal interaction among the participants does more of the work. Both approaches are highly interpretive. Both are called ethnography, but their approach to data is by no means monolithic.

The interpretive nature of qualitative research in general and ethnography in particular places a heavy ethical burden on the researcher. The ethical responsibilities of experimentalists are no fewer, involving first and foremost questions of selectivity regarding data and decisions about the manner in which those data are to be presented. Zentella's research makes use of both quantitative and qualitative findings. In discussing the low frequencies (less than one percent) of codeswitching at certain syntactic boundaries (AP, Pro, PredAdj,

Det, Prep), Zentella could have concluded that the children showed "greater awareness of syntactic hierarchies" (p. 128). But she does not, and her honesty in rejecting this conclusion comes in large part from her knowledge of the children, from the complementary qualitative data she had available. Another place Zentella shows her openness when she reports that for 19 percent of the cases of "crutch-like" code mixing, she was unable to determine whether the child had prior (even partial) knowledge of the word or phrase s/he was trying to retrieve and code mixing was a 'least effort' strategy. This quantity of 'missing data' would never fly in experimental psycholinguistics, where the amount of data from each 'subject' is more limited and less varied.

As with Rampton's approach, Zentella's contributions to educational linguistics and bilingual education will be relevant in the final chapter of the book, for their implications to the study of bilingual acquisition and to the investigation of language disorders among bilingual children. At present I move to experimental laboratories, to a selection of work on psycholinguistic and psychological approaches to bilingualism.

PSYCHOLOGICAL, TASK-BASED APPROACHES TO BILINGUAL PRODUCTION

This second section centers on contributions from psychology, psycho-linguistics, and neuropsychology to the study of bilingual processing. The section begins with a review of de Groot and Kroll's Conceptual Features Model, whose primary focus is the architecture of bilingual memory and the relationships, or 'mappings,' between words and concepts at different levels of processing. We discuss two issues here: the nature of bilingual representation and the role of development in bilingualism, i.e. changes in processing as a function of increased proficiency. The next section deals with Green's Model of Inhibitory Control with its assertions about a variety of processing mechanisms in bilingualism, in particular activation and control. Finally, Grosjean's exper-imental and computational approaches to bilingualism are reviewed with a focus on methodological innovations for examining social aspects of biligualism and generating systematic, valid codeswitching data.

REPRESENTATION AND CHANGE IN BILINGUAL PROCESSING: DE GROOT AND KROLL

De Groot and Kroll (1997; Kroll and de Groot, 1997) review a broad range of issues and a large body of data relevant to bilingual processing in general and bilingual production in particular. While a thorough review of their respective research programs is beyond the scope of this section, their range and depth are an important point to start a discussion of psycholinguistic work in bilingualism and for the proposals presented in the following chapters. After presenting an overview of their Conceptual Features Model, I relate to two issues: the nature of bilingual representation and their developmental hypothesis.

Three generations of bilingual memory research. Two generations of models of bilingual memory preceded Kroll and De Groot's (1997) most recent Conceptual Features Model. In both the first and second generation models, a structural distinction was made between concepts and words, between meaning and form. The differences between these two generations lies in claims about the links between L1 and L2 translation equivalents, and about how second language (L2) words are retrieved. One first generation model, reminiscent of Weinreich's (1953/1968) notion of subordinate bilingualism, is the *Word Association Model*, so named because there are direct links at the lexical (word) level between L1 and L2 translation equivalents. L2 words are not linked directly to concepts and must be accessed via words in L1 (see Figure 2.2). In the other first generation model, called *Concept Mediation*, there is a single conceptual store, and both L1 and L2 words are accessed directly from that store. In this model, there are no direct links between L1 and L2 translation equivalents (see Figure 2.3).

The second generation alternative, the *Revised Hierarchical Model*, was an attempt to capture developmental changes in second language proficiency and to account for data from experimental work involving naming and translation tasks. It is a composite of the two earlier approaches. It posits both lexical links between L1 and L2 words as well as conceptual links between concepts and words in both languages. It claims that the lexical links will be stronger from L2 to L1 (to account for faster and more accurate translation in that direction) and that the conceptual links will be stronger from concepts to L1 words (see Figure 2.4). The data supporting this model cover a wide range of bilingual speakers, stimulus sets, and experimental tasks. In general, when the tasks were more lexically-biased (e.g. translation of cognates, translation recognition tasks), non-fluent bilinguals performed better or showed more interference due to word form, implying lexically-based processing. When the tasks were more semantically-oriented (e.g. categorization judgments, semantic priming), fluent bilinguals performed better or exhibited more interference from meaning, implying conceptually-based processing. The model interprets these findings in terms of differences in the strength of connections between L1 and L2 translation equivalents, and between concepts and L1/L2 words. But the model does not make distinctions between different semantic categories, basically implying that all words and concepts are processed alike.

Figure 2.2 Kroll & Stewart's *Word Association Model* (from Kroll & Stewart, 1994, p. 150)

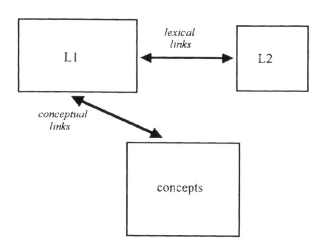

The challenge to characterize semantic distinctions in bilingual processing was apparently what lay behind De Groot and Kroll's third generation *Conceptual Features Model*, later called the *Distributed Feature Model* (Kroll, Michael & Sankaranarayanan, 1998). In particular, the model was stimulated by findings in studies of bilingual picture naming and translation with faster translation times recorded for concrete, animate, and cognate words than for their abstract, inanimate, and non-cognate counterparts. The concrete word effect shows faster translation times for concrete words than for abstract stimulus items, when word frequency and word length are held constant (De Groot, 1992). The authors explain that concrete words are more likely to have "similar or identical subsets of conceptual features" (1997:187) across languages than abstract words, which are said to be more context dependent. Translation is said to be a more conceptually-mediated process, and these similar conceptual features are said to be more accessible for concrete words (pp. 187-188). This same basic finding was documented for animate nouns (Sholl, 1995).

The other major finding that motivated the development of the Conceptual Features Model is that, in general, cognate words are translated more rapidly than non-cognates in experimental tasks. An unqualified finding of this type could serve as evidence that cognates are processed more lexically (less conceptually)

Figure 2.3 Kroll & Stewart's *Concept Mediation Model* **(from Kroll & Stewart, 1994, p. 150)**

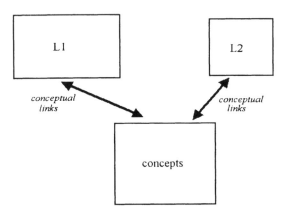

Figure 2.4 Kroll & Stewart's *Revised Hierarchical Model* **(from Kroll & Stewart, 1994, p. 158, Figure 3)**

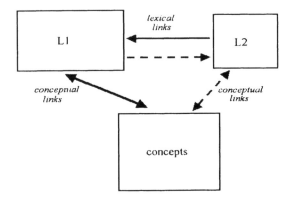

than non-cognates. But Kroll and De Groot (1997) cite a study conducted by Kroll and Stewart (1994), which confirmed the cognate word effect, but also reported differences for what they call forward (L1 to L2) and backward (L2 to L1) translation. When stimuli were presented in blocks organized according to semantic category, more interference was reported in forward translation than in backward translation. The authors interpreted this finding to mean that forward translation (into one's non-native language) is more conceptually mediated, and backward translation (into one's first language) may be more lexically-based.[6]

Representation and development in bilingualism. With this background, Kroll and De Groot (1997) came out with a model of bilingual lexical processing that is differentiated for conceptual features. The functional architecture is displayed in Figure 2.5. That model represents information at three levels: conceptual features, lemmas, and lexical features.

The conceptual and lexical levels contain features unique to L1 and L2 as well as shared features (represented by shaded circles). The model also proposes language-specific lemmas for L1 and L2, adopting "the general assumption that the lemma includes some syntactic and semantic information" (1997:190). The strengths of the links between conceptual features and lemmas vary, with stronger links to L1, weaker links to L2. The authors say that lemmas "are not necessarily a form of symbolic representation that function as an interface between the lexical and conceptual features on the one hand, and semantic or syntactic constraints on the other..." Rather, they view lemmas more as processing agents "to represent the patterns of activation between word forms and meanings" (p. 191). They distinguish between the context-free processing of picture naming and translation tasks, claiming that for these cases lemmas "may reflect only these form/meaning mappings." When context is added to the task (the example they give is a sentence processing task), the lemmas are expected to make use of syntax to give weightings to activate various lexical and conceptual features.

In the Conceptual Features Model *interference* is determined by the similarity in features across languages, as well as by the similarity in within-language and cross-language mappings from meaning to form (more similarity implies less interference). The "costs" of codeswitching for recognition and lexical decision tasks (Grainger & Beauvillain, 1987; Li, 1996) are explained in terms of activation (that both languages are activated) rather than the time it takes to switch from one language to the next. The model also proposes an account of *cross-language priming* phenomena. The available data for these phenomena are mixed, with some studies showing no cross-language priming effects (see Smith, 1997, for a review) and others showing cross-language effects (e.g. Grainger & Dijkstra, 1992). Kroll and DeGroot (1997) account for these apparently contradictory findings through a distinction between lemma level and lexical level processing. Studies that found cross-language priming effects did so because they presumably activated both lemmas and lexical features. In experiments which did not result in evidence for priming (e.g. where stimuli were blocked by language), the authors say that this occurred because subjects activated only the lemma. The data cited from Clyne and others above, where codeswitching in production occurs across a full range of linguistic levels, provides strong corroborative evidence for this account.

Figure 2.5 *Conceptual Features Model* **(from Kroll & De Groot, 1997, p. 190, Figure 6.4)**

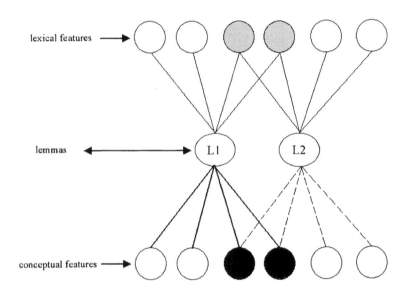

Summary and conclusions*. So what do we know about bilinguals, representation, and processing from this body of research? First, we know that fluent bilinguals show behavioral differences from non-fluent bilinguals. Specifically, fluent bilinguals are more influenced by semantic factors than non-fluent bilinguals in performance on translation recognition tasks. The model that characterizes this difference (concept mediation) does so in structural terms, but the differences are in fact behavioral. Second, we know that bilingual performance changes with increased proficiency. This, too, is a difference related to bilingual behavior, not necessarily connected to the representation of their languages. Third, we know that bilingual performance differs for different types of words, e.g. concrete-abstract, cognates-non-cognates, and animates-inanimates. These differences are grounded in the language and in the structure of the lexicon, and not in bilingualism per se. In fact, processing differences for these phenomena are not unique to bilinguals.[7] Fourth, and finally, we know that bilingual performance differs across task, e.g. translation recognition, picture naming, repetition priming. These are not differences due to the individuals who participate in the experiments. Nor are they due to the nature of representation of their languages. Rather, they are differences owing to processing.

In the words of Kroll, Michael and Sankaranarayanan (1998): "the Revised Hierarchical Model makes some general claims about how interlanguage connections change with increasing expertise in L2, but does not specify how or why these connections may differ for a given person as a function of the type of words and/or concepts that are acquired." In summarizing the Distributed Feature Model, they state: "it does not have much to say about the form of the mappings between words and concepts." The models presented here are conventional ways to represent sources of information and the relations between these sources.

That mental structure is inferred from performance is not necessarily an inadequacy. That processing is inferred from reaction times and accuracy scores is not necessarily a shortcoming. As will be argued below, these data and the models used to present them may get closer to the nature of the phenomenon known as bilingualism than studies using dichotic listening, P.E.T., and functional imaging techniques, which sometimes claim performance to be directly mapped onto brain processing. In fact, if processing can change from word association (accessing L2 words via L1) to concept mediation as a function of an increase in proficiency, this functional change may be the strongest, albeit indirect, support available for claims of neurophysiological or neuranatomical changes owing to the acquisition of knowledge (see Chapter 1).

BILINGUAL PROCESSING AS INHIBITORY CONTROL: GREEN'S NOTIONS OF CONTROL AND ACTIVATION

Green (1986, 1993) goes beyond the functional architecture of bilingualism in an attempt to account for a variety of language phenomena in a general purpose processing model. In the tradition of Garrett (1975) and Levelt (1989) who distinguish three independent, functional processing components (conceptualization, formulation, and articulation), Green (1993) describes the challenge of modeling bilingual processing as threefold:

   ❑ To specify how bilinguals achieve different mappings between
      conceptual representations and word meanings;
   ❑ To specify how language (L1 and L2) is encoded as part of a
      message's intention;
   ❑ To spell out "the means by [which] bilinguals achieve the tasks they
      do"   (Green, 1993:251)

Focusing on lexical processing, the model is intended to account for a range of phenomena in both bilingual and language impaired performance, in particular speech dysfluencies, codeswitching, and translation. A single model is proposed to account for normal as well as pathological processing. Three constructs–control, activation, and resource–are at the core of the model. Language users are said to control, or regulate, "activation levels of various components of the system" by allocating excitatory or inhibitory resources to raise and lower activation levels (Green, 1993:262). The model aims to explain slips of the tongue, dysfluencies, and impaired performance due to brain damage in terms of these same processing constructs, claiming that cognitive and linguistic representations remain "intact."

Control, a construct borrowed from cybernetics and information processing, is defined as avoidance of error. Green claims that slips of the tongue from fatigue and distractions in healthy individuals result from the same lack of control as paraphasic errors in aphasic patients. Previous models of bilingualism (e.g. Ervin & Osgood, 1954; Kilborn & Ito, 1989) are criticized by Green for their lack of detail regarding control processes to account, in experimental translation tasks, for "how it is that the word to be translated is not merely repeated and why it is that subjects can avoid producing words which are similar in meaning" (1993:259). In other words, how can bilinguals to speak one language while filtering out the other? How do bilinguals control or regulate interference? What are the mechanisms that allow a bilingual to codeswitch and to translate? Green's suggested solution is to give the bilingual speaker control over two lexicons by allowing specification of language at the levels of both conceptualization and formulation.

Activation is the construct Green uses to explain pauses, interference, and codeswitching. Hesitation phenomena are said to result from lower activation of certain words and expressions. Interlingual interference is said to result from simultaneous activation of both L1 and L2 systems. Green (1986) also distinguishes between selection and activation. In everyday bilingual processing, when a word or grammatical structure in one language is selected for production, the other language remains activated. Continued activation of the non-selected language is said to lead to longer latencies in bilingual object naming tasks (Magiste, 1979, cited in Green) and to lexical interference errors (Grosjean, 1982, cited in Green). According to this perspective, grammatical interference could be said to be due to activation of the non-selected language. Using the activation construct, fluent codeswitching is said to be a partial function of availability. Fluent codeswitching is distinguished from dysfluent or flagged codeswitching, i.e. the kind that could be marked by a pause or false start. It is also distinguishable from sociopragmatic codeswitching, i.e. the kind accompanied by a focus particle or pragmatic marker. Following this argument about availability in fluent codeswitching, the lexical item, pragmatic expression, or grammatical structure that is most activated, regardless of whether it comes from L1 or L2, is the one that will be produced.

The model does not explicitly address frequency of use, even though it is certainly relevant to various aspects of activation. Green (2000) makes reference to a related construct when he discusses 'strength of pathways' between concepts and words in his discussion of Kroll & Stewart (1994). An account of frequency should include a distinction between societal frequency, as derived from language corpora (e.g. BNC, London-Lund, and Birmingham corpora) and frequency lists (e.g. Kucera-Francis, Thorndike-Lorge) and individual frequency of use, i.e. a person's lexical, pragmatic and grammatical behavioral preferences. Although societal and individual frequency are not identical, there is presumably some overlap between them. Also relevant to activation are the social and demographic factors well documented as sources of identity and determinants of language attrition and loss. The chapters that follow try to deal with the relationships among some of these social factors and psycholinguistic processes in bilingualism.

Green indicates that lack of use will probably lead to lack of activation. Taking from research on non-verbal motor skills (Shallice, 1982, cited in Green, 1986; Shallice, 1988, cited in Green, 1993), he distinguishes three states of activation: selected, active, and dormant. The 'selected' state is what Green means by "controlling speech output" and what may be one of the processing mechanisms behind the matrix language in Myers-Scotton's Matrix Language Model. Selection is defined as "partially a matter of increasing the activation of L1 but, principally, it is a matter of suppressing the activation of L2 words so that words from that system do not get produced" (pp. 216-217). He proposes two kinds of suppression, internal (suppression of L2 words in the L2 system) and external (suppression of L2 words by the L1 lexical system). These two types of suppression are distinguished by different processes. Internal suppression is said to be accomplished by "an inhibitory loop," while external suppression is achieved by "an inhibitory link," that blocks selection of the L1 at the point of "phonological assembly" (see Figure 2.6).

When only one language is both selected and activated, one would expect minimal dysfluency, relatively little interference, and no codeswitching. Basically, this is a description of monolingual speech production. Green (1986) declares that his main interest is in situations in which both languages are active. This state should lead to more evidence of dysfluency, inteference, and codeswitching. For example, when L1 is selected and L2 is the primary language activated, then Green (1986:217) predicts increased dysfluencies in L1 produc-tion. These dysfluencies would include hesitations, false starts, self-corrections, interference and interlanguage phenomena, and 'performance' codeswitches.

Figure 2.6 Green's Model of *Inhibitory Control*

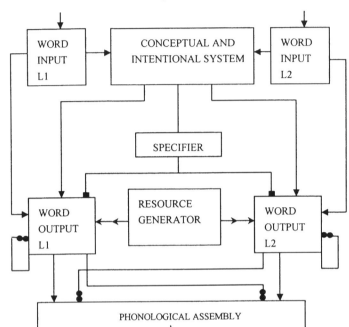

TO SPEECH OUTPUT

When L1 is selected and both L1 and L2 are activated, then fluent codeswitching is predicted. A first pass at investigating the three constructs outlined here might consider 'selection' as a kind of psychological 'set' by asking a bilingual subject to describe an L1-biased setting and event (and in a second condition to describe a unique L2 situation) and speak for 5-10 minutes about his/her feelings in that situation. Then, in an experimental manipulation of 'activation,' tasks involving (a) L1 only, (b) L2 only, and (c) L1 and L2 simultaneously activated can look at the relative influence of selection and activation. The selected-activated distinction may also be helpful for incorporating social and cognitive aspects of processing in the framework proposed in the following chapters.

Resource, the third construct in Green's original model, is defined (1986: 215) as the means "to activate or to suppress the activity of a component in a system." Resources are said to be available for either excitatory or inhibitory purposes. Activities involving control use up resources, and if these resources are not replaced at "the right rate," then control is impaired. Thus, Green posits the existence of a "resource generator" to restock cognitive reserves. Linguistically, bilingualism is assumed to consume more resources than monolingualism. And extra-linguistically, stress and anxiety are mentioned as consumers of resources that affect control of language production. Quite obviously, brain damage is also said to have an influence on resource.

Bilingual processing in a 'control, activation, resource' framework. In accounting for bilingual processing in this framework, Green (1993) says two conditions are necessary to bring about control: explicit intention and language tags on both word meanings (lemmas) and word forms (lexemes). He draws a parallel between language tags in bilinguals and tags for processing style and register switching. His model involves two stages, activation of the lemma and retrieval of the lexeme, with control specified as one of three states of activation. As mentioned above, this general outline is intended to account for a variety of data, including involuntary speech errors, interference, facilitation in experimental tasks, as well as fluent codeswitching. Green discusses how this works for a number of situations, as follows:

In L2 production, activation of both lemmas and lexemes in L2 is increased, while L1 lexemes are suppressed when phonological information is retrieved. In codeswitching, there is competition at the stage of phonological assembly, and the lexeme that "reach[es] threshold first" is the one produced. In monolingual production (presumably when only a single language is both selected and activated and the other language is dormant), an executive attentional mechanism is posited to regulate activation levels, thereby reducing interference and minimizing "the need for attentional control" at lower levels of processing (e.g. at the stage of phonological assembly where inhibitory control operates to regulate selection and activation in bilingual situations).

Inhibitory control. In a further elaboration of his model, Green (2000) frames the main issue of bilingual processing as a problem of control under conditions of multi-tasking, and says the problem of bilingual production is analogous to a Stroop task. In producing a translation of a printed word, Green states: "Bilinguals have to avoid naming the printed word and, instead, produce a translation equivalent as a response." In another formulation of the issue, he asks: "...how do individuals ever manage to avoid producing a word in L1 when they wish to produce its translation equivalent in L2?" Picture naming is also said to be a problem of selection and competition for bilinguals, in this case between the name of the picture in L1 and L2.

The core structural constructs in Green's model are lemmas and language tags. The processing notions in control are competition, selection, and inhibition. Green also makes use of procedural notions, namely, schemas and goals. In describing the multi-level nature of control, he makes three claims, as follows: "...first, one level of control involves language task schemas that compete to control output; second, the locus of word selection is the lemma level...and selection involves the use of language tags; third, control at the lemma level is inhibitory and reactive."

Green's view of language processing, rooted in the work of Norman and Shallice (1986), is that language is "a form of communicative action." In this light, schemas are defined as "networks detailing action sequences...that individuals may construct or adapt on the spot in order to achieve a specific task..." Elsewhere (Green, 2001), they are described in the following way: "The intended sense of a schema is procedural. A schema implements a declarative representation of the instructions in order to achieve the control of action...Schemas can be viewed as methods to achieve goals." Low-level, intermediate, and higher level schemas are distinguished according to the level of specification of action involved. Articulation is considered low-level, translation and lexical decision tasks are intermediate, and business meetings, written production, and conversational interaction are said to involve high level schemas.

One of the structural attractions of Green's model for the present work is that in addition to the conceptualizer, there is a means to deal with goals and intentions. In Green's model the goal to carry out a "linguistic act" is regulated by a coordinated effort among three components: an executive attentional system, which is responsible for non-automatic behavior, a lexico-semantic system, and schemas which are task-specific, e.g. translation schemas, word-naming schemas. In bilingual production, the executive or Supervisory Attentional System (SAS) specifies which language is to be used and makes this known to the task schemas. The schemas are said to "compete to control output from the lexico-semantic system," a process that is carried out by modifying the activation levels of representations and by inhibiting outputs.

In Green's model, which follows Levelt et al. (1999), conceptualization is claimed to be language-independent. Language (L1 or L2) is represented in the lemma, in the form of a 'language tag' along with syntactic information. The model assumes that concepts and lemmas are associated to effect the mapping from thought to language. Green maintains that intentions are "encoded at the conceptualization stage of processing" and that this encoding includes a language tag. But this would seem to contradict the claim that conceptualization is 'language-independent.' It would also seem to preclude the need for additional language tags on the lemma.

Notwithstanding this apparent contradiction (or my lack of understanding of the mechanism), the primary contribution of Green's model is its processing notions, and the exceptionally lucid claims it makes about them. Green posits the construct of functional control circuits that regulate activation and inhibition to handle the competition between language task schemas. To show how this process works, Green marshals both clinical and experimental evidence. From the aphasia literature, he presents an example of a bilingual patient who was able to translate into a language he could not speak spontaneously. The functional control circuit proposed for this phenomenon is described as follows: "a translation schema (L1=>L2) can call and boost the activity of a word production schema (i.e., the one for L2) which can then suppress outputs in

L1..." From the experimental literature, he cites research on translation, codeswitching, Stroop effects, and cross-language competitive priming as further evidence for his model. For example, he explains Kroll and Stewart's (1994) finding that forward translation (from L1 to L2) was more influenced (i.e. it took more time) by category blocking (presenting stimuli in trial blocks grouped by semantic category) than backward translation (L2 to L1) in terms of inhibitory control. He also cites switching 'costs' in studies of numeral naming (Meuter & Allport, 1999) as interpretable within his framework. In this context, the data indicate that translation into one's dominant language under experimental conditions takes longer than translating into L2. This finding raises a question as to why professional simultaneous translators usually prefer to work into their preferred, or dominant, language. There are at least two ways to resolve this: 1. That the costs in terms of time do not extend to more context-rich, simultaneous interpretation; 2. That the automaticity developed from intensive practice such as number use compensates for directionality effects.

Summarizing Green's proposals, the supervisory attentional system (SAS) is responsible for activating language task schemas, which compete to control output. These schemas accomplish the control function by activating and inhibiting language tags at the lemma level by means of functional control circuits. The terms of the model and their instantiation offer explanations for both "*mechanisms* [my emphasis] of control (language task schemas and the SAS) and...*means* [again my emphasis] of control" (reactive inhibition of specified tags on lemmas).

The model I propose in the next two chapters addresses many of the same issues raised in Green's work. Moreover, some of the constructs even have the same names. But there are some essential differences. In particular, those differences relate to (1) the nature of bilingual representation, (2) where language specific information is specified in the model, and (3) the processes and processing mechanisms which contribute to bilingual production. In particular, I draw on the need to build redundancy into the model in order to make the architecture functional and to reflect that aspect of language processing. I also focus on different sets of data, in particular codeswitching and interference. But by far the most meaningful difference will be seen in the social and pragmatic motivations which drive the system and are, thus, the central interest of the model.

MODES AND METHODOLOGY: GROSJEAN'S CONTRIBUTIONS TO BILINGUAL PROCESSING RESEARCH

Grosjean's wide-ranging interests in bilingualism include both experimental and computational approaches (Grosjean, 1997). The core construct in both research programs is the notion of speech modes. *Bilingual mode* is said to underlie CS, where both languages are activated relatively equally, while *monolingual mode* is said to operate when a speaker borrows and incorporates lexical items from one language into the other, with most processing going on in a single language. These studies are focused more on perception than production and generally limited to word recognition processes, but are of interest here for two reasons. One is the innovative methodology for gathering data on codeswitching. The other is their incorporation of social factors (in particular, topic and participants) in the research design. More recent work based on the speech modes construct has been implemented in a computational model of bilingual word recognition (Lewy & Grosjean, ms). Both experimental and computational research programs are clearly focused on processing.

A method for integrating social and psychological factors in codeswitching. Much of the research on codeswitching relies on spontaneous speech samples or interviews as data. This kind of data limits the number of instances of codeswitching available for analyses, and makes it difficult to examine the role of social/contextual factors, such as setting, topic, and participants. In order to gather systematic data, Grosjean (1997) manipulated topic by asking participants to retell stories and describe cartoons, half of which described distinctly French events and places and were presented in French only and half of which described American events and were presented in French with English codeswitching. Participants were asked to retell the stories and describe the cartoons to three different imaginary listeners portrayed as: a new French arrival to the U.S., a French-dominant resident of the U.S., and a relatively balanced French-English bilingual. Both topic and listener were manipulated to generate varying degrees of codeswitching in the production data. Results indicated that both topic and listener influenced the amount of codeswitching. American topics were reported to elicit approximately ten times more English codeswitches and borrowings than French topics. The listener variable also generated varying amounts of codeswitching, tabulated here as follows:

Table 2.1 Frequency of French, English, and hesitation codeswitched syllables as a function of listener (based on data reported in Grosjean, 1997)

LISTENER FREQUENCY	French listener	French dominant BL	Balanced Bilingual
French syllables[8]	245	211	173
English syllables	5	12	25
Hesitation syllables	36	27	23

This study is interesting for two reasons. First, it corroborates, in an experimental framework, a long line of research in micro-sociolinguistics that has documented the importance of social/contextual factors in language choice (see Chapter 3 for a review of some of this work and Walters, 1981, for an earlier attempt at experimental generation of register shift data and a cognitive interpretation of the findings). Second, it provides a systematic and expedient means to collect a large number of instances of codeswitching. The data presented above indicate that almost 15 percent of the syllables were codeswitchings or borrowings. Compare, for example, Dewaele's (2001) labor intensive effort, which took almost 20 hours to conduct the interviews and at least ten times that amount of time to transcribe. That work produced over 50,000 words of data, and generated on average three and nine percent mixed (CS) utterances for formal and informal interviews, respectively. Thus, the retelling paradigm, when manipulated appropriately, can generate large amounts of codeswitching data while providing an opportunity to examine social factors, directionality, and a host of syntactic and pragmatic issues in codeswitching that have previously been addressed mainly by spontaneous speech data and by descriptive and interpretive techniques.

Given the preliminary nature of his report, Grosjean discusses only the increase in codeswitching, not commenting on the apparent complementary distribution of the amount of speech generated and number of hesitations. The monolingual mode seems to generate more verbosity, but it may come at the expense of fluency. With regard to fluency and codeswitching, these data seem to indicate a 'cost' for codeswitching in terms of the amount of speech. Thus, the methodology also offers a way to address new questions in bilingual production.

BIMOLA's constructs. BIMOLA is described as an interactive activation model of bilingual word recognition (Grosjean, 1997; Lewy & Grosjean, ms) with roots in connectionist approaches (e.g., McClelland & Elman, 1986). It proposes two networks, one for each language, to handle a range of possibilities for lexical access among bilinguals. The two networks are said to be both independent and interconnected. Their autonomy is what underlies monolingual mode; their interconnectedness accounts for a range of bilingual phenomena, including codeswitching, borrowing, and interference.

The two networks operate at three linguistic levels: features, phonemes, and words. The feature level is represented by a "shared," or common, system totalling 83 sounds to account for French-English bilingualism. It consists of 16 multi-valued and binary features, drawing on the work of Chomsky and Halle (1968), Dell (1985), and the authors' own research. There are three new features in the model: length, aspiration, and instability. The first two are grounded in acoustic phonetics. Instability introduces a notion of flexibility into the model, which is related to the notion of variation in the processing mechanisms advanced in the present work (see Chapter 4). The other two levels–phonemes and words–include separate representations for the two languages. In order to describe the relation between the two networks, Grosjean adopts Paradis' (1989) subset hypothesis, which postulates: 1. a larger set of connections with features of both languages; and 2. two subsets of connections, one for each language. The primary processing notions in the model are activation and inhibition.

The core construct, 'language mode,' is a processing notion that discriminates activation for all three levels (features, phonemes, and words). The monolingual mode is said to involve "strong activation" of one network and weak activation of the other. The bilingual mode entails activation of both networks, again one more strongly than the other (to account for the base language effect), but here only slightly more strongly. In addition to the base language effect, the model accounts for a variety of experimental data, e.g. phonotactic, phonetic, and phonemic effects, language specific effects, and cross-language homophone effects (Grosjean, 1988). In bilingual mode, the model also distinguishes between codeswitched and borrowed words, the former being less integrated, the latter more integrated. Data supporting this distinction show that codeswitched words are easier to recognize than borrowings.

TWO MORE VIEWS ON BILINGUAL PRODUCTION: POULISSE AND DE BOT

Two more approaches to bilingual production that aim for comprehensiveness, those of Poulisse (1997, 1999) and De Bot (1992, De Bot & Schreuder, 1993), both base themselves on various aspects of monolingual speech production, in particular the work of Levelt (1989). It is understandable that bilingual production research would undertake its initial investigations by first looking at the considerable body of work on monolingual production. By doing so, however, it assumes what Grosjean (1989) calls a 'fractional' view of bilingualism, namely, one that presupposes that a bilingual is basically a combination of two monolinguals.[9]

In reviewing the work of Poulisse and De Bot and the models upon which they are based, I will argue that while certain aspects of the monolingual models may have been a useful starting point, monolingual models provide neither an appropriate functional architecture nor relevant processing mechanisms to account for phenomena unique to bilinguals and bilingualism. More specifically, these models do not have a lot to say about the role of sociopragmatic knowledge in lexical processing, and when they do make claims in this area, they maintain positions that are not very tenable for a sociopragmatic view of language use. In addition, phenomena claimed here to be unique to bilinguals, such as codeswitching, interference, and translation, are not addressed by monolingual models. Thus, the work of Poulisse and de Bot discussed in this section is considered in light of their use of monolingual models to account for bilingual language behavior. As background to this discussion, a brief review of two models of monolingual speech production, those of Caramazza and Levelt, is presented here.

MONOLINGUAL MODELS FOR BILINGUAL CLONES: CARAMAZZA AND LEVELT

Caramazza's (1988, 1997) model and orientation are distinctly structural. The architecture is a linear input-output model, where the lexicon is represented by features for grammatical class, morphology, thematic structure, and meaning. Processing is based on a serial stage model involving passive, parallel activation.

Caramazza focuses on a "modal model" of the lexical system. Three aspects of the lexicon are distinguished: (1) the architecture; (2) the syntactic, morphological, and semantic components of lexical representation; and (3) what he calls "processing structure." The structure, or architecture, of the lexical system is depicted as a schematic diagram with five distinct components: two input components, one each for orthographic and phonological information, flow into a central lexical semantic component that provides separate output of orthographic and phonological information. Lexical representations, labeled lexical features, "play a determining role in the organization of the lexicon" (1988:406). Caramazza proposes distinct components for grammatical class, morphological structure, argument structure, and meaning. He throws up his hands regarding a general model of lexical semantics, claiming that "we do not have the detailed theory of lexical meaning that would be commensurate with the crucial role of this dimension..." (1988:410) and adopts a 'selective impairment methodology' to show evidence for the existence of different structural components. To illustrate this he presents a case in the aphasia literature of a patient who was selectively impaired in a variety of naming tasks for fruits and vegetables but not for other semantic domains. Other studies showed selective impairment of either concrete or abstract words, either inanimate or animate words and names of living things and foods in different patients.[10]

Regarding processing, Caramazza distinguishes between serial search and activation models. He describes, in somewhat more detail, serial stage and cascade models, opting for the former, which involves passive, parallel activation. Finally, both frequency effects and errors are used as evidence of processing. Word frequency is shown to be related to lexical impairment, and types of errors show evidence for impairment of a specific component of the lexical system.

The very label for processing aspects of Caramazza's model is colored by his structural focus. That emphasis can be best seen in his methodology, based on selective dissociations or impairments of various components. Process is inferred from errors, products of the impaired lexical system. Frequency effects alone stand out as direct evidence of processing in this model. Processing mechanisms are presented as assumptions about activation and not explicitly tested in the research program. For example:

❏ "...the assumptions we have made about the address procedures for the input graphemic lexicon and output phonological lexicon (i.e. parallel activation)" (1988: 414);

❏ ...[an] assumption that semantic representations activate lexical-phonological or lexical-orthographic representations...

❏ ...[an] assumption is made that a semantic representation activates in parallel all phonological (or orthographic) entries in the lexicon, in proportion to the degree of semantic similarity each lexical entry has to the access representation..." (1990: 96)

Finally, the structure of the model (e.g. Caramazza, 1988) offers no account of pragmatic concepts, plans or intentions. The model takes the lexical semantic system to be the input to orthographic and phonological output components. But lexical semantic knowledge is not generated in a vacuum or even from a dictionary. It entails an intention, a plan, sometimes a script, and a complex of social and affective knowledge about setting, topic, participants and the like. A model of bilingual production, moreover, needs to account for uniquely bilingual aspects of processing, such as incompleteness, dysfluency, and a host of language contact phenomena such as codeswitching, interference, and translation (see Figure 2.7).

Figure 2.7 Functional architecture of Caramazza's Lexical Model

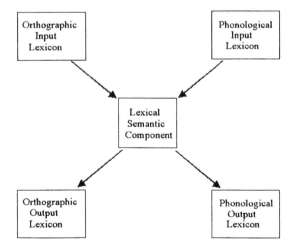

A second major research program in language production is the work of Levelt and his colleagues (Levelt, 1989; Levelt, Roelofs & Meyer, 1999). This model has been the most influential one in bilingual production research to date. The original model (Levelt, 1989) was described as a fairly autonomous, stage-based approach. Its architecture and processing functions are outlined in Figure 2.8.

The more recent version (Levelt, Roelofs, & Meyer, 1999) is labeled a feed-forward, spreading activation model and contains the following components:

- Conceptual preparation
- Lexical selection
- Morphological encoding
- Phonological encoding and syllabification
- Phonetic encoding
- Articulation

Figure 2.8 Levelt's original Model of Language Production (1989:9)

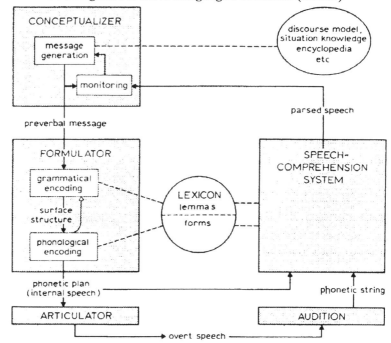

Self-monitoring operates at the phonetic and articulation stages of processing. The most striking difference in the new model is that the elements of conceptual preparation and conceptualization in the earlier formulation have given way to a greater concern for the details of lexical access. Those details have been addressed by a tireless research program, elaboration of the phonetic encoding stage of processing, and development and implementation of a computational component to model the processing stages.

Although the diagram of the original model (Levelt, 1989:9) does indicate that discourse, situational, and encyclopedic knowledge interact with the message generation component of the conceptualizer, these sources of information are not very prominent in any of the monolingual models. A view of language use as purposeful, intentional, and goal-based begs treatment of these aspects of language production. Grosjean's (1997) experimental manipulation of topic and listener is one way to incorporate situational knowledge into the methodology of bilingual production research. The framework proposed in the next chapter attempts to specify identity and discourse information as well.

But even apart from the exclusions of Levelt's model, its view of conceptual preparation and conceptualization is not beyond criticism. The pragmatic elements of communicative intention, macroplanning, selecting information, and microplanning are not reflected in the output of this component, which is restricted to a lexical concept. In defining what has been called the verbalization problem, "how the speaker gets from the notion to be expressed to a message that consists of lexical concepts," Levelt and his colleagues acknowledge that there is "no simple, hard-wired connection between percepts and lexical concepts," stating that this process is "always mediated by pragmatic, context dependent considerations" (Levelt et al., 1999:3). However, those pragmatic elements are not represented in the output of the conceptualizer. In fact, it is not at all clear that the pragmatic considerations should serve a mediating function. Rather, it may be more plausible to assume that they initiate the process and drive the system.

Levelt's solution to the verbalization problem comes in a discussion of what he calls "perspective taking," the observation that there are varied ways to refer to the same object or perform any act of language production (e.g. mare vs. female horse, escort vs. accompany). This issue is clearly germane to bilingual production, and adds another dimension of complexity to the processes of pragmatic, syntactic, and lexical choice in monolingual speech. The processing of conceptual information demands flexibility to handle this kind of variation and indeterminacy as well as to integrate macro and micro sociolinguistic phenomena with information about, for example, frequency of linguistic form. The Monolingual Model is just not set up to do the job.

Finally, the design of the model, in particular, its feedforward, spreading activation mechanism, is intended to allow communication between components, at least in one direction. But even this innovation would not allow a distinction between intentional codeswitching, whose origins can be traced to the conceptualizer, and 'performance' codeswitching, whose origins are more likely to be found in the processes of formulation. To make this distinction, one would need a more interactive, bi-directional feedback mechanism.

On this background, we turn now to bilingual modeling based on Levelt's model.

ACCOUNTING FOR INCOMPLETENESS, DYSFLUENCY, AND CODESWITCHING IN BILINGUALISM

Poulisse (1997) identifies three phenomena that a model of bilingual production needs to account for. One is the fact that second language knowledge is incomplete. Poulisse treats this issue as a structural limitation that bilinguals deal with through compensatory strategies. Lexical and grammatical knowledge are singled out as "incomplete." But, vocabularies are not complete for monolingual users either, and this fact is not accounted for in monolingual models of production. Incompleteness should affect the architecture of the language system, including the nature of lemmas, the connections between lemmas within and across semantic fields, and within and between languages. It should also influence processing phenomena, such as accuracy and speed of lexical retrieval, as well as syntactic choice and stylistic formulation. Thus, incompleteness needs to be built into the architecture of bilingual production, allowing for variability in the way lemmas are represented, among different speakers as well as within speakers and across time. What I mean here is that the lemma for 'hope' is not the same for two speakers and may not be the same for me today as it is tomorrow. This variability also needs to be built into the processing mechanisms, in the way features, sounds, words, structures, and phrases are activated, inhibited, and controlled. The central question for bilingual processing is whether incompleteness is fundamentally different for bilinguals and monolinguals. If so, the terms, definitions, and mechanisms of a bilingual production model need to reflect this difference.[11]

Dysfluency is a second phenomenon that Poulisse says needs to be accounted for in bilingual production. Among the examples she lists for this general category are: hesitation phenomena such as repetitions, corrections, and filled pauses; sentence length, slips of the tongue, speech rate, pause length, and length of run (defined as the number of syllables between pauses). In studies by Wiese (1982; 1984), Mohle (1984), and Poulisse (1999), second language users showed more evidence of dysfluency and slower speech than first language users. Dewaele (2001) shows similar findings for trilinguals. These observations are again not unique to multilinguals, and are found in children's speech and in adults with language and communication disorders. Dysfluency would seem to be handled best by processing approaches speech production, but taxonomies of dysfluencies may also prove useful in identifying the sources of information in the architecture of bilingualism that are most susceptible to this phenomenon.

Levelt's model (Levelt et al., 1999) deals with dysfluency in terms of self-monitoring and speech errors. The main interest there is the nature of the representation that self-monitoring operates on: phonetic segments produced immediately before articulation, syllables produced as prosody is generated, or phonological structures activated during lexical access. Reporting on a series of experiments by Wheeldon and Levelt (1995), the authors demonstrate that self-monitoring takes place during lexical access. Another set of data relevant to dysfluency comes from speech errors and tip-of-the-tongue experiments. While the computational component of Levelt et al.'s model is error-free, the authors claim that the model is consistent with the findings of the speech error literature, and that the "binding-by-checking" procedure offers a way to model speech errors. In particular, simulations show that the following 'ordered' list of speech errors conforms to their model:

- ❏ Segmental substitution errors e.g., the anticipation error 'sed sock' for 'red sock'
- ❏ Perseveration errors like 'red rock' for 'red sock'
- ❏ Exchange errors, e.g. 'sed rock' for 'red sock'

In addition, the simulations show (1) effects of speech rate on error probabilities (e.g., more errors at higher speech rates), (2) phonological facilitation of semantic substitution errors (e.g., 'rat' for 'cat' more likely than 'dog' for 'cat'), and (3) lexical bias (i.e., errors tend to be real words rather than nonwords).

Given the model's primary interest in representation, few of the processing measures identified by Poulisse as relevant to bilingual dysfluency are handled by the model. In fact, it is difficult to see how computational modeling would be able to simulate the variability of hesitation phenomena such as repetitions, self-corrections, pauses, speech rate, and various measures of length indicative of fluency.

The third phenomenon that Poulisse indicates is essential in an account of bilingual production is "that L2 speech may carry traces of the L1" (pp. 206-7). This aspect of bilingualism is referred to as codeswitching, and Poulisse distinguishes between 'intentional' and 'performance' varieties of CS. The former is said to have two potential origins, one socially-motivated to mark identity, topic change, and addressee, to express emotions, or to make a metacomment on the discourse, and one owing to a lexical gap in L2 or greater availability in L1. Performance codeswitches are said to be like slips of the tongue and influenced by both second language proficiency and word frequency, and thus related to accessibility. Poulisse equates performance codeswitching with transfer phenomena, like those discussed from the work of Clyne above and documented in all linguistic domains (phonology, lexis, syntax, and pragmatics).

The language contact phenomena such as codeswitching, borrowing, interference, and transfer are unique to bilingualism and need a unified account. Monolingual models are not fully equipped to handle them. Poulisse's distinction between intentional and performance codeswitching, grounded in social and psychological divisions, requires explicit treatment of information about personal identity and sociopragmatic aspects of language use.

Although Poulisse does not go into great depth in the distinction between availability and accessibility, it may be a useful way to characterize one of the major differences between monolinguals and bilinguals. In this light, both monolinguals and bilinguals should experience problems of accessibility as a function of word frequency (a correlate of exposure), whereas availability could be said to be unique to bilinguals, since it may entail an operation or procedure comparing the two languages.

FOCUS ON THE CONCEPTUALIZER AND VERBALIZER: BILINGUAL LEXICAL ACCESS

De Bot (1992; De Bot & Schreuder, 1993) presents the most orthodox adaptation of Levelt's work to bilingual production, and in doing so comes up with the most explicit model of bilingual production regarding the point at which L1/L2 language specific information is introduced in language production.

De Bot's reading of the Levelt model, based primarily on Bierwisch and Schreuder (1992), can be summarized as follows: The structural components include a conceptualizer, a verbalizer, an interpreter, a formulator, and an articulator. The conceptualizer encodes communicative intentions as message fragments, or what Levelt (1989) calls preverbal messages. These preverbal messages serve as the input to the verbalizer, which performs a many-to-many mapping operation to match message fragments with semantic information in lemmas. Lemmas are said to contain information about semantics, argument structure, and grammar. Even though Levelt admits to a 'verbalization problem,' he does not offer a separate component to handle the 'problem.' De Bot and Schreuder (1993) do, however, state that a verbalization component is needed to handle message fragments larger than a lemma's semantic form, giving this component responsibility for the processes of chunking and matching.

In their bilingual adaptation of the model, De Bot and Schreuder (1993) deal with three topics: language separation and codeswitching; language assignment; and cross-language differences in lexicalization patterns. These are treated in terms of their bearing on the nature of information in the conceptualizer (described as preverbal messages) and the role of the verbalizer in processing information from two languages.

De Bot and Schreuder (1993) opt for a monitoring system and a sociolinguistic perspective in addressing two of the classic questions in bilingual processing: How is it possible for bilinguals to keep their languages apart without random mixing and how is it possible for bilinguals to switch intentionally? Placing this monitor in Levelt's 'Discourse Model Component,' i.e. outside the mechanisms of lexical retrieval, the authors assume that the monitoring system provides information about the conversational setting to the conceptualizer in order to make language choice decisions.

The model refers to Paradis' (1981) subset hypothesis and to Green's (1986, 1993) notion of levels of activation to help explain how bilinguals keep their languages separate as well as how codeswitching works. Drawing on the notion of 'spreading activation,' which is said to be a function of the verbalizer, the authors describe the possibility of separate networks (subsets) of activation as well as "connections between words from different languages" for frequent codeswitching. Activation is said to occur at a variety of linguistic levels: lexical, syllable, and phonological. In this context, the authors say that multi-level activation may be an explanation for Clyne's (1980, 2003) notion of triggering effects, activation spreading along the following route:

L1 lemma → L1 lexeme → L2 lexeme → L2 lemma

According to this hypothesis, activation of an L2 lemma may then trigger other L2 lemmas. The key link in this chain is the central, cross-language connection, between L1 and L2 lexemes, which is effected by similarity in word form. This makes sense for animate and inanimate tangibles–dogs, shoes etc.–but not for abstract concepts like "complexity" or "mercy." Concepts do not have to be fully verbalized, or, dare I say, completely specified words to make the shift. Thus, lemmas of abstract terms may be more variable/less specified, making it harder to translate these concepts out of context, e.g. terrorist, guerilla, freedom fighter, martyr.

Another point raised by this work is that bilinguals, in particular longstanding immigrant bilinguals and beginning learners, show "considerable variation" in sound production. The authors state that this variation from "correct" [their term, p. 200] pronunciation is due to low activation and that it can be compensated for by increased time and attention. In Chapter 4 I propose that variation at this articulatory level, as well as at other levels, is a bilingual fact of life and needs to be accounted for by the mechanisms of the model. Rather than seeing it as an output phenomenon, variation in the present work is considered a processing mechanism; rather than a blemish on production, it is a potential agent of acquisition and processing.

Language assignment. De Bot and Schreuder phrase the question of language assignment as follows: "how does the production system know whether to select elements and rules from L1 or L2?" It is here that De Bot and Schreuder's Bilingual Model diverges significantly from its monolingual progenitor. They state unequivocally: "all information about language choice has to be included in some form in the preverbal message" (p. 201). In other words, language assignment is said to take place in the conceptualizer.

Throughout their treatment of this topic, the authors weave a sociolinguistic subtext. Setting information is said to characterize the difference between what they call random[12] codeswitching and codeswitching "controlled by some higher level process" (p. 202). Information about setting is said to help determine the value of a language cue, and thus the level of that language's activation. Finally, setting is said to determine directionality in codeswitching. In this context, the authors note as a "well established fact" that immigrant bilinguals switch from a minority to a dominant language but not in the other direction.

In processing terms, 'language' is considered one of several cues in lexical retrieval. The central component involved in this process is the verbalizer which, as mentioned above, attempts to match message fragments with lemmas. Semantic cues are presumed to be most important in making this match. But, under certain circumstances 'language' cues may take on higher values than specific semantic cues. When the value of L1 and L2 cues are relatively equal, codeswitching may occur as a result of lack of control from higher level (presumably social and motivational) processes.

In summary, all of the following are said to play a role in bilingual lexical retrieval:

- ❏ the value of the language cue(s)
- ❏ the level of activation of lexical items
- ❏ the need to adhere to a particular language
- ❏ the availability of the intended element
- ❏ the speaker's proficiency in each language
- ❏ the lexicalization patterns of the two languages

Language choice begins in the conceptualizer with a language cue linked to each preverbal message. The verbalizer extracts the language choice information from the preverbal message, divides the message into chunks, gives each chunk a value for each language cue, and finally tries to match each chunk with a lemma and with relevant syntactic information. Language and semantic cues vary in terms of their activation. When the language cues are relatively equivalent for the two languages and/or when the intended lexical item is not available, the bilingual speaker may codeswitch or produce a word that does not meet all of the selectional criteria of the intended item.

Lexicalization differences. One of the greatest challenges to bilingual processing models is to account for how bilingual speakers manage to produce fluent speech, and even fluent codeswitched speech, when the two languages do not have the same morphological, syntactic, semantic, and lexical patterns. Citing data on lexicalization differences between Spanish and English (floated into/entro flotando en) and Korean and English regarding their expression of motion, de Bot and Schreuder place the bulk of the burden for this task on the verbalizer, whose job is to divide the fragments from the conceptualizer into language-specific chunks. They go on to present five types of codeswitching data that appear to argue for the presence of language-specific information at almost every level of processing. In their account, data with this breadth and depth, including the phoneme and syllable levels of processing, require the verbalizer to assign language to individual syllables and phonemes. There is no resolution to this problem in a framework where all the work for language specification is carried out by the verbalizer. It is partially for this reason that the SPPL Model pulls the language choice component out of the lexical retrieval process, making it available to the bilingual production system from the inception of production to articulation.

De Bot's research on bilingual production is wider ranging than his modest claim that it is restricted to lexical processing. As seen in this review, the model incorporates elements of sociolinguistics (setting), general issues in code-switching such as directionality, and reference to variability, a notion pursued in terms of processing in Chapter 4. This approach to bilingual production differs fundamentally from some of the premises of Levelt's model. In particular, language-specific processing begins at the stage of conceptualizing and continues through verbalization. Levelt's (1989:105) model relegates language specific processing to a "set of routine procedures...unlikely [to] require special attentional effort." Codeswitching, language assignment, and resolution of lexicalization differences cannot be handled in a routine fashion. The presence of an independent component to handle verbalization, then, seems to be a basic structural difference between monolingual and bilingual production. Thus, the monolingual-based models might be missing an element that only the presence of another language exposes.

SUMMARY AND SYNTHESIS: FROM CONSENSUS TO SOME CONTROVERSY

The models presented in this chapter were divided, somewhat arbitrarily, along disciplinary lines. Myers-Scotton, Clyne, and Auer were portrayed as linguistic approaches. The work of Rampton and Zentella was called linguistic ethnography. Kroll and De Groot, Green, and Grosjean were offered as psychological perspectives. Those divisions broke down with the work of Poulisse and De Bot, both applied linguists who declared allegiance to a psycho-logical model of monolingual language production, and went far beyond that model in their interests and claims regarding bilingualism. Following are some of the issues and constructs that appear throughout the literature on bilingualism, sometimes centrally and sometimes more peripherally, which are relevant to the SPPL Model and its processing mechanisms.

Partition and integration. One recurrent question addressed implicitly by most of the models reviewed above is formulated explicitly by Clyne, Green, Grosjean, and De Bot: How is it possible for bilinguals to keep their languages separate and produce relatively fluent speech in a single language, on the one hand, and to integrate the two languages and generate utterances involving fluent codeswitching, on the other? Clyne offers three options in response: separation, adaptation, and mixing. Separation is accomplished by the activation of one language and deactivation of the other. Adaptation and mixing are the result of transference of lexico-semantic and phonological elements, respectively. Green explains the phenomenon in terms of control circuits that regulate activation and inhibition to handle the competition between language task schemas. Grosjean's explanation is stated in terms of monolingual and bilingual speech modes, which rely on different levels of activation of a speaker's two languages. In his computational implementation, BIMOLA, the question is addressed in terms of relations between networks for each language. De Bot treats this question from the perspective of sociolinguistic context, proposing a monitoring system to provide setting information to the conceptualizer at the outset of production. He, too, draws on a spreading activation idea, combining it with Paradis' subset hypothesis. The common element here is activation. The ethnographers stand alone on this question, taking the fluent, and sometimes not so fluent, production of codeswitching to be the relevant starting point for bilingual research.

Intentions in bilingual production. Another element found in most of these models is intentionality. There is a consensus that intentions are to be found at the conceptual stage of production. In conceptualization, an intention is the raw material from which a preverbal message is eventually carved up and input to the formulator. Green indicates that intent is a necessary condition for control, further specifying goals and schemas as a separate processing component beyond the stage of conceptualization. Clyne, Poulisse, and De Bot make different use of intentionality with their distinction between intentional and performance codeswitching.

Sociopragmatics in psycholinguistic models. A third element shared by all of the models is a concern for sociolinguistic and pragmatic aspects of bilingualism. The sociolinguistic-ethnographic approaches of Rampton and Zentella deal with most of the parameters that a sociopragmatic model would need to account for. And even the laboratory approaches of De Groot and Kroll and Green refer to sociopragmatic aspects of bilingualism although these do not find explicit expression in their methodologies. The other models do not, however, show a unified approach as to how to handle this kind of information. Myers-Scotton's latest work compares codeswitching patterns of first and second generation immigrants, but her Abstract Level Model reflects no explicit treatment of sociopragmatic information. Clyne provides rich sociolinguistic information about his informants, but does not use that information systematically to interpret codeswitching. Auer uses the terminology and tools of discourse analysis to apply social constructs such as identity and negotiation to his codeswitching data. Finally, De Bot and Grosjean take a more micro-sociolinguistic approach to bilingual processing. Conversational setting is given a key role in De Bot's Processing Model, while topic and listener are built into Grosjean's experimental design. But too much consensus may not be the best thing for a science. It may avoid problems which need to be treated, and it may treat others in a way which does not allow speculation and creativity.

Several issues raised only parenthetically by the bilingual models reviewed above require clarification and further research. One issue relates to language production in general: variability in performance. And three others are unique to bilingualism: directionality, triggering, and the availability/accessibility distinction.

Variation. Poulisse raises the issue of variability in her discussion of incompleteness and dysfluency as two phenomena a bilingual model must account for. De Bot hits on this issue when he mentions variability in pronunciation among non-native speakers. Grosjean builds a notion of flexibility into his BIMOLA computational model. And Rampton's liminality construct gets at the interpretive heart of my notion of variation. I would claim that variability is not unique to bilingualism—more salient, more observable, but not unique. Variability can be seen more clearly at the ends of the linguistic spectrum, in pronunciation and phonetics at one end and in lexis and pragmatics at the other. It is more prominent in the language of special populations, in children, in second language learners, and in those with expressive language disorders. In these cases, variability is a way of describing the products of language use. Chapter 4 shows how variation is processed in the SPPL Model and then attempts a conceptual review of the construct in several related fields. Ultimately, variation is crucial to bilingualism because it facilitates code-switching and translation, which are both ways of compensating for incompleteness phenomena in language processing.

Directionality. Three of the approaches discussed here mention the question of directionality in bilingualism: Kroll and De Groot in an experimental paradigm concerned with translation; De Bot in a statement related to sociolinguistic factors in codeswitching; and Zentella in an analysis of the symbolic meanings of language choice. In their Revised Hierarchical Model, Kroll and De Groot argue that forward translation (L1 to L2) is more concept mediated and that backward translation (L2 to L1) is more lexically-mediated. Lexical links are described as stronger from L2 to L1 in order to account for faster and more accurate translation in that direction. Kroll and Stewart (1994) found that when stimulus words were organized semantically (in category blocks), more interference was reported in forward (conceptually-mediated) translation than in backward (lexically-mediated) translation. De Bot's sociolinguistic assertion, that codeswitching among immigrant bilinguals proceeds from the minority language (L1) to the dominant language (L2) but not in the other direction, is complementary. A working hypothesis based on this work would be: Codeswitching or translation into a second language is meaning-based, grounded in the social world, while translation into one's primary language is basically a lexical operation with codeswitching into L1 being chiefly to facilitate lexical access.

Zentella takes a more balanced and wider-scoped approach to directionality. She calls for looking at the direction of codeswitching in context, in particular the context of interpersonal pragmatics and politeness. In doing so, she rejects the simplified notion that English-to-Spanish codeswitching is a way of expressing solidarity and Spanish-to-English codeswitching is a demonstration of power.

Triggering. Clyne's notion of triggering offers a strongly linguistic alternative to most of the other models. Triggering is described as a structural phenomenon, which is said to facilitate transversion, the activation of one language and deactivation of the other. Four types of triggering are discussed: tonal, phonological/prosodic, lexical, and syntactic. Trigger forms include cognates and compromise/fusion forms, which facilitate a transition from one language to the next. Zentella (1997) reports 12 instances of triggering in her corpus, classifying them in her more psycholinguistic category of "crutch-like code mixing." Neither Clyne nor Zentella would deny the importance of attitudes and social information in language contact. However, both researchers give 'trigger' words and structures a nearly autonomous role in language processing, which would mean independence from social information. As seductive as this idea is, there is a possibility that 'trigger words' are only reflections of more sociopragmatic motivations for their use. This subject requires further examination, in studies that allow a fair competition between social and linguistic motivations for triggering.

Availability and accessibility. Both Poulisse and De Bot mention this distinction. From Poulisse, availability can be understood as a construct that explains why a word is more available in one language because of lexical gaps in the other. Accessibility is linked to performance codeswitching, and said to be influenced by word frequency and L2 proficiency. In contrast, De Bot uses the notion of word frequency to define availability. It might be useful here to distinguish the constructs by using one as a structural property of language and the other as a feature of language use. We could then say that a particular concept is more available in a language because it is lexicalized or because of a lexical gap in the other language. Accessibility, to speakers in general as well as to individuals, would depend on word frequency as well as situational and task parameters such as the particular setting, topic, participants, and experimental conditions.

Towards some Controversy. There is more consensus than controversy in the work reviewed in this chapter. In one sense, this is encouraging, since it is a sign of dialogue and interaction. But for the field of bilingualism to advance, competition and even some controversy are desirable. Grosjean takes the strongest and most explicit stand on behalf of a unique bilingual model. Myers-Scotton's recent adaptation of her model in order to account for a set of codeswitching data, which the Matrix Frame construct could not handle, also indicates a need for a new approach. Certainly Zentella's integrated use of quantitative and ethnographic data is an attempt at integration. And my reading of De Bot's model is that it is structurally and functionally distinct from its monolingual forbear. Despite these encouraging signs, the fact that there is very little cross-referencing over the sociopragmatic-psycholinguistic divide is probably not indicative of benign neglect. With this background, I offer a model that attempts to incorporate some of the components and issues raised in this chapter and to challenge others.

NOTES

[1] This claim is challenged by codeswitches involving, for example, conjunctions (because) and pragmatic markers (well, ya' know, like), which pepper the speech of stable bilinguals. When these apparently system morphemes appear alone in an otherwise linguistically homogeneous utterance, it would be hard to say that they come from the matrix language.

[2] Even though Myers-Scotton (2002) claims to have abandoned this frequency metric for determining the ML (p. 61), her citation of Paradis, Nicoladis & Genesee's (2000) use of this procedure speaks beguiles contravenes this claim. Despite the criticism (e.g. Blommaert, 1992) of Myers-Scotton's model and her own retraction of these aspects of work prior to 1995 (Myers-Scotton, 2002:61-62), I cite this work here in order to give a sense of how the model has developed and, more importantly, because the earlier versions of the model were those that gave expression to social determinants of CS.

[3] The original sources for this phenomenon can be found in Weinreich (1953/1968) and Haugen (1953).

[4] For example, syntactic congruence checking for Arabic/English DET+N constructions, Swahili verb stems inflected with English morphology, English V+PP with verbs which in Japanese are V+accusative; semantic/pragmatic contact phenomena such as Turkish 'elbise' dress and Dutch 'rok' skirt; cross-language differences in the encoding of causation, agent/pro-drop, Spanish-English differences in how manner is expressed in relation to verbs of motion, inchoative/agentive incongruence for the verb 'decide' in Swahili/English CS, double morphology, bare (uninflected verb) forms as a compromise' strategy, quantifiers, lexical gaps and missing lexical categories.

[5] These distinctions correspond closely to the some of the distinctions in the sociopragmatic and psycholinguistic components of the SPPL Model.

[6] The situation regarding cognates in simultaneous interpretation is quite different, in part because the training involves self-conscious awareness of problems with false cognates. Since interpreters generally work into their stronger language (L2 to L1) and are more sensitized to conceptual meaning than lexical meaning, interpreting may be an appropriate place for testing Kroll and De Groot's claim that backward translation is more lexically based.

[7] See, for example, Beauregard, Chertkow, Bub, Murtha, Dixon, & Evans (1997) for neurolinguistic differences in concrete-abstract words.

[8] The linguistic unit of measurement in codeswitching obviously depends on the theoretical orientation of the researcher. Grosjean's use of the syllable as the measurement unit reflects an interest in sound-based aspects of codeswitching.

A comparative study of different units of measurement, e.g. syllables, words, intonation units, clauses, propositions, would be very useful, particular for a contribution to studies of fluency in bilingualism.

[9] It is noteworthy that two other major research programs in monolingual language production, those of Caramazza (1986, 1997) and Garrett (1988) have been largely ignored in bilingual production models except in Caramazza's own recent work (Costa & Caramazza, 1999).

[10] One wonders whether there may be a parallel impairment in the sociopragmatic domain. Investigation of this patient's prior knowledge, experience, and identity might reveal something in his medical or social history related to fruits and vegetables.

[11] Schachter (1990) offers a treatment of this issue in the field of second language acquisition.

[12] Here I would prefer terms such as unavoidable, unplanned, or automatic codeswitching.

3 A Functional Architecture of Bilingualism

SOCIOPRAGMATIC INFORMATION IN A MODEL OF BILINGUAL PROCESSING

This chapter focuses on the structural components of the Sociopragmatic Psycholinguistic Processing Model (SPPL),[1] whose primary goal is to account for a range of sociopragmatic information in bilingual production and integrate that information with psycholinguistic aspects of bilingualism. The first section provides an overview of the model's information components and states some of the key assumptions on which the model is based. The bulk of the chapter is devoted to an explanation of the kind of information the model processes and where that information comes from.

Two information modules make *language choice* and *affective information* available at every stage of language production. The model contains five information components:

1. a *social identity* component;
2. a *contextual/genre component*, which consists of two sub-components, one to specify setting and participants, the other genre and topic information;
3. an *intentional component*, which specifies the pragmatic intention(s) and propositional content of the utterance to be produced;
4. a *formulator* which also consists of two sub-components, one which relates lexico-pragmatic concepts to lemmas and lexemes and another which specifies discourse patterns to handle relevance, cohesion, and sequencing; and
5. an *articulator,* which is responsible for speech output.

The principal differences between this model and those reviewed in the previous chapter are its executive modules for language choice and affect and the components which deal with sociopragmatic information, located in the upper portions of the diagram in Figure 1.1, reproduced here as Figure 3.1.

The *language choice module* (panel A, which runs vertically along the left side of Figure 3.1) selects, regulates, and retrieves information from a speaker's two languages during the entire course of language production and supplies that information to the identity, contextual, discourse, pragmatic, morphosyntactic, phonological, and lexical information components. In other approaches to bilingual production (e.g. Albert & Obler, 1978; Green, 1986, 1998; Poulisse, 1997, 1999), information about language is typically represented as a language tag (L1 or L2) on the lemma during the formulation stage of processing.

Figure 3.1 SPPL Model for bilingual processing

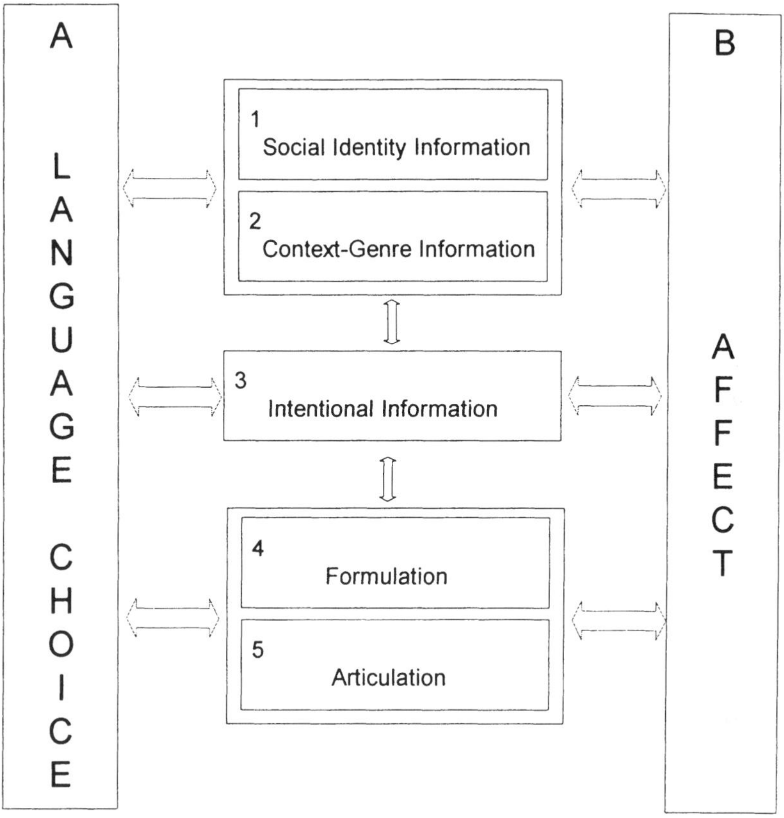

In the present model, language choice information is assumed to be grounded in the social world, and language choices are possible at every stage of production (from identity construction to the generation of intentions and the articulation of speech). Imagine a situation in which a bilingual lecturer has formulated a complete sentence, looks up from her notes, notices that there is somebody who does not speak her L1 in the audience and flips to L2. A tag attached to a lemma does not do a very good job in accounting for the switch because one needs additional layers of modeling to account for the lecturer's recognition of the student's language abilities. In some circles this is called audience design (Bell, 1984). Here, we say that the speaker/lecture has taken into account participant information in making her language choice. That same lecturer may not pay much attention to her audience, may switch to L2 because the term in that language takes less effort or is more salient. That switch would provide language choice information to the formulator and articulator. The SPPL

Model opts for parsimony, with a single language choice regulator to interact with each source of information. One of the arguments for this approach is to show that this language choice module will account for a range of language contact phenomena, including a distinction between sociopragmatic and psycholinguistically motivated codeswitching.

The *affective module* (panel B, which runs vertically along the right side of Figure 3.1) is designed to select, regulate, and retrieve emotion-based information from other components of language processing. This, too, should be viewed as an executive module, operating on every aspect of production, from intention to articulation. It aims to account for a range of affect-based speech phenomena, including humor, cursing, slips of the tongue and tip-of-the-tongue phenomena as well as those associated with clinical syndromes such as schizophrenia and Tourette's Syndrome.

The three major information components proposed as additions to current models of bilingualism include: (1) a *social identity component* (Component 1 in Figure 3.1), which collects, synthesizes, and integrates information from the bilingual individual's social history. This information is combined with the contents of (2) a *context/genre component* (Component 2), which selects, regulates, and retrieves information about external, social context (setting and participants), about genre types (scripts and conversations), and about topic. Cumulative information about social identity and context/genre is merged with (3) information about intentions, derived in large part from various indicators of speech act information in the utterance. The *intentional component* (Component 3) is the primary link between external and internal information, between knowledge of the world and the speaker's intentions, between macro and microprocessing.

All information components and modules are considered both independent and interactive. They are independent in that decisions in language production are made without reference to other components. They are interactive in the sense that they are modifiable by other components of the model and by the processes of language production.

Visual Descriptions. The proposals in this chapter and the next distinguish between structural and processing aspects of bilingualism. In models of this type structure is depicted with rectangles, ellipses and their contents. Processes are rendered by arrows and the direction of arrows. Separation of information into different components implies independence or autonomy. Arrows show the direction of information flow. Linear models imply that information flows in one direction. In many information processing models, that flow of information is from outside to inside, from stimulus to response, from macro to micro. Arrows that point in only one direction make the claim that information flows in only one direction, for example, from the concept to the lemma, from lemma to lexeme, from lexeme to phonetic form. This is considered a feedforward production mechanism. Arrows that feed back to a module from which they originated may represent a control loop or may be a simple feedback mechanism, e.g. a monitoring device (see Chapter 2, the section discussing Green's Model of Inhibitory Control and Chapter 4, the section on perceptual control mechanisms for comparison).

As I walk you through the model, I hope to make explicit what the SPPL Model *can* account for and what it *cannot* do. To summarize, the most fundamental distinction portrayed by the Information Processing Model proposed here is between functional architecture and processing mechanisms. The architecture is dealt with in this chapter, and the processing mechanisms in the next one. The components, or sources of information, constitute the functional architecture. They are relatively simple to represent in two-dimensional graphic diagrams. Processing the relationships between these components is harder to represent as a drawing; so I will add other ways of describing processing phenomena in the next chapter.

ASSUMPTIONS BEHIND THE SPPL MODEL

The model described in this chapter should be viewed as a set of proposals, a way to summarize previous research and to map out my claims and working hypotheses. As such, they are based on several assumptions:

Bilingualism. A monolingual production model cannot account fully and comprehensively for bilingual processing. The principle reason behind this assumption is that codeswitching, interference, and translation are unique to bilingualism. There may be rough parallels of CS, interference, and translation to register/style variation, speech dysfluencies such as false starts, hesitation phenomena and word finding problems, and paraphrase, respectively. But, both the origins and use of CS, interference, and translation are essentially different. In this view, bilingualism is the default phenomenon; monolingualism is an ideal state which does not reflect the same complex sociopragmatic experience and mental processes.

Sociopragmatics. Research on the psycholinguistics of speech production has devoted relatively little attention to the processing aspects of social phenomena, focusing instead on the structure of the lexicon, and in particular on the lemma-lexeme relationship. Models of monolingual lexical production have largely ignored the information components and mechanisms responsible for conversational context, speaker intentions and related social and pragmatic information. In the present work the assumption is that identity and pragmatics are the starting point in speech production.

Autonomy and interactivity. Information is organized in modules and components that are generally autonomous, but which demonstrate specifiable interactions. Evidence for autonomy in language is robust; it comes from philosophy and linguistic theory (Fodor, 1983), from psycholinguistic experimentation (e.g., Ferreira & Clifton, 1986; Bock & Kroch, 1989), and from clinical neuropsychology (Caramazza, 1990). But the autonomy/modularity of syntactic, semantic, phonological and morphological information is only part of the picture in a model of language production. The interaction among these components is another, no less important aspect, of bilingual processing. The evidence here is also broad-based (e.g. McClelland, 1987 on interactivity in processing in general). The *interactivity* of the bilingual system is conceived here as driven by internal motivational forces. They can be modeled in terms of basic algebraic processes (Anderson, 1996) and investigated as perceptual control systems powered by negative feedback mechanisms (Cziko, 2000), which operate on the input and output of the different information components.

Sequential and parallel processing. Some aspects of language production, from the generation of an intention to the culmination of articulation, proceed sequentially; others operate in parallel. Parallel processing is assumed to be more automatic than more goal-oriented, higher-level, serial, and often conscious aspects of cognitive processing (see Duchan, 1983:88-89 for a useful introduction to the contrast between serial and parallel processing and Marslen-Wilson, 1975 for an explanation of parallel processing).

In general, the assumption is that sociopragmatic information is processed before lexico-semantic and syntactic information. First and second language information is accessed to serve social and pragmatic goals. But information interacts within a particular module or component of the model. For example, information about setting and participants interacts in a single situational component, while contextual information interacts with genre and discourse information. In contrast, we will show evidence that illocutionary force, the technical term for a speech act's intention, is encoded prior to propositional content. And both interact with syntactic information. To the extent that these interactive processes are automatic and unconscious, they will be parallel.

The main reason for incorporating a notion of parallel processing in the present model is to allow interaction between and among information components. In particular, parallel processing is intended to allow access to language choice and affective information at every stage of language production and to account for different kinds of codeswitching, spontaneous translation, and attrition.

Two alternatives to parallel processing are offered in the literature on bilingual processing. One says that language choice information is specified in the conceptualizer and is always activated (see my discussion of the work of de Bot and Poulisse in Chapter 2), but this places heavy demands on memory and other general cognitive operations. Another alternative gives the language choice function to language tags attached to lemmas (as in Green's model). Both of these approaches cannot offer a unified account for different kinds of bilingual phenomena such as codeswitching, interference, and translation, nor for different kinds of codeswitching. Thus, a single language choice module, which operates in parallel to the various information components of production and allows language choices to be made and language information to be accessed by any component, is preferred as a way of explaining these complicated kinds of bilingual phenomena.

Redundancy. Language production systems in general and bilingual systems in particular maintain a large degree of redundancy. Redundancy is necessary to accommodate on-line processing demands, especially the exchange of information between modules and components and between and among the various processing mechanisms. Redundancy can be seen as a property of language as well as a factor in language use. From a linguistic perspective, redundancy is a structural phenomenon, "referring to the relationship of predictability among the elements of language" (Cernis, 2001). On the surface of language, it takes the form of lexical repetition, anaphora, paraphrase, and synonymy.

From the point of view of language use, redundancy has been defined in information theory terms as "the reduction of uncertainty" (Shannon & Weaver, 1949). It touches on a wide range of processing issues, including fluency, priming, imitation, familiarity, memory, and word frequency. For example, higher frequency words and expressions produce redundancy by priming copies of themselves in memory, thereby allowing time to be devoted to the processing of new or less frequently said information. Redundancy also restricts alternatives and decreases dependence on linguistic stimuli, thus serving a crucial role in language production. It helps to select, organize, and chunk information so that production of every single utterance is not a unique experience. Hence, while linguistic redundancy is focused more on stimuli and molecular operations, redundancy in language use involves higher level, intentional processes.

Both kinds of redundancy are relevant to bilingual processing. Words and structures in each of a bilingual's two languages generate redundancy, since they are partial copies of each other. False cognates are partial copies of sound-based information; and true cognates are fuller copies of each other. Bilingual phenomena, such as codeswitching and translation, generate redundant material; other bilingual phenomena such as interference or disruptions in fluency may occur because of insufficient redundancy. In both cases, bilingual phenomena are regulated by redundancy processes. In particular, given the importance of frequency and imitation in language processing in general and in bilingual language processing in particular, redundancy is assumed here to play an essential role in understanding bilingual production.

INFORMATION MODULES: AVAILABILITY AND ACTIVATION

Two modules, one for *language choice* and one for *affect*, are offered to handle both sociopragmatic and psycholinguistic information. They run along the entire course of language production, from identity construction to articulation. They are introduced and illustrated in the next two sections.

The next section begins with an overview of the purposes of the language choice module. Then it outlines the major social and motivational phenomena related to language choice. It describes how that social information is incorporated into the SPPL Model and integrated with psycholinguistic information. The following section describes how language choices are made for each of the five information components of the SPPL Model, ending with a case report of a Russian immigrant to Israel to illustrate how language choice interacts with a variety of sociopragmatic and psycholinguistic factors.

A MODULE FOR LANGUAGE CHOICE INFORMATION

The *language choice module* is responsible for selecting, regulating, and retrieving first and second language elements from the various information components of the SPPL Model. These elements include features of identity, context, genre, intentions, morphosyntax, phonology, lexis, and discourse. For example, a speaker may choose to select elements of her L1 (Hebrew) identity and syntax and combine these with L2 (English) lexis to produce an English utterance such as "Not right!" as an expression of disagreement. The speaker's L1 Israeli Hebrew identity and word order are attached to the L2 English words of the utterance. In other approaches to bilingual production (e.g. Albert & Obler, 1978; Green, 1986, 2000; Poulisse, 1997, 1999), language choice information generally plays a role restricted to the lexicon, and language tags are assumed to do this job. The sociopragmatic approach of the SPPL Model ensures that language information is available for language choices at all stages of production, including the initiation of an utterance when identity preferences and pragmatic alternatives are being considered. Language choices are also made during formulation and articulation, and a model that explains these choices needs to make L1 and L2 available at these stages as well. Having just one executive language choice module also makes it much easier to account for specifically different kinds of codeswitching. Socially and pragmatically motivated codeswitching used to express identity, to gain the listener's attention, for pragmatic focus or emphasis would be generated by accessing language choice information in the upper components of the SPPL Model (Figure 3.1). These information components deal with social identity, context, genre, and intentions. Performance codeswitching, occurring primarily from the weaker to the dominant language, would be processed in the formulator and articulator.

Social and motivational factors in language choice. The language choice module is activated by both macro and micro social and motivational factors, and is influenced by psycholinguistic constraints such as word frequency. It operates interactively with all components of the model at any stage of the production process, and allows language choice decisions to play a role in generating intentions, in using contextual and textual information, in speech act formulation, and in lexical retrieval. Social-motivational factors in language choice operate at three levels of processing: a macro-societal level, a micro-sociolinguistic/interpersonal level, and an individual/intrapersonal level. These factors are summarized in Table 3.1.

Macro-phenomena include a list of influences that are the lifestuff for people who live in more than one language environment. Among these are: demographic factors, e.g. the number and relative size of the dominant and minority groups, the extent of in-migration, continued large-scale immigration and/or emigration, and urbanization; prevalence of use of a particular language in a society; the nature of the language contact situation (whether the dominant and minority groups are indigenous or migrant, whether the migration was voluntary or the result of annexation/colonization); the permeability or insularity of the dominant/minority groups, whether enclaves are geographic as well as social; whether insularity is self-imposed, e.g. religious groups, or externally-imposed, e.g. apartheid, segregation; dominant-minority group relations, especially in terms of each group's views about collective goals for minorities, viz. assimilationist, pluralist, separatist; relative status and prestige of the languages in contact; external incentives to learn those languages; presence of diglossia; and ethnolinguistic vitality (e.g. Bratt-Paulston, 1986; Jaspaert & Kroon, 1989; Bourhis, 2001).

Interpersonal phenomena related to language choice have been examined most extensively in the sociolinguistics of 'who speaks which language to whom, when, and where?' (e.g. Broeder, Extra, & Maartens 1998; Fishman, 1965) and more recently via social network theory (e.g. Li Wei, 1994; Li Wei & Milroy, 1995; Milroy, 2001). The data from both kinds of studies are 'reported' language use, in contrast to actual language behavior. A smaller number of studies use role-playing techniques (see Hatch, 1983, for a review). Behavioral evidence of language choice in the interpersonal realm comes mainly from studies of codeswitching (e.g. Blom & Gumperz, 1972; Heller, 1988; Rampton, 1995; Zentella, 1997). Other relevant sources include access and exposure to various languages, in-group and out-group attitudes toward speakers and their languages, and various factors in the communicative situation, especially setting, participants, and topic.

Intrapersonal factors cluster around the constructs of identity and motivation, e.g. an individual's nationality (or multiple nationalities), political leanings, ethnicity, religion, gender, occupation. In Dittmar, Spolsky and Walters (1997) these factors were derived from the concept of 'domain' in sociology and sociolinguistics (Fishman, 1972; Parsons, 1967; Williams, 1995). In Dittmar, Spolsky, and Walters (1998), a paper about social and linguistic identity in processes of grammaticalization, a socio-psychological level was seen as intermediate between macro-sociological factors and micro-linguistic behavior.

Table 3.1 Societal, interpersonal, and individual factors in language choice

Societal phenomena	Demographic factors In-migration Permeability/enclaves Dominant-minority relations Language status Diglossia
Interpersonal phenomena	Setting Participants Topic Social networks Attitudes
Individual phenomena	Ethnolinguistic identity Language use preferences L1/L2 abilities Ethnolinguistic vitality Motivation

Individual psycholinguistic factors in language choice. Owing to a sociological bias, studies of language choice have tended to focus on groups rather than individuals. Data can be found in the findings of language censuses (Lieberson, 1981), language use surveys (Fishman, Cooper & Ma, 1971; Haugen, 1953; Fase & Jaespert, 1991), from factor analytic studies of ethnolinguistic vitality (e.g., Giles & Johnson, 1987), from community studies of social networks (e.g. Milroy & Wei, 1995), and from ethnographies like those of Zentella (1997) which ground their social phenomena in the lives of individual bilinguals. Insofar as samples are representative and random, macro-sociolinguistic studies are reasonable measures of language use and language loss patterns. However, in order to get at individual language processing and individual patterns of language use, one must examine individual data. In the present sociopragmatic model of bilingual processing, individual identity is the initial, driving component of the system. In other words, identity and motivation determine which macro-sociological information gets into the system. Identity and motivation govern choices of interpersonal experience. And identity and motivation even influence a subject's responses in a laboratory experiment.

   Individual language use takes into account macro-sociological and interpersonal factors as reflected in a person's identity. Macro-level social change is most evident for people who have experienced social upheavals such as war, famine, immigration or emigration. Dramatic events of this kind create social changes that alter the known patterns of interpersonal experiences, like shifts in social networks or exposure to new languages. These societal and interpersonal shifts can in turn lead to changes in social identity. The individual is not a passive object in this process. Rather, social phenomena, both macro and interpersonal, serve as the input to individual choices. They contribute to a range of phenomena, including the fact that most communication among bilinguals is monolingual and that much L1 to L2 codeswitching is motivated socially or pragmatically for reasons of identity or for pragmatic goals to indicate emphasis, focus, and attention (e.g. Zentella, 1997).

Psycholinguistic factors constraining language choice include:

1. the frequency and availability of particular words and structures
2. the prevalence of a person's bilingual contacts
3. the individual's L1 and L2 proficiency
4. accessibility of words and structures, as reflected in fluency, e.g. pauses, false starts, speech rate, and codeswitching motivated by a perceived need for relatively automatic lexical access
5. a person's acquisition history and patterns of language use over time, e.g. if and when a language was ever in disuse, whether a word was acquired and attrited or whether it was never acquired in the first place

In the SPPL Model, social and psychological factors are coordinated by an executive monitor through mechanisms of imitation, variation, integration, and control (see Chapter 4 for detailed descriptions of each of these mechanisms). When these factors are harmonious, the result is fluent speech with socially appropriate use of language. When there is dissonance among various sources of social information or between social and psychological factors, that discord can manifest itself in different ways, including interference, word finding difficulties, dysfluencies such as false starts and hesitations, and sometimes "performance" codeswitching. All of these phenomena are a primary source of data about individual language production.

A walk through the SPPL Model. The information from the language choice module is available throughout the course of speech production, from identity construction, to selection of an intention, to the onset of articulation and beyond, to the repository of long-term memory. Walking through the model depicted in Figure 3.1, we see the role of language choice at every stage of production. At the beginning, language choice information is a major determinant of *social identity*. For example, the language choice module enables the speaker to select a form of greeting to project a particular ethnic, religious, or gender identity. Language choice information is also made available to the *contextual/genre component* to decide which language to use for different settings, interlocutors, and genres. Private, more intimate settings like home and neighborhood, and more familiar interlocutors, such as relatives and close friends, usually activate the primary language, while public settings and less familiar interpersonal contacts activate the other language. Regarding genre, conversational interaction usually evokes L1 choices, while more formal and scripted speech is more likely to elicit L2 language choices.

An *intentional component* is responsible for selecting an illocutionary point (the intention) and propositional content (the information conveyed) to instantiate the specific intent and purpose of a speaker's utterances. Language choice is not as transparent in this component as it is in the choices and preferences made as a function of setting and participants in the contextual/genre component. Moreover, language choice plays a less important role in the generation of an illocutionary point than it does in the selection of propositional content to go with that illocutionary point. In planning and generating the intent and content of an utterance, the speaker may be more aware of the content than the illocutionary force, which is generated on a more instinctive and automatic level. Generic requesting, offering, and acknowledging are less language-specific than requesting information about directions, offering a price for a piece of clothing, or acknowledging a gift, where cultural and lexical information from the language choice module to a large extent determine the nature of the propositional content.

During utterance *formulation*, language choice information is made available to lexico-pragmatic concepts, lemmas, or lexemes, as needed. In comprehension, e.g., reading for understanding, where the focus of the reader is on text-based meaning and the expectations for a change in language are minimal, language choice will not be as important as semantic content; it may not even be as important as morphosyntactic elements of the utterance. In contrast, in tasks or in situations where codeswitching is not only expected, but a bilingual convention, information about language will be readily available to the concept, lemma, and lexeme.

One advantage of the availability of language choice information during the entire course of production is to build redundancy into the system. Alternative models, where only the lemma or lexeme are tagged for language information, require deep search procedures and interactive feedback with other subcomponents of the system in order to explain which language(s) is(are) being processed. To access information about a particular language in bilingual models based on language tags on lemmas or lexemes, one would first have to access the lemma, extract the language-specific information, and then transmit that information, for instance, to the context/genre component, where it would determine which language should be used for a particular setting, listener, or genre. The SPPL Model makes that information available already at the outset, prior to the context/genre stage of processing.

Finally, language choice information is available to the *articulator*. At this point in production, language (L1/L2) information is relatively low in salience and not very memorable. This premise would account for findings (e.g. Berkowitz, 1984) that on-line memory for the language of a particular narrative interleaved with sentences from two languages (an experimental form of inter-sentential codeswitching) is relatively poor in comparison to memory for its content.[2] It may also help account for the difficulty that relatively fluent bilinguals have in attaining a native accent in both their languages, and in remembering the language of an utterance when focused on a content-based task.

In order to illustrate the relationship between macro and interpersonal factors in language choice and their role in the construction of social identity, a portion of a case study of a Russian immigrant to Israel is reported in Example 3.1.

Example 3.1 *A case narrative of language choice*

Yulia is a Russian native speaker of Hebrew as a second language and English as a foreign language. She is about to engage in spontaneous conversation (a euphemism for a guided interview) with Tanya, a native speaker of Russian and fluent second language speaker of English and Hebrew, who is collecting interview data for a master's thesis on language attrition.

At the macro level, Yulia brings to the 'conversation' knowledge about the relative size of her linguistic minority group. She knows that she is one of 700,000 new immigrants from the former Soviet Union in a country of 5.5 million Israelis, politically and culturally dominated by Europeans. The level of availability of her three languages is a function of:

(1) Strong preference for using Russian among members of her ethnolinguistic language group, reinforcement of this group preference from continued immigration of Russian-speaking immigrants, connection to the language's homeland through Russian cable TV and satellite stations, and a relatively low intermarriage rate between Russian immigrants and native-born Israelis;

(2) attrition-oriented phenomena such as this group's high motivation to learn and speak Hebrew (Donitsa-Schmit, 1999), ethnolinguistic links between current Russian immigrants and original settlers of modern Israel (e.g. Wexler, 1991), the voluntary nature of a significant portion of the 1990s Russian immigration to Israel (mostly for economic advancement), collective goals of assimilation, and relative tolerance of Russian language maintenance in the society at large. This does not mean that there is no discrimination; on the contrary, a Russian accent is a handicap in everything from health and banking services to employment and dating opportunities, and has been as a factor in more than one violent incident in the 15 years since the beginning of this wave of immigration.

Most salient among these factors are the size of the ethnolinguistic group relative to the overall population (approximately one sixth) and the group's compatibility with the dominant European-oriented forces in Israeli society. Ignoring interpersonal and individual factors in language choice for a moment, a plausible hypothesis regarding language choice on the basis of macro-information alone would yield the following statement: Strong availability of Russian, somewhat less willingness to initiate or respond in Hebrew and meaningfully less availability of English. But individual language users do not always reflect the aggregated data of group patterns. In fact, in studies that report group data, it is often that case that no single language user can be used to represent the group pattern (cf., Runkel, 1990; Rosansky, 1976). Thus, interpersonal and intrapersonal information must also be taken into account to determine the output of the language choice component.

At the interpersonal and individual levels of processing, Yulia's motivations to maintain Russian and to acquire and use Hebrew as well as her attitudes to the demographic, political, cultural, and economic factors mentioned above are all germane. Yulia's interpersonal and intrapersonal profile shows evidence of weak motivation to maintain Russian along with somewhat weaker evidence of Russian attrition.

Yulia learned to read and write in Russian at home, went to school up to third grade in Russia, and immigrated to Israel at the age of nine. She lived in a home where "we began a sentence in Russian and finished it in Hebrew" (Feldman, 1997), logged 16 years of residence in Israel, did all of her remaining schooling, including a Master's degree in music, in Israel, and married a native-born Israeli, a 'language' decision not to be taken lightly. Her primary circle of friends are native-born Israelis (bolstering attrition of her Russian). Her associates at work are almost all Hebrew speakers (also promoting Russian attrition), although at the Music Academy she was employed as a counselor for recent Russian immigrants. She reads newspapers in Hebrew (Russian attrition), but she did read Dostoevsky in the original Russian when assigned one of his novels in high school (Russian maintenance). She currently gets most of her media exposure in Hebrew. Her name, Yulia, and her decision not to change it, are also indicative of both maintenance and shift. It is neither stereotypically Russian, like Genia, Svetlana, and Natasha; nor is it distinctly Jewish or Israeli. On the personal level, her language learning acumen in general and her current skills in Hebrew (her second language) are on a high, even literary, level. These factors add to her positive professional identity as a musician, giving her a multidimensional ethnolinguistic identity, which can be summarized as 'professional immigrant in a multi-cultural society.'

Without hesitation, she introduces herself as an Israeli musician. This form of self-presentation, along with a ranking and weighting of the interpersonal and personal information relevant to maintenance and attrition, make for strong availability of Hebrew, and relatively weak availability of Russian, a profile that contrasts with the output of the macro-level, ethnolinguistic information above.

At this point in the processing of language, macro and micro-level information are assumed to be integrated into a single, weighted hierarchy of language choice information. For Yulia this yields the following pattern: Hebrew is her primary language, Russian is available but to a lesser extent, and English not readily available, but with some effort, accessible.

Summary and conclusion. It is plausible to assume that language choice information is generally stable for a particular individual and for a particular bilingual community. It is also relatively stable for particular plans, scripts and events, but varies significantly in response to contextual constraints, especially setting, topic, and the language background of the participants. Information in the language choice module can be modified to accommodate a temporary, situational change in the weight of one of the factors or a decision of the speaker to modify her identity to adapt to a specific set of conditions, for instance, a new job or new friendship. Similarly, information in the language choice module can be modified more or less permanently, as in some immigrants' rejection of their native language and culture.

A MODULE FOR AFFECTIVE INFORMATION

A second, system-wide module proposed here is an *affective component* to select, regulate, and retrieve emotion-based information and to make it available to other components of language processing. This, too, should be viewed as an executive processor, operating on every aspect of production, from identity to intention to articulation. Among the phenomena this module should account for are: the nature of offensive language, blame, and abuse, including the differences of cursing in native and non-native languages; why a joke in one language, even when translated accurately and appropriately, may not be considered funny in another language; and why French and Italian give an impression of being romantic while German and Hebrew are stereotyped as harsh and brusque.

Affect in bilingual language performance. Affect can stimulate both language production and non-linguistic behavior. For example, if we take liking and disliking as two basic emotions (see Aristotle, *The Rhetoric*, and Frijda, 1986 for taxonomies of emotions), attraction to an individual can stimulate construction or strengthening of social identity. A daughter of holocaust survivors told me once that, for her, the German language meant warmth, cuddling, and other positive memories of her grandmother. She eventually moved to Germany and married a German man, making her feelings and behavior consistent. The affective state that seems to have led to this woman's social identity and marriage preference may or may not have found expression in her choice of accent and lexis in German. In this case, affect was a stimulant to her social behavior.

Another example: a Russian Jewish immigrant to Montreal, fluent in French and a faculty member at a French-speaking university in Quebec, chose a distinctively Moroccan accent in speaking Hebrew, his fourth language. He reported that his choice was due to aesthetics: he liked the sound of the accent. Further probing revealed that his attraction for the relatively large Moroccan Jewish immigrant community in Montreal, and several individuals in particular, was translated into specific language behavior, namely, his choice of accent.

Another common phenomenon among ingroup members is dislike for an individual or group, which may be a factor in failure to acquire a language dialect or native accent. This is a possible reading for the strong maintenance of Spanish accents in English among Puerto Ricans in mainland America, English and Russian accents among American and former-Soviet immigrants to Israel, etc. Their non-native accents in English and Modern Israeli Hebrew, respectively, are hypothesized to be a function of their desire to maintain an identity distinct from the new culture/language. Similarly, affect, in all its forms, e.g. fear, anxiety, hope, and love, is an important factor in choices of settings, friends, genres, and topics in the use of language. Preferences for places, people and language types may be part of the folk wisdom that says that French and Italian are languages of passion, while Hebrew and German are contentious. It's not that the language itself is romantic or callous, or that the speakers of that language necessarily are like that, but rather, that the perceptions of our folk linguists lead to these labels/stereotypes.

The study of language and affect was, until recently, the exclusive purview of the field of psychiatry. Schizophrenia, considered by some (e.g. Goldstein, 1948) to be a disorder of thought and social adjustment, was at the center of the field. The focus on observable behavior and clinical interests in diagnosis and treatment make this body of literature largely irrelevant to a processing model of bilingualism. During the last ten years, however, there has been a move in social science in general and psychology in particular from what has been called 'cold' cognition, i.e. studies of perception, memory, and language that largely neglected emotion and affect, to studies whose primary focus is on 'hot' cognition. This is not the place to review that work, since the concern here is bilingual production (but see Anderson, 1996; Ortony, Clore & Collins, 1988; Murphy & Zajonc, 1993 for background). Unfortunately, hot cognition has not yet made its full impact on current research in psycholinguistics, even though the field can be said to have begun there with Osgood's now-classic research paradigm on the measurement of affective meaning (Osgood, Suci & Tannenbaum, 1957). But current efforts by DeWaele, Pavlenko, and colleagues (2002) and Wierzbicka's (1999) focus on emotion concepts may change the picture for studies of bilingualism.

This section first gives a brief outline of some of the ways affect, like language choice information, plays a role during the course of language production. Next, I look at five ways to examine language-affect relations (tip-of-the-tongue state, curses and offensive language, humor, pragmatic markers, and bilingualism in therapy).

Affect in a model of bilingual production. Motivation, needs, and desires are the traditional constituents in the study of affect. *Social identity*, the driving component of the model proposed here, is an integral of information and emotion. What gets assimilated in one's personality comes in because of strong feelings; and what gets blocked is rejected on the same basis. In the *context/genre component* of the model, affect plays a role in determining which settings and which interlocutors a speaker will choose to interact with. The field of social psychology is full of studies on personal preferences. Social network research is an important framework which has been used to examine personal relationships and bilingualism (e.g. Li Wei, 1994; Dittmar, Spolsky & Walters, 2002).

The *genre sub-component* of the SPPL Model offers some of the best data on the role of affect in bilingual processing. Personal memoirs and biographies of Hemingway, Beckett, W. Somerset Maugham, Milan Kundera, Richard Rodriguez (1982) and Eva Hoffman (1989) and more mundane language learners like those cited in Schumann (1997) are portraits of struggle and pain in acquiring a new language and coping in two worlds. My reading of that literature, as well as my reading of Conrad and Nabokov, is that full flowered expertise in writing in two languages is beyond the reach of even the best. None of these writers, except perhaps Beckett and Kundera, who both work(ed) closely with translators in French, was accomplished in more than one language during a single period of their lives. The only apparent way to become an accomplished writer in two languages at the same time is to divide one's writing along genre lines, as some medieval Jewish scholars did by writing philosophy and/or poetry in Arabic and rabbinic law in Hebrew.

Affect impinges on both the illocutionary force and propositional content of the *intentional component*. The choice of speech act form and accompanying prosodic information is loaded with affect, as seen in the rich literature on linguistic politeness (e.g. Brown & Levinson, 1987; Fraser, 1990; Walters, 1979). Greetings are another source of data on affect, a source particularly revealing in cross-language differences. Verbal information conveyed in a greeting may complement or contradict the body language information expressed in a handshake, a facial expression, or posturing. Arabic, Italian, Japanese, and Finnish greeting behavior is a particularly rich source of data on affect or its apparent absence. Even English greetings vary widely in lexical form and thus offer clues about a speaker's affective state.

Affect is more evident in speech acts that are less explicitly conveyed. Blame cannot be conventionally conveyed through an explicit performative even in languages which are stereotypically blunt (e.g. *I hereby blame you.). Rather, more subtle forms are used (e.g. Why didn't you turn off the soup?), apparently to soften the blow. While the emotions named by Aristotle in *The Rhetoric* or studied more recently by Frijda (1986) and Wierzbicka (1999) may show some degree of universality across cultures, the situations in which they can be conveyed and their linguistic expression are highly constrained by both culture and language.

Pragmatic markers and adverbials (e.g. well, ya' know, eh, really, so) are subtle ways to convey intentions. These little bits of information, called word-parasites in Russian, have recently caught the interest of linguists' eyes and ears (e.g. Fraser, 1996; Schiffrin, 1987) and their inherent relationship to affect has yet to be examined fully. The following excerpt (translated from Hebrew, with pragmatic markers in boldfaced italics and codeswitching to English underlined) from an academic service encounter (Regev, 2004) between secretary and student shows a range of affect, from outrage ("*Yo*" in Turn [13]) to defensiveness ("*Of course*" in Turn [18]) and attempts at conciliation ("*Okay, so...*" in Turn [23]). These pragmatic markers form yet another layer in the information a speaker conveys to a listener.

Example 3.2 *Excerpt from an academic service encounter (Regev, 2004)*

...

[6]   Secretary A (Native Hebrew Speaker): Linguistics goes here [pointing to a blank space on the registration form].

[7]   Secretary B (Native English Speaker): What did you do with the second one? Did you stick a page here? Did you stick a new page on it?

[8]   Secretary B: Yes, yes.

[9]   Secretary A: Um...Can you take me out xxx one (for) (1) direct?

[10] Student: (...) I have (it), I have it here.

[11] Secretary B: Here (2) Direct Track B Linguistics.

[12] Student: [12a] I have it, *um*...[12b] Here, I have it here.

[13] Secretary B: What are you doing with our lists? *Yo*!! [very agitated]

[14] Student: No, they gave it to me.

[15] Secretary B: Who gave it to you?

[16] Student: *Ah*, [Name of] Administrative Assistant (.) I was advised by her (.) I spoke to her.

[17] Secretary B: [Name of] Administrative Assistant gave it to you?

[18] Student: *Of course*.

[19] Secretary B: To take home?

[20] Student: *Sure*.

[21] Secretary B: *Okay*, this is not *at all* [meant] for students. It isn't allowed to be given to anyone.

[22] Student: I came specially and fixed an appointment with her, and she gave it to me, *yes*.

[23] Secretary B: *Okay*, *so*, *ah* come *ah* come first of all, write down all your details.

[24] Student: Where?

The role of affect in the *formulation* and *articulation* of words and utterances can be seen in a variety of paralinguistic phenomena, including pauses, false starts, rate of speech, stammering, and perhaps even in slips of the tongue. Speech errors are seen here as parallel to 'performance' codeswitching (in the language choice module), where breakdowns in fluency can be traced to the lexemic level of processing. Investigations of speech errors (e.g. Fromkin,

1973; Poulisse, 1999) have examined linguistic constraints on their occurrence, largely ignoring affective motivations which, in another research tradition, earned the name of Freudian slips.

Five sources of data for the study of bilingualism and affect

Affect-language relations can be investigated from two directions. One is to select an emotion and then document its linguistic expression(s). This is how we are studying blame. Another way is to infer affect from language use. The investigation of pragmatic markers proposed below illustrates this approach, taking these markers as primary evidence of affect.

Sources of data for examining the role of affect in bilingualism include:

- ❏ tip-of-the-tongue phenomena and slips of the tongue
- ❏ taboo expressions and curses
- ❏ humor
- ❏ pragmatic markers
- ❏ therapeutic sessions

Tip-of-the-tongue (TOT). A study of speech errors coordinated with experimental investigations of the same subjects in a TOT state, where affective factors have been documented and manipulated, may lead to insight about the relationship between affect and lexical production. Such studies could be coordinated with Motley's (1976) procedure for inducing slips of the tongue. In that procedure, the subject is instructed to read compounds and collocations (e.g. barn door) as rapidly as possible. The target word pair is preceded by several pairs, for which the initial phonemes are exchanged (e.g. dart board), thus inducing a slip of the tongue (e.g. darn bore) in approximately 30 percent of the trials. By manipulating L1 and L2 in codeswitched word pairs and by designing experiments with target trials in L1 preceded by priming trials in L2 (and vice versa), one should be able to discover something about the relationship between affect and underlying phonological and monitoring processes in bilingualism. Once some baseline data for codeswitched (and non-codeswitched) word pairs has been established, the interaction of formulation and affect can be addressed by using dirty word combinations as target responses.

Taboo words and curses. The relatively uncharted psychological territory related to using curse words in one's non-native language and avoiding them in the primary language is an area more directly focused on the pragmatics of bilingualism. A first order hypothesis for this phenomenon is to say that non-native curses have less affective potency for the speaker, and thus can reduce social undesirability. But this hypothesis flies in the face of the popular perception that Italian and Spanish are more emotional. Cursing in a non-native Mediterranean language may tease out the plausibility of these competing hypotheses. A study of spontaneous curses in bilingual situations, combined with interviews and perhaps experimental probes in the use of taboo expressions, should further an understanding of the relationship between affect and bilingual production. DeWaele and Pavlenko (2002) have recently reported on one large scale study in this area.

Bilingual humor. Two phenomena are of interest here, one more culturally based and one more closely related to individual bilingual behavior. The fact that jokes that are funny in one community do not elicit the same affective response in another is enough of a demonstration that humor is culturally based. Modern Israeli humor with its extensive jibes at ethnic and dialect differences among its various immigrant groups would be considered politically incorrect in North America. A painful example of the depth of emotion associated with humor comes from an exchange between two middle aged Israelis, one the native-born daughter of Nazi Holocaust survivors employed as an administrative assistant at a university, the other an American immigrant professor at the same institution. Approximately a year after an attack in which 32 Moslems were killed in a mosque by a Jewish doctor from Hebron, a genre of jokes bearing the doctor's name began to circulate. Upon hearing one of these jokes, the American immigrant professor expressed his distaste to the teller. She responded, "C'mon. That's the way the culture takes out its guilt." To which the professor retorted, "Okay, let's tell Holocaust jokes." In both the joke and the listener's response, language use is a window to the identity, attitudes, and cultural values of the interlocutors.

Another kind of bilingual humor relates to jokes that require knowledge of two languages in order to be appreciated. These 'one-liners' are language-based humor such as puns, plays on words, double-entendres and the like. A sampler of humor combining knowledge of computer software with Yiddish-English bilingualism is drawn from one of several Jewish humor lists on the world wide web (e.g. http://www.mazornet.com/jewishcl/humor/humor-jokes-03.htm).

Example 3.3 *Bilingual humor*

If Microsoft© were a Jewish company, some things about the firm might be different. Here, for example, are some things that might change:

- ❑ Instead of getting a "General Protection Fault" error, your PC would get "Ferklempt."
- ❑ Hanukkah screen savers will have "Flying Dreidels."
- ❑ When disconnecting external devices from the back of your PC, you would be instructed to "Remove the cable from your PC's tuchis."
- ❑ After 20 minutes of no activity, your PC would "Go Schloffen."
- ❑ When your PC is working too hard, you would occasionally hear a loud "Oy!!!."

Here the humor is lodged in the use of Yiddish expressions from a slightly different semantic field. The humor is generated partly by the perception of the Yiddish language as a source of frivolity and jokes, and partly by the semantic/pragmatic variation, i.e. the use of a meaning slightly inappropriate for the context, as above in "Schloffen" (lit., 'sleep') for the "pause" or "shut down" state of a computer.

Pragmatic markers. Pragmatic markers and related phenomena (e.g. discourse markers, focus particles, sentence adverbials, interjections) have recently been looked at more closely in the fields of pragmatics and discourse analysis (e.g. Blakemore, 1992; Fraser, 1996; Jucker & Ziv, 1998; Köenig, 1991; Schiffrin, 1987). This line of research has focused on linguistic properties and constraints and has yet to be formulated in an integrated psycholinguistic theory. Moreover, even fewer studies have investigated these markers among bilinguals.

Maschler (1994, 1997, 1998), Matras (2000), and de Rooij (2000) are exceptional in this literature for a number of reasons. First, in addition to a classification scheme, Maschler's (1998) treatment goes beyond individual discourse markers, their frequency, and their meaning in context. Her studies are based on 'talk-in-interaction.' They report on the use of discourse markers to segment or frame conversation, clustering patterns, and the way they function in bilingual codeswitching. Her approach is fundamentally structural, i.e. the "correlation between moments in interaction–namely, the beginnings or endings of particular types of conversational action–and the frequency and type of discourse markers employed at those moments in interaction" (Maschler, 1998:14).

Three kinds of studies of pragmatic markers are needed to address bilingual aspects of affect:

1. the affective bases for their use and distribution, probing the intentions and explanations of language users during and following production of expressions such as *like, ya' know, kind of, for sure, really, well,* etc.
2. the nature and extent of the use of these expressions in second languages.
3. the interaction of pragmatic markers and codeswitching.

One wants to know the kinds of affect conveyed when a speaker uses a pragmatic marker, what this does to the illocutionary force (intent) of the utterance and whether it creates another layer of communication. For example in monolingual production when we say "I kind of like your new sweater" we could be expressing jealousy, making a mitigated compliment, or both. When the answer is 'both' we have interesting indications of multi-functionality. Initial findings from Dittmar, Spolsky and Walters' (2002) investigations of Russian immigrants' acquisition of German and Hebrew show that non-natives, even advanced level second language speakers, use a smaller range of pragmatic markers to cover a wider semantic/pragmatic range. We have yet to understand

the affective implications of their use. Based on previous studies, we feel that
here too the bilingual story will not just be an add-on to descriptions of
monolingual production, but rather something essentially different.

The following excerpt, Example 3.4 (divided into major segments for
illustrative purposes), is taken from an interview with a 45-year-old biologist
from Moscow, who is telling his immigration story to two graduate students, one
a native speaker of Hebrew and one a Russian immigrant. It is full of affect
distinguished by accompanying pragmatic markers (bolded and italicized).

Example 3.4 *Pragmatic markers in an immigration narrative*

[1] ken, ani yodea, hu *derex agav* haya, *eh afilu* she'hu b'gili,
    yes, I know, he *by the way* was *uh even though* he was my age,
[2] hu haya more sheli harishon shel ivrit, b'ivrit.
    he was my first Hebrew teacher, in Hebrew
[3] *v'gam* more harishon sheli b'ya'hadut,
    and also my first teacher in Jewish subjects,
[4] v'ani lo ha- ha- hafaxti l'ish *eh* dati,
    and I didn't tur- tur- turn into *uh* religious man
[5] *ulay* lo haya li maspik koax,
    maybe I didn't have enough energy
[6] *aval eh* lo kmo barux,
    but uh not like Barux,
[7] *eh aval* ah, *adayin, aval* ani, *ma she'omrim* m'sorti.
    uh but ah, *still, but* I [am] *what they call* traditional.
[8] v'ze *derex agav* biglal *eh* barux,
    and this *by the way* is because of *uh* Barux.

Particularly noticeable in the excerpt above is the defensive comment in
segment [5], distinguished by the pragmatic marker *ulay* ('maybe') and the
repetitive, stammer-like use of *aval* ('but') and *adayin* ('still') in segment [7],
where the speaker gives a label to his identity. More speculatively, the use of
derex agav ('by the way') in segment [8] accompanying the credit he gives to
his first teacher could indicate of mixed feelings, perhaps a conflict between his
identity and his gratefulness.

Therapeutic situations A final source of data on affect in bilingualism comes
from therapeutic situations in which therapist and client have the option to use
either L1 or L2 or both languages. On first brush, one might think that the
bilingual therapist would allow the client to choose the language of therapy to
put him/her at ease and to facilitate openness. But therapy in a second, even non-
preferred language can set up a situation similar to role-playing. Painful,
emotion-laden issues may be easier to express when the language allows some
detachment. Similarly, a practiced therapist, aware of the client's language use

patterns, can use L1, L2, and codeswitching as a way of helping the client through various moods and situations. Awareness of language and affect of this type has been noted in the clinical literature and has begun to be investigated systematically (Altarriba & Bauer, 1998; Santiago & Altarriba, in press).

To conclude, affective information is culture-specific and highly variable across individuals and cultures. It figures meaningfully in an individual's social identity. Knowing when to be humorous and when to be offensive are both part of a bilingual's second language proficiency and bilingual identity. Knowing how to be humorous and how to be appropriately insulting is also part of sociopragmatic competence. The affective module selects intonation contours, word stress information, pragmatic markers and the like and integrates them with other aspects of language at the various stages of production.

Information in the affective module, like information in the language choice module, can be modified temporarily and adapted to preferences and choices regarding identity, settings, topics and genres, and intentions, which are related to changes in affect, e.g. dealing with a new boss or new aspects of a personal relationship. Moreover, like language choice which can be modified to accommodate more or less permanent changes such as immigration, affective choices are adapted to take into account relatively permanent emotional changes resulting, for instance, from marriage, the birth of a child, divorce, or death of a loved one.

INFORMATION COMPONENTS IN BILINGUAL PRODUCTION

Overview. The first and second major components of the SPPL Model, depicted in Figure 3.1 as *identity* and *contextual-genre information*, specify sociopragmatic information relevant to message selection. These components are the primary links between external and internal information, between knowledge of the world and the speaker's intentions, between macro- and micro-level processing. These sociopragmatic components of the model consist of three sources of information:

- ❏ Information about the language user's social identity, integrated from internal, motivational sources and external experience;
- ❏ Information about the setting and participants in a bilingual speaker's environment, derived largely from external sources;
- ❏ Genre-based knowledge, internal representations generated from exposure and experience with social, cultural, and linguistic knowledge related to a diversity of oral and written text types.

Among bilinguals, social identity can be monolingual, based on a rejection of the first or second culture. It can take the form of biculturalism, where social identities are grounded in each of a bilingual's two cultures and deployed in a way similar to language use in diglossic situations. A third kind of identity would be a composite of first and second culture identities, with some elements coming from one culture, some from the other, and some an amalgam of both. In this composite, integrative view, social identity undergoes changes or shifts in weighting, with certain aspects of identity taking on less importance at the expense of others.

Identity is an abstract construct, and as such less accessible to observation than its components, like language, dress or social networks. Among these elements, language, while observable, is nevertheless subtle in its expression of identity. Despite its subtlety, language presents a rich set of possibilities for examining the less accessible aspects of identity. In this model, then, language production is a partial reflection of the less observable construct, identity. Conversely, identity is expected to have a strong influence on language production, acquisition, and attrition.

The *intentional component*, based on speech act theory in philosophy of language (Austin, 1962; Searle, 1969) and linguistics (e.g. Bach & Harnish, 1979; Geis, 1995) is the framework that converts intentions to utterances. In language processing, an illocutionary force or intention is generated first, and then propositional content is selected to express that intention. In bilingual speech, information about social identity in general and the identity projected in a given situation is essential in determining the nature of the illocutionary force for a given speech act. Among the most salient linguistic clues to illocutionary force are the language/dialect choice, linguistic expressions of affect (e.g. intonation), pragmatic markers, and lexical choice.

The remaining two components of information in the SPPL Model are known in the language production literature as the *formulator* and the *articulator* (e.g. Levelt, 1989; Levelt, et al., 1999; Poulisse, 1997). In the extensive body of research on the formulator, the lemma (semantic and syntactic information) and the lexeme (morphological and phonological information) have usually been investigated without reference to their sociopragmatic context.[3] As mentioned in the previous chapter, Levelt, Roelofs and Meyer (1999) "do not claim completeness for their theory." They acknowledge that they have no neat solution for that what they call the 'verbalization problem,' stating that there is "no simple, hard-wired connection between percepts and lexical concepts... [they are] always mediated by pragmatic, context dependent considerations." The authors' stance comes from two limitations in their model: a restricted view of social and pragmatic information and the model's inability to handle variation. Conceptual information is grounded in pragmatics and as such demands flexibility to handle variation. It also needs a way to integrate macro and micro information about sociolinguistic identity with information about linguistic form. The present model derives the lemma from a lexico-pragmatic concept, which serves as input to the formulator.

We turn now to a more detailed explication of the various components of the SPPL Model.

1 SOCIAL IDENTITY IN BILINGUAL PRODUCTION

As a construct, social identity has its origins in personality psychology (Erickson, 1968; Mead, 1964), in social psychology (Tajfel, 1982; Stets & Burke, 2000) and in sociology (Goffman, 1959; Waters, 1990). Unidimensional views of identity, based on classical variables such as social class, gender, ethnicity, nationality, territory, religion, family, and occupation are giving way to more dynamic approaches which allow for multiple, fluid identities. This section reviews a selection of the rapidly proliferating research on bilingualism and identity.

Institutional origins of social identity. An individual's social identity is in part a reflection of his or her interaction with various social institutions. Contact with those institutions or lack thereof will lead to maintenance or shift of native identity or acquisition of the identity features of the new culture. Parsons (1967) divided sociological structure into four domains: economy, polity, kinship, and culture, and Williams (1995) adopted these domains as a framework for his introductory textbook in sociolinguistics. Economy, polity, and kinship are readily adaptable to the present model and are reflected in one or more social institutions as described below. Culture, on the other hand, is defined to include a wider range of constructs, like friendship networks, other extra-familial relationships, role and status, leisure activities, interaction with various forms of media and attitudes. Due to the broad range of these constructs, they cannot be applied directly to clusters of settings and events, and thus 'culture' is a less useful construct in this model where we want to represent a scaffolding across levels. Most of the interpersonal and attitudinal information associated with cultural aspects of identity is included in the SPPL Model in an expanded view of 'kinship,' restricting culture to more manageable, empirically examinable notions such as leisure and media activities.

Economy. Social settings which are most closely affiliated with 'economy,' include: workplace, casino, bank, street corner (e.g. black market), supermarket, corner grocery, open-air market. In our study of former Soviet immigrants in Israel and Germany (Dittmar, Spolsky & Walters, 2002), the conventional western office, with its desks, telephones, coffee machine and 8am-to-6pm work day, along with its accompanying social hierarchy, was a reasonable description of the Israeli workplace environment in the hey-day of high tech. It consumed a large proportion of the fully employed immigrant's time and language use. In contrast, Russian-speaking immigrants in Berlin, and now many in Israel's economy of recession, generally do not have jobs in their pre-immigration occupations. In Berlin, their economic institutions can be characterized by a complex of morning visits to government welfare and social security offices and evening employment as "runners" in the *spielhalle* on the eastern side of the city. These institutional differences lead to distinct patterns of identity. Successful immigrants to Israel apparently adopt multiple identities along the lines of home and work, or public and private domains, showing clear evidence of convergence toward the host culture and indications of both attrition and maintenance of Russian identity. Immigrants to Germany, lacking involvement in conventional 'workday culture,' show more evidence of maintaining their Russian identity. In both societies the vitality of the economy is a major factor in identity construction.

Polity. Political institutions tend to dilute an immigrant's native national identity and lead to convergence to the new culture. Voting for an ethnic candidate is one way of maintaining native identity. Formal political institutions are usually less regularly frequented than the places that make up a person's economic identity. This does not mean they are less meaningful to social identity. On the contrary, the prototypical Western political institution, the voting booth, is the center of national as well as individual life on Election Day, and the first vote in a new country is more often than not a significant marker in an immigrant's personal story about himself. Polity also invades the home in the form of pamphlets, surveys, and telephone canvassing. Political identity is also developed through interpersonal and media contact, perhaps to a greater extent than through formal contact with political institutions. A person on her way to complete assimilation in the new society might vote the same way as a person who lives in an immigrant enclave, speaking and hearing the "old" language and still consuming only "old country" media products. Thus, for bilingual identity, in particular immigrant bilingual identity, political behavior on its own may not be very useful to predict language maintenance and attrition.

Kinship. Kinship is viewed here in the broadest sense of social and interpersonal relations, and not restricted to the nuclear or even extended family. Among the most common family settings studied in bilingual homes are dinner table narratives (e.g. Blum-Kulka, 1997). Relatively little research has documented telephone conversations, kitchen talk, parlor meetings, and the more intimate settings of bedroom and bathroom. Reports of home-school diglossia in the early research of Gumperz and Hernandez-Chavez (1972) and the public-private dichotomy in Richard Rodriguez' (1982) bilingual memoir tend to simplify L1 as a home language, ignoring some of the complexities of codeswitching and other polyphonic phenomena in that setting. More careful behavioral documentation of the speech events and topics in the home, like the social network studies of Li Wei and his colleagues (e.g. 1994) might help shed light on how individual bilinguals use various locations in the family setting for negotiating language choices and specificying intentions. Furthermore, investigation of kinship relations beyond the confines of the home should provide insights that current data have not. For example, mother-daughter conversations in a home where the mother speaks in L1 and the daughter responds in L2, may engender more L2 data from the mother when the conversation moves to a shoe store. Thus, language choice may be primarily a function of the setting, or it may be an integrative function of the setting, participants, and speech genre. A model of bilingual production needs the flexibility to handle single as well as multiple sources of information and to handle different weightings of each source.

Behavioral manifestations of individual identity: Accent, names, and greetings. Among the most relevant yet subtle indicators of an individual's social identity is the use of language. Accent and lexical choice are the features of language use that have lent themselves most readily to sociolinguistic investigation. People and place names, child naming practices, and greetings are strong indicators of social identity. Other linguistic units which are used for establishing identity, for presentation of self, and for sustaining interpersonal relations include grammatical patterns, pragmatic phenomena such as metaphor, sarcasm, irony, politeness, and lexical items (e.g. pragmatic markers, ethnic vernacular). In conventional social interaction, all of these phenomena, most notably the use of lexical items, adverbials, and pragmatic markers, are the structural manifestations of social identity.

Bilinguals struggling with a dual character or attempting to take on a new identity may find it difficult to acquire a native accent in the second language, even though they may be relatively talented at learning languages. Rather, for some people, an accent in the second language may be too much of a threat to the already endangered native culture. For others, that non-native accent may be useful–to project a minority image. And for still others, it may be an embarrassing feature of one's past. These same profiles are expressed in personal name use. One bilingual alternates between his given name and a name adopted from the new environment (Carlos-Charlie); another may only use an indigenous name strategically for recognition of minority status; and a third makes an official name change with the appropriate government authority. Greetings are still another way to examine these identity options. In modern, assimilated western Israeli culture, colloquial Hebrew greetings alternate with borrowings from English and Arabic. In more traditional surroundings, *shalom* and *kif haalek* or one of their variants may be the default option. And in some cases, foreign greetings may replace native language variants entirely.

Social identity is conceived here as a multidimensional construct. Its origins can be traced to social domains and social institutions, in particular to economy, polity, kinship, and culture. Individual social identity is expressed in a variety of ways: in particular in one's language behavior in all linguistic domains, especially in accent, names, and greeting behavior. Imitation (social and linguistic) is the primary process underlying the expression of social identity. General goals and intentions are derived from social identity and supported by processes of social and linguistic imitation. The output of the social identity component of the present model can be conceived as a set of individual preferences and goals. These goals and preferences, along with language choice and affect information, help determine choices in speech formulation and which settings and participants one will interact with.

Towards a composite social identity. Returning to our story about Yulia, her choices and decisions regarding work, finances and shopping and her social contacts in various institutions (e.g., workplace, bank, supermarket, corner grocery, market) help generate her economic identity. Her voting behavior, political affiliations and attitudes, and the like constitute her political identity. Birth order, gender, interaction and attitudes toward family are some of the constituents of family identity. Friendship networks, extra-familial relationships, her role and status at school and university, in leisure activities, her interaction with various forms of media form a complex of information sources that is the input of her cultural identity. Processes of immigration and urbanization impinge on Yulia's composite identity. Industrialization, secularization and alienation do not apply to Yulia. In her particular case, immigration is only important as the baggage she inherited from home and parents. She herself quickly integrated, and from late adolescence never really perceived or presented herself as an immigrant. Thus, her immigrant identity is memorial, but not relevant in her daily social identity as an Israeli.

Notes on method. Ethnography and case studies are the current methods used to get to deeper levels of analysis. These approaches could be followed up with tightly designed experiments focused on individual bilinguals, for example, in the framework of personal design (Anderson, 1990, 2001). Experiments allow examination of specific hypotheses and relations among selected variables. Here I would like to persuade the reader that multiple methods may be an effective research strategy, especially if the search for variance is an important endeavor. Another way to investigate social identity, goals and intentions is to examine narratives and memoirs in literary works. Good examples of this type of portrait are Erik Erikson's psycho-histories of Luther and Gandhi, or more recent non-native memoirs like Eva Hoffman's (1989) *Lost in Translation* or Richard Rodriguez' (1982) *Hunger for Memory.* Techniques of content analysis and text/discourse analysis from corpus linguistics, systemics, pragmatics, and social psychology can be applied to the bilingual aspects of these works. Content analysis can provide insight into the relative amount of material devoted to a topic and the salience/relevance of key concepts, while discourse approaches permit deeper insight into an individual's attitudes and motivations.

Recent increased interest in narrative psychology has led to the use of autobiographical reports to investigate bilingualism. Marian and Neisser (2000) modified a technique introduced by Schrauf and Rubin (1998) involving single-word prompts to elicit life experience narratives from different periods of Russian immigrants' lives to examine coding and retrieval in episodic memory. The immigrants remembered more experiences when the prompts were in the same language as the interviews, than when prompts and interviews were in two different languages. Moreover, the kind of things they remembered changed according to the language that was used for prompts. The authors took this as evidence for language dependent encoding and retrieval.

One ancillary finding is relevant to this work, in particular for what it can teach us methodologically. The finding relates to the age at which the life experiences were drawn from. Marian and Neisser noted that "participants recalled relatively few memories from the period around and just after immigration, fewer than from either their childhood in Russia or their adult lives in America" (p. 367). This finding was interpreted as perhaps additional evidence of a mismatch of the language of the experience (presumably a mixture of Russian and English) and the language of the interview, which was restricted to a single language. An additional interpretation involved schema theory, with the authors claiming that during immigration, life experiences may not have been consistent with childhood Russian schemata. It should be noted that, in eliciting their data, the authors proscribed the use of codeswitching. Thus, the task restrictions may not have allowed an opportunity for each of a subject's multiple identities to be expressed. This may have been especially true for those four subjects (out of 20) who stated no language preference. It is also noteworthy that, despite sanctions against codeswitching, a full 20 percent of the memories generated in each of the two experiments reported involved codeswitching. Thus, while the authors were not necessarily interested in codeswitching data for a study of the role of language in episodic memory, the existence of these data is quite relevant for those of us interested in finding ways to generate fluent, natural data about codeswitching.

Another approach in social identity research is to examine identity as a list or cluster of traits. That list can then be submitted to sociometric and/or psychometric analyses. Peter Weinreich's (1986) 'identity structure analysis' is illustrative in this regard. His studies of ethnic identity in Irish and British minority and majority culture members combine data from semi-structured interviews with rating scales. These data are computationally assessed for their goodness-of-fit to a model of identity based on psychodynamic, individual, and symbolic interactionist components. Unfortunately, language use and language attitude data do not have a formal role in this model, but the computational and methodological innovations are noteworthy.

The study of social identity is spread across a variety of disciplines (sociology, social psychology, literary studies) but cannot yet be said to be an integrated interdisciplinary endeavor. In addition, the best efforts at computational modeling of social identity are still elementary. My preference is for multiple methods of data collection, gathered in different situations, including a range of social, psychological and actual language behavior and attitude tasks, all where the unit of analysis is the individual language user (case studies). In an exploratory study of Tatiana, a Russian immigrant adolescent, Walters and Popko (1996) described the girl's identity as very strongly Russian, mildly Israeli, and negatively Jewish. In that study, a stark contrast was found between largely anti-Israeli *attitudes* (from the content of the interview data) and thoroughly integrative (Israeli/Hebrew) language *behavior* in performance on a role-playing discourse completion task eliciting greetings, where Tatiana performed exactly like native-born Israel counterparts.

The difference between the attitudinal and behavioral findings here and throughout the literature in social psychology indicates the need for multiple data gathering approaches and flexible interpretive frameworks. While trying to understand some of this cross-disciplinary complexity in work with Russian immigrants in Germany and Israel, we have experimented with different profiles of personal information (e.g. profiles for language proficiency and use, for attitudes, for identity, etc.) summarized from sociolinguistic interviews. These profiles were complemented by content analyses of what the immigrants said about immigration and identity and linguistic analyses of phonetic, lexical and pragmatic features of their speech. The content, discourse, and quantitative lexical and phonetic analyses in this work offer guidelines for developing an overall framework and a working model of social identity in bilingual production (Dittmar, Spolsky & Walters, 2002).

2 CONTEXT AND GENRE

The contextual/genre component depicted in Figure 3.2, like the social identity component described in the previous section, is fundamentally sociopragmatic. It contains elements which are roughly parallel to two of Halliday's (1994) three meta-functions (the interpersonal and textual), but in the SPPL Model, context and genre are imbued with social content–from the social identity component and from societal and institutional knowledge.

2A EXTERNAL CONTEXTUAL INFORMATION: SETTING AND PARTICIPANTS

The importance of setting and participants as factors in language use in general and bilingualism in particular, from pragmatic considerations down to the tiniest phonetic detail, is well documented. Ferguson (1959) lists twelve speech functions in his classic definition of diglossia. Three of these functions, the sermon, the political speech, and the university lecture, which might be labeled genres or events in different disciplinary traditions, are strongly grounded in the 'setting' construct. A second set of constraints on diglossia is included in the participant function, viz., speech variation to listeners of different types. A third category is more clearly genre- or text-related, e.g. newpapers, personal letters, poetry, news broadcasts. Setting and participants are also the lead terms in Hymes' (1974) mnemonic for investigating the ethnography of speaking (Setting, Participants, Ends, Acts, Key, Intent, Norms, Genre). Some of the earliest work in both psycholinguistics and sociolinguistics made use of these constructs (e.g. Ervin-Tripp, 1964) before disciplinary divisions caused a parting of ways.

Whether setting and participants are determinants of language use, as claimed implicitly or explicitly in most sociolinguistic research (see Walters, 1979b for a review), or whether they are subordinate to internal motivations and social identity, as modeled here, are questions that have not been investigated empirically. Unlike social identity, which is an internal representation of external information, information about setting and participants is external, mostly observable, and relatively easy to document. What has been variously called setting, situation, speech event, script, schema, plan, and topic is typically subsumed under a single notion. Before trying to wade into the distinctions relevant to the processing of information about bilingual language choice and social identity, a selective review of this terminology and some of the issues may be useful.

Figure 3.2 The context/genre component of the SPPL Model

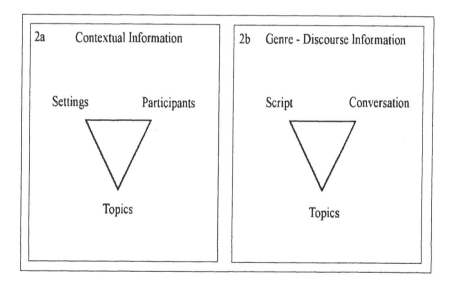

What Hymes (1974) labels setting in his taxonomy of communicative competence, what Halliday and the systemicists call 'context of situation' in the tradition of Malinowski and Furth, and what cognitive psychology and artificial intelligence research have referred to as plans, scripts, schemata, and events (e.g. Bower, Black & Turner, 1979; Schank & Abelson, 1977) include information that goes far beyond physical location. In their more comprehensive sense, scripts have included general and culturally-based background knowledge, procedural knowledge, expectations, and beliefs about status and role relationships. Investigations of plans and scripts have looked, for example, at ordering in a restaurant and planning a trip. Studies of non-native scripts and schemata include processing of information about weddings, doctor-patient interactions, and service encounters. In its more restrictive sense in micro-sociolinguistics, setting has been limited to information about the time and place of an interaction (e.g. Walters, 1981; Rintell, 1981).

Two kinds of studies are relevant here to capture a distinction between macro- and micro-sociolinguistics. The two differ both in the range of information included in their notions of setting and in their methodologies. The studies from a macro, societal perspective can be illustrated by Fishman, Cooper and Ma's (1971) investigation of Spanish-English language use in the Puerto Rican community of Jersey City, New Jersey. In that study, the domains of 'family,' 'friendship,' 'religion,' 'education,' and 'employment' were used to summarize initial observations and data. It was from this study that Fishman's question, "Who speaks what language to whom and when?" emerged. The way this question is phrased emphasizes the participants in the interaction ('Who' and 'to whom'). Information about 'where' the interaction takes place is not differentiated from 'when,' which is apparently a general term for all situational information. In contrast, Cooper's (1969) model specifies three sources of information for 'social situation:' time, setting, and role relationship. In the SPPL Model, these notions are modeled separately as setting and participants.

The other kind of investigation relevant here comes from micro-sociolinguistics. In early studies of codeswitching (e.g. Gumperz, 1967; Blom & Gumperz, 1972; Gumperz & Hernandez-Chavez, 1972) setting and participants figured prominently in the interpretation of the data. In a more experimental vein, Walters (1981a) examined variation in politeness of requests as a function of setting and listener in Puerto Rican bilingual children. This study elicited requests in Spanish and English using role playing techniques, which presented four settings, two at school (cafeteria and playground) and two in a neighborhood setting. In each setting, subjects made requests on two topics, to eight different listeners, who were presented as puppets. The listener puppets varied as a function of age (adult/peer), gender (male/female) and race (African-American/white). Using Edwards' (1957) method of paired comparisons, the requests elicited in the study were assigned politeness scores, based on independent ratings of the speech act forms (e.g. would you, could you, can you, etc.) by native speakers of Spanish and English. These scores were submitted to analyses of variance to assess the relative effects of setting and the age, gender and race of the listener. Results showed main effects for setting in every experimental arrangement; moreover, effects for setting were always the largest. That finding has been replicated across of wide variety of studies of contextual information (e.g. Walters, 1981b for a review).

Diaries in the investigation of language use data. Another approach to the study of setting and participants, motivated by the framework proposed here to examine identity, is the use of language diaries (Walters et al., 2003). Diaries could (perhaps should) be complemented by sociolinguistic interviews as well as ethnographic and phenomenological studies in order to assess the relevance of specific situations and preferences for particular genres in particular bilingual communities. At first, individual case studies are recommended, with large amounts of data collected from each subject. Later, longitudinal and cross-sectional group studies can be conducted to assess generality.

Using the methodology of personal design (Anderson, 1990) we should ask bilingual participants to keep a diary of the places they frequented on a given day, logging the time, setting, people present and the event. Records should be kept for each participant by taking three samples (over a six-month period) of two weekdays and one weekend day. The following table proposes a way to organize information from a hypothetical language diary of a Ukrainian immigrant to Israel. As can be seen from the information in Table 3.2, the immigrant teaches high school English and participates in various religious activities. The data here are "reported language data," and like the findings for "language use," are highly correlated with setting and topic.

Table 3.2 Contextual information in an immigrant language diary

Day	Time	Language	Setting	Participants	Event/Topic
6.11.98	5:00	no speech	Home/bedroom	Wife	dressing
		no speech	Home/bathroom	Alone	shower/teeth
	5:30	Hebrew/Heb-R CS	Synagogue	rabbi, 3 other men	talmud lesson
	6:40	Hebrew	Synagogue	40-50 men, God	prayers
	7:30	R-H CS	Home	daughter, 14/son, 5	eating, dressing, Sabbath plans
	7:45	H	School/teachers' room	5 other teachers	gossip about pupils
	8:00	H/E	School/classroom	35 grade 11 pupils	attendance
	8:10	H/E	School/classroom	35 grade 11 pupils	lesson on poetry

A methodological note. In the Fishman study mentioned above, the data come from questionnaires eliciting *'reported language use.'* The same is true of the data from language diaries. In the micro-sociolinguistic studies referred to here, the data come from *'language behavior'* in role-playing situations. Effects for setting across all three methods are an important first-step toward generality.

Identity is captured in these research paradigms via language use, reported or actual. Individual bilingualism is not explicitly represented in the data and must be inferred from preferences a speaker has for particular settings and participants. Two ways are suggested here to capture bilingual aspects of social context. One is the use of the social networks paradigm; the other is examination of both social and speech phenomenon in spontaneous code switching data.

Social network research in bilingual settings has made use of both actual language behavior collected via ethnographic observation (Li Wei, 1994) and reported language use via questionnaires (Pong, 1991, cited in Li Wei, Milroy & Pong, 2000). The social network paradigm has provided scalable data for looking at language choice and a host of social and stylistic variables including age, generation, and gender. These data on social networks and language use offer a way to scaffold social/demographic information onto interactional data about the relationship between speaker and interlocutor, making them relevant to the connection between the social identity and contextual components of the SPPL Model. Pong's data via questionnaires confirmed the findings in Li Wei's ethnographic study.

In a social network task involving reported language use in the framework of sociolinguistic interviews, we (Dittmar, Spolsky & Walters, 2002) examined the number, density and importance of social contacts of Russian immigrants in Berlin and the greater Tel Aviv area. Findings showed that even though the overwhelming majority of social contacts were with fellow immigrants, the participants in the study reached a fairly high level of proficiency in the non-native language. Nevertheless, language behavior data from the interviews indicated that the high level of proficiency was still marked phonetically and pragmatically by certain aspects of non-native pronunciation and usage.

The social network paradigm lends itself to ethnographic, interview, and questionnaire procedures. In all cases it allows information about language use to be placed in the background, away from the center of attention. In this way, participants can make uninhibited, presumably honest responses to questions about social contacts with the data about language use provided almost incidentally.

The study of bilingual codeswitching could benefit from the application of one of the research strategies above where information about codeswitching comes with information about setting and the language background of participants. Diary and social network studies that combine setting, participant, and codeswitching in a single framework would illuminate questions about the distinction between socially and psycholinguistically motivated codeswitching. With these descriptive findings, experimental designs could be arranged to test specific hypotheses about the role of setting and participants in codeswitching. One useful approach would be to provide rich contextual information for these speech phenomena, thereby allowing a comparison with ethnographic and naturalistic data gathering techniques.

2B GENRE INFORMATION

The genre construct, like context, is seen here as fundamentally sociopragmatic. This view challenges text-based approaches. Historically, from Aristotle and Isocrates to Bakhtin in the west, from Saadia Gaon and Al-Farabi in the Mediterranean, genre has been called everything from text type to social discourse. Isocrates' notion of genre has been defined as "a literary category defined in terms, for example, of theme, style (e.g. language, metre) and/or occasion of performance (e.g. drama, lyric, epic)" (Too, 1995:13). Too cites Hieronymus Wolf's (1570) categories (hortatory, deliberative, epideictic, and forensic) as exemplary of a medieval view. The jump from this view to the Russian formalists' taxonomy and modern English rhetoric textbooks (narrative, expository, descriptive, and argumentative) is not a large jump.

Literary scholarship has gone beyond these structural categories, as Too (1995) shows in his work on identity in the work of Isocrates. He notes the "continual revision of generic boundaries," drawing on Hirsch's (1967) view that this fact is based on subjectivity. Citing Todorov's social-institutional approach to genre ('reveal[ing] the constitutive trait of the society to which they belong,') Too claims that "Genre is a product of personal and social prejudices and assumptions about particular literary identities." This perspective also echoes Bakhtin (1986), who states that "notions of genre are in any case themselves shaped and determined by a complex set of assumptions and prejudices...[he] favours plurality, advocates increasing the number of genres, perhaps indefinitely, so that our descriptions of discourse become more detailed and less systematic" (18-19).

Current work on genre is a far cry from the restricted notion of text type still prevalent in English composition classrooms, where the focus is on structural differences in discourse, syntactic, semantic, and lexical features. Today, the genre construct has been expanded to include knowledge and information about discourse community, script, schema, event, writer's purpose, and topic. The literature treating these constructs–from Miller (1984) in literary theory, from Bazerman (1989) and Berkenkotter and Huckin (1994) in rhetoric, from Freedman (1993) and Swales (1990) in applied linguistics–does not usually make a rigorous distinction between social and textual information. In contrast, for Bakhtin (1986), structure is primary:

> Language is realized in the form of individual concrete utterances (oral and written) by participants in the various areas of human activity. These utterances reflect the specific conditions and goals of each such area not only through their content (thematic) and linguistic style, that is, the selection of the lexical, phraseological, and grammatical resources of the language, **but above all through their compositional structure** [my emphasis]. All three of these aspects– thematic content, style, and compositional structure–are inseparably linked to the *whole* of the utterance and are equally determined by the specific nature of the

particular sphere of communication. Each separate utterance is individual, of course, but each sphere in which language is used develops its own *relatively stable types* of these utterances. These we may call *speech genres* (Bakhtin, 1986:60).

Freedman (1993) makes the relationship between textual and social information explicit with the balance in favor of the latter: "...the recurring textual regularities which characterize genres are themselves seen as secondary to, and a consequence of, the action that is being performed through the texts in response to recurring socio-cultural contexts" (Freedman, 1993:225). The subordination of text information to socio-cultural considerations fits with the SPPL Model, in which social identity drives the system. However, Freedman's notion of the genre/text as a "response to recurring situations or contexts" does not correspond with the purposive, goal-driven, self-motivated approach taken here. Thus, the SPPL Model attempts to distinguish between social and textual aspects of genre, subordinating both of these sources of information to individual social identity.

The sources mentioned above do not deal directly with genre processing issues per se, and are not concerned with how bilinguals process textual aspects of genre information. (For exceptions, see Ford Meyer, 2000:254, who discusses a continuum of spontaneity and "transparency of cognitive function" for conversation, oral monologue, and written texts and Hanauer's, 1995, work on poetic texts.)

There are a series of procedural questions one would want to address first to sharpen the focus around the larger question of what constitutes a genre. Among these questions are: To what extent is the speaker aware of genre information? Is it more incidental than explicit? Is a genre decision, albeit unconscious, even made by the speaker, or can genre choices be subsumed under other sub-components of processing? Some clarity on these questions is needed before we can move to an understanding of the role of bilingual language choice and affect in the processing of genre information.

Studies in contrastive rhetoric have also moved the focus of genre from the text outward to the social context (e.g. Kaplan, 1966; Connor, 1996, Chapter 8). The skewed concentration of this subfield on academic and written language makes these studies less useful for a general model of bilingual production. The discourse structures and data do, however, provide important information for answering the declarative/structural question raised above, namely: What constitutes a genre? Narratives and scientific journal articles are among the most commonly investigated forms. The structural components of narratives have been examined in reading comprehension research in the context of schema theory and the story grammar paradigm (e.g. Stein & Glenn, 1979; and Carrell, 1984; Walters & Wolf, 1986 for non-native schema). The structural elements of a story include setting, initiating event, internal response or goal, attempt to reach the goal, consequence of that attempt, and an ending. These six sources of information are said to be organized hierarchically in the mind of the reader/writer. Robust findings show that both natives and non-natives recall settings, initiating events, and consequences better than information from the other three categories. One could make a parallel statement about the nature and processing of academic research articles, which consist of four explicitly labeled structural elements: introduction, method, results, and discussion. Choice of content, syntax, and lexis differs meaningfully from genre to genre, as well as across the structural categories of a particular genre (e.g. Berkenkotter & Huckin, 1994).

With this in mind, we distinguish here between scripted language and conversational interaction. Both *scripts* and *conversations* are based on mental representations or schemata, and they themselves are derived from the integration of social experiences with social identity and goals. These two genre types fall at either ends of a continuum of explicitness in terms of their sociolinguistic rules or norms of interaction. Scripts for classroom lessons, service encounters, doctor-patient interactions, and ordering meals in a restaurant are more constrained and distinctive than conversational interactions, in terms of who can initiate and who can conclude, which topics are permissible and which are not, how long a topic can be maintained, when a switch is permissible, and what constitutes an interruption versus when an utterance is considered uptake or back-channeling. While scripts and conversations are apparently universal structures, with both types being found across cultures, their instantiation is far from universal. And it is precisely because of their language and culture-specific patterns of discourse that bilingual interference and miscommunication can arise.

Scripted language. In a study of doctor-patient scripts among Hmong immigrants to the United States, Ranney (1992) extends earlier notions of setting within a speech acts framework and modifies Schank and Abelson's (1977) notion of a script as a "schema which accounts for stereotypes of routine activities occurring as a sequence of actions." Her study examined multiple sources of data, including 'free elicitation' of a doctor-patient script, a cued elicitation task, an interview involving norms of interaction, and a discourse completion task. The findings for nine native Hmong speakers and nine native English speakers were aggregated in the form of a 'composite script,' that specified five discrete stages in a doctor-patient encounter: (a) a preliminary encounter stage where the patient waits to be greeted by the doctor, (b) elicitation of the problem, (c) investigation of the problem (including interrogation and examination), (d) communication of the diagnosis, and (e) recommended treatment.

The most striking difference between American and Hmong scripts was the absence of the fourth stage, i.e. communication of the diagnosis. An American English speaker who has been examined by a Hmong doctor could request a diagnosis or even issue a complaint if not provided with one. A Hmong patient in an American clinic may not understand why the diagnosis is being communicated to him/her; but, unlike an American in Laos, it may or may not register as cross-cultural miscommunication.

One way to approach bilingual processing of script information is to treat the phenomenon like other kinds of disturbances due to language contact (see Walters & Wolf, 1992). In this vein, when trying to process a target culture script that lacks a structural element from a parallel native script, as in the case of the Hmong user of English, the first exposure to the missing element will probably go unnoticed. After hearing verbal statements of the diagnosis several more times, the Hmong immigrant might develop a metalinguistic awareness of an additional element in the doctor-patient script. At the point that the Hmong patient completed integrating other elements of American language and culture into his genre knowledge, the American English doctor-patient script could become part of that knowledge, and with this, the expectation that the doctor should tell the patient what's wrong with him or her.

Now let's fit this into a model of bilingual processing. Script information is seen here as a genre type. Social and contextual information enters the model from other components. Scripts can be distinguished from conversations in terms of repetition and variability. The language of scripts is more repetitious and less variable than the language of conversations. Moreover, scripts are more closely tied to settings, participants, and topic. Thus, scripts should generate less overt interference, fewer instances of codeswitching, and less integration of first and second language patterns than conversations. Culturally distinct scripts, like the wedding narratives investigated by Steffenson, Joag-Dev and Anderson (1979) and Johnson (1982) should show still less evidence of language contact phenomena such as interference and codeswitching, since they are distinct in terms of setting and participants as well as language.

Conversational interaction. For bilingual interaction, Auer's (1995) work offers perhaps the best access to some of the processing questions we wish to address in the present model. Auer rejects approaches that try to correlate language choice and speech events as well as functional typologies, conversational loci, or listings of verbal activities where code-alternation can be expected (e.g. reported speech, meta-comments, role, mode, and topic shift, focus, reiteration). In doing so, he opts for an interpretive, conversational approach to bilingual speech within a more general theory of contextualization (Gumperz, 1992; Auer, 1998). Code-alternation is seen as "but one of an array of devices such as intonation, rhythm, gesture or posture which are used in the situated production and interpretation of language" (Auer, 1995:123).

To review briefly the presentation from the previous chapter, Auer (1995) distinguishes four patterns of code-alternation. In the first two patterns, language choice is clearly marked by each speaker. In the other two, language choice is not readily apparent. The first pattern, labeled 'discourse-related code-switching,' involves a switch to another language at a certain point in the conversation or within a single speaker's turn, due to "contextualization" of a conversational feature such as topic shift or change in participants. Pattern II, called 'preference-related code-switching,' begins with a rule of 'one-speaker, one-language.' Following one or more exchanges in this mode, one of the speakers accommodates to the language of his interlocutor. According to Auer, the initial preference for a particular language and the ensuing negotiation towards a single language offer insight into a speaker's confidence, language proficiency, or even political attitudes. The third pattern is characterized by switching within a speaking turn. It can involve discourse-related as well as participant-related switching. The main feature of this pattern is that the speaker is apparently holding his/her cards close, not giving away information about language preference. The fourth pattern of code-alternation is labeled transfer/insertional. It is defined as turn-internal and described as a "momentary lapse into the other language" with a "predictable end." It does not affect language choice.

Auer (1995) goes on to show how the constructs and tools of conversational analysis inform negotiation of language choice. Re-analyzing several classic excerpts from the literature on conversational code-switching (Heller, 1988; Alvarez, 1990; Myers-Scotton, 1990), he shows how one can use notions such as first-pair part, repetition, and cohesion to gain insight into expected differences between monolingual and bilingual interaction. The results of his analyses show that these constructs are useful in determining language choices and in directing the course of language negotiation.

In contrast to scripted language, where the setting and participants are more distinctive and identifiable, conversations are more variable. The same conversational structure (e.g. greetings, turn-taking patterns, repairs) can be found in many settings and participants, but they vary more than the patterns in scripts. Thus, conversation should generate more interference, more codeswitching, and more integration of first and second language patterns. Culturally distinct conversational patterns, such as Au's (Au & Jordan, 1981) Hawaiian talk stories, Schiffrin's (1984) New York Jewish conversational style, and Zupnick's (2000) interruption patterns in Israeli-Palestinian dialogues provide more evidence of cross-cultural miscommunication than scripted language (see also Gudykunst & Ting-Toomey, 1990, for related research from the field of speech communication).

Topic. Conversational interaction, whether face-to-face, via telephone, or by means of electronic chat, is initiated by an individual decision and the availability of an appropriate setting and participants. One of the most prominent differences between scripted language and conversation is related to topic. In the SPPL Model, topics originate at all levels of processing down to and including the formulator (cf. lexico-pragmatic concepts). Topic is the link between contextual/genre information (settings, participants, and genres) and internal linguistic knowledge (in particular, propositional content), between social identity and grammatical and lexical options. Topic is also the bridge between social/textual information and lexico-pragmatic concepts.

According to Pinker (1998), eighty percent of the average speaker's lexicon can be accounted for by the 2,000 most frequent words and almost 90 percent of lexical knowledge can be accounted for by approximately 4,000 words. The number of topics, then, is a still smaller set of concepts, mentally tagged for frequency of use and availability, and hierarchically organized around the individual's social identity, experiences, and social networks. Topic, for the scripts discussed above, is more constrained, and thus may lend itself more readily to computational modeling. In bilingual production, the language choice module plays the major role in determining whether the speaker uses L1, the second language, or both in generating topics.

Summary. The genre component is an attempt to fill a gap in bilingual production research and help clarify some of the unclear boundaries between and among constructs such as context, setting, participants, genre, topic, and discourse. Setting and participants are fundamentally external, interactional phenomena, subsumed in SPPL's notion of 'context.' They are distinguished as contextual information in that they are external to an individual language user's social identity. They are interactional in that they provide input to the language user from his/her physical and social environment and from other speakers and listeners in that environment. The genre component is also external, but it involves interaction between the language user and more abstract, symbolic phenomena, namely texts and their properties. Within the genre component, the SPPL Model distinguishes between scripted language and conversation.[4] Finally, topic is the construct that links both context (setting and participants) as well as genre (scripts and conversations) with internal linguistic representations.

The output of this component is derived from input on attitudes, use, and behavior. The integration of these varied sources of information is a complex conceptual and methodological challenge. Very tentatively, I would say that in a model where sociopragmatic information drives the system, setting and participant information may already be incorporated into a bilingual's identity before the genre is selected. A first pass at how to process this information would be to envision it as a ranked or weighted lists of settings, participants, and genres. In accordance with this approach, the output is conceived as:

- ❏ a set of specific situations which the speaker has already been exposed to, each rated for familiarity and/or preference;
- ❏ a social network of actual and potential interlocutors; and
- ❏ a listing of genre options and preferences.[5]

Each of these components comes with a set of topics, which can be conceived as concept maps (Novak, 1998). The ranked or weighted lists, along with their topics, are integrated to yield a set of scripts or conversational norms/rules which are made available to the speech act component, whose job is to specify an illocutionary point and its accompanying propositional content.

I began this section by referring to the roots of the genre construct in philosophy and rhetoric, then tried to give some of the social flavor of more recent scholarship in applied linguistics, and finally presented the SPPL's way of cutting up the genre pie. We see that 'contrastive rhetoric' and non-native schemata do not lead to anything close to a uniquely bilingual genre. Research on pidgins and creoles, kanaksprache, and World Englishes such as Spanglish, Hebrish, and SAE gets us a little closer. Distinctions among speaker and voice, author and narrator draw on notions of identity and context. The script/ conversation partition allows for both ends of the linguistic sprectrum. Scripts, like words and collocations, are bottom-up, grounded in the features of language. Conversations are speaker-generated, top-down. Scripts promote fluency; conversations add propositional content. Scripts draw more from the imitation mechanism, conversations require variation for sustenance. Information about scripted and conversational speech is integrated, along with the other sociopragmatic components of the SPPL Model, forming the basis for the knowledge which makes up a speaker's intentions.

3 INTENTIONS IN BILINGUALISM

Intentions come from within; they are speaker-based. They are distinguished from context, which was defined above as external. In the SPPL Model, intentions and context are processed by independent components in language production. This autonomy is grounded historically on research in various sub-fields in psychology and sociology. Studies in personality, motivation, and identity are different attempts to get at intentions. Ethnographers who have examined the cultural bases of intentionality question whether it is possible to understand the intentions of someone from a different culture. In the SPPL Model, intentions are separable from the social, interactive aspects of language, which belong more properly to the domain of sociology and social psychology. In this view, intentions are centered on the individual, conceptualizing personal characteristics, desires, and needs independent of their social dimensions.

The *intentional* component was originally conceptualized as grounded in speech act theory in linguistics (Walters, 2001), but as the range of disciplinary research on intentions has broadened from philosophy and linguistics to psychology, computer science, and anthropology, the current model takes a wider perspective. The purpose of this component in the SPPL Model is to identify the various sources and features of intentions. In language production an intention is generated from within, and propositional content is then selected to express it. Illocutionary force is a primary source of information about intentions (Austin, 1962; Searle, 1969). Pragmatic markers are another source (Fraser, 1996). The former is an abstract construct; the latter are more transparent. The intentional component draws from other information components of the SPPL Model and uses that information to formulate intentions, which are envisioned to be a good deal more complex than even the dichotomous notion of primary and secondary illocutionary force. The illocutionary force of some speech acts is considered to be, on the whole, universal (e.g. requesting, blaming). On the other hand, the manner (i.e. the surface syntax and semantics) in which speech acts are expressed is language specific. Many, perhaps most, speech acts exhibit cross-cultural differences (e.g., greetings). Still others may exist in one culture but not in another. For example, an explicit, formulaic, verbal response to an acknowledgement or a thank-you is obligatory in British, Spanish, and Israeli culture but optional in many American settings.

In bilingual speech, information about social identity in general and the identity projected in a given situation are indispensable in determining the illocutionary force for a given speech act. Among the most salient linguistic clues to illocutionary force are language/dialect choice, linguistic expression of affect (e.g. intonation), pragmatic markers, lexical choice, and intonation. Production research in a speech act framework, due to its focus on linguistic form, may pass over valuable insights into processes that do not lend themselves to observation. In the present model, evidence of illocutionary force is a reflection of an individual's social experiences, attitudes, needs, and motivations. It can be read off language use phenomena such as adverbial modifiers, pragmatic markers (e.g. anyway, so, well, kind of, etc.), personal and deictic pronouns, and the lexis needed to support these means.

Stages in the processing of intentions. Poulisse (1997, 1999), in her adaptation of the conceptual stage of Levelt's (1989) model to the study of bilingual production, outlines five processes:
- ❑ conception of a communicative intention
- ❑ planning the content (macro-planning)
- ❑ selecting information to achieve goals
- ❑ planning the message's form (micro-planning)
- ❑ output of a preverbal message to the formulator

Following a speech act approach to language production, the first of these processes, conception of a communicative intention, seems to be most closely related to selection of an illocutionary point (Searle, 1975), or what Ninio (1986) has called meta-meaning. For bilingual production, we would argue that each utterance potentially expresses multiple illocutionary points (e.g. Ninio, 1986; see also Hovy, 1995, on the multifunctionality of discourse markers). That same potential for multiplicity is built into the present model such that an intention involves various aspects of a speaker's social identity, contextual, genre, and discourse information, as well as input from the language choice and affective modules. As proposed in the next chapter, mechanisms of variation and integration attempt to explain how multiple sources of information are processed.

The second process in Levelt and Poulisse, macro-planning of content, seems to presuppose a conscious, top-down hierarchical plan. Such a procedure would necessitate, or at least be facilitated by, availability of lexical concepts, which in the Levelt et al. (1999) model are not generated until a later stage of formulation.

But not all speakers plan to the same extent before they speak or write. Some plan on-line, adapting an original plan of content as they go along; others first need to do some brainstorming and shuffling of lexical concepts before they come up with a macro-plan. In the SPPL Model, this function is conceived as concept mapping (e.g. Novak & Gowin, 1984; Novak, 1998). It involves selecting, linking, and organizing lexico-pragmatic concepts. In scripted language this might occur earlier than in spontaneous conversation. But even in written production, the system needs flexibility in order to allow modification. The SPPL Model, through its processing mechanisms described in the next chap-ter, allows for a dynamic, modifiable approach to intentions (cf., Perrault, 1990).

Selecting information, the third process, involves choosing concepts, or propositional content. 'Information' is equated here with lexico-pragmatic concepts. The kind of micro-planning, described in Levelt's model as the choice of speech act, the marking of given or new information, and assignment of topic or focus, would all fit into a single formulator in his model. In the present approach, the speech act is selected before formulation. Moreover, lexical access and discourse formulation (i.e. marking given-new information, cohesion, relevance) are separate sub-components of the SPPL formulator. In any case, to choose a speech act and perform the other operations named here, both illocutionary force and propositional content are required. The SPPL Model proposes that illocutionary force and propositional content are more than a "preverbal message" (Roelofs, 1992; Poulisse, 1997, 1999). Rather, they are combined to produce a lexico-pragmatic couplet, incorporating both sociopragmatic information from previous stages of processing as well as syntactic and semantic information in the sense of Levelt and others.

To summarize, then, the SPPL Model differs from previous work in terms of macro-planning, micro-planning, and discourse processing. Macro-planning is envisioned here in terms of lexical networks and concept maps; it is a process that can be started before and after the onset of an intention, and can be modified throughout conceptualization as well as during formulation. A discussion of macro-planning is beyond the scope of the current presentation, and the reader is referred to the extensive research program involving WordNet (Fellbaum, 1998) and its bilingual implementations. Micro-planning, the central focus of the next section, is restricted in the present model to the selection of speech acts, which consist of illocutionary force(s) and propositional content. Finally, marking of given or new information and management of cohesion and relevance are treated as discourse functions and are handled by the discourse component of the formulator (see below).

Intentions in a model of bilingual production. To show how intentions might be encoded, I draw from the methodology and findings of Walters (1980, 1981a) on requests and some of my current work on blame and refusals. The data on requests come from role playing studies of bilingual children (native speakers of Armenian, Puerto Rican and Chicano Spanish), who were engaged in structured conversations in a variety of settings (school, home, neighborhood) with puppets varying in age (adult/child), gender (male/female), and race (African American/white). Individual (one-on-one) data collection procedures were used. Each bilingual child was introduced to a 'friend' (a puppet of the same age and gender) who was described as being in need of assistance. After a brief, 'spontaneous' conversation, the 'friend' puppet initiated a structured conversation, which was conducted from a written dialogue. Example 3.5 is the transcript of one of those conversations, along with the responses of one bilingual child, given the pseudonym Carlos. (The relevant utterances, i.e. the ones that indicate the illocutionary force, are printed in boldfaced upper case letters.)

Example 3.5 *Transcript of script for eliciting speech act information*

'Friend' puppet:	What're you gonna do on your vacation?
S (Carlos):	I don' know.
'Friend' puppet:	My mother is gonna take us to the zoo. Do you wanna go?
S (Carlos):	Yeah.
'Friend' puppet:	Hey, Carlos. I have to go to the supermarket. I have to buy some milk and some rice for my mother. Will you come with me?
S (Carlos):	Okay.
'Friend' puppet:	Well, here we are. Hey look. That (<u>man</u>/woman/boy/girl) over there has some rice. Go ask (<u>him</u>/her) to show you where the rice is, and I'll go get the milk. I'll meet you back here in a minute.
S (Carlos):	**MISTER, CAN YOU GOT RICE?**
Listener puppet 1 (adult, white, male):	
	It's over there…on the top shelf.
'Friend' puppet:	Oh good…Wow! The lines are really long. I've got to get home by three or my mother will punish me. Ask this (man/woman/boy/<u>girl</u>) in front of us to let us go first.
S (Carlos):	**CAN WE GO IN FRONT OF YOU?**
Listener puppet 2 (young, AfrAm, female):	
	Sure, you only have two items. Go ahead.

In this conversation, personal identity, needs, motivations, etc. are all relatively unimportant in the child's utterances. Even the setting and genre information are inconsequential in comparison to the information in the task itself. The role playing scenario attempted to simulate a spontaneous conversation in a supermarket. But the addressee's identity, as defined by the age, gender, and ethnicity of the addressee puppet, and the illocutionary point of the target utterances (in both cases requests) capture most of the speaker's psycholinguistic attention, making the specific intention of the speaker transparent. A child who is earnestly engaged in this task has little room to invoke his own language choice, affect and social identity unless he wants to violate the social rules of the school-like task. As a result, in four studies involving approximately 120 bilingual children, very few codeswitched utterances emerged. A great deal of non-fluent, non-native speech did, as evidenced in the first request in the above example ("Mister, can you got rice?"). But the children mostly stuck to the task, not displaying the social and affective information one usually finds in spontaneous speech in the form of pragmatic markers and lexical choice.

Analysis of more than a thousand requests from studies of this type in terms of Canale and Swain's (1980) Model of Communicative Competence indicated that every speaker was able to convey an illocutionary point (Walters, 1980). The least proficient subjects did so simply by naming the object of their request or by attaching a rising intonation to that name (e.g. Rice...Rice?). Further analysis showed the independence of intentions from grammatical formulation. The method used to show this independence was to provide examples of utterances where the intention was dissociated in various ways from the grammar and the semantic form. There were utterances in which the intention was clear but the grammar was violated:

Can you tell me where is the can openers, please?

There were others, where the speech act form could be used conventionally as a request, but not with the grammatical formulation that followed:

Do you give me 35 cents for the lunch?

May you give us the towels to clean up our milk?

Are you have some rice?

And there were others, where the speech act form was self-corrected before grammatical formulation:

Can we/Do you have any ball?

Will you/Can we get in front of you?

Do you/Can you tell us the word for ball in Russian?

This last group of examples is perhaps the best evidence that the intention and its semantic/conventional form are encoded prior to grammatical formulation, as specified in the present model.

But the role playing methodology used in these studies does not provide an opportunity for the language choice, affect, and identity components of the SPPL Model to express themselves linguistically. More natural settings and more spontaneous conversations, such as guided sociolinguistic interviews, generate richer data regarding identity. The following is an excerpt translated from an interview with a Russian immigrant in Hebrew (conducted by two interviewers, one a native-born Israeli and the other a Russian immigrant).

Example 3.6 *Transcript of an excerpt from an immigration narrative*
And, really, I believe in it, even though I'm not all that religious, so this is what I wanted to say. Maybe a few words about..uh..my family...because also..uh..[they are] important.. uh my wife she works at the P-- Institute, also in the finance department. She's an economist, uh also she works in [her] profession, also I expect very much, expect, I know she is very satisfied with her work...[[I09 GIF]]

The specific intentions, in terms of illocutionary point, are less salient than in the role playing data illustrated above. Sometimes it is difficult to discern whether the speaker is expressing a social attitude toward Israeli society or an emotion about his own personal state, or both. Whatever the case, social identity and affective information are strikingly present in the key words "works in [her] profession." It reflects strong occupational identity and pride, since 'working in one's profession' is a strong indicator of success for Russian emigrants all over the world. Nevertheless, the illocutionary point is not as clear as in the structured conversations, above where the speaker is led down a garden path to produce a request.

Output of the intentional component. The intentional component is a bridge between social information and psycholinguistic information, between external phenomena, which have been internalized as identity, and utterance meaning. The output of this component is conceived as a complex of illocutionary points and their propositional content. The integration of the illocutionary points with the propositional content is what converts this production unit into an utterance. This does not mean that inventories of illocutionary possibilities, concept maps, and individual concepts do not have psychological reality. On the contrary, in a dynamic system where all decisions maintain traces in memory and are to some extent recoverable, an utterance is an integral of all this information.

For bilingual processing, an illocutionary act takes language choice, affect, and social identity information into account, first because this act was previously experienced in a particular context (language, affect, identity) and also because it is expressed in a real context, where language, affect, and identity are relevant. This kind of information may be less obvious when it comes to specification of illocutionary points and propositional content in international, Westernized contexts. The function of the intentional component as a bridge to formulation may also make language, affect, and identity information less salient than a particular illocutionary point and its propositional content. Even in language- and culture-specific situations, such as blessing and greeting in traditional societies, verbal dueling in African-American culture (Labov, 1972), and the Hawaiian talk story (Au & Jordan, 1981), the illocutionary point and propositional content of a particular utterance may not reveal a great deal of language choice, affect, and identity information. Thus, one may not find very much in the way of bilingual processing phenomena in the intentional component. The evidence we seek is likely to be more subtle, taking the form of subtle semantic and pragmatic deviations from native speaker usage, like the combination of a native culture speech act and second language propositional content illustrated by the Hebrew/English "Not right!" example at the beginning of this chapter.

A note on method. In a refreshingly candid discussion of methods at the end of her paper, Ranney (1992) states: "The combination of the interview data with the speech act data provided a basis for comparing subjects' intentions with their choices of language forms" (p. 44). From this statement and others in the paper, especially from her examination of the interview data, Ranney assumes that the *content* of the transcribed utterances provides an accurate portrait of her subjects' intentions. The history of research in social psychology, however, shows discrepancies and even contradictions between attitudes and behavior for phenomena much less subtle than language behavior (e.g. Petty, Wegener & Fabrigar, 1997). And this discrepancy may underlie some of the controversy over intentions in anthropology as well as psycholinguistics (e.g. Duranti, 1993; Gibbs, 1999).

In this section, we have referred to three kinds of data: narrative scripts, sociolinguistic interviews, and conversations generated via structured role playing. Each method allows access to a different component of information relevant for production. Scripts highlight genre/discourse structure while interview data is richer, allowing access to a full range of language, affect, and identity information. The role playing study described in this section focuses on the illocutionary point, the nexus between the speech act performed and the language chosen to express the act.

For an examination of bilingual processing where language choices themselves are the main source of data, language contact phenomena will differ across these three methods. One can get at behavioral aspects of codeswitching and interference in a sociolinguistic interview, depending on the social identity, language proficiency, manipulative talents, and empathy of the interviewer(s). But the intentions behind these language contact phenomena are not transparent in the data from an interview. Intentions need to be investigated from several angles, and even when all roads lead to the same conclusion, one doesn't really know whether the interviewees' statements were honest opinions, with behavioral implications, or whether they were merely trying to please the interviewer. Ethnographers (Duranti, 2000) describe this problem as the inability to go beyond one's own culture.

Experimental and quasi-experimental techniques, in the form of role playing, discourse completion, metalinguistic judgments, and even elicited imitation are some of the ways to compensate for these limitations. These techniques are not intended as a substitute for rich, qualitative interview data, but are recommended as complementary tools for confirmation of focused hypotheses. They allow intentions to be evaluated across both qualitative and quantitative methods and at different levels of linguistic processing, viz. phonetic, lexical, and pragmatic markers of intention. Thus, language behavior data like names of people and places, greetings, pragmatic markers, and the like, can supplement explicit statements of intent and more traditional attitudinal measures to give a more precise picture of a speaker's intentions. (For a more audacious attempt to incorporate underlying intentions into a theoretical model with a built-in methodology, see my handling of codeswitching in the section on Perceptual Control Theory in Chapter 5.)

4 FORMULATION IN BILINGUALISM: INCOMPLETENESS AND VARIABILITY
4A LEXICO-PRAGMATIC CONCEPTS, LEMMAS, AND LEXEMES

In the extensive body of research on processes involved in the formulation of utterances, lemmas (said to contain semantic and syntactic information) and lexemes (morphological and phonological representations) are usually investigated without reference to their sociopragmatic context. As mentioned earlier, formulation is said to be preceded by 'conceptual preparation,' which is defined as "how the speaker gets from the notion/information to be expressed to a message that consists of lexical concepts." It is labeled the 'verbalization problem' by Levelt, Roelofs, and Meyer (1999). In this view, there is "no simple one-to-one mapping of notions-to-be-expressed onto messages" and "no simple, hard-wired connection between percepts and lexical concepts...[they are] always mediated by pragmatic, context dependent considerations." The SPPL Model in general, and its formulation component in particular, are attempts to account for pragmatic, context-dependent information and to recognize the inherent variation in the mapping of intentions to form.

The model (see Figure 3.3) distinguishes between two sub-components in the formulator, one to handle lexical information (Component 4a) and one for discourse formulation (Component 4b). The conventional distinction in the architecture of the lexicon is between lemmas and lexemes. This is an attempt to render the conceptual autonomy of semantic/syntactic information and morpho-phonological information. In the present model, the input to lemma selection is considered to be a lexico-pragmatic concept. A conservative modification of the conventional approach would take lexico-pragmatic concepts, encode them for syntactic and semantic information (producing lemmas), and then instantiate this product with morpho-phonological information as a lexeme.[6] Lexemes here are conceived broadly, as words, collocations, or multi-word phrases.

The discourse sub-component of the formulator is responsible for sequencing, relevance, and cohesion. It interfaces with information from the lexical component by means of word order constraints, collocational properties, and specification of argument structure.

Figure 3.3 Formulation component of the SPPL Model

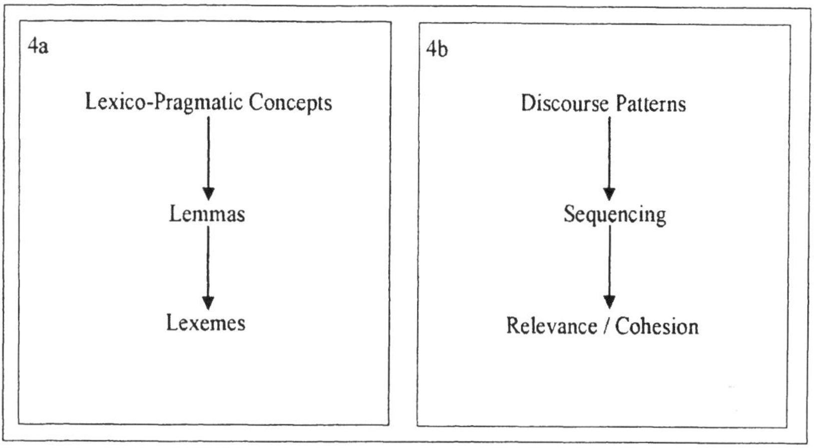

```
┌──────────────────────────────────┬──────────────────────────────────┐
│ 4a                                │ 4b                               │
│                                   │                                  │
│      Lexico-Pragmatic Concepts    │       Discourse Patterns         │
│                │                  │               │                  │
│                ▼                  │               ▼                  │
│           Lemmas                  │          Sequencing              │
│                │                  │               │                  │
│                ▼                  │               ▼                  │
│           Lexemes                 │       Relevance / Cohesion       │
│                                   │                                  │
└──────────────────────────────────┴──────────────────────────────────┘
```

The SPPL Model differs in a number of ways from other approaches to bilingual production. First, the lexical-pragmatic concept integrates linguistic and experiential knowledge. Thus, both linguistic (syntactic and semantic) information and world knowledge are input to the lemma. This is related to the notion of episodic memory in cognitive psychology. In this view, the lemma is not a simple dictionary entry, but is more encyclopedic in nature. In addition, lemmas in the bilingual lexicon are not necessarily the same for each speaker. The lemmas of more proficient speakers may approach those of native speakers, but even the most advanced second language users will show evidence of lexico-semantic and lexico-syntactic language contact. 'To *secure* reservations,' 'to *endure* unacceptable service;' '...the problem *occurred probably* after the chocolate has been *passed* to the store which sold you the product' are examples of the ways in which non-natives might alter English expressions.

The SPPL Model claims that at least some of these examples result from different representations of syntactic and semantic information, at the lemma stage of processing. This is what I believe Poulisse (1999) means by the need to account for incomplete knowledge in a description of bilingualism and what Clyne (2003) means by incomplete grammatical integration. The bilingual memory literature allows for the dynamic, changing nature of concepts (De Groot, 2000; Francis, 2000). The present work makes that same claim for lemmas. Finally, the SPPL approach maintains that the lemma has access to both languages (L1, L2, etc.) and to affective information. The primary rationale for making 'language' information available to the lemma is to account for different kinds of language contact phenomena, viz. different types of codeswitching, interlanguage forms, lexical innovations, etc. And, in parallel, an important reason for making affective information available to the formulator is to account for psycholinguistically-motivated speech errors and slips of the tongue.

The present conception differs from those models of bilingual processing (e.g., de Bot, 1992; Poulisse, 1997) which are based on monolingual models of language production (Caramazza, 1990; Levelt et al., 1999), and even from bilingual models designed to capture some of the unique aspects of bilingualism (Clyne, 2003; Green, 1998; Grosjean, 1997; Myers-Scotton, 1995, 2000). These models claim that the conceptual stage of processing does not refer to language-specific information. The proposal here is more interactive at all levels of processing than models where autonomy restricts the kind of information within and between components. In the more recent model of Levelt et al. (1999) "diacritic parameters" (e.g. number, person, tense, mood) of lemmas and the encoding of these features, are said to partially "derive from the conceptual representation." This would seem to imply a direct link from concept to lexeme, or at least that lexemes draw on conceptual knowledge without having to refer to the lemma.

Among the most widely researched issues in bilingual production is a range of language contact phenomena investigated under labels such as interference, transference, codeswitching, code-mixing, code-blending, code-copying, and translation. While these phenomena vary from community to community, from speaker to speaker, and across settings, topics, and speech acts within speakers, they are presented here as unique reflections of bilingual formulation.

By way of illustration, in a study of attrition of Russian (L1) among immigrants to Israel at varying stages in the acquisition of Hebrew (L2), Feldman (1997) found evidence for individual language contact at both the lemma and lexemic stages of processing. Using a variety of data collection procedures, including six different production tasks (picture naming, naming from definition, semantic opposites, category naming in response to a series of nominal stimuli, locative naming, and synonym production), she reported that approximately a third of the responses of her subjects involved codeswitching to Hebrew, the salient, but non-native language for most of them. In a large number of cases (again approximately a third), this switch assisted in the search for the target lexical item.

As an explanation for the prevalence of codeswitching data, Feldman (1997:192-3) proposed the following sequence of processes based on Levelt (1989): "activation of the lexical concept associated with the stimulus picture/item, selection of an appropriate lexical item (lemma) from the mental lexicon, and subsequent failure to access phonological encoding of that item (lexeme) in the appropriate language (Russian), thus yielding the retrieval of the L2 (Hebrew) lexeme." The first two processes, activation of the concept and lemma selection, were presumed to be language independent, while access of the lexeme was claimed to be language-specific. Feldman goes on to report that none of the codeswitched responses were semantically-related approximations and all were translations of target items. This lack of semantically related codeswitching from L2 was cited as evidence that "the lemma has already been accessed and the blockage occurs at the lexeme (word-form) level...The interfering influence of L2 is presumed to occur when word forms of a stronger language (L2) pass the threshold faster than L1 words affected by attrition."

However, one could argue for another explanation. The lemma is presumed to encode syntactic and semantic information. For a bilingual, however, the representation of that information may not be a polished entry from a monolingual dictionary. Rather, lemmas could be conceived as idiosyncratic, approximative (cf., Nemser, 1971), interlanguage forms (cf., Selinker, 1972), whose representation of syntactic and semantic information is incomplete. There is no shortage of evidence for syntactic and semantic interference and for the role of syntactic and semantic influences on intrasentential codeswitching. In fact, one of the primary interests of linguistics in both interference and codeswitching has been its syntactic properties. From Weinreich's (1953) classic treatise on interference to Myers-Scotton's (1999, 2002) Matrix Frame Model, linguistic research has attempted to provide a description or typology of various kinds of interference and codeswitching and an account of the syntactic constraints of its occurrence. But the various literatures on language contact have become mired in terminological battles, and methodological innovation has lagged behind other sociolinguistic and psycholinguistic areas of investigation.

A refreshing alternative can be found in Clyne's (1980; 2003) longstanding interest in triggering, facilitation, and integration. Clyne takes these same language contact phenomena, investigated as constraints on codeswitching and the separation between languages, and develops a taxonomy for examining their points of contact and how they are triggered. He calls for a single framework to handle phenomena heretofore treated as unrelated: interference, transference, codeswitching. He also argues that dichotomies such as borrowing/code-switching "tend to accentuate the assumption of two or more fairly discrete systems in contact rather than a more dynamic relationship between languages that are interconnected and constantly changing..." (p. 4). Despite strong structural biases (e.g. his unit of processing is the syntactic phrase), he consistently emphasizes the need to examine interaction of language contact phenomena with linguistic structure. In developing his transference terminology and in discussing convergence (p. 9) and integration (p. 15-16), his focus on processing issues such as facilitation and integration goes beyond an architecture of bilingualism. It is to these issues that I turn in the processing mechanisms of the model presented in the next chapter.

4B DISCOURSE FORMULATION

The discourse information handled by this component takes the social knowledge assembled from the context and genre components and relates it to linguistic features. Discourse information includes the way(s) a language marks importance via given-new, topic-comment, theme-rheme, and foregrounding and the ways these uses of language indicate cohesion and relevance. At more macro-levels of processing this component includes discourse rules for how to begin a script or conversation, how to continue it, how to bring it to an end, and how to get it to sound coherent. Among the features that relate to this kind of discourse information are length (of utterance, speaking turn, or written paragraph), adverbial modifiers, focus particles, discourse and pragmatic markers, and features of speech such as loudness, pitch, rate, and pauses.

Bilingual discourse formulation draws on information processed by the social identity, contextual/genre, and speech act components as well as information from the lexico-pragmatic sub-component of the formulator. In the course of integrating that information and planning an utterance, the same kind of bilingual phenomena that occur in lexical formulation result. Thus, when an attempt is made to mark importance or focus in a way that can accommodate the discourse preferences of both languages, dysfluency or codeswitching may result. Codeswitching or dysfluency can also be a result of a change in utterance planning or an inability to negotiate the lack of congruence in the discourse rules of the two languages. Examples of language contact at this level of processing are not as easy to detect as, for example, lexical codeswitching and lexical non-equivalence. They may show up as pragmatic violations, but more often, other types of codeswitching and dysfluency only hint at deeper discourse phenomena.

A note on research method. Bilingual discourse formulation is an area which has witnessed vigorous research from Auer, Maschler, and others working in conversational analysis. It remains fertile ground for further integrated studies of bilingual processing. For example, language contact data regarding given-new, topic-comment, theme-rheme, and foregrounding across pairs of languages that express these phenomena in similar (and distinct) ways could provide another source of data and perspective that would need to be accounted for in a general model of bilingualism. These phenomena go beyond observable linguistic forms and cut across syntactic and semantic categories. As such, they are in need of a more processing-oriented approach (e.g. de Rooij, 2000; Matras, 2000; Walters, 2002). Studies of relevance, importance or salience, and the role of pragmatic markers in bilingual production offer similar opportunities.

5 THE BILINGUAL ARTICULATOR

I begin this section with an observation, an assumption, and a proposal, each of which is based partly on theoretical considerations, partly on data, and partly on intuition:

❑   Bilinguals produce language at a slower rate than monolinguals.
❑   Bilinguals are assumed to show more evidence of speech dysfluency, in the form of hesitations, false starts, lexical repetitions, and perhaps overuse of certain pragmatic markers.

❑   Bilinguals are hypothesized to have smaller vocabularies in each
     of their languages than do monolinguals, but taken together, have
     a larger overall lexicon.

Each of these phenomena is phrased in terms of a horse-race question, comparing bilinguals and monolinguals, bilinguals coming up short on all counts. But the horse-race analogy, maligned throughout this work as methodologically ailing due to its reliance on group data and the accompanying problem of between-subject variance, could be rehabilitated by viewing it in terms of social comparison, from the perspective of the individual bilingual. Thus, when the individual bilingual interacts with monolinguals and perceives that his/her rate of speech, fluency, and vocabulary are not the same as the listener's, the conclusion is a social, not a linguistic one. In this way, surface linguistic phenomena are converted to social phenomena and internalized as such.

Flege (1995) has proposed an adaptive system for bilingual articulation, arguing "that phonetic systems reorganize in response to sounds encountered in an L2 through the addition of new phonetic categories, or through the modification of old ones" (p. 233). The concerns of that research program are wide-ranging, and include a speech learning model, an interest in age of second language acquisition, and discussion of the relationship between perception and production among bilinguals. In the latter context, Flege begins by citing data (Nooteboom & Truin, 1980; Koster, 1987) that non-natives need to be exposed to a greater portion of a word than natives to attain recognition of the word (p. 236). He goes on to review the argument in first language acquisition that production, or articulatory, errors are based in perception. In doing so, he invokes a "motor theory of speech" explanation for the phenomenon.

For bilingual production, however, the powerful influence of L1 phonology is said to play a major role in second language production. Notwithstanding this influence, Flege makes a claim consistent with the processing aspects of the SPPL Model when he points out that speech perception in a second language may not be invariant. To make this argument, he cites data from feedback training experiments (Logan, Lively, & Pisoni, 1991; Strange, 1992) that "perceptual patterns are modifiable to some extent" (p. 237). The important implication of this statement for the present model is that bilingual speech may be better characterized by flexibility, modifiability, and variability.

At the heart of the Speech Learning Model (SLM) in Flege's research program are questions of phonetic representation. That model is directed largely at issues of critical period and "ultimate attainment" of pronunciation in second language acquisition. But the model and its accompanying research program go far beyond these issues, articulating an urbane approach to contrastive analysis and addressing problems concerning the relationship of perception to production and the psychological reality of various phonetic, phonemic, and syllabic units.

Of particular interest to the present work are Flege's repeated remarks about variability in bilingual production, especially at the level of what he calls "position-sensitive allophones." He notes a number of primordial identity factors (age and gender) and individual, situational, and affective factors (style, clarity, speech rate, and stress) that contribute to this variability. In the SPPL Model proposed, the identity factors are processed in the identity component (see Figure 3.1), while the remaining factors draw on information from the contextual component (style and clarity) or (in the case of speech rate and stress) can be seen as articulatory reflections of information from the affective module.

Flege (1995) summarizes his SLM by means of four postulates and seven hypotheses. The most important of these for the present work states that "Bilinguals strive to maintain contrast between L1 and L2 phonetic categories, which exist in a common phonological space" (p. 239). This postulate is complemented by a hypothesis which presumes that phonetic segments, in particular vowels, tend to "disperse so as to maintain sufficient auditory contrast" (p. 242). This premise and the accompanying claim imply a merged phonetic system, a view that runs counter to most other approaches to bilingual processing (see, for example, Bohn & Flege, 1992).

Some of the best evidence for the uniqueness of bilingual processing, i.e. that bilingual processing cannot be accounted for by a model of monolingual processing, comes from voice onset time (VOT) studies of production (and perception). Flege (1993) reported that when bilinguals spoke in L1, their stop consonants had VOT scores similar to those expected in their second language. Flege (1995) summarized case study data from Mack (1990) where a French-English bilingual produced "short-lag" VOTs in both languages. Although these measurements differed from expected monolingual values, they still "maintain[ed a] *phonetic contrast* among the three stop consonants investigated." Further evidence that bilinguals produce unique sounds, which are identical to neither L1 nor L2, comes from a variety of languages and a variety of phonemic contrasts (e.g. Caramazza et al., 1973; Obler, 1982; Peng, 1993).

In the SPPL Model, articulation is conceived as the last stage of a complex of cognitive processes involving social, psychological, and linguistic decisions, which are based on attitudes and affect, preferences and feelings. Articulation is both planned and automatic. Its molecular processes include attention, discrimination, recognition, identification, classification, and categorization; selecting, associating, organizing, valuating, and integrating; conceiving and planning. One assumption in this work is that the same bilingual phenomena documented for other components of the model should also show up for articulation.

The approach suggested here needs to be grounded in studies of false starts, hesitations, and what appear to be dysarthria and stuttering among normal bilinguals, with careful attention to social and contextual information accompanying the articulatory variation. An important beginning in this direction is the work of Towell, Hawkins, and Bazergui (1996) in second language acquisition. Experimental techniques such as TOT studies of bilinguals (e.g. Gollan & Silverberg, 2001) should be complemented by fine-grained, computerized speech analysis of bilingual discourse. Clinical studies of bilinguals with dysarthria and stuttering disorders would also be relevant.

Another issue that has been kicked around anecdotally for years and which recently gained more scientific prominence is the question of *accent*. Lenneberg (1967) formulated the issue in neurolinguistic terms, claiming, in a one-sentence comment on bilingualism, that attenuation of brain plasticity can explain why older language learners maintain a non-native accent. Neurolinguists have examined this phenomenon in adult aphasia (Blumstein et al., 1987). Psycholinguists have taken up the issue in studies of critical period (Flege, 1995; Johnson & Newport, 1989). Sociolinguists (Wardaugh, 1998) and speech communication researchers (e.g. Bradac & Wisegarver, 1984) claim the subject of non-native speech as their own, hinting at its relevance to the study of social identity. A unified account of accent would begin in the articulation component of the SPPL Model and should pave the way to integrate neurolinguistic, psycho-linguistic, and sociolinguistic hypotheses into a single, testable framework.

CHAPTER SUMMARY

This chapter began by declaring the goals of the proposed model of bilingual information processing:
1. To distinguish between structural, information components of the model and its processing features;
2. to specify the sources of sociopragmatic and psycholinguistic information;
3. to indicate the specific phenomena the model aims to account for, viz. codeswitching, interference, and translation; and
4. to suggest methodological guidelines and approaches for carrying out research in the framework of the model.

Next the chapter discussed five assumptions:
1. That bilingual phenomena cannot be accounted for by monolingual models of language production or their clones;
2. that sociopragmatic information, in particular information about the speaker's identity, is the starting point for a model of bilingual production;
3. that the information components of the model are both autonomous and interactive;
4. that certain kinds of information are processed serially (e.g. social identity information is processed prior to lexico-semantic and syntactic information), while information from the language choice and affective modules are processed in parallel; and that redundancy needs to be built into the model, in terms of the

sources of information as well as the processing mechanisms.

The detailed description of the SPPL Model began with two modules that are available and activated through the entire process of language production. A *language choice module* acts as an executive monitor to select, regulate, and retrieve identity, contextual and genre, intentional, lexical and discourse, and articulatory information from a speaker's two languages during the entire course of language production. A second, *affective module* performs the same functions in the affective domain. It was argued that the availability and activation of information from these two modules would help account for, among other things, a distinction between intentional and 'performance' codeswitching and the difference between phonologically-based (TOT) and affect-laden speech errors (slips of the tongue).

The chapter then proceeded to describe the five information components and their contents. Their overall structure is a tripartite division into (1) sociopragmatic information, which includes social identity, external context, and genre elements, (2) a central intentional/speech act component, and (3) psycholinguistic information, which includes the formulator and articulator.

The *social identity* component, containing information that a bilingual language user brings to the speech situation, was portrayed as grounded in social institutions, defined in terms of economics, politics, kinship, and culture. Bilingual identity was characterized as a composite of information from these domains, along with input from the language choice and affective modules. Three cues to bilingual identity, accent, greetings, and names, were discussed and illustrated by referring to a case portrait of a Russian immigrant to Israel. *External contextual* and *genre* information are housed in a single contextual component to capture the relationship between interpersonal and textual information. External context is further specified as information about setting and participants. Genre information, viewed here as a social construct, is classified in terms of scripts and conversations. Information about conversational topic is included at this point in the model.

The central component of the SPPL Model (*intentional information*) is an attempt to get at the intentions of individual bilingual speakers. It serves as a bridge between sociopragmatic and psycholinguistic information, an integral of information brought from the environment and information generated from inside the bilingual speaker's head. After grounding the intentional component in speech act theory and positioning it with respect to models of language production, this section goes on to describe how bilingual intentions are derived in large part from linguistic cues such as language/dialect preferences, pragmatic markers, lexical choice, and 'accent.'

The output from the intentional to the *formulator* is an integral of illocutionary and content information, which takes the form of a lexico-pragmatic concept. This concept is claimed to be language specific, or at least language-dependent. It differs essentially from the more conventional notion of a lemma, which is claimed to be a universal syntactic-semantic representation. Thus, in the present model, formulation operates on language-specific information, which is both 'incomplete' (in comparison to a lemma) and variable. These characteristics (incompleteness and variability) allow the model to place a wide variety of language contact phenomena (codeswitching, interference, transference, and lexical invention), in a single framework.

The fifth information component of the model, the *bilingual articulator*, was described as part of a complex of phenomena that could be relevant to bilingualism at the output stage. These phenomena include bilinguals' presumed slower rate of speech, presence of dysfluency markers such as pauses, false starts, and repetitions, and larger total vocabulary size than monolinguals. After speculating about how these matters might help give bilingual articulation research a more social direction, I turned to Flege's Speech Learning Model. This model is relevant to the constructs and processes here for two reasons. One is its hard-nosed empirical approach; the data on speech errors and voice onset time (VOT) among bilinguals and second language learners, in particular, argue for the existence of phonetic categories that do not exist among monolinguals of either of a bilingual's two languages. The other relevant construct is variability, used by Flege in its classical, sociolinguistic variationist sense. The data amassed by his research program, which contribute to the importance of building variability into a model of bilingual production, include identity (age and gender) and individual, situational, and affective factors (style, clarity, speech rate, and stress).

While explaining the SPPL Model, I have referred to the need to account for mimetic aspects of language use such as accent, greetings, and names as well as the use of pragmatic markers and lexical repetitions for fluency. I have also referred to the need to incorporate variability into the model. In addition, the various components and subcomponents of information need a mechanism of integration that could merge this information into a unified utterance. It is to the processing mechanisms underlying this information that I now turn.

NOTES

[1] A previous version of this model was introduced at Third International Conference on Maintenance and Loss of Minority Languages in Veldhoven, 1998 and published in the proceedings of that conference (Klatter-Folmer & Van Avermaet, 2001).

[2] This finding should be contrasted with recent work on long-term episodic memory among bilinguals, which shows that information about language may be encoded along with significant life events (Schrauf & Rubin, 2003; Marian & Neisser, 2000).

[3] See, however, the recent controversy over concepts and meanings in bilingualism addressed in a special issue of *Bilingualism: Language & Cognition, 4*(2), 2000.

[4] In written production, text types considered narrative, expository, descriptive, and argumentative all show elements of both scripted discourse and conversation. The classical examples of these genres (the ones illustrated in rhetoric and composition textbooks) are more scripted; the kinds of writing concerned with audience design (Bell, 1984) are more like conversation.

[5] See Jackendoff, 1983 on preference rules and Spolsky's 1989 application of this construct to second language learning.

[6] A more radical approach might do away with the lemma-lexeme distinction entirely, and allow intentions to be encoded directly as words and phrases, with a full range of pragmatic, syntactic-semantic, and morpho-phonological properties.

4 Four Processing Mechanisms in Bilingual Production

One of the themes of this chapter is that imitation and variation, repetition and novelty, mimesis and creativity, are not polar contrasts. Rather, the latter are nurtured, supported and sustained by the former. There can be no creativity without repetition, no novelty without imitation, and no originality without mimesis.

It is particularly important to invoke this theme at the beginning of a chapter that deals with bilingual processing mechanisms because these elements are so much part of a bilingual's daily fare. The bilingual plays both consciously and unconsciously with copying and variation as he or she processes language to communicate or, especially, to overcome problems. The problems are out there in the world or inside the bilingual's head, and require solutions in one or both languages. It is a case of difficulty begetting solutions.

This theme is captured by Tannen's query on a provocative quotation from Bolinger, who asks: "How much actual invention...really occurs in speech we shall know only when we have the means to discover how much originality there is in an utterance" (1961:381). Tannen challenges: "If it can be shown that repetition in conversation is evidence of automaticity, rather than of 'originality' in utterance, then this study may contribute in a modest way to answering Bolinger's question" (Tannen, 1989:88).

In this same vein, Waugh (1976) discusses Jakobson's notion of the dynamic nature of language, delineating two kinds of creativity. One is an individual's use of "...a variety of sub-codes...in different situations...which he can creatively alter as new situations arise" (1976:22). The other, considered more important, presumably by Jakobson as well as Waugh, is: "the creativity of language seen...in the new combinations which any speaker can make (phrases, clauses, sentences, utterances, discourses) including the creation of new linguistic and extralinguistic contexts for old words." The first kind of creativity involves differences in register and sociolinguistic variation, and accounts for the linguistic component of interpersonal relations, social attraction and the like. The latter is illustrated with poetry, metaphor, and metonymy; it focuses more on individual linguistic attributes than on social relations. Lower level linguistic units such as phonemes, syllables and words, are claimed to be less open to creativity than higher level structures, such as phrases, sentences, utterances, discourses, exchanges. This perspective stands in stark contrast with Chomsky's (1957, 1965, 1986) more static view of creativity as the innate capacity to generate an infinite set of sentences.[1]

But if we need notions like creativity and its mimetic roots to explain one aspect of bilingual production, the other side of this pattern must be those mechanisms that create order out of the chaos of two tongues chasing each other's tails in the bilingual's head. The two mechanisms are integration and control, the mechanisms that draw it all together and interact with possible solutions to understand input and oversee output. These two mechanisms are needed to explain how bilinguals overcome the difficulties associated with producing one or both languages in an intelligible form in appropriate circumstances.

The chapter begins with a brief generalized description of imitation, variation, integration and control. This is followed by a close and detailed walk through the processing aspects of the SPPL Model. The graphic depiction of the model is in a series of boxes and arrows. In the last chapter, we looked at the boxes, and now we will follow the arrows that describe the processes. Each of these arrows describes information flow and makes use of one of the generalized cognitive processing mechanisms that either help or hinder the production of bilingual speech.[2] Next the chapter returns to show some of the ways these constructs interact with research that makes use of similar ideas. The thematic focus on imitation and variation draws us to a more detailed demonstration of how these mechanisms help explain bilingual phenomena. I follow the same pattern with integration and control, tracing first the roots of these constructs in other fields, then describing the specific notion intended here. With integration, I review some of the research I have conducted, suggest its potential and point to some of its limitations. The section on control is more speculative, looking at Perceptual Control Theory more for its theoretical appeal than for the data it has generated.

BASIC LEVEL PROCESSES AND GENERAL PROCESSING MECHANISMS

The four processing mechanisms discussed in this chapter: imitation, variation, integration, and control are all general cognitive mechanisms, with relevance beyond the study of language, bilingualism, and their application to language acquisition, attrition, and language disorders. This broad conceptual scope allows them to handle both sociopragmatic and psycholinguistic information. These mechanisms are supported by a set of more fundamental processes which include: attention, discrimination, recognition, identification/ recall, classification/sorting, categorization/organizing. *Recognition* and *recall*, the concepts most relevant to the imitation mechanism, have roots in a behaviorist psychology (Woodworth, 1938) but have been refreshed as it were in the connectionist paradigm. The variation mechanism used here is grounded in the processes of *discrimination* and *classification*.

Integration and control are executive mechanisms. The integration idea is taken from Anderson's Information Integration Theory; the control notion is based on Powers' (1978) Perceptual Control Theory and other advocates of this approach (e.g., Cziko, 1995, 2000; Runkel, 1990). The integration mechanism has two functions, operating on information as well as on basic processes. Information that is subject to integration in bilingual production includes those sources of information specified in the SPPL Model. Processes that are subject to integration include those specified above: discrimination, recognition, identification, classification and categorization. Control is an executive mechanism responsible for regulating and calibrating the balance between intentions and perceptions. Behavior is considered a variable means to control perception, not a response to a stimulus or the outcome of some combination of innate and environmental factors.

These four mechanisms are central to phenomena claimed here to be unique to bilingualism: codeswitching, interference, and translation. As such, they have potential for contributing to a relatively comprehensive account of issues that are generally not brought under the same roof. Interference has been mostly at the purview of structural linguistics, contrastive analysis, and second language learning (e.g. Weinreich, 1953; Walters & Wolf, 1992). Codeswitching has been addressed independently with very little cross-disciplinary dialogue by generative linguistics and sociolinguistics. And translation was at one point labeled "a separate skill," thus excluding it from the mainstream of linguistic and psycholinguistic research (but see Massaro & Shlesinger, 1997 for a psycholinguistic orientation to the field of interpretation and Wadensjo, 1998, for a social-interaction approach to the field).

WALKING THROUGH THE SPPL PROCESSING SCHEMATA

The following section spells out in detail how the SPPL Model accounts for processing. It is best read while referring to the model in Figure 3.1. These descriptions are of necessity very brief, and most are followed by an example to make the pathway clearer.

Graphic conventions:

❏ Upper case letters describe the processing mechanism (e.g. IMI for Imitation).

❏ Modules are labeled: Lg Choice for language choice and Affect for Affect

❏ Arrows show the linkage between the Modules and the five Information Components

❏ Numbers (1-5) refer to the information components (with the suffix "a" or "b" as necessary if the central box is double headed, as in context-genre and lexical-discourse formulation)

Thus, the processing involved in the SPPL description of how Imitation helps language choice create associative linkages between certain Genres would be described as: "IMI 2b Lg Choice→Genre," meaning that the imitation mechanism regulates the flow of language information from the language choice module to the Genre information component.

FROM LANGUAGE CHOICE TO BILINGUAL PRODUCTION

Imitation in Language Choice

The imitation mechanism enables bilinguals to replicate speech elements from L1 to L2 and vice versa under the influence and/or guidance of various sociopragmatic and psycholinguistic factors.

IMI 1 Lg Choice→Identity

L1/L2 elements (e.g. names, greetings, and more subtle indicators of social identity such as pragmatic markers and pitch contours) are copied to the Identity component in order to express linguistic aspects of social identity. For example, high front vowels like the [i] in 'si' (yes) are part of Carlos' native (L1) Puerto Rican identity; they are made available/copied to the social identity component when he wants to project his Puerto Rican identity. The name Boris is copied to the identity component when this Russian immigrant wants to feel like/act like a Russian. etc.

IMI 2a Lg Choice→Context

Information about L1/L2 patterns flows from the Lg Choice component to the Contextual Component, setting up associations between language and particular settings and participants, L1 with the home, family, and more intimate matters, L2 with work, school and more public domains.

IMI 2b Lg Choice→Genre

Information about L1/L2 patterns flows from the Lg Choice component to the Contextual Component, setting up associations between particular languages and particular genres. For Russian immigrants to the US, prose or poetry from Pushkin, Dostoyevski or Akhmatova is associated with classic high literature, while the Gettysburg Address, Pledge of Allegiance, and the numerous government forms an immigrant fills out become the L2 genres. L1 or L2 information is copied to conversations largely as a function of topic.

IMI 3 Lg Choice→Intentions

The Lg Choice Module makes L1/L2 information available to the intentional component. For example, in a recent email message I received from a Chinese colleague thanking me for agreeing to send him reprints of several of my articles, he included a lengthy apology for putting me out. The Imitation Mechanism makes it possible for the speech act of apologizing to be copied from Chinese (L1) to the Intentional Component.

IMI 4a Lg Choice →Lexical Formulator

L1/L2 information is made available to syntactic, semantic, morphological, and phonological representations in the lexical formulator. These L1 and L2 features are called language tags in other models of bilingual lexical processing. They are what produces inter-language structures and lexical inventions such as "offer you to dinner" and "learning English at the university" and codeswitched forms such as 'brushti et ha-teeth' (Hebrish for "I brushed my teeth" literally, 'brush+1st person+past the-teeth').

IMI 4b Lg Choice →Discourse Formulator

L1/L2 information is copied at the discourse level of processing from the Lg Choice Module to the Discourse Formulator to yield given or new information, cohesion, and relevance patterns which characterize a particular language. For example, lexical repetition in the English of Hebrew-English bilinguals is a cohesion pattern which is more characteristic of Hebrew, English preferring cohesion via anaphora, synonyms and other structures.

IMI 5 Lg Choice →Articulator

At the level of articulation, copies of L1 and L2 pitch contours, aspiration patterns, and voice onset time thresholds are input to the articulator, yielding speech which is uniquely bilingual, not L1, not L2, but rather, somewhere in between.

Variation in Language Choice

The variation mechanism facilitates discrimination, classification and categorization of L1 and L2 information as it operates on all information components. These processes enable the speaker to make distinctions among all kinds of information and to organize them for retrieval.

VAR 1 Lg Choice →Identity

The variation mechanism takes L1 and L2 information from the Lg Choice module and uses it to distinguish language-dependent features that mark identity from these two cultures. Language related identity features include accent, names, greetings, and pragmatic markers. Less linguistic markers of identity, which may still be marked with incoming Lg Choice information, include clothing, gait, and the like. When Lg Choice information enters the Identity Component, it enters as an L1, L2, or codeswitched variant. The variation mechanism directs the flow of L1, L2, and bilingual information and enables the bilingual to discriminate and classify L1 and L2 information within the Identity Component.

VAR 2a Lg Choice →Context
L1 and L2 information from the Lg Choice module enters the Contextual Component and is directed by the variation mechanism to settings, participants, and topics that are distinguishable on the basis of language or cultural features. For example, the variation mechanism distinguishes home, school, work, church settings. It also discriminates participants on a range of variables, e.g. levels of intimacy of family members, friends, work associates, etc.

VAR 2b Lg Choice →Genre
The variation mechanism discriminates and classifies various texts into scripts and conversations and then into one of more than a hundred different genres. This mechanism then makes use of Lg Choice information to examine a genre's L1/L2 features and designate each text as L1, L2, or characteristically bilingual. It is information from the Lg Choice module that distinguishes L1 from L2 features and enables a bilingual to make the overall categorization judgment about a particular text. This connection between the Lg Choice Module and genre may have been what led medieval theologian-poets like Ibn Ezra to write his Rabbinic-legal treatises in Hebrew and his philosophy in Arabic.

VAR 3 Lg Choice →Intentions
The variation mechanism takes L1 and L2 information from the Lg Choice Module and uses it to discriminate among speech acts. An immigrant to Quebec from just about any country or language background will muster whatever limited French he may have to communicate with an immigration officer, employer, school official. The variation mechanism classifies, weighs, and ranks L1 and L2 information, enabling him to select the appropriate language to convey his intention, i.e. that he wants to stay in Quebec.

VAR 4a Lg Choice →Lexical Formulator
The variation mechanism discriminates lexical information (i.e. semantic, syntactic, morphological, phonological) based on language and classifies it as L1, L2, codeswitched. It does so by taking the L1 and L2 information from the Lg Choice module and assigning it to the structural representations in the formulator. That information flows along L1 and L2 pathways into the formulator, where classification, weighting, and ranking take place. This is the mechanism that distinguishes among L1 and L2 and codeswitched words, between codeswitching and codeblends.

VAR 4b Lg Choice →Discourse Formulator
The variation mechanism discriminates discourse patterns for distributing given and new information in an utterance, for creating cohesion, and for expressing relevance. Discourse patterns are distinguished and classified by

making use of L1 or L2 information from the Lg Choice module. It is the Variation Mechanism which allows us to distinguish the native language of a Yiddish speaker of English when new (rather than given) information tends to be more focused, more fronted, and clefted in an utterance "It's my mother, she gave me to eat that."

VAR 5 Lg Choice →Articulator
The variation mechanism monitors and regulates L1 and L2 pitch contours, aspiration patterns, and Voice Onset Time thresholds by discriminating, classifying, and categorizing the L1/L2 features of an utterance. Although L1/L2 information may not always be detectable to the ear, psycho-acoustic measurement gives insight to the bilingual nature of articulation, e.g. VOTs which are neither L1 nor L2, but rather a merger of the two.

Integration in Language Choice

The integration mechanism takes L1 and L2 information from the Lg Choice module and combines it with various information sources in the five information components of the SPPL processing Model.

INT 1 Lg Choice →Identity
Integration is the mechanism that combines L1 and L2 information from the Lg Choice module, takes the sum/product and combines it with information from the Identity Component. For example, the Lg Choice module channels native (L1) Russian into the intellectual/literary portion of the Identity Component while L2 (American English, German, or Israeli Hebrew) language choices are directed into the occupational aspects of the Identity Component.

INT 2a Lg Choice →Context
L1 and L2 information from the Lg Choice Module flows into the Contextual Subcomponent, combining with the sum/product of information about settings and participants to yield the output of this stage of bilingual processing. For example, L1 Spanish comes to church from the Lg Choice Module, while English goes to school, and both languages are found on the playground.

INT 2b Lg Choice →Genre
The Lg Choice module supplies L1 and L2 information to the Genre Subcomponent, integrating L1 and L2 information with each other and with genre information. For example, L1 Syriac, the traditional language of Maronite Christians, is made available to the Genre Subcomponent in order to read prayers. It is combined in the Church setting (see Int 2a above) with the colloquial Arabic of the congregants and the standard Arabic of the priest (for sermons) inside the Maronite churches of Lebanon and Israel.

INT 3 Lg Choice →Intentions

L1 and L2 information is merged in the Intentional Component to yield speech acts that show evidence of multifunctionality. For example, a request for a favor may be combined with a justification, excuse or apology for putting the listener out. The Integration Mechanism performs this combinatorial function.

INT 4a Lg Choice →Lexical Formulator

The integration of L1 and L2 information from the Lg Choice Module at the level of Lexical Formulation produces a variety of bilingual phenomena. Examples include codeswitching across morphological boundaries (brush+ti), lexical semantic interference (lakaxti shower) and fusions or compromise forms, e.g. 'noce' = no (Eng) + roce (Heb); 'mima' = Mommy + ima.

INT 4b Lg Choice →Discourse Formulator

The Lg Choice Module makes L1 and L2 information available to the Discourse Formulator. The Integration Mechanism combines those two sources of information with each other and with the information about how to formulate a cohesive, relevant, and cooperative utterance. In bilingualism, for example, integration at this level of processing might occur when a speaker takes an L1 cohesive device (e.g. lexical repetition in Hebrew) and integrates it in an L2 (English) essay, producing a 200 word English text with 17 instances of the word 'climate.'

INT 5 Lg Choice →Articulator

The Lg Choice Module supplies L1 and L2 acoustic and phonetic information to the Articulator, which merges this information to generate bilingual VOT patterns, intensities, and pitch. An example: The characteristic singsong Hungarian accent in English is produced by taking L1 Hungarian pitch and intonation contours from the Lg Choice Module and integrating them with information which flows from the lexical and discourse components to produce English with a Hungarian accent.

Control in Language Choice

The Control Mechanism operates on all levels of language production to create a homeostatis between L1 and L2 information within the Lg Choice Module (not pictured in any of the diagrams yet) as well as between the L1/L2 information and the linguistic information in each of the five Information Components. This section describes the control processes underlying the relationship between the Lg Choice Module and the five information components.

CON 1 Lg Choice →Identity

Control is the mechanism that compares the amount and quality of L1 and L2 information from the Lg Choice module with information about the particular social identity the speaker wants to project. If the amount and quality of L1/L2 information are congruent with the speaker's social identity, information will flow through the model smoothly without disturbance, and language production will proceed fluently. Disturbances will show up as problems in the flow of information, e.g. hesitations, false starts, blocks in lexical access. (Continued disturbances should result in reevaluation of the weighting of L1/L2 information that enters from the Lg Choice Module and/or the social identity of the speaker.) For example, the Control Mechanism compares the amount and quality of (L1) Russian and (L2) English entering the Identity Component from the Lg Choice Module with the amount and quality of the desired levels of Russian intellectual/literary identity and American work ethic identity. To the extent that these sources of information operate in tandem, information will continue to flow smoothly. To the extent they do not, disturbances will result, showing up as dysfluency, changes in L1/L2 language use patterns, or even changes in social identity. For example, a Russian employee of a Russian-owned business in Toronto is encouraged to talk about work related subjects in English. In a bar, however, he talks with his boss in Russian about music. At the point the conversation veers back to work-related subjects, it is the control mechanism that jerks the language choice back to English after an interregnum characterized by a lot of codeswitching and hesitation.

CON 2a Lg Choice →Context

L1 and L2 information from the Lg Choice Module is compared with information about settings, speakers, and listeners. The Control Mechanism is responsible for making sure there is an appropriate balance between L1 and L2 language use and the various settings and participants a speaker comes into contact with. An imbalance between L1 and L2 information and information about context may cause a disturbance, and the Control Mechanism will then adjust the L1 to L2 ratio to stabilize the system. For example, a Spanish-speaking child who goes to a monolingual English-speaking school (setting) with a monolingual English speaking teacher (listener) may emit a few words in Spanish on the first day. But the incongruence between language choice (Spanish) and school context (English) will probably generate a disturbance in the child's control mechanism. This may result in: i) a decision to remain silent; ii) a decision to learn English; iii) a decision to avoid this context; iv) some combination of these and other behaviors to control the child's perceptions.

CON 2b Lg Choice →Genre

The Control Mechanism regulates L1 and L2 information flowing from the Lg Choice Module into the Genre Subcomponent by comparing L1/L2 language use with the type of scripts and conversations a speaker produces. A stable flow of L1/L2 information depends on the amount and kind of speech events/text types the bilingual interacts with. For example, the Maronite Christian who knows only how to pray in Syriac will find it disconcerting if a Lebanese physician begins taking a medical history in this language. This may result in more intensive efforts to learn spoken Syriac, a request to switch to another physician, a request to change languages, a feeling of confusion, or all of the above. Conversely, prayer in the colloquial language may arouse anger from congregrants who expect this genre to be conveyed in the sacred language.

CON 3 Lg Choice →Intentions

The Lg Choice information is compared with the intended speech act(s). If these bits of information are congruent (e.g. greetings and blessings in standard, literary Arabic and casual conversation in the colloquial variety), then language production will proceed fluently, the speaker then moving to the formulation stage of processing. If however, a speech act is uttered in the 'wrong' language so to speak, as in 'language crossing,' the control mechanism declares a 'disturbance' and attempts to bring Lg Choice into line with the intended speech act. The control mechanism stabilizes the system by: i) adapting the kind and/or amount of information flowing from the Lg Choice Module; ii) modifying the speech act selected; iii) appending additional intentions or concealing others; iv) some combination of i-iii.

CON 4a Lg Choice →Lexical Formulator

The Control Mechanism compares L1/L2 Lg Choice information with the semantic, syntactic, morphological, and phonological information in the Lexical Formulation component. Disturbances in the balance between these sources of information are managed by adjusting the amount and quality of Lg Choice information and the various linguistic components of lexical information. In addition to monolingual speech in both L1 and L2, the Control Mechanism theoretically allows all possible combinations of L1 and L2 semantics, syntax, morphology, and phonology. In reality, however, only some of these combinations actually result in real bilingual language data for a given pair of languages. Examples include: '*deny the invitation*,' *externities*, *brush-ti et ha-teeth*, *red casa*. On the other hand, one is less likely to hear: '*contradict the invitation*,' *externic*, *ti-brush*, *casa red*, and *party made I*.

CON 4b Lg Choice →Discourse Formulator

At this stage of language production, the Control Mechanism compares L1/L2 Lg Choice information with discourse information (e.g. given-new, cohesion, relevance) to see if the intended balance of language information fits the discourse features of the utterance. When there is a fit between these sources of information, the Control Mechanism allows the information to flow freely. When there is not, the Control Mechanism handles the imbalance by modifying the relative amount and quality of L1 or L2 information and/or the discourse options available. Referring to the same example presented above in connection with the Integration Mechanism, the Control Mechanism may, in the interests of fluency, let the Hebrew-English bilingual student writing a composition for an exam in English use more lexical repetition than English discourse might generally allow. Otherwise, a general system fault might bring about such a major disturbance to fluency that the bilingual could be left speechless in two languages.

CON 5 Lg Choice →Articulator

The Control Mechanism monitors and regulates the flow of L1 and L2 acoustic and phonetic information between the Lg Choice Module and the Articulator. It does so by comparing the amount and kind of L1 and L2 information with the acoustic and phonetic features of the utterance. When these jive, there is no disturbance in the Control Mechanism and no disturbance in fluency. In fact, at this stage of language production small disturbances may not even be noticeable. Bilingual Voice Onset Times and intensities may only show up under fine-grained acoustic measurement. Bilingual pitch contours may be more noticeable, showing up in the intonational and prosodic aspects of foreign accent. In terms of 'control,' a foreign accent can be said to include an imbalance of L1/L2 acoustic phonetic features.

FROM AFFECT TO BILINGUAL PRODUCTION

Language related affective information represented in the Affective Module usually comes from one or more of the following linguistic domains: (1) lexical-pragmatics (emotionally-laden expressions, in particular nominals, adverbials, and pragmatic markers), (2) phonetics (e.g. intensity, pitch); and (3) paralinguistics (rate of speech, pauses, length)

Imitation in Affect

The imitation mechanism recognizes and recalls affective information in driving the flow of information between the Affective Module and the other information components. These processes are used to copy affective information from emotional experience and to organize them for retrieval.

IMI 1 Affect →Identity

Affective elements (e.g. facial expressions, hand motions, pragmatic and paralinguistic language features such as pragmatic markers, loudness, rate of speech, and hesitations) are copied to the Identity Component to express affective aspects of social identity. For example, the differences in the ways Finnish, Japanese, and Italian nationals greet each other can be seen in the degree and quality of affect they express. One Finnish applied linguist once remarked that the affect of a Finn can be detected in his toe nails. Japanese, at least those less Westernized, are known to bow. And Italians, like other Mediterranean peoples, kiss. Bilinguals tend to alter at least some of these elements according to the identity they deem appropriate.

IMI 2a Affect →Context

Information about affect flows from the Affective Component to the Contextual Component, setting up links between affect and particular settings and participants. In some homes, warmth, love, and comfort reign; in others, the norm is hostility, blame, and abuse; most settings, however, involve a complex of subtle affective elements that can be very difficult to discern. This arrow indicates how features of affect are copied from the Affective Module to settings and to individuals, to be used in language production.

IMI 2b Affect →Genre

For this aspect of language production, affective information is copied from the Affective Module to the Genre Subcomponent of the Contextual Component, setting up associations between particular emotions and particular text types. A boring lecture, a French love song, a dirty joke are examples of genres that help establish associations between affect and genre. The link between a particular emotion and a particular genre creates a representation that characterizes this emotion in memory. For a bilingual the Affective Module houses this set of representations and makes them available in the appropriate language in the genre component of language production.

IMI 3 Affect →Intentions

The Affective Module copies affective features into intentions and speech acts. For example, the condescension expressed in the utterance, "Who are you, anyway?" copies affect into the speech. Literally, this speech act is a request for information, but the affect expressed here, in the intonation as well as the pragmatic marker 'anyway,' consume most of the listener's cognitive attention. In a bilingual context, this mechanism is essential to insert the language features in the right language(s) to mark the affect.

IMI 4a Affect →Lexical Formulator

Affective information is made available to syntactic, semantic, morphological, and phonological representations in the lexical formulator. These affective features are one of the sources of slips of the tongue, particularly those called Freudian slips, and are claimed here to be responsible for morphophonologically based verbal tics in Tourette's Syndrome. Angry words uttered when arguments get out of hand produce slips of the tongue. Slips also show evidence for of the influence of affect on lexical formulation (e.g. "he glue a basket" instead of "he blew a gasket").

IMI 4b Affect →Discourse Formulator

Affective information is copied at the discourse level of processing to yield associations between particular discourse patterns (e.g. foregrounding, cohesion devices) and corresponding emotions. The short, staccato utterances of Israeli news commentators in Hebrew convey the frenetic lifestyle of that country, while conversations between astronauts and their handlers in Houston convey calm assurance.

IMI 5 Affect →Articulator

At the level of articulation, copies of arrogant, angry, empathetic and compassionate pitch contours, aspiration patterns, and Voice Onset Time thresholds are input to the articulator, yielding speech which is characteristic of these emotions. Combined with information from the Lg Choice Module, these affective features are part of what make French and Italian 'sound' romantic while German and Hebrew are perceived as 'harsh.'

Variation in Affect

The variation mechanism facilitates discrimination, classification and categorization of affective information as it enters all information components. These processes enable the speaker to distinguish subtle and not so subtle differences in emotions and to organize them for retrieval.

VAR 1 Affect →Identity

The variation mechanism takes information from the Affective Module and uses it to distinguish affective identity features from the speaker's two cultures. Lexical-pragmatic, phonetic, and paralinguistic information is used to distinguish detachment from friendship and intimacy, anger from frustration, and condescension from conceit in a speaker's greetings. The variation mechanism directs the flow of affective information towards language-specific pathways to an appropriate place in a person's social identity. The variation mechanism enables the bilingual, not always successfully, to discriminate and classify affective information within the Identity Component.

VAR 2a Affect →Context

L1 and L2 information from the Affective Module enters the Contextual Component and is directed by the variation mechanism to settings and participants that are distinguishable based on language or cultural features. For example, the variation mechanism distinguishes levels of intimacy suitable for home, school, work, and church settings, and does the same sifting of interlocutors, non-active participants and topics in verbal interaction. For bilinguals certain emotional states like love or prayer are contexts of one language only.

VAR 2b Affect →Genre

The variation mechanism discriminates scripts and conversations and various oral and written texts by identifying their affective features and classifying each text as belonging to a particular genre. For example, it is information from the Affective Module which, in part, distinguishes Romantic poetry from comedy in Shakespeare, a joke from a sarcastic remark, etc. Bilinguals who may or may not have complete command of their L2 genres, use affective information as yet another clue that can lead them to the right discrimination about the kind of genre they are encountering and the appropriate response.

VAR 3 Affect →Intentions

The variation mechanism takes information from the Affective Module and uses it to discriminate among speech acts. To take a mundane example from the speech act literature, a person about to be late for an important interview for a job he wants desperately will insert a great deal of affect into a request to change a dollar to fill a parking meter. If he arrives late to the interview, he will insert a measured amount of affect into his apology in order to elicit empathy from the potential employer. The variation mechanism, by classifying, weighing, and ranking affective information, enables him to select the appropriate amount to convey his intention. For a bilingual this is particularly important. To continue the parking meter example, urgency in one language can sound like hostility in another and not yield the required result.

VAR 4a Affect →Lexical Formulator

The variation mechanism discriminates affectively loaded lexical information (i.e. semantic, syntactic, morphological, phonological) and classifies lexico-pragmatic concepts and lexemes into what could be called affective fields (cf., semantic fields). The Variation Mechanism enables a speaker to distinguish lexical items based on affective information. It is the mechanism that allows the advertising writer to choose among the names for a new product (e.g. *Cheer, Soft 'n White* laundry detergents) and the student of poetry to see the alliterative contrast between sibilants [s, sh] and stops [p, t, k]. The distinctions among Jerusalem, Il-kuds and Yerushalayim make use of the variation mechanism to elicit affect of various levels among Christians, Muslims, and Jews.

VAR 4b Affect →Discourse Formulator

The variation mechanism discriminates discourse patterns for expressing given or new information, for creating cohesion, and for expressing relevance by identifying their affective features and classifying each pattern according to these features. For example, Broca's aphasics, given their limited fluency, tend to have a characteristically frustrating affect, which clinical neurolinguists call 'press of speech.' Affect may be the way these patients compensate for lack of syntax and fluency in language production. The expression of frustration may be an unintentional side effect of language impairment in the other domains. For many bilinguals this mechanism is apparent in what they describe as discourse problems related to specific patterns that usually reflect some kind of "black hole" in L1 or L2 language acquisition and development.

VAR 5 Affect →Articulator

The Variation Mechanism regulates affective information in pitch contours, intensity peaks, and rate of speech by means of the Affective Module. It does so by discriminating, classifying, and categorizing affective information. For example, investigative reporters are said to be good at detecting evasiveness. A bilingual investigative reporter whose interlocutor knows both languages could start aggressive codeswitching to throw the interviewee off balance to elicit responses in the language in which the reporter is best at sensing lies or insincerity.

Integration in Affect

The integration mechanism takes affective information from the Affective Module and combines it with various information sources in the five information components of the SPPL processing Model to yield the necessary understanding and produce output.

INT 1 Affect →Identity

Integration is the mechanism that combines information from the Affective Module and merges it with information from the Identity Component. For example, the Affective Module integrates feelings of cultural pride and intellectual fulfillment with the features of a Russian immigrant identity, especially those related to intellectual identity in contrast to L2 identity.

INT 2a Affect →Context

Affective information is combined with information about setting and conversational participants to yield a sum/product of Affect and Context information. For a bilingual this is a game of integrating non-affective language context decisions with affective context decisions. Many native Israeli technology professionals tend to converse with each other in English in settings that demand English (their L2) like professional conferences. But in the midst of this English language choice context, strong emotions for or against a particular person trigger a shift back to Hebrew.

INT 2b Affect →Genre

The Affective Module integrates affective information with information in the Genre Subcomponent. Hymns classically do this in Christian liturgy. For the bilingual, affect is used to distinguish genres. To feel holy it must be in the language associated with prayer and meditation. A trilingual (English-Spanish-Hebrew) friend who had learned Spanish from the literature of Miguel de Unamuno and Garcia Marquez told me that when he listened to Rabbinic sermons in Spanish, in particular words such as *sagrado* (sacred) and *fe* (faith), he felt deep-seated linguistic anomie.

INT 3 Affect →Intentions

Affective information is integrated with information from the Intentional Component. In most languages, linguistic expressions of affect are detectable in pragmatic markers and adverbials (e.g. sort of, ya' know, anyway), where linguistic options are integrated with (sometimes latent) intentions, e.g. defensiveness, intimacy.

INT 4a Affect →Lexical Formulator

The integration of affect and syntactic, semantic, morphological and phonological information at the level of Lexical Formulation is not readily observable and may not be very common. The Freudian tradition claiming affective motivations for slips of the tongue has given way to a more 'cold cognitive' approach that accounts for these speech phenomena in terms of linguistic features. The study of morphological and syntactic manipulations of curses (e.g. abso-fucking-lutely) may be a productive source of data on the integration of affect and lexical information.

INT 4b Affect →Discourse Formulator

The Integration Mechanism combines affective and discourse information at the level of Discourse Formulation. An example plays on the Gricean pragmatic maxim "Be relevant": When a friend comes up on the street and instead of greeting you conventionally, says: "Your husband/wife was faithful last night." Knowledge of the discourse feature of relevance is integrated with what may either be malice or humor to produce the effect on the listener.

INT 5 Affect →Articulator

Information from the Affective Module is integrated with acoustic and phonetic information to generate characteristically emotional pitch and intensity. Sarcasm is flatter pitched than straightforward speech; anger is louder than friendly speech. At the level of articulation, the integration of affect is essential for the bilingual to comprehend the language-specific emotional meanings and riders on given statements.

Control in Affect

The Control Mechanism regulates the relationship between affect and the linguistic information in each of the five Information Components. This section describes the control processes underlying those relationships, which are of importance to bilinguals because they represent the dynamic management mechanisms needed to regulate and adjust output in one or both languages.

The arrows in this section represent a somewhat different relationship than in other sections because the notion of control incorporated into the SPPL Model is inherently interactive.

CON 1 Affect ⇔ Identity

Control is the mechanism that compares the amount and quality of information from the Affective Module with information about the particular social identity the speaker wants to project. If the amount and quality of affective information are congruent with the speaker's social identity, information will flow through the model smoothly without disturbance, and affective aspects of language production will proceed fluently. Disturbances will show up as problems in the flow of information, e.g. hesitations, false starts, lexical access difficulties. For example, a bilingual could try to express, say, professional determination and capability in L1, start stuttering as he feels the message is not getting through, and then shift to L2.

CON 2a Affect ⇔ Context

Affective information is compared with information about settings, speakers, listeners, and topics of conversation. The Control Mechanism is responsible for making sure there is an appropriate balance between affect and the various settings, participants and topics with which a speaker comes into contact. An imbalance between affect and contextual information will result in a disturbance, and the Control Mechanism will then adjust the amount of each source of information in order to stabilize the system. For example, a monolingual Spanish-speaking child's fear and dread (perhaps even panic) upon first entering a monolingual English speaking school (setting) with a monolingual English speaking teacher (listener) may lead the child to remain or to avoid going to school the second day. These behaviors, and others even less socially acceptable, are used to control the child's perception of incongruence between language and context and reduce the disturbance from the fear generated by that incongruence.

CON 2b Affect ⇔ Genre
The Control Mechanism regulates the flow of information from the Affective Module to the Genre Subcomponent by comparing affective aspects of language use with the type of texts a speaker produces. A stable flow of affective information depends on the amount and kind of speech events/text types the bilingual interacts with. For example, a Maronite Christian recently described to me how she felt knowing that she prays in the language of Jesus. Her involvement in a project to revive Aramaic in Maronite kindergartens can be seen as a way to expand the range of genres she can function in. The Control Mechanism apparently indicates that she has a need for more use of her ancestral language; using that language in other genres will make her feel more Maronite and more Christian.

CON 3 Affect ⇔ Intentions
Affective information is compared with the intended speech act(s). If these elements of information are congruent and balanced (e.g. greetings and blessings imbued with warmth and empathy and requests for information expressed with relatively flat affect), then language production and emotional communication will proceed in tandem, with the speaker then moving to the formulation stage of processing. If, however, a speech act is uttered with the 'wrong' affect so to speak, the control mechanism declares a 'disturbance' and attempts to bring affect into line with the intended speech act. The control mechanism stabilizes the system by modifying i) the kind and/or amount of information flowing from the Affective Module, ii) the speech act selected, or iii) some combination of i) and ii). This is important in bilingual situations because the detection of disturbances also has to declare in which language these take place to fix them as the processing moves into formulation.

CON 4a Affect ⇔ Lexical Formulator
The Control Mechanism compares affective information with the semantic, syntactic, morphological, and phonological information in the Lexical Formulation component. Disturbances in the balance between affect and linguistic information may produce slips of the tongue, tip-of-the-tongue phenomena, stuttering, and dysarthria. These disturbances are managed by adjusting the amount and quality of affect information and the various linguistic components of lexical information. For bilinguals, affective feedback regarding "permissible" levels of codeswitching is modified with instructions from the control mechanism.

CON 4b Affect ⇔ Discourse Formulator

The Control Mechanism compares affective information with discourse patterns (e.g. foregrounding, repetition, cohesion, relevance) to see if the intended quality and level of affect fit the discourse features of the utterance. When there is an appropriate fit between these sources of information, the Control Mechanism allows the information to flow freely. When there is not, the Control Mechanism handles the imbalance by modifying the relative amount and quality of affective information and/or the discourse options available. For example, a request for a favor in Hebrew with elaborate justification and several markers of politeness will make the native English speaker come off as a wimp. The Control Mechanism monitors and regulates the relationship between utterance length and affect, allowing the speaker to come off as appropriately casual and confident for most Israeli contexts.

CON 5 Affect ⇔ Articulator

The Control Mechanism monitors and regulates the flow of acoustic and phonetic information between the Affective Module and the Articulator. It does so by comparing the amount and kind of affective information with the acoustic and phonetic features of the utterance. When these are congruent, there is relatively little disturbance in the Control Mechanism and an appropriate degree of fluency. In terms of 'control,' a foreign accent can be said to include an imbalance of affective features at the acoustic-phonetic level of processing, resulting in loud (acoustic), arrogant (affect) speech.

SEQUENTIAL PROCESSING IN BILINGUAL PRODUCTION

The vertical arrows linking the five information components to each other try to describe the flow of information in language production from identity formation to articulation. Obviously, there is some interactive ebb and flow of information between each pair of components, and a complicated feedback mechanism is described below in the section on control. But mostly, the information flows downwards from the sociopragmatic components to the psycholinguistic ones. Both language choice and Affect come into play in the ways described above as the information flows downwards. The exposition here, unlike the previous sections, is selective, and is intended to show how one or more of the processing mechanisms guide information from identity to articulation.

From Social Identity to Context and Genre

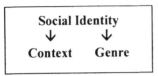

The speaker takes his/her social identity, including demographic, economic, political, religious, family, and cultural features into a context. Those identity features constrain the settings, participants and genres a speaker chooses to interact with. For example, a Tigrigna-English bilingual from Eritrea will prefer to interact in Tigrigna in spontaneous conversation (genre) at home (setting) with family and friends (participants), but will speak in English when traveling abroad, especially in service encounters and in contact with government personnel, where the genre of interaction is largely scripted and the settings are more formal and participants are strangers. This is the place in which bilinguals are most conscious of their two languages and the implications of using either or both languages.

From Context and Genre to Intentions

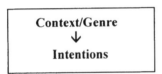

The composite of social identity, contextual, and genre information becomes the input to the Intentional information component. This information is integrated, along with relevant language choice and Affective information to yield the intentions underlying utterances like the following:

Hijo de mi alma, did you see that homer to left?

Sir, now can you please explain the difference between quarks and gluons?

The first of these is an opinion, reflection or observation, the second a request for information or possibly an attempt to trip up the listener or make an impression. Both indicate a great deal about the social identity of the speaker, the setting, and the basic genre. All of that information is integrated into a single intention with its accompanying speech act that in many cases, "exposes" the bilingual's lack of fluency in the less frequented language.

From Intentions to Formulation

Formulating an utterance involves a complex set of processes. It includes selection and retrieval of words and discourse patterns and matching these structures to the intentions/speech acts generated in the previous stage of processing. Most lexical processing studies describe selection and retrieval as a process involving representation of syntactic, semantic, morphological, and phonological information. In bilingualism (and in my opinion monolingualism as well), the speaker does not always have a single, transparent intention in mind. Moreover, sometimes there is more than one intention, e.g. a single utterance can convey interpersonal, informational, affective information simultaneously. Thus, the arrow here conveys both ambiguity and multiple intentions.

Lexical and discourse selection and retrieval rely on the Imitation Mechanism; matching of structures and intentions entails processes of comparison governed by the Variation Mechanism. The Integration Mechanism is responsible for bringing together the multiple sources of information within and between the lexical and discourse sub-components while the Control Processes regulate the balance of these multiple sources.

From Formulation to Articulation

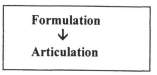

The lexical (semantic, syntactic, morphological, and phonological) and discourse (length of utterance, cohesion, given-new, relevance) information are assigned acoustic-phonetic features at this stage of processing, bringing the process to a boundary point with articulated speech.

ALTERNATIVE APPROACHES IN PROCESSING

If the present work were not so intensely interdisciplinary or if the various sub-disciplines in the cognitive sciences could agree on definitions of constructs like physicists do about protons and quarks, then the following section might not be necessary. However, to clarify and further illustrate how my own notions of imitation, variation, integration, and control operate in a model of bilingual processing, I pick up here some of the research in related fields on these processing notions. The SPPL Model aims to serve researchers in a variety of fields related to bilingualism. It uses notions from these fields and places them within a framework that enables both mapping and isolation of the key dynamic elements. Within the structure of the model, this is relatively easy, as described in Chapter 3. But structure is nothing without systematic description of the dynamic linkages between the "boxes." This was done functionally in the walk through the model above. Now we have to take each one of the processing elements and flesh it out both in the terms of the discipline from which it is derived and in the operational terms of the SPPL Model. It is neither convenient nor easy to combine sociopragmatic and psycholinguistic dimensions of bilingualism. But these hurdles are there for good reason. Leaving the sociopragmatic and psycholinguistic out on separate branches of the tree makes less sense than bringing them together because bilinguals do, after all, articulate phonemes in social contexts.

IMITATION, REPETITION AND MIMESIS

Imitation has been mostly neglected in modern linguistics because of the focus on creativity and excitement over the child's infinite capacity for understanding novel sentences. Imitation may have even suffered 'guilt through association' due to its centrality in behaviorist theory, but it seems that there has been some recent interest in using this construct in a variety of fields.

From a socio-psychological perspective, processes of imitation are at the basis of Speech Accommodation Theory. This research program attempts to explain the similarity of various speech and communication patterns in social interaction. Speech Accommodation Theory (Giles, 1977) and its successor Communication Accommodation Theory (Giles, Coupland & Coupland, 1991) try to explain how speakers select and modify speech and other behavior to converge towards their interlocutor. Convergence at the interpersonal level is comparable to "interactional synchrony" (Argyle, 1969; Erickson & Schultz, 1982), "listener adaptedness" and other directedness (e.g. McCann & Higgins, 1990) in social psychology and "positive politeness" (Brown and Levinson, 1987) and listenership (Tannen, 1989) in linguistics.

Giles, Coupland and Coupland (1991) define convergence as "a strategy whereby individuals adapt to each other's communicative behaviors in terms of a wide range of linguistic-prosodic-nonverbal features including speech rate, pausal phenomena and utterance length, phonological variants, smiling, gaze, and so on" (p. 7). In social-psychological terms, convergence is said to reflect conformity and identification. Imitation, then, can be viewed as a processing mechanism that underlies the more observable notion of convergence. Most of the work in the Speech Accommodation paradigm draws on attitudinal data, mostly excluding the purposeful and intentional dimensions of imitation.

Imitation processes are also fundamental to the construct of *cultural memes* in neo-Darwinian thought (Dawkins, 1989). More recently, imitation has begun to be treated in a neuro-biological framework. Skoyles (1998) presents evidence for what he calls *mirror neurons*. Gabora (1998) proposes autocatalysis as an explanatory framework in an evolutionary model of the cognitive mechanisms in the transition from episodic to memetic culture. Her notion of a meme as "anything from an idea for a recipe to a memory of one's uncle to a concept of size to an attitude of racial prejudice" is useful background for a discussion of imitation processes. She identifies three characteristics of memetic processing that distinguish it from episodic processing. First, memetic processing is integrative, combining information from perception and memory. Second, "memory is sparse, content addressable, distributed, modular, and habituates to repeated inputs." According to Gabora, these properties are what lead to the generation of abstractions. A third feature of memetic processing is the conscious and recursive manipulation of abstractions. These features of mimesis are very far away from the habit and reinforcement ideas in early behaviorist psychology.

In a cognitive examination of primate behavior, Byrne and Russon (1997) present imitation in what can be called a revisionist construct in cognitive science. Drawing from their research on orangutan behavior, they distinguish action and program levels of processing. Action level imitation is restricted to the surface form of behavior, more or less analogous to what an analog camera might do, while the program level involves copying the organizational structure of behavior. Their terminology and analysis focus on motor learning but are useful beyond non-human primates and beyond motor skills. Especially relevant to language processing is their notion of a "diagnostics of hierarchical organization," a component of program-level imitation which they say involves a mechanism for handling interruptions in the main line of processing, a procedure for self-correction, and "substitution of functionally equivalent components." This work makes meaningful advances toward an understanding of some of the non-observable component processes in behavior and learning in general, which can be examined analogously for language processing. However, it too falls short of recognizing the role of purposefulness and goals in imitation, essential constructs in the SPPL Model.

IMITATION AS A LINGUISTIC CONSTRUCT

In linguistics, imitation has been treated as a stylistic and discourse phenomenon (e.g. Bolinger, 1975; Joos, 1961; Tannen, 1989) and as relevant in second language learning (Coulmas, 1981; Hakuta, 1974; Ohta, 2001). Tannen (1989) delineates five functions of repetition in conversation:
1. for fluency in production;
2. to facilitate comprehension, i.e. to make the discourse less dense, thereby allowing more time to think;

3. to forge connective links as cohesive devices (e.g., Halliday & Hasan, 1976);
4. as interactive links, e.g. to get or keep the floor, to show 'listenership,' for back-channelling (Duncan, 1974; Yngve, 1970), to bide for time prior to speaking, to be humorous, or to show appreciation of the speech of one's interlocutor, to ratify the interlocutor's statement;
5. for interpersonal coherence, i.e. to keep a conversation going, to show one's response or acceptance of someone else's utterance, or to indicate one's own participation in a conversation.

Among these categories, "connective and interactive links" and coherence phenomena, in particular lexical repetition and grammatical parallelism, figure most prominently in language production. In lexical repetition, a word or part of a word is repeated to effect the cohesive link. In anaphora, where a pronoun makes the connection between two entities, the form changes from noun to pronoun, while the meaning (referent) is repeated. Along a dimension of salience, phonological repetition in the form of alliteration, assonance, and rhyme, sound play (in child language), and lexical repetition, are perhaps most important. In the domain of phonology, meter may be a somewhat less common kind of repetition to the untutored. Even less salient examples of repetition include grammatical parallelism, which involves repetition of structure and variation in meaning, while in pronominalization, synonymy, and analogy, the structure varies and a portion of the meaning remains constant (Waugh, 1976).

Given the prevalence of repetition in language, it should not be surprising that Hymes (1981) defines structure as the interplay between repetition and contrast. This definition notwithstanding, the linguists who have taken an interest in this topic, Jakobson, Bolinger, Fillmore and Coulmas, are not famous for their orthodox structuralism; they are not from the same linguistic stock as the Bloomfields, Chomskys, Halles, and Jackendoffs. Even in her lone structural category cited above, Tannen (1989) slips into the functional aspects of repetition, pointing out that it is more related to rheme than theme, more to comment than topic, and then notes its function for emphasis. She is clearly more at home in a functional framework and more insightful in her use of analogies of linguistic repetition to the "comfort of a familiar chair" and as "a source for building trust."

Pronunciation and lexical choice are the most prominent features of spoken language that can be imitated. But these are not the only aspects of language use selected for imitation, nor are they necessarily the most noteworthy in language production. Grammatical patterns, metaphors, sarcasm, irony, politeness, virtually all aspects of language use, are motivated by needs to establish identity, for presentation of self, and to sustain interpersonal relations. In conventional social interaction, there is a measured degree of imitation, most notably in the use of nominals and pragmatic markers. Imitation imparts feelings of familiarity and solidarity. This is part of the psychology behind the marketing strategy of Howard Johnson's© and similar franchise stores. When you see the orange cupola from a distance, when you enter the restaurant and see the ice cream parlor on the right, the cash register front and center, and the bathrooms beyond the tables down the hall, the familiarity is supposed to put you at ease. Imitation fosters familiarity, and familiarity engenders satisfaction and comfort. Linguistic imitation operates in tandem with social processes of imitation, convergence and identity and inculcates the same feelings of comfort and satisfaction.

Bilinguals, especially immigrants, seek familiarity to compensate for those parts of their lives filled with the strange and the alien, with dissonance and distress. Imitation is the most readily accessible process to help overcome these feelings. The non-native imitates the new culture as well as the old. Names, dress, proxemics, and language are all vulnerable to change for the non-native. Ricardo becomes Richard, Irena Irene, Zhanna Jane; the turban and the toga are removed entirely or exchanged for more Western dress.

All of these distinctive features of identity (dress, proxemics, names and other features of language) are socially determined, copies of existing patterns. None are generated from innate primitives. They represent a set of choices for the bilingual, sometimes conscious and deliberate, and always intentional. Selection from among various options is more limited for names and dress. But variation in the number of options is not the only difference between language and non-verbal markers of social identity. Complexity also plays a role. Linguistic markers of identity include phonetic, lexical, and grammatical options. The non-native has to choose from these options, often not knowing either the relative importance of each domain or the potential value of various options within a domain. The claim here is that the same attitudes and motivations that lead to convergence or divergence in name selection and choice of dress operate in making linguistic choices.

Acts of linguistic choice, motivated internally by the social needs and externally by pressures of social comparison, draw heavily on processes of repetition and imitation. These processes can be either deliberate or unconscious. A speaker's conscious selection of a particular lexical item to converge towards the speech of a listener includes, for example, codeswitching to show ethnolinguistic solidarity. The unconscious choices of accent or grammatical patterns involve retrieval of a known pattern from memory, copying the pattern to the planning component of production, and, finally, integration of the copy into the linguistic context of the sentence or utterance produced.

IMITATION IN LANGUAGE CONTACT

The products of codeswitching, intereference, and translation can all be considered partial copies of their L1 sources. More specifically, the kinds of speech phenomena that are labeled interference result from an attempt to produce a second language form (a phoneme, a word, or a syntactic structure), but instead, a first language copy results. Codeswitched language can be seen as copying a structure (a phoneme, a word, or syntactic frame), from one language system onto the other. Translation ideally involves a mapping of second language meanings onto the first language. Sometimes the mapping is incomplete, and non-natives language forms and meanings are 'copied' onto first language forms, resulting in some difference from native speaker meaning or structure.

Clyne's (2003) notion of transference is similar. Rather than seeing the structures of two contact languages as interfering with each other, he says that a particular linguistic element (like syntax, lexico-semantics, phonotactics, morphology, pragmatics, tonemics, etc.) is transferred to the language being produced. The term transference maintains the structural notion of two relatively independent systems (to account for the fact that the overwhelming amount of processing even among bilingual individuals is unilingual). But beyond the terminology, Clyne describes transference as an attempt to capture the linguistic process whereby a structure in one language is incorporated into another language. In the context of this work, transference is a product while incorporation is a process. The notion of incorporation is important because it gives us a processing account for codeswitching, interference, and translation, all of which involve some form of transference.

The SPPL Model looks at *imitation* as a psycholinguistic mechanism that underlies these structural phenomena. It might not be the mechanism or process most comparable to Clyne's notion of incorporation; *integration* could be closer (see the section on integration below). The focus here, however, is on imitation because despite the structural differences among syntactic, lexical, lexico-semantic, tonemic, and pragmatic transference, all these forms of transference involve a singular imitation process.

For example, a Spanish-English bilingual speaker, rather than use a Spanish form 'Casa Blanca' in a Spanish utterance about the US President's residence, may intentionally switch to 'White House.' In doing so, she accesses the relevant intention, its corresponding lexico-pragmatic lemma, and copies further lexico-semantic features on to that lemma. The intention and lemma are in a certain sense an abstraction, i.e. not all details are specified. In particular, the lexico-semantic details, including the English instantiation of those details, are not yet encoded. In another sense, the intention and lemma contain non-abstract information, namely, pragmatic features which, in this case, lead the speaker to the codeswitched English expression. The same kinds of examples have been documented in psycholinguistic studies of translation and interpretation (see Shlesinger, 2000).

Thus, codeswitching, interference, and translation are claimed here to rely on roughly same processes. They begin with an intention to replicate the meaning of a source language expression. That source language expression contains a combination of abstract, sometimes incomplete, referential and language-specific pragmatic features (a lexico-pragmatic lemma). During the course of production, output is directed to the other language for one of the reasons detailed in the SPPL Model, and the imitation mechanism is used for the replication.

In addition to the imitative, reproductive aspects of language production there is a reconstructive and integrative process involved. For example, in phonological interference or transference, a native Spanish speaker's pronunciation of the English verb 'hit' with a long (high) vowel (as in the English word 'heat') mimetically retains the lexico-semantic and syntactic information from the L1 source. In doing so, the bilingual combines and reconstructs that information with his/her perception of the phonological shape of the L2 target item. Codeswitching and translation also involve integration of certain features of one language with the features of the other language. For codeswitching from L2 to L1, memorial representation of L1 features are integrated with a combination of memorial and perceptual features of L2. Given the incomplete nature of the second language, a fair amount of reconstructive processing will probably be involved. In simultaneous interpretation, where production is usually in L1, a more or less immediate representation of L2 features (the source language) is integrated with memorial features of L1. Thus, while the same imitative processes work for codeswitching, interference, and translation, they may be distinguishable by the integrative processes operating on the copies or representations being processed. For interpretation, the integration process is assumed to involve less reconstruction of L2 than for interference and codeswitching.

IMITATION IN A MODEL OF BILINGUAL PRODUCTION

To illustrate how imitation operates in the SPPL Model, we shall discuss three of its information components. In the *social identity component*, names and greetings, among the first ways to project identity, are mimetic in their essence. To give and to use a name involves a model and a replica. The model is selected, copied, then adapted (phonologically, morphologically, and/or semantically) to the new language. For example in Hebrew "Hashem sheli Binyamin," is a copy of the utterance "My name is Benjamin," with the name changing slightly in English enunciation, to project a different identity. Structurally, greetings can be looked at as frozen forms or routine formulas. This same terminology captures the imitative aspects of greetings. In the Israeli context, two of the most prominent greetings among adolescents and young adults in Modern Hebrew are the English '*hi*' and the Arabic '*ahlan*,' both products of language contact. In the idiom of one tradition in bilingual research, these are borrowings. In the present context, they are the products of a social and psychological process involving a large degree of imitation. First and foremost, they involve imitation of a social and pragmatic nature. In using a greeting borrowed from another language, the Hebrew speaker to some extent identifies with that language and its speakers. Linguistically, imitation is a derivative of social identity. A copy of the lexical model from the source language is integrated with copies of phonological and pragmatic features accessed from the target language. As with names, greetings do not involve a great deal of manipulation and adaptation. They are taken from one language, as chunks (Dittmar, Spolsky & Walters, 1997), imitated, and imported to the other language, as in the Khalabi "merci ktir" a French-Arabic codeswitched way to say 'thank you very much.' The primary and prevalent processes they make use of are recognition and recall, molecular processes underlying the mechanism of imitation.

Imitation is involved in the **intentional component** in several ways. Representations or copies of social identity, contextual, and discourse information are integrated, and the product is used to select a speech act. That speech act itself is copied from a mental list of viable intentions and integrated with an appropriate propositional content, which is generated from available lexico-pragmatic concepts. In bilingual processing, we saw above that copies of L1 speech acts are sometimes combined with L2 propositional content (or, alternatively, L2 speech acts are combined with L1 propositional content) to yield utterances that have elsewhere been described as interference. Imitation is at work here, replicating the speech act and propositional content from each of the bilingual speaker's languages.

In the *formulator,* lexico-pragmatic concepts and lemmas are abstract, mental representations of syntactic, semantic, and pragmatic features. Lexemes are words, which are comprised of syntactic, semantic, and pragmatic features in combination with morphophonological information. Imitation is the processing mechanism that takes the abstract information from the concept and lemma and copies or maps it onto morphophonological information to yield the lexeme. In bilingual lexical processing, information is copied from different linguistic levels and integrated to yield forms that have been described as interference and codeswitching. The following exchange may be illustrative:

Native English speaker: What's your major at the university?

Native Hebrew speaker: I am *learning* English.

In this example, the native Hebrew speaker uses the word 'learn' in a context that requires the word 'study.' In terms of the imitation mechanism, the speaker has selected the syntactic and semantic information from the Hebrew lemma 'lilmod' (to learn) and copied it onto the English lexeme, resulting in the word 'learn.' Hebrew does not make a lexicalized distinction between process and result for this particular verb. In the terminology of contrastive linguistics, this might be called an interference or transfer error. Studies of codeswitching might ignore this phenomenon, since it seems that there is only one language in the example above. In Clyne's terminology, this is lexico-semantic transference.

And, in the present context, this form shows evidence of the same underlying imitation process as examples of interference, interlanguage, and codeswitching.

Imitation has been presented here as a processing mechanism that underlies sociopragmatic as well as psycholinguistic aspects of bilingualism. Language production entails representation, which is analyzed for its structural features, i.e. sounds, morphemes, meaning. Certain features are selected, copied, and adapted, based on social, psychological, and linguistic preferences. Phenomena unique to bilingualism such as codeswitching, interference, and translation all rely heavily on imitation. Studies that restrict their focus to formal, structural properties of language contact do not need to get into the language user's mental processes. Studies of language use, acquisition, and attrition, however, do need to relate to the processes that underlie these phenomena.

VARIATION, VARIANCE, AND OTHER CLOSE COUSINS

Like imitation in cognitive science, variation is a construct that does not attract a lot of good feeling among most researchers. In behavioral science, variance is something you want to get rid of. In statistics, it's what produces large errors and stops data from reaching significance. In much of linguistics, variation is considered an impediment to generalizations and universals. In sociolinguistic research, however, the correlation of linguistic and social variation is a tool for examining regularity, systematicity, and rule-governedness (e.g. Sankoff & Labov, 1979).

In this section I offer yet another approach to variation. I build on the constructs of diversity or richness of linguistic forms, strategies, and patterns from sociolinguistics and the social psychology of language, and add to these the notion of variation as a mechanism involved in language use. My fundamental claim is that richer variation allows a speaker to generate more and different utterances in a larger number of contexts. The idea for variation as a processing mechanism is derived from the psychology of William James (1890) and William Powers (1973), for which the primary maxim is 'Consistent ends by variable means.' One not-so-kind idiomatic version of this postulate is: 'There's more than one way to skin a cat.' Variation operates in a dynamic and complementary relationship with imitation. Both mechanisms drive language use. Together they explain some of the processes underlying acquisition, attrition, and language disorders.

As background, three (very different) approaches to variation are presented here. The first focuses on linguistic form, the second on pragmatic range. To illustrate these types of variation I draw from studies in corpus linguistics, sociolinguistics, and my own studies of bilingual children. The third approach to variation comes from Perceptual Control Theory (Powers, 1973). On this background I show how the variation mechanism operates in the different components of the SPPL Model of bilingual processing, with a particular eye on the language contact phenomena of interest throughout this work: codeswitching, interference, and translation.

VARIATION IN LINGUISTIC FORM

The study of linguistic variation, in lexis as well as in syntax, is focused on observable, countable forms. Lexical diversity has been used as a measure in various ways in corpus linguistics (Biber, 1995), in vocabulary acquisition (Laufer & Nation, 1995), in sociolinguistics (Sankoff & Lessard, 1975; Walters, 1980) and in social psychology (Bradac & Wisegarver, 1984). Although calculation of the measure is much the same across fields, the use and implications of that measure differ.

In corpus analysis, for example, type-token ratios (the number of different words divided by the total number of words) have been used to determine the homogeneity of a text. Shorter texts produce higher type-token ratios than longer ones. In corpus-based studies of lexis, high variability is considered undesirable, unstable (Richards, 1987). In some of my own corpus research with a relatively small corpus (approximately 600 texts of mostly non-native written English totaling 20,000 words), I have explored the use of lexical variation as a way to examine differences among non-native writers: as a measure of written proficiency, as a measure of how they relate to different genres (e.g. narrative, expository), and as a way to assess creativity. In this work, variation is considered lexical diversity. It is a positive (welcomed) construct in the interpretation of the data.

Sankoff and Lessard (1975) examined "vocabulary richness" in 120 interviews drawn from a corpus of spoken French in Montreal. Defining richness as a comparison of the number of different words (D) in each interview with the total number of words (T), the authors conducted a multiple regression analysis of this measure with six demographic variables: age (15-85), sex, mean income (inferred from the speaker's neighborhood), educational level, status within the household, and the speaker's occupational status. Only the age-education interaction term emerged as significant in the regression analysis. Two of the authors' conclusions are relevant to the interest here in bilingualism:

❑ Vocabulary knowledge increased with age "at a slowly decreasing rate over time, but this rate can be magnified up to five times through extensive education;"
❑ Vocabulary was found to increase at least up to age 50.

In this work, variation is the number of different words a speaker uses, or more technically, the proportion of different words to total words (D/T) in a speaker's overall corpus.

Turning to studies of bilingual children, in my earlier studies of requesting (Walters, 1980), the number of different speech act forms for performing a request was the measure for calculating variation. This measure can be seen as analogous, at a semantic level of processing, to Sankoff and Lessard's measure of vocabulary richness. Speech act variation consistently differentiated between native and non-native speakers of English across a variety of ages, languages, and social groups (see Table 4.1). In a range of studies conducted within this framework, fourteen different speech act forms were elicited, e.g. *may I, can you, could you, would you, will you, I need, you have to.* The number of different speech act forms produced by each speaker in a series of role-playing scenarios was taken as a measure of linguistic versatility. Higher variation scores were assumed to predict the bilingual speakers' abilities to function in a greater variety of contexts. Here, as above, the variation idea is based on frequencies and proportions of language produced.

Table 4.1. Variation as diversity of speech act form (mean number of different speech act strategies) (based on Walters, 1980: 343, Table 1)

Study	Native Eng/Bilingual	n	Mean(sd)	Non-native English	n	Mean(sd)
1	Anglophones	10	5.4 (1.08)	Armenians	10	4.8 (1.69)
2	Mainland Puerto Ricans	32	5.7 (1.38)			
3	Middle class Anglophones	8	5.1 (0.84)	Non-natives	8	4.5 (1.51)
4	Anglophones	24	5.0 (1.84)	Chicanos	24	4.3 (1.40)

VARIATION IN PRAGMATIC RANGE

In an effort to give a more pragmatic basis to the variation construct, each of a speaker's requests was assigned a politeness score based on the "method of paired comparisons" used in attitude theory (Edwards, 1957). This procedure involved pairing each of fourteen different speech act strategies (elicited in the above studies of requesting behavior) with each other, submitting the pairs to native speakers for judgments of relative politeness, and normalizing and standardizing their judgments (see Walters, 1979, for a description of the procedure). The standardized score for each request was taken as a 'normative' measure of politeness. Then the range of politeness for each speaker was computed, and those ranges averaged across the subjects in each group.

Table 4.2. Variation as pragmatic range (mean group politeness) in four studies (based on Walters, 1980: 343)

Study	Native Eng/Bilingual	n	Mean(sd)	Non-native English	n	Mean(sd)
1	Anglophones	10	.458 (.36)	Armenians	10	.056 (.21)
2	Mainland Puerto Ricans	32	.152 (.30)			
3	Middle class Anglophones	8	.259 (.47)	Non-natives	8	.283 (.32)
4	Anglophones	24	.174 (.47)	Chicanos	24	.068 (.71)

As can be seen in Table 4.2, variation in politeness was greater for native speakers than for non-natives in two of the four studies (Studies 1 and 4). But the most striking aspect of the data is the variability, both within and between studies, as indicated by the standard deviation scores in Table 4.2. That intra-group variability, along with a fundamental interest in the individual language user, led me to explore other ways of examining the pragmatic range of individual speakers.

In order to bring the group data in Table 4.2 to an individual level of analysis, Table 4.3 compares three measures of variation, one based solely on semantic form (speech act variation), one based on pragmatic range (range of politeness) and one based on sociolinguistic appropriateness. For this analysis, I selected those bilinguals who showed the most and least evidence of speech act variation. Those with greater speech act diversity used 7 or 8 different strategies (can you, could you, would you, etc.) in eight role playing situations. Those with the least diversity used only four or fewer different strategies. I compared these individuals both for their range of politeness as well as for the extent to which they varied their strategies 'appropriately' according to the age and gender of their listener, i.e. whether they were generally more polite to older listeners than younger ones and more polite to female listeners than to males. The individual data in Table 4.3 show that those with higher variation scores (column 2) commanded a greater range of politeness (not surprising) and also tended to vary the use of their request strategies according to norms of social appropriateness (not so obvious). The speakers with lower variation scores, even those who commanded a moderate range of politeness (subject nos. 105, 110, 112), were just as likely to use normatively inappropriate strategies as appropriate ones, i.e. to use polite requests to younger and male listeners and impolite requests to older and female listeners.

For these analyses, the measure of variation is not read directly from the frequency or proportion of the language produced; rather, it is grounded in the judgments of native speakers and social norms. In this way, both the speaker's utterances and the listener's perceptions are incorporated into the measure of variation, affording it a more pragmatic foundation.

Table 4.3. Individual analysis comparing speech act variation with range of politeness and appropriateness in 13 subjects from Study 2.

	Subject Id Number	Speech Act Range	Variation in politeness score	Appropriateness for addressee's	
				Age	Gender
High variation subjects	108	8	.982	+	+
	120	7	.837	+	+
	128	7	.891	+	+
	103	7	.910	+	+
	106	7	.859	-	+
	115	7	.789	+	+
	131	7	.730	+	+
Low variation subjects	110	4	.608	-	-
	105	4	.580	-	+
	112	4	.498	+	+
	102	4	.321	+	-
	127	4	.194	-	+
	104	1	0	-	-

VARIATION IN CONTROL OF PERCEPTION

The basic idea of Perceptual Control Theory (see Powers, 1973, 1978) is that perceptions, goals, and intentions are maintained or kept stable by variable means. In this view, behavior is not an end, but a means, and a variable means. The more ways available and accessible to accomplish a goal or carry out an intention, the more likely that an internal standard will be maintained. Variation is a means to maintain a goal. This is not the variance of statistics, the source of error in the search for rule-governed behavior, the impediment to significance. Rather, here variation is a processing mechanism, to be sought after, to be taken advantage of, to be manipulated, in the service of one's goals and intentions.

Runkel (1990:147-8) identifies three sources of variation in behavior in the terms of Perceptual Control Theory:

1. The nature of the environmental event, i.e. whether an event opposes or supports an intention or internal standard.
2. The opportunities or possible actions available in the environment.
3. The means selected to oppose a disturbance to an internal standard.

In less technical terms, the notion of variation here is in the way the individual perceives the environment and in the way he or she chooses to interact with it. All three sources of variation, i.e. determination of whether an event is disturbing or maintaining an intention, the opportunities available, and the means selected, are crucial to an understanding of behavior.

The first of Runkel's sources of variation is dichotomous; it doesn't involve the same kind of continuum of diversity discussed in the research above. The second source, the "opportunities or possible actions" does involve diversity, the idea that 'more is better.' Finally, the third source depends on what actions are perceived to be successful, on whether another internal standard is threatened, and on the individual's resourcefulness in thinking up creative ways to oppose the disturbance. Here "the individual's resourcefulness" is closer to the kind of variation we are after.

This selective review of literature on variation from linguistics, sociolinguistics, and psychology was meant to advance the notion of desirable variation. I have tried to ground the construct in language form, in social norms, and in the psychology of intentions. With this background, I turn to the ways the variation idea plays itself out in bilingualism.

VARIATION IN BILINGUAL PHENOMENA

The language contact phenomena highlighted here, namely, codeswitching, interference, and translation, are all considered variants. When the bilingual speaker codeswitches, when she experiences interference, or when he translates, a variant is produced.

In one sense, the word, meaning, or structure produced is a variant of the L1 form or pattern. In another sense, it is a variant of the target form. In the SPPL approach it is a variant of both. This is the structural sense of variation. In functional terms, language production in bilingualism involves a set of choices from among different social identity options, settings, participants, genres and topics, speech acts, lexico-pragmatic concepts, and discourse patterns, all of which depend on language choice. In this sense, the options, concepts, representations, and patterns are also variants. One of the mechanisms through which options are selected and choices are made is variation–variation in choosing a topic, in selecting speech acts, in accessing a lexical representation, and in picking a discourse pattern. The variation mechanism generates input by selecting a representation from memory, and manipulating it to fit the speaker's social identity, general goals, and specific intentions. Selection and manipulation may be conscious or unconscious. They involve even more basic psycholinguistic processes, in particular *discrimination* and *classification*. The remainder of this section describes how the variation mechanism and its component processes work for the information components of the SPPL Model.

Discrimination and classification are basic and general; they are processes that operate on information in all components of the Model of Bilingual Production presented in the previous chapter. For example, in the expression of *social identity* a language user's clothing, name, pronunciation, and lexical preferences both distinguish that individual from certain groups and classify him/her as a member of a particular group. If a speaker's identity is anchored in a single culture, very little codeswitching, interference, and translation are expected at this stage of processing. But, if a language user has had even minimal out-group exposure, then language contact phenomena are possible, even likely.

Similarly, for *settings* and *participants* involving in-group members only, acts of greeting, naming, and pronouncing are not likely to generate much codeswitching or interference, but if the conversation takes place on 'foreign' territory or the listener projects a different identity, then language contact phenomena will result. Discrimination and classification also operate in processing information about *genre*. Scripts are discriminated from each other and classified as first or second language phenomena. Clearly distinguishable genres will engender less interference and codeswitching than those that are more difficult to classify as L1 or L2. Monolingual conversations are of the former type; service encounters, doctor-patient scripts are of the latter.

The *intentional* component of the SPPL Model involves selection of an illocutionary act from among a large inventory of possibilities (over a thousand by some counts). Some of these are readily discriminated from others especially across languages, e.g. commands, invitations, suggestions. Others are less discriminable, e.g. orders and commands, invitations and offers, suggestions and recommendations. This complexity lends itself to bilingual phenomena, e.g. an L1 speech act attached to L2 propositional content. The following example illustrates a Hebrew (L1) speech act (disagreement) attached to English (L2) propositional content:

Native English speaker: "I think that Israeli economic independence is impossible given the present international situation."
Native Hebrew speaker: "Not right."

The process of accessing propositional content and formulating concepts, lemmas, and lexemes also induces language contact phenomena. Among all the information components of the SPPL Model, *formulation* may engender more interference and performance codeswitching than other aspects of production for a number of reasons. One factor is the sheer amount of information that must be processed to formulate an utterance. Another factor is that the frequency of lexico-pragmatic concepts and lemmas is rarely the same across languages, even for cognates and translation equivalents. Finally, lexical formulation involves processing of both symbolic (e.g. syntactic) and statistical (e.g. frequency) information. This is difficult (for a bilingual) to do and for us (researchers) to understand. The combination of symbolic and statistical information does not lend itself to unified treatment in current models of language processing (but see Klavans & Resnick, 1996, for papers which try a synthesis). This problem may, then, be a cause of language contact phenomena.

The symbolic-statistical distinction mentioned here may also help clarify differences between variation and imitation. Imitation is a conservation process. It is based on recognition and recall, processes grounded in learning theory, associationism, and connectionist models. From the bilingual perspective, it is this mechanism that allows things that happen in one language to be duplicated in another language as well.

Variation is dynamic, based on discrimination and classification, and rooted in notions of contrast in structural linguistics and symbolic approaches in generative theory. From the bilingual information processing perspective, it is the ability to route varied notions and inputs to the correct processing address. Language production involves a dynamic relationship between imitation and variation. Integration and control are the central mechanisms that forge this dynamic relationship.

INTEGRATION PROCESSES IN BILINGUALISM

The integration idea in bilingual processing has been conceptualized in different ways. One way, which we used in previous work on second language comprehension (Walters & Wolf, 1992), saw integration as "the role of first language information in second language understanding." For that view, the first language was seen as operating in service of the second. A more bilingual orientation, like the one advanced in the previous chapter (and in the work of Grosjean, 1997), takes information from both languages and looks at how that information is integrated in bilingual processing. This picture of bilingualism should also be seen as an alternative to the notion of transfer in the field of second language acquisition.

THE INTEGRATION IDEA: INTEGRATION OF INFORMATION

Anderson (1981, 1996) bases his Information Integration Theory (IIT) on the assumption that "...all thought and behavior has multiple causes, being integrated resultants of multiple sources of stimulus information" (p. 4). The theory is grounded in a functional perspective, which finds expression in its theoretical constructs as well as in its approach to methodology. Functionalism, for Anderson (1996), is "purposiveness of thought and action." In other words, thought and action are goal-oriented, goal-directed. Anderson's theory distinguishes observables (stimuli and responses) and non-observables, which he labels "intervening processing operators." These operators and the other terms of his theory—valuation, integration, and action—explain how one gets from observable stimuli to an observable response. Figure 4.1 characterizes the relationship among these processes.

Valuation is the process that converts observable stimuli into subjective representations by extracting information. Because these values are in the head of the individual, not in the stimuli, the definition of valuation relies heavily on goals. Thus, it is a purposive and constructive process. Integration is the process that converts subjective stimuli into a unitary, implicit response. In doing so, it is the process that brings about multiple determination. Integration, in this theory, takes the form of basic algebraic rules. Finally, the action operator is the process that converts an implicit response into an observable one. IIT has been applied to a wide range of problems in social psychology, psycholinguistics, child development, moral judgment, and psychophysics. It was chosen as the appropriate tool for the study of bilingualism because of its conceptual ability to handle multiple sources of information, its functional (goal-oriented and constructivist) orientation, its derivative methodology, and its broad range of applications.

Figure 4.1 Schematic diagram of Anderson's Information Integration Theory (from Anderson, 1981)

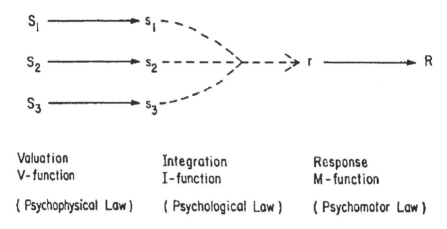

For an IIT approach to bilingualism, all of the sources of information outlined in the SPPL Model in the previous chapter, from information about social identity to phonetic forms, are potential candidates for stimulus information. In the terminology of IIT, the information from each of these sources is "valuated," i.e. examined, assessed, and given a subjective value, and that value is integrated with information from other sources. Each of the information sources in the model has access to and makes use of information from both L1 and L2. Thus, both valuation and integration processes operate on information about identity, context/genre, intentions, lexico-pragmatic concepts, etc. as well as on the L1 and L2 language information that goes into these.

Three kinds of studies have been conducted to examine how integration processes work in bilingualism. These include sociopragmatic studies of identity among immigrants (Ellinger, 1997), psycholinguistic studies involving metalinguistic judgments of unfamiliar idioms based on bilingual hint words (Walters & Wolf, 1988, 1992), and studies involving comprehension of codeswitched metaphors, which combined sociopragmatic and psycholinguistic information in a single task (Walters & Wolf, 1992).

In the *sociopragmatic studies*, Anderson's (1982) person perception paradigm was used to investigate the role of non-native accent, names and employment in the social integration of Russian immigrants in Israeli society. University students, ages 20-27 (16 native-born Israelis and 17 immigrants, 11 from Russia and 10 from English speaking countries), were presented person descriptions like the following:

> Alex is a 25-year-old Russian immigrant who grew up in Moscow. He is a successful lawyer. He speaks Hebrew with (no Russian accent/a mild Russian accent/a heavy Russian accent). And he (uses his Hebrew name exclusively/alternates use of his Russian and Hebrew names/uses his Russian name exclusively). How likely is it that he will integrate into Israeli society?

Subjects made judgments on a 20-point graphic scale, ranging from 'very unlikely' at one end to 'very likely' at the other. In a second experiment, information about use of personal names was replaced by information about employment (unemployed/part-time employment/full-time employment).

With regard to valuation of the different sources of information, findings showed that more importance was assigned to information about *accent* than information about *names* in judgments about how likely immigrants would be absorbed into Israeli society; Israeli born subjects and English-speaking immigrants tended to valuate *employment* information about the same as *accent*, while Russian immigrants tended to valuate *occupation* as slightly more important than *accent* in their judgments about immigrant absorption.

In the ***psycholinguistic studies***, of unfamiliar words and idioms, subjects were asked to make metalinguistic judgments of the relative contribution of pairs of L1 and L2 hints in helping them understand the meaning of an unfamiliar idioms, 'hit it off' and 'be off.' With regard to valuation of stimulus information, both L2 (English) and L1 (Hebrew) information were considered important in understanding the unfamiliar idiom. Fluent bilinguals ascribed greater importance to L1 (Hebrew) hint items than to L2 (English) items, while no consistent pattern of integration emerged in another study involving intermediate proficiency students. When it came to integrating information from the two languages, synonymous pairs of hints elicited were integrated by a simple averaging process, while judgments of pairs of translation equivalents showed a somewhat more complex integration process, described in the terms of IIT as 'differential averaging.'

In the combined sociopragmatic-psycholinguistic studies, we investigated the relative contribution of L1 and L2 in the comprehension of codeswitched metaphors like the following:

An encyclopedia (ENG) hino   mixra't zahav (HEB).   (stimulus sentence)
'An encyclopedia   it (is) mine   gold.'   (gloss)
An encyclopedia is a gold mine.   (translation)

The topic conveys the subject of the metaphoric sentence, in this case 'encyclopedia.' The vehicle provides a means for making a non-literal interpretation; in the present example this vehicle is 'gold mine.' Just about every philosophical, linguistic, and psychological treatment of metaphor makes this distinction, either implicitly or explicitly (e.g. Black, 1962; Fraser, 1979; Ortony, 1980). Sixteen codeswitched sentences were generated from a 4 by 4 factorial combination of topic and vehicle information, where the main interest was the contribution of L1 and L2 information in a judgment as to how valuable the reading material was.

Twenty native Hebrew speakers and 20 native English speakers made judgments of codeswitched sentences with different combinations of Hebrew and English topics and vehicles, summarized in Table 4.4.

Table 4.4 L1 and L2 topic and vehicle information for codeswitched metaphor experiment

Topic information	Vehicle information
ensiklopediya/encyclopedia	mixre zahav/gold mine
sefer/book	mixre kesef /silver mine
milon/dictionary	mixre nexoshet/copper mine
iton/newspaper	mixre barzel/iron mine

Bilingualism found expression in two ways in this study. First, bilingualism was manipulated in the two languages in the codeswitched stimulus sentences. It was also represented in the native and second languages of the subjects. The language (L1 or L2) of the stimulus items showed no consistent pattern in the results; the pragmatic nature of the task captured most of the variance, subjects attributing more importance to vehicle information than to information about the topic of the metaphor. In other words, the fact that the stimulus sentences were codeswitched was not as important as the metaphoric nature of the task and the distinction between topic and vehicle. The bilingualism of the subjects did show significant differences, however. When the topic was presented in the native language (L1), it was ascribed less importance, and the vehicle received a great deal more importance.

As far as integration processes are concerned, both simple averaging and multiplying rules were found in the data. Native English speakers applied rules of simple averaging, while native Hebrew speakers showed more of a tendency to integrate topic and vehicle information differentially. Simple averaging implies roughly equal weighting of the two sources of information and an independent process of integration; differential weighting implies that topic and vehicle information are integrated in a more ad hoc manner, perhaps because the task or the stimulus material was not as familiar to this group of subjects.

In codeswitching, integration operates well beyond the level of single sentences in the relatively artificial tasks described here. Integration takes into account sociopragmatic information related to identity, contextual factors and genre as well as information from the formulator. The integration mechanism also operates on lexical, syntactic, and to a lesser extent phonological information. It also serves an executive function to combine information and processes from both sociopragmatic and psycholinguistic sources. It is to this other function of the integration mechanism, as an integrator of processes, that I turn now.

INTEGRATION PROCESSES IN CODESWITCHING

Codeswitching involves integration at more than one level. It entails integration of basic level processes. In the language choice module, information is stored or marked for 'language,' including L1, L2, and/or codeswitched language. Storage and marking entail *discrimination* and *classification*. When a lexical item from one language is selected from the language choice module and inserted into an utterance in the other language, that lexical item must first be *recognized* among the pool of available items. The *recognition* process involves searching for a word or expression that matches, or comes close in meaning and form, to the one intended and fits (not necessarily perfectly) the syntactic frame into which it will be inserted. When the particular word being sought is produced and inserted in the context of an utterance, we can say it has been *identified*.

Discrimination and classification processes are directed at and operate on differences or variations in structural features. Recognition and identification also make some use of the variation mechanism in the search-and-match process in order to distinguish the intended word from those not intended. However, recognition and identification make more use of the imitation mechanism, since the search for a match or near-match and the decision following that search is based more on similarity than on differences.

In codeswitching, each basic level process is valuated and integrated by the integration mechanism. This valuation function involves weighing the importance of the distinctions and classifications that are made, and the categories into which words and expressions are placed (e.g. L1, L2, codeswitch). It also involves assessing the relative importance of the basic level processes (discrimination, recognition).

In simple terms, integration can be pictured as part of the bilingual decision making process during the production of language. Information is fed into this hopper as described above. But that information is not all that's needed in specifically bilingual speech production. The distinctive bilingual experience includes many decisions that make up uniquely bilingual phenomena like codeswitching. Among these are decisions about what fits the desired L1/L2 correspondence using the imitation mechanism, and what is different or stands out using the variation mechanism. These too go into the hopper for valuation. Hence, this picture of the integration mechanism includes both processes and information.

FOUR NOTIONS OF CONTROL

This section reviews different approaches to the construct of *control*, first briefly in generative grammar, developmental psycholinguistics, and the psycholinguistics of bilingualism. It ends up with a proposal to incorporate some of the ideas and methods of Perceptual Control Theory into a model of bilingualism. A bilingual model needs a control mechanism to provide high level response and 'governmental features.' Each of the first three notions below has something valuable for the perspective of bilingual processing; the last provides a picture broad enough for the scope of the SPPL Model and powerful enough to account for all the necessary processing.

CONTROL IN GENERATIVE GRAMMAR

The origins of the notion of control in generative grammar come from discussions of equi-NP deletion, a transformational rule in Chomsky's (1965) *Aspects* Model. In more recent work, the EQUI rule is labeled subject or object-control. In sentences such as 'John promised Mary to resign' (subject-control) and 'John persuaded Mary to resign' (object control), the empty category PRO in the lower clause is said to be controlled by the subject or object in the higher clause (Radford, 1992:323-4). What is being controlled in these sentences is the reference of PRO. The idea of control here is regulatory and abstract. It operates on grammatical categories, which are abstract, structural notions. In grammatical theory, processes are inferred from the relationships among structures.

CONTROL IN DEVELOPMENTAL PSYCHOLINGUISTICS: ANALYSIS AND CONTROL

Bialystok's (1978, 1990, 1994) model of second language processing includes a notion of control relevant to the present review. Drawing on the work of Schneider and Shiffrin (1977), who distinguish between automatic and controlled processing, she describes control as "the component of processing specialized for governing the attentional procedures necessary to performance" (1990:128). Two of the toughest concepts to get a handle on in language processing, fluency and intentionality, are referred to. High levels of control are said to "confer the impression of fluency or automaticity..." and to lead to intentional processing. More specifically, according to Bialystok, performance becomes intentional "when attention can be deliberately directed towards relevant information in the service of solving a problem" (p. 125). The defining feature of control in Bialystok's model is "selective attention." Comparing conversation, reading, and metalinguistic language tasks, she concludes that the language user "must direct attention to a specified portion of the available possibilities" (p. 126).

A variety of tasks are presented to illustrate the notion of control of attention: the Stroop task (Stroop, 1935; MacLeod, 1991), Piagetian tasks such as the sun/moon problem, the class-inclusion task, conservation tasks, and the embedded figures tasks (Piaget & Inhelder, 1966). In other work (e.g. Bialystok, 1988) judgment and correction of semantically anomalous sentences are considered to represent 'control of cognition.' In more recent work on early literacy, focusing attention on larger issues and monitoring of comprehension are seen as control-based strategies.

As should be apparent from the SPPL Model discussed in the previous chapter, I strongly agree with Bialystok's assessment of language use as a problem involving "multiple sources of information, both linguistic and non-linguistic." I disagree, however, with her focus on competitive aspects of attention in language processing, which is apparently what leads her to claim that "part of effective language processing is being able to attend to the required information without being distracted by irrelevant or misleading cues" (p. 125). That same perspective is reflected in the Piagetian data collection procedures, which impose unidimensional, forced choices on the child, not allowing an opportunity for more than a single stimulus dimension to contribute to the response (see Anderson & Cuneo, 1978, and Wolf, 1995, for a full critique of Piaget's methods).

Beyond the intentional and attentional aspects of control, Bialystok (1988, 1990) offers an innovative notion of 'switching.' In the context of reading, she states that the "ability to switch back and forth between forms and meanings, between graphemes and phonemes, between words and intentions, is a crucial part of fluent reading" (1988:562). Unfortunately, her notion of switching here, like her notion of control in general, is said to involve "Deliberately suspending the meanings..." Again, unidimensional processing is assumed. The child is presumed to be incapable of relating to more than a single piece of information. This view is further elaborated in her work on control-based communication strategies, where codeswitching is described as follows:

> ...communication is achieved by holding constant the initial intention but altering the means of reference. The predominant means of effecting this manipulation is through switching the language. In processing terms, the strategy is to switch attention away from the linguistic system being used and focus instead on some other symbolic reference system...The primary mechanism of control of processing is selective attention (1990:133).

The position taken in the present work gives more credit to the language user, in particular to allow for simultaneous processing of multiple sources of information, as laid out in the previous section on integrative processing. Codeswitching, according to this perspective, would involve processing both languages, or at least aspects of both languages, rather than selectively attending to one of them.

CONTROL AS TRADE OFF BETWEEN ACTIVATION AND INHIBITION

The construct of control in information processing comes from cybernetics (Weiner, 1950) and, in the most general sense, is conceived as "avoidance of error." Green (1986, 1993, 2000) has applied a version of this construct to bilingualism, focusing on lexical processing. Citing both slips of the tongue in normal language use and aphasic speech in brain-damaged patients as resulting from lack of control, Green's take on the nature of control in bilingualism is to address the question of how it is possible for bilinguals to speak one language while filtering out the other one. In Green's model, control operates at two levels of processing: during conceptualization and during formulation. During conceptualization it involves "explicit intention" to activate one language or the other; during formulation control involves activation and inhibition of lemmas and lexemes. An executive mechanism is assumed to be responsible for regulating activation levels in bilingual situations.

Like Bialystok, Green's (2000) notion of control is seen as the way to handle multi-tasking and is analogous to a Stroop task, involving selection from and competition between the lexical entries of the two languages of a bilingual. To handle multi-tasking and competition, functional control circuits are proposed to regulate activation and inhibition. See Chapter 2 for a review of the evidence Green marshals for these control circuits from experimental work on translation, codeswitching, Stroop effects, and cross-language competitive priming.

In Green's theory "the intention to perform a specific language task is expressed by means of the supervisory attentional system (SAS) affecting the activation of language task schemas which themselves compete to control output." These schemas coordinate into "functional circuits and exert control by activating and inhibiting tags at the lemma level...because the mechanism of inhibition is reactive, the activation of specific lemmas requires input either from an external source (hearing words or reading them) or from the conceptual system" (2000:14-15). To paraphrase, intentions serve as the input to an executive control mechanism, which activates competing language task schemas. The schemas exercise control over the output by regulating activation and inhibition of lemmas. The schemas perform this regulatory function by a process of "coordinat[ing] into functional circuits." The architecture for this process is depicted in Figure 4.2.

The details of this coordinating process and how the circuits operate are not specified in the model. But based on the statement that "inhibition is reactive," the circularity in the model's diagram is unclear. In fact, the question Green

Figure 4.2 Green's Model of *Inhibitory Control*

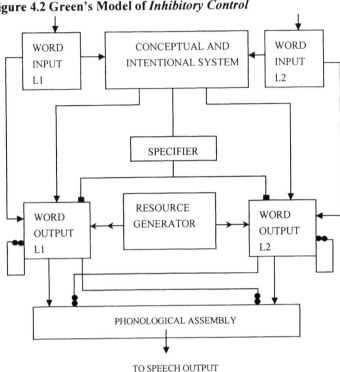

TO SPEECH OUTPUT

poses regarding language tags gives the impression that inhibition is more of a
stimulus-response, linear reaction to activation than the circular control loop of
classical control theory.

Given that a language tag is just one feature, how do we ensure that the
correct response controls speech output? The IC Model supposes that this is
ensured ultimately by suppressing lemmas with incorrect tags. This process of
inhibitory control through tag suppression occurs after lemmas linked to active
concepts have been activated...Inhibition is assumed to be reactive though
previous episodes of suppression may exert their effects since it takes time for
the effects of prior inhibition to be overcome. (Green, 2000)

Intentions are built into this model as input, stimulating and activating
language task schemas. The schemas are the core control construct in the model.
They perform the regulatory function, operating on activation and inhibition, in
order to inhibit one language and facilitate fluent speech in the other.

PERCEPTUAL CONTROL THEORY

Powers' Perceptual Control Theory (PCT) is the control perspective which
seems best at handling speaker intentions and accounting for sociopragmatic and

psycholinguistic information in a single framework. In general terms, PCT states that intentions and perceptions are kept stable by variable means. Behavior is not the end product of a linear chain beginning with a stimulus or set of stimuli, but rather, a means to control perception. Behavior is variable, not static or constant. Grounded in Jamesian psychology and in the maxim of 'consistent ends by variable means,' Perceptual Control Theory adopts the cybernetic notion of a negative feedback circuit as an operational model for living control systems in general and for human information processing in particular. Robertson and Powers (1990) described the model as follows:

> A feedback circuit is one in which some condition of a phenomenon is sensed or detected, and variations in its degree or magnitude are controlled by the system's mechanism, working to keep the sensed signal matched to a specific value or reference signal. The intensity or magnitude of the sensed signal is compared with the reference signal, and any mismatch is corrected as the output varies, however necessary, to drive the controlled condition back toward its reference state (p. 14, footnote 3).

This model is based on the same constructs and principles as the negative feedback mechanisms involved in temperature-regulated home heating systems and cruise control technology in large automobiles. It is not restricted to electromechanical applications. As recorded by Cziko (2000:74), a series of conferences in the United States in the late 1940s and early 1950s brought together leading scientists to discuss circular causality and negative feedback mechanisms. Those meetings considered applications of the basic model in communication and information theory, biology, and social and behavioral sciences. The importance of the model for information theory is well-known (Shannon & Weaver, 1949); its applications to human physiology include body temperature and weight, calcium levels, and acidity, gaseousness, and pressure in blood (Mrosovsky, 1990). Human behavior was to wait for Powers' (1973) explication of a model of behavior based on control.

Cziko (2000:71-73) defines control as "maintaining some variable at or near a specified fixed value or pattern of values despite disturbances" (p. 72). He reviews four basic characteristics of control systems.

- ❑ "…although…control systems…compensate for…disturbances …they need not perceive the disturbances themselves."
- ❑ "a control system does not control what it does. Rather, it controls what it senses," in other words, what it perceives.
- ❑ "…whereas…behavior is clearly influenced by…environment, it is not determined solely by…environment. Rather…behavior is determined by what it (control system) senses/perceives of the environment in comparison with its goal or reference level."
- ❑ "…control systems behave in a clearly purposeful manner, varying behavior as necessary in the face of unprecedented disturbances to

control some perceived variable…This is not achieved by some
future state having present effects, but by having a goal state
(reference level), comparing it with current conditions (perception),
and acting on the difference (error) until it disappears or is made
very small."

According to Cziko (2000:71), the main difference between
mechanical/engineered control systems and those of humans is that the reference
levels (goals, purposes, intentions) for humans "originate somewhere inside the
brain" and therefore, are "not subject to direct environmental control." This is a
direct rejection of the view that holds that behavior is caused by external stimuli
in a linear stimulus-response chain.

A role for intentions. PCT calls for a reversal of the equation in conventional
psychology, be it behaviorist or cognitivist, connectionist or symbolic
representationist. In those camps, behavior is the endpoint (the so-called
dependent variable) in a linear chain, beginning with a stimulus (or a set of
stimuli), acted on or processed by the organism (in the case of humans, by the
brain-mind), and leading to a behavioral response. In these approaches, the
human is passive and assumed to be controlled by the environment, by the
stimuli. In PCT, behavior is the way to control perception. Intentions, goals, and
purposes are reference signals in the above model (Robertson & Powers, 1990:
3). They come from within the mind of the individual. They are compared with
the individual's perceptions. And behavior is the way that variation between
intentions and perceptions is brought under control.

Bilingualism in PCT

PCT offers a unitary mechanism based on control systems to handle a variety
of levels of language processing. While identity and fluency do not fit neatly
into a single one of PCT's levels of perception, sociopragmatics/identity clearly
belongs in the upper levels of the hierarchy and psycholinguistics/fluency in the
lower levels. In this way the PCT hierarchy, like the SPPL Model, can
distinguish between intentional codeswitching for the purpose of identity and
'performance' codeswitching carried out to maintain fluency. It does so with a
single control mechanism.

Another question regarding the relevance of PCT to the study of
codeswitching is whether it can offer an empirical approach derived from the
theoretical constructs of the model. The basic methodological approach is to try
to identify the individual's internal standard or reference signal, and then to
change something in the environment and see if the individual acts to maintain
the environment according to their standard or reference signal. This is called
"testing for the controlled variable." Two examples of how to test for controlled
variables in codeswitching are offered, one related to sociopragmatic issues and
one to psycholinguistic concerns.

In the sociopragmatic domain, in the literature on bilingualism and identity, the methods tend to be more qualitative and descriptive, e.g. ethnography, sociolinguistic interviewing, social networks. PCT calls for a more hypothetico-deductive approach: guessing at the variable, predicting the results of not maintaining the reference level, applying disturbances to the variable, measuring the effects of these disturbances, and attempting to identify the variable under control (Runkel, 1990). Following Runkel's outline:

1. We first *select a variable* for which a bilingual individual has a particular reference level. For this step, we choose bilingual codeswitching (CS), and distinguish between program or principle level CS on the one hand and event or category level CS on the other. We quantify this input variable as high L2-to-L1 codeswitching and low to moderate L1-to-L2 codeswitching. These settings are an attempt to characterize someone maintaining a strong level of native identity, while still attempting to maintain a moderate level of second language identity and a moderate level of fluency.

2. Next we *predict* what might happen if the person does not maintain the reference level (high L2-to-L1 and low to moderate L1-to-L2 codeswitching). In the present example, failing to maintain the intended levels of codeswitching may bring about an increase in the amount of each type of codeswitching and an increase in the relative amount in each direction. It may also lead to higher level results, including anomie, a decision to emigrate, closing oneself off in a native language enclave, or a decision to change the reference level of the variable.

3. The next step is to "Apply various amounts and directions of disturbance directly to the variable" (Runkel, p. 118). These disturbances can take the form of a direct expression of negative attitudes to codeswitching, or more subtle diversion, like a simple lack of codeswitching by an interlocutor in a setting or for a topic where it would be likely to occur. Another way to influence the codeswitching variable would be to find a way (artificially or naturally) to get the individual bilingual to speed up the rate of speech.

4. Measurement of the effects of the disturbances. Both qualitative and quantitative measures are desirable. They may include written records of observations, audio or video tape recordings, and analysis of the amount and type of codeswitching that occurs, before and after disturbances are applied.

5. Identifying the variable.
   a. If the bilingual person is "controlling for" codeswitching, and the disturbances introduced do not lead to any measurable differences in codeswitching, then we have selected the wrong variable.

b. If the effects of the disturbance are minor (less important than predicted), we then need to look at what the bilingual does to "oppose the disturbance." For example, regarding sociopragmatic aspects of codeswitching, does she/he refute, reject, or contradict the interlocutor's claims about codeswitching? Regarding speech fluency, does the bilingual individual use codeswitching as a way to increase speech rate or avoid dysfluencies? In other words, is CS used to influence (control) perception of identity and fluency?

c. Another approach to help identify the variable is to find the way the bilingual "senses" codeswitching and to "block" the means to sense the phenomenon. One way to do this has been to present codeswitched texts to be read and recalled. Berkowitz (1976) showed that subjects, when presented with these kinds of materials and asked to perform a comprehension task, attend to the content and not to the language. Playing around with the rate of input and hesitation phenomena may be another way to block a bilingual speaker's "sensors" for codeswitching.

This is no doubt a simplification of a very complex procedure, a far cry from more conventional methods in the study of bilingualism. Nevertheless, the potential insight of this theory and its accompanying method offer a fresh approach to the study of control processes in bilingualism.

A Perceptual Control Theory approach to codeswitching would claim that CS is a "variable means to achieve consistent ends" regarding maintenance of identity and fluency. In this view, codeswitching is a continuous, not a categorical variable. Thus, language contact phenomena such as interference, codeswitching, borrowing, etc. can be seen along a variable continuum of behavior. PCT sees this continuum as a hierarchical network of negative feedback loops. Within each loop, reference levels of identity and fluency (the speaker's goals or intentions) are compared to sensory, or perceived, levels of these phenomena. If the two (the reference and perceptual levels of identity/fluency) are not in relative equilibrium, and codeswitching is in fact a behavior the speaker is using to control identity and fluency, then the speaker will increase that behavior in the direction and in the quantity that will oppose the disturbance which is creating the instability. If the disturbance persists and the speaker cannot bring it into line, it is possible that he/she will change the reference level. In this way, PCT brings together goals and intentions (regarding identity and fluency), perception, and behavior (codeswitching) in a unified theory whose method is derived directly from its constructs.

CHAPTER SUMMARY

This chapter has discussed four processing mechanisms deemed relevant for bilingualism, and shown how these mechanisms operate within the SPPL Model.

The detailed script describing "movement" between the information boxes of the SPPL Model was intended to show how the model accounts for process, and to create a reference map for discussion of bilingual processing. Four processing mechanisms—imitation, variation, integration and control—were discussed.

Imitation was shown to be a linguistic and cognitive mechanism, likely to involve multiple levels of processing, perhaps even hierarchically organized. The imitative aspects of pronunciation/accent, name preferences, greetings, and codeswitching at all linguistic levels highlighted the importance of this mechanism and its constituent processes for the study of bilingualism. The section on imitation ends with a description of its role in processing information about social identity, in converting intentions to speech acts, and in lexical aspects of formulation.

The *variation* mechanism was motivated by comparison to research in other disciplines. Three approaches to variation were described. One was drawn from variationist sociolinguistics and corpus analysis; it saw variation as rooted in linguistic form. A second approach took from my own work in micro-sociolinguistics and focused on pragmatic variation, i.e. the range of contexts a speaker is able to function in. A third approach described the notion of variation in Perceptual Control Theory (Powers, 1973), focusing particularly on how intentions are kept stable by variable means. The section concludes with a look at variation in bilingual phenomena, especially codeswitching.

Imitation and variation are grounded in more basic level processes, with recognition and recall for integration, and discrimination and classification for variation. Integration and control, on the other hand, are executive mechanisms.

For the *integration* mechanism, I used Anderson's Information Integration Theory, illustrating its usefulness for investigating the processing of both social and linguistic information. On the social side, findings are presented from person perception studies on the role of name use, accent, and occupation in the absorption and integration of immigrants. On the linguistic side, two types of studies are presented to illustrate the integration mechanism. One type shows the relative contribution of first and second language lexical information in the comprehension of an unfamiliar idiom. The other type focuses on how two languages are integrated in codeswitched utterances. The section concludes with a discussion of processing aspects of integration in codeswitching.

In the last section I discussed four types of *control*. In grammatical theory control is an abstract notion. It operates on grammatical categories. In this view, process is inferred from structure. Bialystok's control concept is taken from the literature on the psychology of attention. Her tasks involving metalinguistic judgments and correction of semantically anomalous sentences are characterized as involving 'control of cognition.' These, and her more recent application of control to literacy and comprehension monitoring, show the executive nature of control mechanisms. Green's notion of control comes from cybernetics. It is an attempt to account for how bilingualism, particularly at the lexical level of processing, inhibits the use of one language and activates the other. Control also deals with multi-tasking. In Green's model, language task schemas are organized into "functional circuits" which exercise control by activating and inhibiting language specific tags on lemmas. Thus, control serves an executive, regulatory function. The relationship between inhibition and activation in this model is more linear and reactive. This view stands in contrast to the circular causation of classical cybernetics and Perceptual Control Theory (PCT), the fourth approach to control discussed.

Perceptual Control Theory is introduced as a processing model to handle the control aspects of bilingualism. First, I presented a brief history of the origins and development of the model, highlighting the centrality of intentionality and explaining the nature of its negative feedback mechanism. Next, I conducted a Perceptual Control Theory analysis of bilingual codeswitching behavior for both sociopragmatically and psycholinguistically motivated codeswitching. A discussion of the hierarchical nature of language behavior followed. The section ends with a discussion of the compatibility of PCT methods for the study of bilingualism.

The next chapter returns to the issues introduced at the outset of this work—codeswitching and interference, translation and interpretation, computation, and cursing—in an attempt to show how the structural and processing components of the proposed SPPL Model account for these phenomena.

NOTES

---

[1] See Duranti (1993:224) for an anthropologist's view of creativity.

[2] Since thinking and speaking are highly complicated affairs, two-dimensional representations of processing, even Jackendoff's (2001) use of curvilinear arrows, do not fully capture the dynamic nature of linguistic processing. To describe this complex set of processes in a database form, one would probably need a relational or object-oriented database; a hierarchical database could not do the job. This is the direction I would take to get to a computational implementation of the SPPL Model.

5 Accounting for Bilingual Phenomena with the SPPL Model

I began this inquiry by identifying a number of phenomena that show evidence of being processed uniquely among bilingual speakers. These were: *codeswitching* and *interference, translation* and *interpretation, computation* and *cursing*. The first four phenomena are unique to bilingualism, and the latter two are processed uniquely by bilinguals. In this chapter, I will summarize the main issues related to these phenomena, and describe them with the functional architecture and processing mechanisms presented in the previous two chapters.

This chapter should be seen as a first step in meeting the challenge set out by Poulisse (1997, 1999) to account for incompleteness, dysfluency, and codeswitching in bilingual production. The functional architecture presented in Chapter 3 identifies the locus of these phenomena, while the processing mechanisms spelled out in Chapter 4 explain how these phenomena operate.

When data exist, they will be cited. When there are not enough data, and unfortunately that is true in too many cases, I will suggest possible research avenues that would yield what I would describe as valid data. Along the way, other issues raised in the literature will be referred to, sometimes incorporated in the current account, and other times left as unaccountable at present.

First, a brief reminder. I described codeswitching as both a sociopragmatic and psycholinguistic phenomenon, and compared it on the one hand with register and style switching, which I defined as exclusively sociopragmatic, and, on the other hand, with interference, which was described in psycholinguistic terms. Translation has been investigated primarily as a linguistic phenomenon, but, as will be seen below, there are those who have begun to take an interest in the cognitive, communicative, and sociopragmatic questions in translation and interpretation. Computation and cursing have not been treated widely up to now in the field of bilingualism; they are discussed here, not for their inherent connection to bilingualism, but for the unique way they interact with two languages.

CODESWITCHING AND INTERFERENCE IN SPPL

Codeswitching and interference have been presented throughout this work as different kinds of language contact. In order to make this argument, several issues were raised. The initial and perhaps primary concern is the underlying motivation for these phenomena. In this connection, the SPPL Model distinguishes between sociopragmatic and psycholinguistic motivations. Within this framework, codeswitching was said to be motivated socially, by the aspects of *identity* the bilingual brings to the speech event and by the *contextual* parameters of the interaction like setting, topic, and participants. Codeswitching was also shown to be structurally and psycholinguistically motivated by lexico-semantic features of the two languages as they come into contact (e.g. lexicalization differences) and/or irregularities in *formulation* and fluency, in particular lexical access. Interference was described as a subclass of language contact phenomena, a reflection of linguistic structure and performance.

A second issue raised was the directionality of codeswitching, from L1 to L2 and from L2 to L1. Here, too, the SPPL Model's sociopragmatic/psycho-linguistic distinction was useful. Finally, these issues are related to the more difficult problem of how to get at veridical data about a speaker's *intentions*. I could not offer a unitary, convincing solution to this problem, but did suggest two potentially valuable research strategies–investigations of speech acts and pragmatic markers. The present section offers a synthesis of my treatment of language contact and an account of codeswitching according to the terms of the SPPL Model and its accompanying processing mechanisms.

Codeswitching has been shown to implicate a complex of social, structural, and psycholinguistic issues. The most fundamental distinction is between intentional and 'performance-based' codeswitching. In the SPPL Model, intentional codeswitching, motivated by internal as well as external considerations, is grounded in social identity, conversational context, genre, and speech act information. This is codeswitching meant to express one's ethnolinguistic identity, to bond with a listener, or to show awareness and cognizance of a particular setting, listener, or topic. The description of performance codeswitching, due to difficulties in lexical access or lexicalization differences and/or competing morphosyntactic constraints, is grounded in the formulation and articulation structures and processes.

SOCIAL AND PRAGMATIC ASPECTS OF CODESWITCHING

On the intentional side of the phenomenon, it may be instructive to reexamine Jake and Myers-Scotton's (2000) comparison of first and second generation Arabic-English codeswitching. Their not-so-surprising finding was that first generation speakers used more monolingual Arabic utterances (actually the unit of measurement was the complement phrase) and more Arabic matrix language utterances, while second generation speakers used more monolingual English and English matrix language utterances. But there was an additional interesting difference between the two generations: For utterances where a matrix language could not be pinned down, they proposed a category called the 'composite matrix language.' All instances in this class (38 out of a total of 1591 codeswitches) were produced by second-generation speakers. From Jake and Myers-Scotton's (2000) data, we know quite a lot about the syntactic patterning across the two generations. For example, among embedded language constituents in Arabic matrix language utterances, more examples of noun embedding were found in the data of second-generation immigrants, but more instances of an embedded adjective/adverb, verb, and INFL phrase were reported for first generation immigrants. We also know some general things about Arabic language maintenance, and about social and ethnolinguistic identity. Among these, the authors mention the international status of Arabic, its political and economic importance in the Middle East and North Africa, and its prestige as the language of Islam. And from the fact that the first generation informants in the study were immigrants, we are told that they "identify strongly with their experience as political refugees." In the SPPL Model, all of this information serves as input to the initial component, resulting in the identity the bilingual speaker brings to the interaction.

Jake and Myers-Scotton make a general assessment of identity from these sources of information, and then correlate this information with codeswitching data. They conclude that the type of codeswitching of their first generation immigrants shows "that they feel very comfortable with a dual identity" (p. 19), while the second generation immigrants in their study "are more oriented toward the identity symbolized by the use of English..." Two types of evidence are cited to support the generalization about second-generation speakers: the overall prevalence of English in their speech, even in bilingual interaction, and a greater tendency to merge the two languages into composite matrix language forms. Identity is read directly from language use, in this case codeswitching. What is missing here is micro-sociolinguistic information about setting, topic, and participants. Such information would help clarify a bilingual's specific intentions when codeswitching, thus complementing more macro-sociolinguistic information such as the prestige of Arabic and sociological group factors such as the generation to which the speakers belonged.

Grosjean's laboratory approach and Auer's field-based methods help fill this gap, adding an interpersonal level of analysis to the macro-social aspects of codeswitching. As discussed in Chapter 2, Grosjean (1997) investigated the role of *setting/topic* and *listener* information by having subjects retell stories about uniquely French places and events and about American places and events. The participants were asked to direct their narratives to different imaginary listeners, one a new French immigrant to the U.S., one a French-dominant resident of the U.S., and the third a French-English bilingual. As summarized in Chapter 2, the original stories were presented in French in the case of French events, and using French with English codeswitching in the case of American events. Results showed that both topic and listener influenced the amount of codeswitching: American topics and bilingual listeners generated more codeswitching than French topics and new immigrant listeners. The experimental conditions set out the parameters to which the bilingual subject was asked to direct his or her attention. Thus, the methodology is able to tap into speaker intentions, and be reasonably assured that the codeswitching elicited is intentional.

Two of Auer's (1995) patterns of codeswitching capture the same kind of interpersonal information via the structural tools of conversational analysis. In

Auer's Pattern I, "discourse-related" codeswitching, the language switch from speaker to speaker or within a speaking turn indicates a shift in participants, events, or topic. Pattern II, labeled "language negotiation" and "preference-related" switching, adds a dimension to the discussion here. It moves from a speaker-centered approach to codeswitching, where the setting, topic, and listener are objectified, to a more balanced approach involving negotiations between speaker and listener. These patterns are structural descriptions of bilingual interaction. They are influenced, and perhaps governed, by social and contextual factors. But such factors do not fully determine the patterns.

Auer's (1995) claim that social factors "underspecify language choice," Heller's (1988) notion of "strategic ambiguity," and Reynolds and Akram's (1998) "sustained divergence" all raise the question as to whether codeswitching phenomena, at least some codeswitching phenomena, may be a deliberate, perhaps unconscious, attempt to negotiate social relations and meaning via language choice. The SPPL Model accommodates this range of possibilities by making language choice information available to all the processing components, from identity to articulation. Thus, a bilingual speaker can make language choices before coming to an actual setting, while interacting with a specific listener, and engaging in a particular topic, or she can keep her options open up to, and including, the moment of articulation.

STRUCTURAL AND PSYCHOLINGUISTIC ASPECTS OF CODESWITCHING

When codeswitching is a performance issue, a further distinction may help clarify the ground. This is the distinction between L1 to L2 codeswitching and switching in the other direction, i.e. from L2 to L1. *Directionality* has only recently been addressed systematically in psycholinguistic and sociolinguistic studies of codeswitching (e.g. Francis, Tokowicz & Kroll, 2003; Zentella, 1997). This is somewhat surprising, given that in training programs for translators and interpreters, it has long been common practice for professionals to work from their weaker into their stronger language. The classic sociolinguistic position is that switching into the native language strengthens indigenous language maintenance identity, while switching into the non-native language, especially when that language is English, is meant to assert power and authority (Valdes, 1981; Zentella, 1997). But, other hypotheses are possible. It would also be plausible to assume that switching from a weaker to a stronger language, from a second to a primary language, is more likely for reasons of lexical access and other processing phenomena, while switching from L1 to L2 may be more prompted by interaction, by micro-sociolinguistic factors. It should be noted that this working hypothesis is not symmetrical, and the psycholinguistic part may be more plausible than the sociolinguistic one.

In the SPPL Model of bilingualism, an understanding of 'performance' codeswitching is found by using the processes underlying formulation and articulation. Intentional, socially-motivated codeswitching is explained by the identity, contextual, and pragmatic aspects of bilingual production. L2 to L1 codeswitching should reflect more evidence of dysfluency, in the form of accompanying hesitation phenomena, than L1 to L2 switching, which may be marked by other pragmatic and sociolinguistic phenomena. Here Poplack and Sankoff's (1988) notion of flagging is relevant, and directionality might help clarify some of the issues and controversy surrounding the notions borrowing and codeswitching. These factors can be built into the design of a study; they are measurable, and worthy of research.

Clyne's notion of *triggering* may also be useful for addressing some of the issues raised here. An exploratory study of triggering (Baumel & Walters, ms) has looked at several structural issues in codeswitching. University students (n=19) whose native languages were Hebrew, English, and Russian were asked to make metalinguistic judgments about the likelihood that codeswitched sentences would be heard. The stimulus set consisted of 24 sentences manipulated along five axes:

1. The initial language of the sentence (Hebrew/English)
2. The language of the trigger word (Hebrew/English)
3. Whether the trigger word was a true or false cognate
4. The presence of an infinitive as a trigger
5. The locus of the codeswitch (before, at, or after the trigger word)

Due to the exploratory nature of the study and the individual variation across small numbers of subjects from each native language group, only two findings are worthy of note here. One is the overall preference for Hebrew, the dominant language of social interaction in Israel, as the "triggering" language. The other is that, with regard to the locus of the codeswitch, subjects generally preferred sentences where the switch occurred *at* or *after* the trigger word. This latter result, if corroborated (and further research is certainly needed involving behavioral data with examples of actual codeswitching), would mitigate Clyne's proposal that triggering is indicative of an anticipatory process. In fact, we might then have to look at triggering as a reflection of psycholinguistic processes rather than a cause of them.

When examining the processing mechanisms involved in triggering, I would distinguish between text-based features of triggering and mental operations. Linguistic, text-based characteristics of triggering include a notion of similarity, equivalence, or congruence, based on likeness in orthographic, phonological, and semantic form. Mental operations in triggering are bottom up, whereby lexical items, in particular cognates, jog the language production mechanism.

Another construct that may shed light on some of the psycholinguistic aspects of codeswitching is the distinction between horizontal and vertical processing. That distinction can be illustrated by comparing bilingual and monolingual dictionaries (see Walters & Wolf, 1992, and the references there for a fuller discussion). A good deal of translation involves the kind of analogic, horizontal processing one finds in bilingual dictionaries. Monolingual dictionaries, on the other hand, use more vertical processing. Entries are superordinate terms or examples, going from a specific case to a more general category or vice versa.

Codeswitching, especially in its mimetic aspects described in the previous chapter, certainly involves horizontal processing. But the fact that it can also involve multiple levels of processing (like syntax, semantics, pragmatics) means that the bilingual must be able to maneuver among vertical levels. Reflecting this (and other factors as well, of course), the information components in the SPPL Model are stacked vertically, from identity down to articulation. Codeswitching, then, entails both horizontal and vertical processing. Horizontally, it involves cross-language mimesis and variation, copying and substitution. Vertically, codeswitching involves processing at every level of production and a need to gain entry to the information processed by the model.

PROCESSING MECHANISMS IN BILINGUAL CODESWITCHING

In terms of the functional architecture involved in processing deliberate, L1-to-L2 codeswitching, information is drawn primarily from the identity and contextual components. On the other hand, performance codeswitching and language contact resulting in structural interference are generated mainly during the formulation and articulation stages of production.

The processing mechanisms underlying both kinds of language contact are the same: imitation and variation, integration and control. Deliberate, L1-to-L2 codeswitching is accomplished by taking relevant social identity and contextual (setting, topic, and participant) information and applying it to a speaker's intentions. That information is largely copied. When the speaker also intends to codeswitch (for ethnic solidarity, pragmatic focus or other sociopragmatic reasons), the copying mechanism gives way to variation (usually in the speech act component), permitting access to the language choice module and entry of the L2 word or expression. That word or expression will then show up as an L2 lexical word or phrase in the formulator. The transition from processing via imitation to processing via variation results in a switch from L1 to L2, and may be marked in ways other than the language switch. There may be signs of dysfluency, like pauses, self-corrections and the like, and pragmatic fluency markers can also mark this transition. These may appear at the speech act level of processing, as shown in Chapter 3.

When the switch is phrase or utterance-internal, or in unusual cases, such as fusion or compromise forms when the switch is word-internal, integration processes take central stage in the analysis. We are talking here about two kinds of integration.

One involves the integration of information, the set of processes that combines first and second language structural features to yield codeswitched forms. The features integrated in bilingual codeswitching cover the full range of information, from identity, attitudes, and context to lexical and discourse pragmatics and segmental, syllabic, and tonal phonemes. These information sources, according to Information Integration Theory (Anderson, 1996), are assigned subjective values and are then integrated with information from other sources. Thus, a structurally based kind of integration operates on information about identity, context, intentions, lexico-pragmatic concepts, etc. as well as on the language information that goes into these.

The second kind of integration involved in codeswitching involves integration of processes. Basic level processes such as discrimination, recognition, identification, classification, and categorization were defined and discussed in Chapter 4. Recognition was related to search strategies, and identification connect to retrieval. Both rely primarily on processes of imitation and mimesis. Discrimination, classification, and categorization were explained in terms of storage and 'language' marking or language tagging. These rely more on variation than on imitation. The integration mechanism valuates each basic level process that is being used, weighing the importance of recognition, identification, discrimination, classification, and categorization, and then, generating either L1, L2, or codeswitched utterances.

In discussing the last of the four processing mechanisms, control, I attempted dialogue with Green's (2000) notion of inhibitory control, but ended up by offering a more orthodox view of the construct in terms of Perceptual Control Theory (Powers, 1973; Cziko, 2000). In Green's model, control was proposed to handle multi-tasking and competition, both of which are important aspects of codeswitching. In that model, functional control circuits regulate the relationship between activation and inhibition. Control finds expression during both the conceptualization and formulation stages of processing. For conceptualization, control is described in terms of intentions to activate one or more language. Thus, during formulation, both activation and inhibition (of lemmas and lexemes) are said to be involved. To summarize, intentions are seen as responsible for activating competing language task schemas. These schemas are then organized into "functional control circuits" in order to control output, which they do by regulating activation and inhibition of lemmas.

At the outset, I had envisioned a similar kind of control mechanism to regulate and coordinate processes of imitation and variation. At that stage of thinking, I viewed imitation and variation as mechanisms in the service of goals and intentions, in particular the goals of accuracy and fluency. A closer look at the origins of the control construct and its instantiation in PCT led me to question the 'reactive' nature of inhibition in Green's model, and my own view of the relationship between imitation and variation. Thus, while intentions may be what initiate activation in Green's model, they are not built into the mechanism of control in the same integral way they are in PCT. Rather, they simply stimulate and activate language task schemas. And the schemas are the central functional units in the model. They perform the regulatory function, coordinate activation and inhibition while inhibiting the lemmas of one language and facilitating those of the other.

In a PCT view of control, intentions are systematically connected to perceptions. More generally, behavior is the way to control perceptions (Powers, 1973). In particular, intentions and perceptions are synchronized and balanced by a hierarchical set of negative feedback loops. Behavior is a variable means to achieve consistent ends (James, 1890). In terms of this discussion, codeswitching is a means to accomplish two different purposes: to express identity and to maintain fluency. Within the identity loop, the bilingual speaker specifies a particular level of identity and compares it to his/her perceived level of identity. If intentions and perceptions are not relatively balanced, and codeswitching is one of the behaviors used to control identity, then the speaker increases or decreases the use of codeswitching in order to maintain stability and to avoid disturbances. A classic example is a politician feeling a not-too-warm response from a bilingual immigrant crowd, and then using more words from the immigrant language to express her identification with the potential voters.

In most situations, stronger L1 identity should lead to more codeswitching, while stronger convergence to the target culture should lead to less codeswitching. Speakers who set high goals for maintaining both languages and high standards of fluency should also tend to use codeswitching to maintain the intended level of fluency. Other means available to bilingual speakers to control perceptions of identity and fluency are to choose or avoid settings, topics, and conversational partners where codeswitching will promote the speakers' standards of identity and fluency. If the bilingual speaker detects a lack of equilibrium between the intended and perceived levels of identity and/or fluency and that instability persists, the reference levels for the 'controlled' variables (identity and fluency) may be modified. In this way, PCT offers an integrated model for combining intentions and perceptions of identity and fluency with behavior (codeswitching).

INTERFERENCE AND FLUENCY IN BILINGUAL PROCESSING

Not much has been said about interference so far, other than to declare that it belongs to the same class of language contact phenomena as codeswitching. In this sense, interference is also multidimensional, encompassing linguistic, psycholinguistic, and sociopragmatic features. This view transforms the construct radically from the structural, behaviorist view of linguistic interference of the 1950s (e.g. Fries, 1945; Lado, 1957) and even moves it beyond later cognitive modifications (see Walters & Wolf, 1992 for a review).[1]

Related psychological and psycholinguistic research on bilingualism includes notions such as *inhibition* and *suppression*. These constructs are attempts to get at basic psychological processes, not just language processes and those related to bilingualism.

Raising the issue of interference here means that we have to wrestle with questions of *fluency*, *automaticity*, and *completeness*, all of which are relatively underdeveloped topics in the context of bilingualism research, but all of which are nevertheless crucial to a comprehensive model of bilingual processing.[2] As an entry point to these constructs, we can draw on the fundamental distinction made in the present work between structure and process. Incompleteness, in this light, can be seen as a structural phenomenon. The products of second language use are incomplete because the phonological, lexical, syntactic, semantic and pragmatic representations are incomplete, or in Poulisse's (1999) terminology, due to "an incomplete knowledge base." Fluency and automaticity, on the other hand, are processing terms. These constructs can be viewed both as the products or reflection of completeness or incompleteness and/or as explanations for them. As reflections of incompleteness, fluency and automaticity become sources of data about language contact. As explanations for incompleteness, they need to be given operational definitions and subjected to systematic study.

Fluency has been investigated in a number of ways in bilingualism and second language studies, both in spontaneously generated natural settings, and experimentally induced under laboratory conditions. Fluency phenomena include: speech errors (Poulisse, 1999; Baars, 1992), length of utterance (Blum-Kulka & Olshtain, 1986), self-corrections/falsestarts/repetitions (Walters, 1980), rate of speech (Cook, 1997; Shlesinger, 2000), pauses/hesitations (Goldman-Eisler, 1972), and tip-of-the-tongue state (Gollan & Silverberg, 2001). None of these studies have looked at fluency phenomena in conjunction with codeswitching and interference. An investigation where data collection involves both spontaneous speech and experimental procedures would help clarify how fluency interacts with bilingualism. Acoustic-based speech analyses would be useful in the interpretation of spontaneous speech data. Elicited imitation and story retelling where the stimulus materials are designed to target pragmatic as well as syntactic and semantic features would also be useful.

Fluency and automaticity can be distinguished as follows: Fluency can be seen as a linguistically-defined construct,[3] while automaticity is a more general psychological process that cuts across all perceptual and cognitive domains, and as such will not be treated here. Imitation, variation, integration, and control, the mechanisms proposed in Chapter 4 as core constructs of bilingual processing, can be used here to make the link between bilingual phenomena such as codeswitching/interference and more general linguistic processes like fluency. Along these lines, dysfluency can occur when:

❑   information from the two languages has not been accurately or appropriately copied from memory (perhaps due to deficiencies in storage, search, or retrieval)

❑   there are inadequate or inappropriate use of the imitation and/or variation mechanisms (e.g. underuse, overuse, inappropriate use)

❑   imitation and variation are out of balance, i.e. when the control
mechanism indicates disturbances (e.g. unstable relations between
intentions and perceptions)

All of these processes could, perhaps even will, lead to incompleteness,
which can manifest itself as pauses, false starts, repetition, the use of pragmatic
markers as space fillers, lexical inventions, and a host of other codeswitching
and interference phenomena, all of which are surface reflections of language
contact. In terms of the processing mechanisms in the SPPL Model, underuse,
overuse, or an imbalance of imitation and variation can lead to incomplete
representations. As stated earlier, bilingual speakers' lemmas are not full-scale
OED (Oxford English Dictionary) entries. Rather, they are potentially
'incomplete'–phonologically, syntactically, semantically, and pragmatically.
The notion of incompleteness is a problem for static, monolingual models of
language production, but not for the approach presented here. In the SPPL
Model, incompleteness and dysfluency and the processing mechanisms
underlying them are tools for attaining deeper insight into bilingual phenomena
such as codeswitching and interference. As a sideline that has been raised
several times previously in this book, bilinguals as people are usually more
aware of their mistakes and difficulties in speech products than monoglots.
Likewise, research on bilingualism is deeply focused on the fault lines of speech
production. This focus on so-called problems can gratuitously shed light on
linguistic models whose often unexamined assumptions about completeness can
hold as much water as the fallacy of "correct speech."

Two additional observations about bilingual speakers relevant to interference
and fluency are *size of lexicon* and *rate of speech*. Apart from their interaction
with codeswitching, these phenomena are fairly easy to assess, and as such,
should be more prominent in bilingual research than they are at present. In the
terminology advanced here, vocabulary size is more closely related to structure,
and rate of speech is a construct closer to processing. Both contribute to fluency.

Lambert and Tucker, in their classic studies of bilingual immersion programs
in Quebec, reported that children educated bilingually did not attain vocabulary
levels commensurate with those of monolingual peers (see also Schaerlaekens,
Zink, & Verheyden, 1995). This observation, one likely to be confirmed in
children raised bilingually from birth, would be another piece of evidence
arguing for a model of bilingualism which is not just an add-on or a clone of a
monolingual model. A comparison between bilinguals and monolinguals is not
likely to lead to a deeper understanding of bilingualism per se, and it may lead to
a methodological dead end. Actually, the history of research on bilingualism and
cognitive development, from Darcy's (1953) review portraying bilinguals as
'retarded,' to Peal and Lambert's (1962) equally unreasonable implication that
bilinguals are more intellectually endowed, is a horse-race metaphor with no
finish line. The variance between subjects, even in studies where subjects are
matched one for one, cannot be brought under proper experimental control. The

appropriate comparison in bilingualism is a within-subject comparison, where the stimuli, tasks, and conditions can be experimentally manipulated.

Laboratory studies of bilinguals (de Groot & Kroll, 1997; de Bot & Schreuder, 1993) and simultaneous interpreters (Shlesinger, 2000) maintain that bilinguals speak slower than monolinguals in both of their languages. Here the point is the same. Until there is a baseline rate of speech for the individual, comparisons of bilinguals and monolinguals are not likely to offer much insight into either the nature of the bilingual representational system or the processes that underlie it.

Incompleteness and fluency have been presented here as reflections of structure and processing. Incompleteness can be observed in the VOTs of bilinguals' phonetic representations, in their imprecise argument structure, in their lexical malapropisms, and in the structure of their overall lexicon. Dysfluency is manifest as hesitations, pauses, false starts, repetitions, and slow rate of speech. A structural view of language production would see incompleteness as the causal origin of dysfluency phenomena. The approach recommended here is that the complex relationship between incompleteness and dysfluency, between representation and retrieval, between structure and processing, be investigated on a single platform.

INTERPRETATION AND TRANSLATION

There have been surprisingly few systematic and scientific studies of interpretation and translation (Shlesinger, 2000), particularly in the fields of applied linguistics and psycholinguistics. One reason for this neglect may be due to the respective biases in these fields. Translation studies were predisposed historically toward written language and much of the rest of linguistics was biased in favor of spoken language. Another reason for this neglect may be that early programmatic work in bilingualism and second language learning labeled translation a "special skill," not related to supposedly 'normal' processes of second language acquisition. We may be able to rehabilitate the notion of the special nature of translation in more current terminology by looking at interpreters/translators and ordinary bilinguals as experts and novices, respectively. A further reason for neglect of this phenomenon might be that the strong professional orientation of the field and the desire to find better ways of training interpreters and translators may have blocked or delayed investigation of more theoretically and empirically challenging questions. A fourth reason may be the sheer complexity of the phenomenon–involving hidden social agendas, non-explicit pragmatic considerations, unbridgeable cross-linguistic gaps, and awesome memory and time demands.

More recently, cognitive psychology has taken an interest in some of the processing aspects of simultaneous translation (e.g. Gernsbacher & Shlesinger,

1997; Massaro & Shlesinger, 1997). And translation theory itself has attempted to place communicative, social psychological, and interactive aspects of the phenomenon on the research agenda. Wadensjo's (1998) interactive, discourse-oriented approach attempts to balance a field that she claims has been dominated by normativity and prescriptivism, a discipline oriented to developing strategies for training professionals and focused on accuracy and adequacy. She does acknowledge more communicative approaches in modern translation theory (Roy, 1999; Toury, 1995) and a growing body of literature on cognitive processing in translation, but she herself opts for an examination of what she calls "the social order of real-life interpreter mediated conversations" (p. 5).

Interpretation and translation are not viewed here as a single, unified discipline. The existence of the two terms provides prima facie evidence for the need to elaborate on the two constructs and to describe their differences. But the two constructs *are* related–sociopragmatically, linguistically, and cognitively. Both involve a complex, multidimensional set of skills, where the interpreter/translator is called upon to process information on several levels (some simultaneously and some sequentially) under conditions of heavy cognitive demand, i.e. dense information input, restricted time to perform and the requirement for accurate output. The SPPL Model advanced in this work may be useful in distinguishing the two constructs, as follows: Interpretation is more dependent on social and pragmatic processes, in particular, interaction and affect; translation is more linguistically and cognitively oriented. In the graphic representation of the SPPL Model (see Figure 3.1), interpretation draws on information from the upper components, i.e. the identities of the speaker/deliverer and the interpreter, external contextual information (including setting, topic, and participants/audience), and genre-discourse information germane to setting and topic. Translation is concerned more with the illocutionary act, especially the propositional content, and with formulation. As such, interpretation is more ostensibly social and interactive, while translation is more individual and psycholinguistic.

This distinction can also be seen in the difference between children raised bilingually and professionally trained translators. At the early stages of bilingual development, children with two parents who speak different languages or whose parents speak a home language different from the language of the street have been known to engage in spontaneous interpretation behavior. I use the term interpretation deliberately, since their linguistic activity shows a preference for pragmatics over lexical accuracy. Harris (1992) calls this phenomenon 'natural translation.' But there are other, perhaps more spontaneous, less obvious, examples of natural translation. When a mother asks one of her children to find out what the other child is doing, the parent-to-child interaction will usually take place in the parent's preferred home language, but the child-to-child interaction is more likely to be in the 'language of wider communication,' the idiom more dominant outside the home. Another example of natural translation from within the home comes from children who engage in unprompted translation during language play (Swain, 1972). This activity will usually stress attitudinal and pragmatic aspects of the parent-child interaction. In contrast, training programs for professional translators (simultaneous as well as written) tend to emphasize textual comparison and lexical accuracy, often ignoring pragmatic and interactional aspects of translation.

The remainder of this section attempts to raise some of the issues that should be addressed by a model that combines sociopragmatic and psycholinguistic information, while trying to show how these issues are related to some of the questions in bilingualism treated throughout this work. I begin with an examination of interpretation and translation in light of the language choice and affect modules, which are depicted vertically along either side of the information components in Figure 3.1. Next, I discuss interpretation and translation in light of the various information components in the model: identity, context, genre, speech acts, formulation, and articulation. Finally, I examine interpretation/translation in terms of the model's processing mechanisms.

LANGUAGE CHOICE IN INTERPRETATION AND TRANSLATION

The language choice module, proposed to make (L1 and L2) language information available at all stages of production, serves interpreters/translators most noticeably to encode goals and intentions and to carry out the processes of formulation. Interpretation/translation can be seen as a form of intentional codeswitching. As such, the switch from source to target language, typically from L2 to L1, is regular, planned, and conscious. The illocutionary force and propositional content are always identified in the source language. They serve as the basis for lexical and discourse formulation, which hopefully takes place in the target language. The process of identifying speech act information in the source language and formulating it in the target language, while regulated by the language choice module, requires much less in the way of cognitive energy than bilingual conversation. It is not to be confused with the most taxing aspect of interpretation/translation, which is the processing of large amounts of information under limited time constraints. It is exactly this regularity, where the source language is primary in comprehension and the target language is fundamental in production that makes interpretation/translation unique. Contrary to the innovative claims of Wadensjo (see below), it also makes this phenomenon different from language processing in normal conversational interaction. In fact, if one of the most distinguishing features of bilingualism and bilinguals is 'choice,' then this feature is severely constrained in the bilingualism of interpretation/translation.

AFFECT IN INTERPRETATION/TRANSLATION

The affective module may also have a relatively restricted function in interpretation/ translation. In simultaneous interpretation, the professional is presumed to be dispassionate, and in written translation the specialist is considered objective. In the former situation, what develops is a more or less formal, conference-like affect, and the text gets interpreted in a filtered fashion without the original affect of the speaker. Among dozens of examples that could be cited to illustrate this phenomenon are the impassioned speeches of Yoram Sheftel, defense attorney in the Israeli trial of John Demenjuk, accused (and acquitted) of crimes as a Nazi concentration camp officer. One of the interpreters in that trial, Miriam Shlesinger, reports (personal communication) that in order not to disturb the expectations of the judge and other court personnel, she would substitute less affect-laden lexical items in places where the defense attorney had used intonation, pitch, and rate of speech with a relatively high level of emotion. In written translation, especially literary work, there may, perhaps should, be more evidence of the emotional involvement of the translator. This will depend in part on whether the translation has been commissioned by the original author, the publisher, or some other party. What matters even more when one looks at affective opacity/transparency in written translation is the translator's personal and professional involvement.

IDENTITY AND CONTEXT IN INTERPRETATION/TRANSLATION

The interpreter's/translator's identity is presumed in some contexts and for some genres to be anonymous, objective, and even omniscient–no mean task for a mere mortal who has sometimes been compared to an airport control tower operator. In reality, the interpreter/translator is human, male or female, with a fixed age, professionally-trained, and may have come to work today with a host of personal and circumstantial qualities that have greater or lesser relevance to the task at hand. Among the most important information about identity is the interpreter's/translator's language acquisition history. This information usually determines the direction of the interpreter's/translator's career. In particular, it is conventional for interpreters/translators to 'work' into their stronger or dominant language (Dodds, 1999; but see Campbell, 1998). That language is determined as much by preference as by proficiency, since language acquisition history does not always progress linearly, from one language to another. Rather, our interpreter/translator may have been born into one language environment, spent early and later childhood in another, high school back in the homeland, and adult life in one of the childhood language environments. An interpreter's/translator's linguistic identity is constituted by input from and interaction with parents, siblings, other relatives, other adults (such as W. Somerset Maugham's nanny, his main source of input for French[4]), and most all peers. In this way, our interpreter/translator may be no different than any other bilingual. But then again, she may. It would be useful to come up with detailed profiles of the language acquisition history of a variety of interpreters/translators and investigate whether there are a critical set of features that make a successful professional. This could be done initially along the lines of studies of good/bad language learners (e.g. Stern, 1975). Methodologically, I would choose less breadth and much more depth, probing small numbers of interpreters/translators via interviews, language diaries, and observations. In summary, even though some interpretation takes place without visual contact with the interpreter, the professional certainly brings a linguistic and social identity to the interpretation event, and that event is in turn undoubtedly influenced by the identities of all participants.

Wadensjo devotes an entire chapter of her book to the exploration of interpreters as intermediaries, mediators, gatekeepers, and non-persons. This complexity is a far cry from the nameless, faceless, covert, glass-booth conference interpreter, heard but never seen. In the context of Wadensjo's work, these labels are better descriptions of interactive patterns than they are of identities. Drawing heavily on the work of Bakhtin (1986), Goffman (1959), Erickson and Schultz (1982) and others, Wadensjo focuses on the interactive aspects of interpretation, primarily in face-to-face communication. She argues against a normative bias in most of the writing about interpretation/translation, favoring a Bakhtinian, dialogic, interactionist approach over what she condemns as "an underlying preconception of language use as monological" (p. 79). Wadensjo likens the 'non-person' role of the interpreter to the photographer who moves freely around an audience and commands a certain degree of authority for controlling the ecological space. She points out that, even in the 'non-person' role, the interpreter takes a more active role in the communicative situation than is assumed by the participants. The most obvious confirmation that the interpreter/translator is an active member of the linguistic exchange is the fact that s/he engages in speech. Moreover, that speech is public, and its form and content influence and are influenced by the speech of the others (p. 67). Thus, the non-person aspect of the interpreter/translator is only in the perceptions and expectations of others; in reality the interpreter/translator is involved in the active, construction of meaning.

Although Wadensjo does not mention participants, setting, and topic per se in her work, these notions are implicit throughout. Her treatment of interpreters as intermediaries, mediators, gatekeepers, and non-persons and their relationships to the speakers in a translation event are the 'stuff' of micro-sociolinguistics. One starting point for research in this area would be to interview interlocutors and their interpreter in attempt to gain insight into respective perceptions of the role of the interpreter. In addition, language data from actual translation sessions should be used, with an eye on metadiscourse comments from the interpreter and any utterances that an interlocutor directs toward the interpreter/translator. These language data are expected to be particularly revealing, since they provide a behavioral basis for comparison with perceptual and attitudinal data from interviews. The general orientation here, as in some of the studies of bilingualism cited above, is to gain access to the same phenomenon (in this case interpretation/translation) through multiple sources of data.

In conference interpretation, while the *setting* and *topic* are generally assumed to be neutral, or at least relatively unimportant, the *participants*, i.e. the interpreter, the speaker, and the audience, are party to a special set of relationships, with each one privy to different kinds and amounts of information. The respective relationships and information may, and in fact, *do* influence the contents of the translation and consequently affect the audience as well. More specifically, the speaker is visible to the interpreter, but in some sense, the speaker is reduced to an oral text. The interpreter is not visible, but to a certain extent controls the content. Thus, the relationships between and among speaker, interpreter, and listener/audience are not typical of everyday, face-to-face conversational interaction. In addition, the interpreter has knowledge about his/her own performance, which is not accessible either to the speaker or the audience. Furthermore, the interpreter may not have any contact with the speaker before the conference, and usually has no contact with either the speaker or audience after it. These last two features of the setting afford the interpreter a degree of control not available to interlocutors in more typical conversational interaction. Finally, in conference interpretation the interpreter may be given a transcript or a précis of the lecture/speech before the event. The professional's knowledge about or preparation of the topic can influence everything from the pragmatics of delivery to lexical access and fluency. Thus, participants, setting, and topic (contextual information, external to the identities of the interpreter and her clients) all contribute to a sociopragmatic understanding of conference interpretation.

The distinction raised above between children and adult interpreters/ translators, between natural, spontaneous translation and professional work, can be applied to participants and setting as well. Sociolinguistically, this distinction draws on the formal/casual continuum. Face-to-face interpretation, for example, in the courtroom, in the hospital, or even in less formal settings like banks, restaurants, and on the street, is clearly different from conference interpretation or written translation, where the products of the translation are heard or read, but the interpreter/translator herself is not seen.

GENRE ISSUES IN TRANSLATION

Although traditionally the genre construct was synonymous with text type, e.g. narrative, expository, etc., genre is treated here in a broader perspective, including social as well as text-based information, spoken as well as written language, and within the oral modality, scripts as well as conversations. Among the questions delineated in the discussion of genre (see Chapter 3), all are relevant to an integrated examination of interpretation/translation in a sociopragmatic-psycholinguistic framework. These questions include:

> To what extent is the interpreter/translator aware of and makes use of genre information in on-line processing? Does genre information, social as well as textual, influence the processes and products of translation/

interpretation explicitly? And if so, how? Does an interpreter/translator make a genre decision, albeit unconscious, or can genre choices be subsumed under the other sub-components of processing?

These questions, while perhaps important for basic research into the mechanisms and processes of interpretation/translation, are not necessarily the first or most relevant questions for those interested in applications of the present model to training and practice in this field. In this regard, it might be more useful to focus on genre distinctions and genre features. In practice, the oral/written distinction is the first cut. Schools of translation and interpretation and more modest training programs generally specialize either in simultaneous interpretation or written translation, or at least offer separate courses along these lines of genre and modality. In terms of the social-textual distinction, training in the field of interpretation/translation is focused almost exclusively on the text. It might be useful here to compare medical education, which twenty years ago basically ignored doctor-patient relations and today, when communication is perceived as an integral part of a physician's training at most medical schools. In the field of translation, professional-client relations may be treated informally or in ad hoc fashion in courses for interpreters/translators; nevertheless there is certainly room for integrating social discourse issues more explicitly and extensively into the curriculum. Wadensjo's recent book is a long first step in that direction.

A third genre distinction in the SPPL Bilingual Model, the one between conversations and scripts, is not directly relevant to a treatment of interpretation/translation. The idea of interpreting as conversational interaction is pertinent, however, and here I would take issue with Wadensjo. Given the complex, often unspecified relationships between and among speaker/interpreter/audience or writer/translator/reader and similarly unspecified notions about setting and topic, the role of participants, setting, and topic in interpretation/translation may be more like the characters, staging, and content in a Shakespeare play than mundane conversations. In particular, the interpreter's privileged access to knowledge and power are not sufficiently exposed and made explicit, even via the tools of Bakhtinian dialogics and Goffman's symbolic interactionism. These theoretical and methodological approaches need to be supplemented by phenomenological and experimental procedures, particularly those which address speakers', interpreters', and listeners' perceptions of their roles, their behaviors, and their relationships. Examining triangulated data will provide multiple insights to the phenomenon. Such triangulation can be achieved by looking at language behavior data (in the form of a transcript of the interpretation or the source and target texts of a written translation), data from sociolinguistic interviews with the participants, and judgments of critical social and linguistic information from the transcripts/translation and these interviews.

SPEECH ACTS IN INTERPRETATION/TRANSLATION

The speech act, in particular its illocutionary force and propositional content, serves as a bridge between sociopragmatic and psycholinguistic aspects of bilingualism. The suggestion, here, is that the same is true for interpretation/translation. The illocutionary force, which can be broken down into attitudinal and affective information, leans more heavily on the sociopragmatic aspects of the Bilingual Model presented in this work. The propositional content can be associated better with aspects of formulation and articulation, although it does draw from social and pragmatic information components as well. Recognition of the illocutionary force in the source language and evaluation of its appropriateness in the target language is likely to be more straightforward and accurate than recognition of the full extent of the propositional content in the source language and identification of parallel content in the target language. Illocutionary force is read from speaker/writer intentions. It involves a great deal of redundancy from multiple social cues and mutually supporting linguistic indicators. In contrast, propositional content requires attention to a myriad of syntactic and semantic details; its redundancy cues are fewer. The way to target language propositional content is not as smooth and predictable as the road to illocutionary force. Thus, propositional content in the target language undergoes a reduction due to the sheer amount of material and the perceived need to 'get on with the show' (Shlesinger, 2000).

ASPECTS OF FORMULATION IN INTERPRETATION/TRANSLATION

Reviewing the main assumptions and claims made in Chapter 3 about formulation, the present model distinguishes between two subcomponents, one to get from concepts to lexemes and one to handle discourse patterns. The conceptual stage of processing was assumed to involve language-specific and sociopragmatic information, integrated prior to lemma selection. Concepts were said to be lexico-pragmatic and to be an integral of both linguistic and experiential knowledge. Lemmas in the bilingual lexicon were claimed to differ across and within speakers, and to be subject to modification as functions of proficiency and use. Lemmas were also said to have access to language-specific information as well as to information about affect. Overall, the model is more interactive at all levels of processing than strictly autonomous models, which limit the kind of information that passes between components.

Two issues are relevant to skilled translation. One relates to the assumption that language-specific information is available at every stage of formulation, from conceptualization to lexical access and articulate production. The other relates to the variability of concepts and lemmas across and within speakers. These two, apparently opposing, characteristics of bilingual production should differ for skilled translators and run-of-the-mill bilinguals. In order to stand up to the cognitive demands resulting from large amounts of input, the need to convert that input to another language and to do so within a limited time frame, the skilled translator develops a set of strategies to make access of language-specific information efficient. In formulation, this efficiency can be envisioned as strong links between source and target concepts, lemmas, and lexemes, with the target member of the pair being more salient, and thus, more accessible. In terms of variability, it should not be too difficult to show that skilled translators are less variable and more internally consistent in matching source-target pairs than untrained bilinguals. When cognitive demands increase–due to the density of input, the speed of delivery, and unfamiliarity with the content–then the inherent variability of concepts and lemmas may appear in a translator's product. If the translator has perfected various compensatory strategies (e.g. reduction of information via summarizing rather than proposition-by-proposition interpretation), then the source-target links will prevail over conceptual-lemma variability.

For discourse formulation aspects of interpretation/translation, the same basic constructs are relevant. However, discourse patterns, for example sequencing and cohesion rules, do not lend themselves to the same kind of source-target linkage as concepts and lemmas. Thus, there should be more evidence of variability in discourse patterns.

Among the most significant contributions to psycholinguistic aspects of interpretation/translation, and to formulation in particular, is Shlesinger's (2000) Ph.D. dissertation. The author, an expert bilingual herself, used conceptual tools from models of working memory to design and conduct four experiments to examine the effects of linguistic and temporal factors on attentional resources in expert simultaneous interpreters. She described the central problem of the thesis as follows: How to get at "the systematic tradeoffs that seem to figure in abiding by the sacrosanct 'keep talking' norm of SI [simultaneous interpretation]…while maintaining an output which, by and large, matches the semantic input of the source message and the syntactic patterns of the TL [target language]." The findings were wide-ranging and can be summarized briefly as:

- Better performance at a faster rate of delivery (input)
- Use of "generics" (semantically reduced, underspecified target language words) increased as a function of rate of delivery
- Effects for word-length
- A deleterious effect of norm-driven strategies on less frequent words
- A recency effect for input strings, which appear in string-initial position in output (last in, first out)
- Greater retention of string-final items at slower rates of delivery
- A tradeoff between the number of items retained and error rate

The SPPL Model of bilingualism, in particular its processing mechanism focused on variation, may be useful in understanding how simultaneous interpreters cope with special cognitive demands. Six of the seven findings in Shlesinger's study can be said to be related to 'variation' phenomena. Use of "generics," retention of shorter and less frequent words, recency effects, retention of string-final items, and retention of fewer words can all be seen as ways of reducing variation and its cognitive load.

ARTICULATORY STRATEGIES OF INTERPRETERS AND TRANSLATORS

In the context of the SPPL Model, by the time the interpreter/translator gets to the point that s/he is ready to articulate, whether through a spoken or a written medium, there is not much room for maneuvering. Shlesinger's "the show must go on" maxim is the overriding force at this stage of processing. And that maxim is largely a function of the three factors outlined as most relevant to bilingual articulation in Chapter 3. There I characterized the articulatory aspects of bilingual production as follows:

- Bilinguals produce language at a slower rate than monolinguals.
- Bilinguals show more evidence of speech dysfluency, which takes the form of hesitations, false starts, and lexical repetitions.
- Bilinguals have smaller vocabularies than monolinguals in each of their languages, but taken together have a larger overall lexicon.

All of these phenomena were said to distinguish bilinguals from monolinguals. In the present context, they distinguish everyday bilinguals from professionally trained interpreters/translators. Interpreters speak faster, with fewer dysfluencies, and are probably more lexically endowed than monolingual counterparts. By lexically endowed, I mean that their domain-specific vocabularies are larger, more differentiated, and have stronger links among entries than non-trained bilinguals or monolinguals. Lexical richness and fluency are probably the major contributors to speech rate and the ability of interpreters to access and retrieve words rapidly and fluently. Thus, in order to be counted as an expert bilingual, a cognitive as well as professional elite, years of training and practice are devoted to compensating for what ordinarily might result in slower speech, more dysfluency, and undistinguished lexis.

PROCESSING MECHANISMS IN INTERPRETATION/TRANSLATION

Imitation. Despite their complexity, interpretation and translation offer perhaps the simplest and purest way to examine imitation and variation. As stated in the discussion about imitation in Chapter 4, the products of translation can be considered a partial copy of the source language. From a structural point of view, the imitation mechanism in interpretation and translation ideally involves a mapping of meaning from the source language to the target medium. When meaning is accurately copied, the translation is considered successful. When it is not, the professional is accused of malpractice. In simultaneous interpretation in particular, there is probably a great deal of phonetic and syntactic mimesis as well. From a processing perspective, among the mechanisms proposed here, imitation is the one most responsible for promoting 'the show must go on' phenomenon. This phenomenon is related to fluency, frequency and to automaticity. 'The show must go on' is a deliberate intensification of rate of speech and reduction of content, instituted in order to keeo up with the delivery of input. It is a preference for, or perhaps reliance on, automaticity over accuracy.

A study of the motivational aspects of this aspect of interpretation ought to shed light on some of the less transparent fluency processes in ordinary bilingualism. Two kinds of frequency contribute to fluency and its intensified expression in interpretation/translation. One is societal frequency, the prevalent use of a lexical item in a language. This is the kind of frequency measured by word lists and corpora (e.g. Kucera & Francis, 1967; British National Corpus). It varies as function of geography, genre, speech event, and other social factors. The other kind of frequency is grounded in the language use of the individual. Individual word frequency is difficult to investigate, since it requires documenting a person's exposure to a variety of audio and print media as well as recording the individual's speech, transcription of both of these sets of data, and some means of calculating frequency differences. A more practical, first step in an examination of these two kinds of frequency would be a comparison of interpreters and translators' self-reports of exposure to and active use of words selected from a relevant corpus or frequency list. My guess, based in part on Shlesinger's (2000) research, is that individual interpreters make use of a highly repetitive, generic vocabulary, which may not necessarily reflect the societal norms found in established corpora.

Variation. Like imitation, the variation mechanism provides a framework for distinguishing ordinary bilingualism and translation. Variation was characterized both structurally and strategically as 'diversity of linguistic forms and patterns' as well as 'the range of strategies' for using them. More variation means greater lexical, grammatical, and pragmatic versatility, and ultimately the possibility of functioning in more contexts. Ordinary bilinguals trade off freely between imitation and variation. For interpreters/translators, however, variation is expected to be more limited. To achieve fluency in the face of heavy cognitive demands (fast rate of delivery and large amount of content), the professional interpreter compensates by limiting the degree of variation. Linguistic and strategic diversity are sacrificed, and speech is produced in the target language with fewer forms, patterns, and strategies.

Integration. The integration mechanism described in the previous chapter may be less relevant to the study of bilingual aspects of interpretation and translation than to an examination of codeswitching. It is certainly important in looking at the integration of various sources of information–identity, context, genre, lexis, pragmatics, syntax, etc. But in translation, the speaker at some point needs to disengage the source language and switch to monolingual target language processing. From the point of view of integration, it would be of interest to examine whether the same range and kinds of language contact phenomena occur among proficient interpreters/translators. My educated guess is that sound-based and syntactic slips are more likely than those from lexical, semantic, and pragmatic domains, given the extent of monitoring interpreters engage in for accuracy and fluency. Given the typically uni-directional (L2-to-L1) nature of interpretation/translation (in contrast to bilingual codeswitching), an investigation of VOT contrasts, tip-of-the-tongue phenomena, and experimentally-induced slips of the tongue among professional interpreters would shed interesting light on bilingual articulation processes.

Control. The notion of control discussed throughout this work, grounded in Powers' Perceptual Control Theory, states that goals, intentions, and perceptions are maintained or kept stable by variable means. Behavior is not an end, but a means to control those goals, intentions, and perceptions. Behavior is variable, not constant or even static. The goals of interpreters/translators are to produce a fluent, accurate semantic copy of the source language. Their intentions are to identify the phonemes, grammatical patterns, and speech acts in the source language, and convert these to the appropriate target language forms. Behavior, namely the on-line language behavior generated by the interpreter, controls the perceptions of incoming words and speech acts. To achieve the overriding goal of fluency, accuracy may be sacrificed by producing a translation that includes less precise, more generic lexis and eliminates what is perceived to be expendable. The target language material, which is the product of translation, varies from the source material in several ways–first and foremost in its phonological and grammatical form. It also varies semantically and pragmatically, hopefully not too much. Thus, variation is a means to maintain a goal. As stated more than once in this work, this is not the variance of measurement error and standard deviations, the obstacle to significance differences. Rather, here it is both a construct in Perceptual Control Theory and a processing mechanism in the SPPL Model.

BILINGUAL ASPECTS OF COMPUTATION AND CURSING

The remaining two phenomena, unlike the three that preceded them, are not unique to bilinguals. They do, however, interact uniquely with bilingualism, thus offering insights that other cognitive phenomena do not. The exposition here is not linked as closely to the SPPL Model as the previous sections on codeswitching and translation/interpretation, due to both limitations of space and the more speculative nature of the discussion. Thus, for both computation and cursing I try to zero in on those information components and processing mechanisms that will clarify the bilingual aspects of these two phenomena.

COMPUTATION AND BILINGUALISM

Walk up and down the aisles of a local grocery store in a multilingual neighborhood; linger at the checkout counter in the duty free shop at a major international airport. Whatever the lingua franca and whatever the context, you will probably see highly fluent bilinguals reverting to what appears to be their native language to count the change. I say 'what appears to be' because initial anecdotal findings show that the 'language of instruction' in basic arithmetic may be preferred over the mother tongue or native language.

Two immediate explanations come to mind to start a systematic examination of this phenomenon. One is sociopragmatic; the other is psycholinguistic. Computation is a learned skill, acquired in most of the Western world in classrooms via explicit instruction, and in the marketplaces of the non-Western world through the exchange of money and goods. Those social experiences, school and marketplace, are relatively untapped sources of data, offering potential insight into why bilinguals, even those who make relatively little use of their native language, revert to that language to add, subtract, multiply, divide, and count.

A sociopragmatic explanation for this phenomenon is that there is something in the learning context that drives the bilingual to use the primordial language for this purpose. A contrasting, psycholinguistic explanation focuses on the fact that the most prominent psycholinguistic feature of computation, be it sequential counting or one of the four basic operations in arithmetic, is automaticity. In this case, the language that has been learned the earliest and used the most frequently for computation will be chosen.

These two hypotheses are not necessarily competitive or mutually exclusive. A first step towards examining them would be self-report survey data from bilinguals who do not compute in the same language they typically interact in. A second step might be to examine the validity of self-report data by asking the same bilinguals to perform a variety of tasks involving counting and computation. These data would minimally include various kinds of bilinguals, who are raised in one language (let's call it L1) and arranged according to the following profiles, each with its own underlying hypotheses:

1. math education in L1, primarily interacts in L2, and computes in L1
2. math education in L1, primarily interacts in L2, and computes in L2
3. math education in L2, primarily interacts in L1, and computes in L2
4. math education in L2, primarily interacts in L2, and computes in L2
5. math education in L2, primarily interacts in L2, and computes in L1

The first two kinds of bilinguals are equated for home language and the language of arithmetic education, but use a different language for social interaction. Two examples, selected to illustrate the bilingual profiles in A and B, may be useful in considering the hypotheses raised below: 1. A French Canadian who attended French-medium schools, received arithmetic instruction in French, but whose main social interaction is with English-speaking people. 2. An Hispanic American who attended a transitional bilingual education program in the US, received arithmetic instruction in English, but whose main social interaction is with English-speaking people.

Profile A. If counting and arithmetic are performed in L1, it would appear to be related to preference for the home language and/or the language of the arithmetic classroom (perhaps due to a positive educational experience). This may be because computing in L1 means to some extent rejection of the language of social interaction, which is currently L2. French Canadian and Hispanic American bilinguals may engage in social contact in L2 at work due to perceived expectations and obligations or perhaps even due to motivation for outgroup mobility. It would be interesting to probe the reasons for maintenance of L1 arithmetic performance in light of persistent social interaction in L2.

Profile B. If, on the other hand, the same language/arithmetic history leads to computing in L2, then preference for the language of social interaction (L2) would prevail over the native language as well as the language of arithmetic instruction. This possibility would show a clear preference for social functions of language over more symbolic cognitive functions such as arithmetic. This finding is expected to be more prevalent in situations where a minority language is endangered or where there are strong social pressures to conform to the majority language.

Profile C/the converse of Profile A. Here, there is a match between native language and the language of math instruction, but a mismatch between the language of math instruction (L2) and the language of social interaction (L1). Counting and arithmetic in L2 would show a preference for the language of instruction over both the language of social interaction and the mother tongue. Data favoring this hypothesis would be the best evidence to show that basic arithmetic was a unique cognitive phenomenon in bilingualism.

Profile D, where computation is performed in the same language as the language of arithmetic instruction and social interaction, shows a mismatch between the native or home language and the language of the other two relevant functions (arithmetic and social interaction). This profile is quite common. Its converse, Profile E, is expected to be extremely rare, since this bilingual would have to overcome both school-based cognitive and social obstacles in order to perform arithmetic tasks in a language in which s/he neither received instruction nor currently uses. One possible situation which could give rise to this profile is an academically 'pushy' family environment, where counting and basic arithmetic were introduced in the home. English-speaking immigrants to non-English-speaking countries or foreign service personnel who send their children to local schools but have high expectations for English language maintenance, would be one way to get to this profile. Another example might be a geek or autodidact with an endangered mother tongue, who learned math from electronic games and internet. but even internet is social; A study of the language histories of math geniuses, from Euclid to Einstein may offer insight here.

In order to test for the validity of the hypotheses behind these profiles, one would want to document them among indigenous as well as immigrant bilinguals, among bilinguals raised in homes where two languages are spoken as well as those where the second language is acquired outside the home, and in situations where the second language is a minority and a majority language. In a survey study of 552 college-age bilinguals in Texas, Vaid and Menon (2000) came up with 32 students who reported counting and computing in both of their languages. My hunch is that these 32 would be spread across several of the profiles outlined here. Tasks in future studies should be tied to sociopragmatic as well as cognitive aspects of basic arithmetic and extend across a range of automatic operations (e.g. counting, adding, multiplying, etc.) as well as more complex verbal problems that involve language skills and more explicit planning.

One of constructs most relevant to understand the interface of bilingualism and computation is automaticity. Above, for language processing, automaticity was distinguished from fluency as follows: fluency was taken to be linguistic and grounded in the structure of language; automaticity was labeled a general psychological process and said to make use of the structural elements of language. By analogy, fluency in computation includes knowledge of numbers and basic arithmetic operations. That knowledge involves basic syntax of mathematics, e.g. knowing the difference between single digits and two-place numbers, the order of operations in addition, etc. If fluency is based on structural aspects of mathematics, then automaticity is a component of arithmetic language use, i.e. it involves the use of this knowledge. The underlying processes most relevant to automaticity include discrimination, recognition, identification, classification, and categorization. These are clustered in two of the four fundamental mechanisms outlined in Chapter 4: imitation and variation. Recognition and identification are basic to the mechanism of imitation. Discrimination, classification, and categorization are component processes of variation. Timing features, including stimulus duration, the length of time between stimuli, and response time are also relevant to automaticity. Some of these parameters have been investigated by Frenck-Mestre and Vaid (1993).

If bilingualism makes additional cognitive demands to handle the presence of additional words, additional grammatical patterns, and additional sounds, those demands should be most evident in their effects on automaticity. Computation in bilinguals should then be slower, more prone to false starts, peppered with cross-language interference, in general, subject to the same dysfluencies that other language contact phenomena reveal. Frenck-Mestre and Vaid (1993) have confirmed some of these phenomena in mental arithmetic and lexical decision tasks, others (e.g. Hunt & Agnoli, 1991) have argued for a linguistic relativity interpretation of articulatory differences, for example, between Chinese and English. Generally, computation is protected from language contact phenomena. It is largely free of hesitations, false starts, slower rate, interference, and codeswitching. The question is why. This is what makes computation in bilinguals a unique psycholinguistic phenomenon. Another way to phrase this query is as follows: How is it possible that bilingualism intrudes in so many ways but counting and arithmetic computing are so insulated? The way this question is formulated is reminiscent of the classic query in bilingualism: How is it possible for the bilingual to filter out one language in order to produce monolingual speech? The original proposal to answer this question, the so-called bilingual switch which operated categorically on the speaker's entire language system (Macnamara, Krauthamer, & Bolgar, 1968) has given way to more continuous notions of activation and deactivation (e.g. Green, 1986, 1993).

In addition, we are left with a question as to why automatic, arithmetic operations lead to the relatively complete deactivation of one language system (in some bilinguals), allowing the other language to operate freely. Shall we look to the neuroanatomy or neurobiology of counting and computation for an answer? Perhaps computation is particularly localized in the cortex; perhaps it is not localized, but a particular autonomous circuitry underlies its normal functioning. Or perhaps the neurobiology is not initially all that unique for computation, but continual, recurrent operations on a very limited set of primitives (numbers) with a restricted syntax (e.g. associative/commutative laws) facilitates the development of an autonomous computational system, and one way of supporting that autonomy is through language. Thus, repetitive activities in a single language, frequent or perhaps excessive use of the imitation mechanism, may bring about a separation of languages in the bilingual mind.

Computation requires no originality. There is no need for an interplay between imitation and variation; no need for codeswitching and pragmatic markers and no need for social identity and contextual information. Computation in and of itself is pure cognition. It has none of the social, contextual, and affective aspects of bilingualism. Thus, it has no need for mechanisms beyond imitation. No need for variation, a hallmark of bilingualism. Thus, no need for bilingualism. But mathematics is different. So is the acquisition of mathematics, and even the acquisition of computational skills. These involve social identity, learning contexts, situational variables. In fact, they involve most of the sociopragmatic information outlined in Chapter 3.

One way to study computation, then, may be to see it as a unidimensional issue, engulfed by automaticity and isolated from the sociopragmatic influences of bilingualism. Once computation moves beyond the restricted confines of counting and basic arithmetic, however, to the investigation of higher level processes in mathematics and the acquisition of mathematical skills, the name of the game is sociopragmatics.

CURSING AND BILINGUALISM

The interface of bilingualism and cursing, swearing, cussing, or the use of what is regarded as foul language is viewed here as a branch of the general study of language and emotion. Bilingualism is a special case of language, and cursing is a special case of emotion, i.e. verbal emotion. In this brief section, intended only as an entrée to the field, I would like to address two topics in light of previous bilingual issues raised. One is related to directionality, the other to triggering. These topics have both sociopragmatic and psycholinguistic ramifications, but the latter are more interesting here.

The directionality of bilingual cursing. Bilinguals often report the use of their second, non-preferred language when the need arises to use an expletive. Thus, a native English speaker may prefer to use Spanish curses when frustrated, agitated, infuriated, or angry. This phenomenon offers an unusual opportunity to examine the interaction of the language choice and affective modules of the SPPL Model (Figure 3.1).

Based on the hypothesis raised earlier that L1-to-L2 switching may be more socially and pragmatically motivated than switching into one's native language, a question which arises centers on the motivation for swearing in a non-preferred language. One plausible answer is that the weaker, non-dominant language may be less emotionally encumbered than the primary language. By cursing in this medium, the speaker creates a distance between himself and the "bad" words he uses. In terms of social identity and affect, the speaker who curses in a second language is, in a way, saying that the primary or native language is a more integral part of his identity, that he is more emotionally invested in it. In speech act terminology, he is admitting to the illocutionary force of the expletive expression, but is partially denying ownership of the form and content. While the affective module has already provided input regarding the nature of the emotion as well as the degree of feeling, a decision regarding language choice may be reserved to a later stage of processing. Based on the assumption that cursing in L2 is motivated by social considerations, like a need to temper or modulate the level of affect, language choice information will be made available to the speech act component, and the input to the formulator will be a lexico-pragmatic concept for whichever language (L1 or L2) is already specified. If, for some reason the level of affect changes during formulation or the speaker experiences a lexical access problem in the second language, the language choice module may facilitate production of a first language expletive. There are sociopragmatic considerations here as well, including setting, listener, topic, and genre considerations. Soon after arrival on sabbatical in North America, I was called into the principal of my 13-year-old son's religious school. He spoke to me embarrassingly about a 'cursing' problem in school. I asked whether the problem was in English or in the boy's native language, to which the principal didn't respond, understanding that cursing in English was a function of the North American school environment the boy had quickly assimilated to.

Triggering. The other bilingual issue worthy of mention in the context of cursing is the notion of triggering. Clyne (2003) defines triggering as a linguistic phenomenon that facilitates transversion, his term for the activation of one language and deactivation of the other. He distinguishes four linguistic domains where triggering has been documented: lexical, tonal, syntactic, and phonological/prosodic. Triggering is said to occur when cognates and fusion forms are used to facilitate a switch from one language to the next. Clyne does not explicitly reject a role for sociopragmatic information in triggering, but he does restrict his discussion to structural and processing aspects of the phenomenon. In discussing his work (see Chapter 2), I raised the possibility that 'trigger words' may reflect sociopragmatic motivations. Thus, bilingual cursing may be a way to gain access to sociopragmatic aspects of triggering. As a first step, it would be useful to see whether switching to a second language for cursing is maintained, and the curse operates as a trigger, or whether the speaker switches back to the native language, the curse taking the form of an island insertion.

The best data for an issue of this sort would be naturally occurring production of curses in a second language, which are supplemented by intensive probing via interview and metalinguistic judgments of the speakers who produced the original curses. Unfortunately, naturally occurring codeswitching itself is difficult enough to record; the frequency of cursing as a subclass of codeswitching phenomena may not turn up more than a dozen examples in several thousand utterances (see, for example, the incidence of codeswitching in Rampton, 1995, Zentella, 1997). Alternative paradigms include elicited imitation and tip-of-the-tongue experiments, which could generate expletives in much greater numbers. These procedures would need to be supplemented by metalinguistic judgments incorporating sociopragmatic information regarding setting and participants into the stimulus material.

Coda. There are other important issues related to the study of bilingualism and cursing, which may provide insight to the interface of bilingualism and affect. In particular, this dimension of bilingualism may offer new approaches to therapist-client interaction, where the choice of the two languages is directed by the therapist in order to influence the client's degree of involvement in the therapeutic situation and the therapeutic narrative. Altarriba's work offers one promising application (Altarriba & Bauer, 1998; Santiago-Rivera & Altarriba, in press). A study of bilingual patients with Tourette's syndrome would offer exceptionally valuable data about the relationship between contextual factors and cursing. Tourette's is a thought disorder marked by inability to control offensive language in the presence of contextual cues. A Tourette's patient predisposed to ethnic prejudice is apparently unable to control racist language in the presence of a person from the target ethnic group. In this light, it might be valuable to investigate the strength of three-dimensional objects, two-dimensional pictures, and verbal descriptions in eliciting curses and insults. And, for insight into bilingualism, it would be useful to examine whether the same manifestation of Tourette's disorder occurs in both languages of bilinguals.

METHODOLOGICAL PERSPECTIVES ON THE INVESTIGATION OF BILINGUALISM

An important subtext in this book has been a concern with method. Among desirable first principles is the Aristotelian maxim that method should be derived from theory (Walters, 1990). Unfortunately, the study of bilingualism has not been particularly blessed with its own theories. Rather, it has drawn theoretically and methodologically from a variety of disciplines, including anthropology, sociology, psychology, and linguistics, sometimes without the realization that picking and choosing unsystematically, or sometimes even indiscriminately, may lead to incompatibility of theory and method, or may even lead to incongruous methods.

A brilliant little book which has guided my thinking in this direction is Phillip Runkel's (1990) *Casting Nets and Testing Specimens: Two Grand Methods in Psychology*. The distinction between "casting nets" and "testing specimens" may help put some order in methodological options for research on bilingualism. The more scientific name for "casting nets" is called the "method of relative frequencies" (Runkel, 1990:5). It involves frequency counts, statistical estimates, clustering of data, correlation of conditions with those clusters, in short, most of what is considered quantitative research in the social sciences. In this method, the data are aggregated. These methods provide information about groups, not individuals. The method of relative frequencies is characterized by the following assumptions:

❑ Individuals are considered to be interchangeable, substitutable for each other. A recent convention in some journals, although still not universally applied and relatively rare in studies of language use and bilingualism is the presentation of individual data to support group analyses. Zentella's (1997) work has been cited throughout the present work as an exception in this regard.

❑ All subjects in an experiment (whether data are collected via questionnaire or behavioral performance, in the laboratory or in the field) are assumed to "act in the ways called for by the experimental design, even though most experimenters know that cannot be the case" (Runkel, 1990: 45).

❑ The method "requires us to conclude that the people in an experimental group, or at least a statistically significant number of them, have behaved in a certain way, even though by its very procedures, the method usually fails to demonstrate that any single person has actually behaved that way" (1990: 44-45).[5]

❑ The language of interpretation frequently overstates its conclusions or makes claims which cannot be justified by the data. Statements such as "Bilinguals are..., second language learners show..., high proficiency speakers demonstrate..." are preferred over more conservative, and accurate phraseology, such as "The bilingual children tested in this study..., the Greek speakers of English investigated here..." Only true random samples of both subjects and stimuli would justify generalizations with this scope. The samples in most, if not all, research on bilingualism are opportunistic, or what Anderson (1996) more generously calls "handy samples."

In "testing specimens," the other "grand method," the individual is the focus of attention. The method attempts to predict behavior of individuals, in particular how internal processes operate within and across individuals. To get inside the head of the individual language user, it is not enough to rely on observable behavior. Moreover, to describe that behavior, one needs to scaffolding a theory of the role of behavior in general onto the role of language behavior in particular. Behaviorist psychology, and even much of what has passed as cognitive psychology in the last 30 years, has viewed behavior as the response to a stimulus. All linear models, which attempt to measure behavior, make this assumption. But, a simple demonstration will show that an individual's intentions are not readily observable. Intentions are part of a complex of processes that can be modeled by very few theories. Speech Act Theory in linguistics and role playing methodologies were an attempt to get at structural information related to intentions (see Chapter 3's description of the intentional component of the SPPL Model). But this is not a "testing specimens" approach. Perceptual Control Theory is. Applying control theory terminology, Runkel (1990:163) phrases the central problem in social psychology as follows: "...the way individuals can use a common physical and social environment and, while doing so, maintain the necessary degrees of freedom so that every individual can avoid inner conflict." The environment does not cause behavior. Rather, behavior is used to control perceptions (Powers, 1978), where control is the reduction of conflict between an internal standard (goal, intention) and a perceptual signal, i.e. between motivations and perception, between internal and external forces.

In sociology, psychology, and linguistics, the study of bilingualism, until recently, was seen merely as a source of data to explain more general phenomena or to advance particular theories like intergroup/interethnic relations, social planning and policy, pro-active memory, lateralization of language in the brain, generative studies of second language acquisition, and many more. This supporting role meant by default that the data were not suitable for studies of bilingualism per se, and in the event that they were, they were not comparable.

The issue is complicated by the different disciplinary foci of the various sources of insight on bilingualism. Sociology, much of social psychology, and macro sociolinguistics opt for "casting nets," to use Runkel's metaphor for their interest in broader scope. These approaches tend to gather more data, from larger numbers of subjects, utilizing questionnaire and survey analysis techniques to examine 'reported language,' and they rely on generalizations based on statistical inference to interpret the data.

Psychologists and psycholinguists, on the other hand, prefer depth over breadth, collecting smaller amounts of data, from fewer subjects, designing materials and procedures to conduct experimental tasks which require subjects to comprehend or produce language, but often grouping subjects to achieve the same kind of statistical generalizations as their sociolinguist counterparts.

Linguists, structuralists and functionalists alike, tend to focus on language as an entity unto itself, largely independent of speakers and their environment.

The integrated study of bilingualism must cope with these divergent and sometimes contradictory, orientations. This is the central methodological challenge of the field. More specific methodological issues in the study of bilingualism include:

❑ How to attend to the balance between structure and process in our descriptions of bilingual phenomena, and how to ensure that these "soft" descriptions and linkages are grounded in countable data;

❑ How to deal with definitional problems as to who or what is a bilingual (e.g., early/late and simultaneous/sequential bilinguals, natural/formal acquisition contexts, how to measure proficiency);

❑ How to equate stimulus texts/words from two languages;

❑ How to collect data from both languages without giving preference to one of them (order effects, which language to present instructions in, which field site to visit first/second/last).

Ideally a fully integrated theory and method is desirable. But, unfortunately, that doesn't exist yet. Thus, we offer here a set of principles and guidelines from those who see methodology as inseparable from theory (e.g. Aristotle, Anderson, and Runkel).

With this background and by way of summarizing some of the methodological notes and comments made throughout this work, the following guidelines are offered, more to make them explicit as a basis for dialogue on the issues they raise than to suggest their adoption as standards and benchmarks.

1. *Interface of theory and method.* As a first principle, one of the desirable methodological goals is that the method (choice of subjects, materials and stimulus design and selection, and development of tasks and procedures) be derived from, or at least firmly grounded in, the theoretical assumptions. More modestly stated, the methods should be conceptually related to the assumptions of the research.

2. *Linking structure to process.* As said above, the issue of linking static architecture to dynamic process is not only a matter of theory. It must infuse thinking on the methodological level. All good researchers are part theorists and part plumbers. The theoretical part of their persona invents dimensions to describe phenomena along axes of interaction. The plumber must insist that these dimensions fit into a measurable and comparable framework. For example, in studies of blame and avoiding blame, Anderson the theoretician distinguished among intent, damage, and recompense. Anderson the empirical scientist went on to measure these constructs by embedding them in short narratives in a person perception paradigm and asking his subjects to rate the degree to which a person with a measurable amount of intent should be blamed for causing a measurable amount of damage, given a certain degree of recompense. He did this by asking his subjects to make subjective ratings on graphic rating scales or

by means of magnitude estimation (e.g. Anderson, 1996). The processes are then inferred from the way a participant integrates information. The gross oversimplification here is intended only to illustrate how process is inferred from the measurement of structural constructs. Below I talk about what to count and what to measure in bilingualism.

3. *Bilingualism as a multidimensional phenomenon*. Ideally, methods should be able to handle multiple sources of information in a unified framework (see Anderson, 1981, 1996). In addition to the integration of first and second language information (e.g. Walters & Wolf, 1992), bilingualism has been shown to involve a complex of sociopragmatic and psycholinguistic phenomena and to operate at a variety of levels of processing. This should not be interpreted as disapproval of studies restricted to only one of these domains or to a single level of processing. On the contrary, the integrative purpose in this work led me to review, for example, studies of bilingual lexical processing that ignore social context and to studies of identity which are only peripherally concerned with processing. At the same time, I have taken a special interest in studies of lexical processing which do take into account social context (Grosjean, 1997) as well as to micro-sociolinguistic studies which address issues in social cognition (Walters, 1981).

4. *Group and individual data*. At the end of the day, sociolinguists are interested in societal trends, which means data collection from large numbers of bilinguals and attention to group patterns. Psycholinguists are ultimately interested in what is going on inside the head of an individual bilingual. Some of the fiercest academic battles have been fought over this aspect of methodology, more so than over substantive issues.[6] Both sociolinguistic and psycholinguistic studies of bilingualism tend to present findings in terms of group performance. In order to allow valid interpretation of findings, group patterns should be shown to reflect individual performance, not simply by reporting standard deviations and conducting significance tests. Minimally, this means presentation of individual data, where the reader can see how many bilinguals conform to the group trend and how many do not, as well as the special characteristics of those that do and do not fit. It also means looking at data which do not fit the general pattern, e.g. Myers-Scotton's 38 instances of a composite matrix language, Maschler's (1997) 62, and Vaid and Menon's (2000) 32 respondents who reported doing arithmetic in two languages. Attempts at innovative individual data analysis, which go beyond narrative case descriptions, are to be encouraged. It should be kept in mind that the burden of this proposal rests not only with the researcher and writer but also with journal editors and reviewers, the gatekeepers of published research.

5. *Data collection procedures*. A review and analysis of every method that has been used to collect data on bilingualism is obviously beyond the scope of this work. As a first step toward such an end, Table 5.1 presents a list of procedures. These cover a wide range of techniques, including field-based and

laboratory methods as well as observational, experimental, and quasi-experimental approaches. These techniques have been used to investigate spoken or written language, ranging from large segments of text to individual phonetic features. The range of methods listed here also covers the distinction between actual behavior and reported language use. In an effort to summarize and simplify some of this complexity, the list of procedures are divided here roughly along sociopragmatic and psycholinguistic lines.

Table 5.1. Data collection procedures used widely in bilingual research

Sociopragmatic procedures	
Qualitative	Ethnographic field notes
	Sociolinguistic interview data
	'Spontaneous' speech samples
	Diaries/journals
	Role playing elicitation techniques
Directive	Self-report of language behavior
	Media (newspaper, radio) surveys
	Attitude questionnaires
	Person perception procedures
	Free and cued elicitation of scripts/interviews
	Social network data
Psycholinguistic procedures	
Identification/Recall tasks	Written discourse synthesis
	Story recall
	Translation
	Paraphrase
	Discourse completion
	Oral reading
	Sentence imitation
	Picture/object naming
Recognition tasks	Sentence comprehension tasks
	Metalinguistic judgments (of frequency, availability)
	Lexical decision
Discrimination tasks	Categorical perception of voicing (VOT) contrasts
	Same-different judgments

In the sociopragmatic section in Table 5.1, the methods at the top are more 'naturalistic' and 'qualitative,' while from the middle on down they become more calculated and directive. The psycholinguistic list is divided into three groups (identification, recognition, and discrimination) assumed to range from more global and complex processing (identification) to more molecular, elementary tasks (discrimination). Similarly, within each of the three groups the tasks are ordered from larger to smaller segments of linguistic material, again assumed to be along a continuum of complexity. The state of the art in bilingualism research is such that we do not yet have a direct link from bilingual phenomena such as CS and translation to specific tasks.

     6. *What to count and how to measure.* Another feature of methodology, which should also be linked to theory, research questions, and task, is the choice of performance measure, namely, what gets analyzed or counted. In sociopragmatic research on bilingualism, frequency counts based on linguistic categories are the norm (see the section 'Notes on Data and Method' at the end of the review of Myers-Scotton's work in Chapter 2). For psycholinguistic performance, the standard measures are accuracy, time, and errors in performance. Accuracy is conventionally measured as 'correct/incorrect' or with a point system to allow for partial correctness. Timing measures include latencies and rate of speech. For laboratory studies, time is usually measured in milliseconds, while in classroom-based research, performance may be measured in turn or utterance length, word counts, or duration of pauses. Quantitative measures of errors are roughly in complementary distribution with accuracy measures, while qualitative analyses of errors are meant to shed somewhat different light on the data. All of these psycholinguistic measures imply a normative or criterial standard of performance, which for bilingualism is usually the performance of the monolingual speaker. The accuracy of the bilingual is typically compared to the standard expected or achieved by the monolingual on the same task. The speed of performance of the bilingual is similarly compared to the monolingual. Both 'errors' and 'accuracy' carry prescriptive overtones.

     The measures described in the previous paragraph are attempts to characterize bilingual speech. While grounded in their own theoretical orientations, they do not make much of an attempt to map structure onto processing. That mapping, as indicated throughout this work, is not easy to bring about. It would take a lot less effort for ethnographers to continue counting instances of codeswitching to measure identity, for social psychologists to continue calculating type-token ratios as measures of lexical diversity, for pragmaticists to assess the distribution of pragmatic markers in a corpus, and for experimental phoneticians to measure VOTs. Unfortunately, some of the constructs in bilingualism are abstract and complex, thus not so easy to measure. We saw that code crossing (Rampton, 1995) required information about inter-personal and role relationships as well as knowledge about race, ethnicity, and multilingualism. Fluency, even if we define it as a processing phenomenon, remains a multidimensional construct, including lexical, prosodic, and pragmatic constituents.

     Dealing with these phenomena in the kind of comprehensive fashion demanded by the SPPL architecture means that we have to link structure and processing yet again through constructs that have a strong, countable bedrock.

To do this we will outline several dimensions of bilingual speech and point out how these can be described in metric terms.

Table 5.2 presents a list of structural measures, some gathered from the literature on bilingualism, others proposed in this work, all organized according to the information components of the SPPL Model.

Table 5.2 What to count to measure biligualism in the SPPL framework

Language choice	instances of codeswitching
	switch points
	direction of codeswitching
	trigger words
Affect	pragmatic markers (sort of, ya' know, well)
	vocatives
	pitch/intonation contours
	intensity/loudness
	verbosity
Identity	personal and place names
	person deictics (we, us) and their referents
	greetings, responses, blessings, 'leave-taking'
	accent
Context	settings a bilingual speaker interacts in
	listeners a bilingual speaker interacts with
	speaking opportunities
Genre	topics of conversations participated in
	topics of scripts (e.g. bank, medical,
	supermarket checkout line)
	'genre' tokens and types
Intentions	speech acts
	pragmatic markers
Lexical formulation	word tokens
	lemmas
	type token ratios
Discourse formulation	given and new information/ foregrounding,
	backgrounding
	cohesion markers
	relevance
Articulation	VOT
	rate of speech
	pauses
	dysfluencies

The measures in the table illustrate both the range of different phenomena across the components of the model as well as some of the diversity within each component. They do not, however, say how to identify each one, nor how to relate one measure to another in a more comprehensive approach to bilingualism.

For that we need to go one step further. Taking that step, beyond the list in the 'context' component in Table 5.2, we can ask what to count for settings and participants that would get at bilingual processing. We begin by following bilingual speakers, or asking them to follow themselves with microphones or by writing cognitive, sociolinguistic diaries, listing the different settings and participants they spoke with for a given day or set of days, the times they spoke, and the topics they spoke about, and the languages they spoke in. Then we reckon the amount of exposure to each language, for each setting, each participant, and each topic. We're still dealing with structure.

To get us to processing, we need measures of the processing mechanisms and basic level processes in the SPPL Model. For example, to assess 'imitation,' we want to look at the number of times a setting, listener, and topic repeated itself. To evaluate variation, we want to know how many *different* settings, listeners, and topics a bilingual 'experienced' in each language. To further ground the processing mechanisms of the SPPL Model, we recall the discussion of variation and control in the previous chapter. Measures of variation in performance are grounded in the notion that richer variation implies the ability to produce more and different utterances in a greater number of contexts. These measures are based on the notion that 'more is better.' Three types of variation were presented in Chapter 4. One was centered on linguistic form, and included measures of lexical diversity, vocabulary richness, and variation in speech act form. A second dealt with pragmatic range, attempting to bring together linguistic form (speech act form), pragmatic intent (politeness), and external context (the age and gender of the listener). The third measure, 'variation in control,' was more speculative, albeit grounded in Perceptual Control Theory (Powers, 1973) and William James' (1890) maxim, 'consistent ends by variable means.' The general approach, called "testing for the controlled variable," is to identify the individual's intention, change something in the environment, and observe whether the person acts to maintain a balance between intentions and perceptions of the environment. Two examples, one sociopragmatic and one psycholinguistic, were offered for how to test for controlled variables in codeswitching. The 'test' for a controlled variable involves five steps, summarized as follows:

1. Selecting a variable to be tested
2. Predicting what will occur if the individual does not maintain his/her goal or intention
3. Applying different amounts and kinds of disturbances to the variable

4.   Measuring the effects of the disturbances

5.   Identifying the variable

Both variation and control measures were illustrated with examples from language contact phenomena, in particular codeswitching and interference. Measures of codeswitching which were shown to be relevant included: structural variation–in phonological shape, syntactic form, and meaning–and functional variation–in terms of the bilingual speaker's choices, of social identity options, settings, participants, genres and topics, speech acts, lexico-pragmatic concepts, and discourse patterns. Procedures for examining sociopragmatic aspects of codeswitching might include measurement of the effects of negative attitudes to codeswitching on a bilingual speaker's use of this discourse mode. Psycho-linguistic aspects of codeswitching could be assessed by measuring the effects of demands for an increase in speed on the degree and kind of codeswitching.

Conclusions. As stated at the beginning of this section, the particular methodological approach should be derived from the theory and integrated with the research questions and tasks. Corpus analysis techniques and frequency counts are more appropriate for investigating societal trends, while social network analysis, Information Integration and Perceptual Control Theory are more fitting for the study of individual bilingualism. Studies that combine behavioral and attitudinal data are always better than those with attitudinal or behavioral data alone. Longitudinal inquiry is preferred over cross-sectional investigations. Laboratory and field-based settings are generally not combined in a single investigation, but there is no reason why they cannot be. Recognition of the limitations of each approach in terms of observational bias is an important part of the interpretive process. Finally, the methodological contributions of linguistic argumentation, even when the data are quantitative and not necessarily linguistic, are not to be overestimated.

The issues discussed in this section and in the methodological subtext set forth throughout this work have led to divisions in the field of bilingualism where, at best opposing camps ignore each other and at worst they are a greater source of antagonism than substantive issues. The strongest division falls along a dimension related to research setting–between experimental, laboratory approaches on the one hand and phenomenological, field-based approaches on the other. This division is not likely to lead to any constructive rivalry. The argument between those who collect actual language behavior and those who rely on reported language use, on the other hand, is more likely to lead to productive competition in the field of bilingualism.

CHAPTER SUMMARY

This chapter has attempted to show how the SPPL Model can account for phenomena claimed to be unique in bilingualism, namely codeswitching, interference, translation, computation, and cursing. The information components, or functional architecture of the model, attempted to locate these phenomena in the course of bilingual production. The processing mechanisms were directed toward explaining how they operate.

Two kinds of codeswitching were distinguished: sociopragmatic codeswitching, shown to be motivated by sociolinguistic factors, and structural-psycholinguistic codeswitching, motivated by lexicalization and grammatical-ization differences between the two languages in contact as well as by disturbances in formulation. Two constructs were used to distinguish these different types of codeswitching: intentionality and directionality. Socio-pragmatic codeswitching is more top-down, goal-driven, and influenced by external, contextual factors; psycholinguistic codeswitching is governed more by internal, individual processes. The directionality of codeswitching was raised as a related issued. It was argued that L1-to-L2 codeswitching should be more prevalent when codeswitching is sociopragmatically motivated and marked, while L2-to-L1 codeswitching should be more prevalent when there are difficulties in lexical access and fluency. Four processing mechanisms, imitation, variation, integration, and control, were applied to a discussion of codeswitching. The interplay between imitation and variation was proposed to explain how codeswitching operates. Two kinds of integration were mentioned as relevant: integration of structural information about and integration of processes. Finally, two views on control processes were presented, Green's Model of Inhibitory Control and Perceptual Control Theory.

Interference was defined as a subclass of language contact phenomenon, closely related to codeswitching. Three relevant constructs, fluency, automaticity, and completeness, were discussed in this regard. These were distinguished in terms of the structure-processing distinction made throughout this work. Completeness was described as a structural feature of language. Fluency and automaticity were characterized as processing-oriented, the former language-specific and the latter more general. These notions served as background for discussion of a variety of interference-related issues in bilingualism: size of vocabulary, rate of speech, and cross-language transfer in repetition priming.

Interpretation and translation were presented here as two independent, but related constructs. Interpretation was defined as motivated more by social and pragmatic processes, while translation was more grounded in linguistics and cognitive psychology. The section on interpretation and translation in this chapter presents an analysis of the major information sources and processing mechanisms relevant to these phenomena in terms of the SPPL Model. Research on interpretation, e.g. regarding the identities of the speaker and interpreter, the context of interpretation, etc., should draw more on the upper components of the model (identity, context, genre-discourse information), while research on translation should focus more directly on the psycholinguistic components of the model (formulation and articulation). Discussion of the sociopragmatic components of the model are compared with Wadensjo's (1998) interactive, discourse-oriented approach to the field; psycholinguistic sources of information are seen in light of Shlesinger's (2000) findings on linguistic and temporal factors in simultaneous interpretation.

Two final issues, mental arithmetic and cursing, while not necessarily unique bilingual phenomena, interact in special ways with bilingualism. Again, the major dimensions of the SPPL Model are found to be useful. Sociopragmatic aspects of the model are expected to provide insight into the learning contexts of bilingual arithmetic, while automaticity is expected to be relevant to both language processing and computation. The other issue, the use of racist, sexist, and otherwise offensive language, is offered as relevant to some of the same questions raised throughout the chapter. In particular, preference for cursing in a non-native language may shed light on matters raised regarding directionality in codeswitching. Sociopragmatic motivations for cursing may afford insight into triggering processes.

The chapter ends with a discussion of methodological issues and a set of guidelines for conducting research on bilingual processing. After reviewing a distinction between "two grand methods" (Runkel, 1990), I bring together the comments made throughout this work under the heading "Methodological Notes." In particular, I address the importance of a tight interface between theory and method; the nature of bilingualism as a multidimensional phenomenon; and some critical differences between group and individual data. Finally, data collection procedures, task variables, and measurement issues are addressed.

NOTES

[1] The work in contact linguistics (e.g. Thomason & Kaufman, 1988; Myers-Scotton, 2002) also maintains a structural view of interference.

[2] In the field of second language acquisition, however, the past decade has witnessed a fresh interest in these topics, e.g. Schmidt, 1992; Segalowitz, 1991; Towell, Hawkins & Bazergui, 1996; Cucchiarini, Stik, & Boves, 2000; Wray, 2002.

[3] Fillmore (1979) offers a broad programmatic treatment of fluency.

[4] Maugham's autobiography, The Summing Up, is a gold mine of bilingual data, from his deliberate efforts to translate Cicero to his failed attempts to learn Arabic.

[5] Rosansky (1976) pointed out the hazards aggregated data in second language acquisition morpheme studies).

[6] See Schoenfeld's (1974) American Psychological Association Presidential Address for a sharp critique of the issues in the argument. In bilingualism, methodological battles are latent in the 'differences' between and among second language acquisition, cross-linguistic, and bilingualism research.

6 Acquisition, Attrition, and Language Disturbances in Bilingualism

This chapter tries to show that the study of bilingualism is not just for the benefit of scholars and scientists. Bilingualism is about real people, people learning and losing languages, people choosing languages to communicate and people with cognitive limitations and language disorders.

The idea here is to organize the valuable practical knowledge of teachers and educators, social workers and psychologists, and speech and language clinicians into a framework in which professionals can see the larger picture and begin to talk to each other. The social worker and psychologist may be working with an immigrant client on acculturation problems related to negotiating mixed identities. The language teacher might be teaching advanced learners how to formulate compliments and complaints and fit them into appropriate contexts. And language clinicians working with bilingual children on lexical retrieval problems will hopefully see the potential value in doing their work in both of the child's languages. For these everyday situations, the SPPL Model and its processing mechanisms offer a common platform that hopefully will be of use both in connecting the questions and clarifying the issues.

We have found over the years that most of the problems met by professionals and researchers in the field can usually be understood as an interaction between one of several processes and a structure that tries to make sense of the problem by placing it somewhere within either a sociopragmatic or psycholinguistic context. As noted earlier in this book, many professional differences of opinion rest at least in part on terminological issues that can be resolved if one does not want to turn terminology into territory and researchers into predators. There might be another way to go about it. It is hardly surprising that so many of the terms in the SPPL Model have their direct or less direct equivalents in other formulations of the issues involved in researching bilingualism since many of these terms are infused by the work of so many other experts in the field. Since these equivalents are so readily available, and since one of the most powerful uses of the SPPL Model is a viewpoint that looks simultaneously at structure and process, it is hoped that the theoretical framework, as spelled out in chapters three and four, could be used as shown below by the real people of bilingualism, the bilinguals.

This chapter deals with applications and implications. The applications are for the study of language disorders in bilingual populations; the implications for research on acquisition and attrition. The first two sections are relatively brief, touching on questions of theory and practice. The third section, on language disorders, begins by outlining two apparently competing hypotheses: cognitive advantages of bilingualism and the limited processing capacity of language disordered populations. It then raises three sets of questions related to how conventional research would investigate these positions. I end by illustrating how the SPPL Model would handle some of the language-related issues in Down Syndrome, PDD/Autism, and Specific Language Impairment.

ACQUISITION IN BILINGUALISM

As most people in the field know there is a large measure of controversy among researchers in first and second language acquisition. An in-depth treatment of the contentious issues in either first language acquisition (e.g. Pinker, 1995; Tomasello, 1992) or bilingual language acquisition (e.g. Meisel, 1994; Lanza, 1997) is clearly beyond the scope of this work. I try here to go beyond the controversies. I am interested in both the acquisition of bilingualism and the acquisition of a second language that turns a person into someone who lives in a world distinctly different from a person with only one language, in early as well as late bilinguals, in simultaneous as well as sequential acquisition, and in children as well as adults.

In this section, I first raise questions regarding acquisition related to identity, language choice, and affect, and then move to processing issues, explaining how SPPL processing mechanisms might be useful in understanding lexical acquisition. Specifically I point to the relevance of codeswitching and translation in language acquisition. Next, I talk about fluency in bilingual acquisition and about lexical fluency in particular. Finally, I consider translation and translation equivalents in bilingual child language acquisition in light of an issue in first language acquisition (the 'principle of contrast') that might benefit from a bilingual perspective and bilingual data. Along the way, there are some practical suggestions for language teachers and parents raising bilingual children or whose children are studying second and foreign languages. These topics are not related to the latest research in bilingual language acquisition. Rather, they try to remind us that if most of the people in the world are not bilingual now, they probably will be so in a generation or two, and that we need to find way to integrate the societal and individual concerns and challenges that this creates in a in a single framework.

SPPL INFORMATION IN SECOND LANGUAGE ACQUISITION

Some of the major issues in the field of second language acquisition have been addressed in this work under the heading of language contact. Historically, studies in second language acquisition (SLA) tended to adopt research strategies and assumptions that mimicked research on first language acquisition. The generative orientation concentrates on language structure and on finding second language evidence for structural claims about how language is organized or represented in the mind (e.g. Epstein, Flynn, & Martohardjono, 1996). This has been the basic focus of the research program in generative linguistics and in first language acquisition research, two of the three domains outlined in Chomsky's (1986) Managua Lectures. Data in these two areas of generative linguistics have primarily come from linguistic analyses, laboratory experiments, and clinical reports to support claims about principles and parameters, both constructs that are grounded in language structure. In a 'principles and parameters' framework, 'process' is inferred from 'product,' i.e. from linguistic structure and/or the products of comprehension. The third area Chomsky (1986) said was relevant to an understanding of language was the study of language use. At best, this area has suffered from benign neglect, as pragmatics and sociolinguistics have followed their own tracks, largely independent of the generative enterprise. The present work has been more interested in language use in its processing dimensions because of the unique light they shed on bilingualism.

In stark contrast to the generative strain in second language acquisition, Rampton and Zentella both argue against an anti-bilingualism bias in their respective societies' views on the role of English and the mother tongue in educational programs[1]. Their work is no less important for social policy than it is for English language instruction. Rampton attacks ESL and transitional bilingual education programs as inherently racist, citing British government commissions and policy documents which are highly critical of ESL programs for pulling children out of the mainstream classroom and socially stigmatizing them as "language minorities," non-native speakers of English, or "bilingual." Zentella traces some of the history which led to the "English only" movement in the US, decries the labeling of bilingual children as LEPs (Limited English Proficiency), and tells the heart-rending story of Isabel "in and out of special education" and her battle for a high school equivalency diploma.

One can deplore, praise or tolerate the fact that people tend to make normative judgments about the manner of using language, or, in the case of bilingualism, about which languages are used in various contexts for different purposes. The fact is that these judgments occur, and often inform or influence political or educational policy and debate. Frameworks like the SPPL Model create, almost by default, an arena for such debate because of the clarity they seek, especially in the distinctions and bridges they construct between sociopragmatic and psycholinguistic elements of language production. Rather than avoid the questions with their risk of labeling, it might be helpful, in passing, to refer to those areas where the SPPL Model might illuminate the context surrounding these issues.

The acquisition of bilingualism, as a first language[2] or second tongue, simultaneously or sequentially, in the home or in the daycare center, in a natural environment alone or in both formal and informal contexts, can be described with the information components of the SPPL Model. The term acquisition is wider here than in most models of second language acquisition (for a review see Ellis, 1994) because we are dealing with the acquisition of a second identity, or at least various components of identity, and that goes far beyond the didactic range of the traditional second language classroom. As such, the SPPL framework points to some tough ethical questions that touch on decisions regarding teaching methods. One issue is whether the second or foreign language learner should be asked to adopt a new identity, even for classroom purposes. For example, in the audiolingual language instruction environment of the 1960s, it was taken for granted that the language learner would receive a name in the new language. Andrew, Pat, and Steve became André, Patrice, and Etienne. While this practice was not necessarily explicit policy, it generally went unquestioned in the heyday of substitution drills, memorization of dialogues, and language laboratories. In the current era in which pluralism and the rights of language minorities enjoy similar sway, changing a student's name or even offering the pupil a second name would raise a multitude of of uncomfortable questions for language teaching professionals in a rich country. The fact that many educators today are leery of such impositions does not, however, mean that the identity issues highlighted by the SPPL Language Choice Model go away. On the contrary, it is the speaker herself who adopts an identity, an identity often designed with stars, stripes, and union jacks–as one can see in the global proliferation of schools teaching business English as a second language.

Perhaps less political, but no less controversial, are other issues raised by the SPPL Model's language choice and affective modules. The model reflects a reality in which language choice and affective factors influence speech production from the topmost, conscious levels to the most subtle and automatic levels of articulation. If we make some fairly simple assumptions–that not all students learn in the same ways, that each student should bring her best to the fore, and that mixed languages are an ever increasing fact of life in multicultural societies–then we might also say that translation and codeswitching should be encouraged, or at least not delegitimized, in second language acquisition and teaching. Endorsement of translation as a technique for acquiring a second language would, however, open one to 'guilt by association' with the late nineteenth, early twentieth century grammar-translation approach. And codeswitching would be attacked by monolingual purists from both languages. The critics of the grammar-translation approach need not even be answered in an era when translated subtitles on TV are such an important part of some people's language learning experience. And the monolingual purists may have powerful aesthetic arguments, but less of a solution to the reality most children meet during their formative years.

I would propose that stimulation of the language choice module in the form of translation and codeswitching should be good for at least two aspects of second language acquisition. Translation could support lexical acquisition by helping to establish strong cross-language links and fine-tuning of within-language semantic distinctions. In second language writing, translation offers one of the best ways to overcome limitations in lexical access. The popularity of online translation dictionaries of various kinds like Babylon shows that this strategy has been endorsed by millions of people with the most pronounced interest in improving lexical access in a second or third language. Charles Ferguson once described a teacher in a Delhi English class who himself knew four or five Indian languages, but more notably facilitated the use of the other six languages represented in the class and in doing so maintained a high level of attention and activity.

The encouragement of codeswitching should benefit the development of second language fluency, a facet of language learning that has only recently begun to receive extensive attention in linguistic research and has yet to be addressed seriously in pedagogical techniques. Allowing codeswitching in the second language classroom, especially in diglossic situations such as the large Spanish-speaking communities in the United States, offers a message that fluency (in the form of speed and density) is important in language production. Fluency and fluency training should be looked at from sociopragmatic as well as psycholinguistic perspectives to determine its role in building certainty and confidence, and perhaps ultimately, second language identity.

School violence is an issue potentially relevant to classroom language acquisition. The day-to-day reality in most Western schools includes the defacement of property, verbal insults and abuse, and physical violence or the threat thereof. This reality, of course, leads directly to information in the affective module of the SPPL Model of bilingualism. A broad-based investigation of how violence plays itself out in context, intentions, and formulation would be useful in mapping the sociopragmatic and psycho-linguistic aspects of this phenomenon. One area that could be particularly promising would be a study of cursing, which could tell us a lot about bilingualism, as well as contributing to an understanding of the limits of context, intent, and formulation.

PROCESSING FOR FLUENCY IN SECOND LANGUAGE ACQUISITION

One of the main working elements of the SPPL Model is creating a systematized way of cross relating structural and processing aspects of bilingualism, allowing us to make use of valuable focused research in a broad integrative framework. Among the least structural and most processing oriented approaches in language acquisition is Aitchison's (1987) treatment of lexical acquisition. In that work, Aitchison delineates three tasks in the acquisition of meaning: labeling, packaging, and network building. Labeling is considered more than pointing to an object and saying its name or associating object and word (Aitchison, 1987:87-88). It is said to be grounded in 'symbolization,' an ability that develops relatively slowly between the ages of one and two. It is characterized as "the realization that a particular combination of sounds 'means' or symbolizes a certain object" (p. 88). Packaging is defined as classification, i.e. the organization of objects under a particular label" (p. 96). And network building is the process involving refinement of meaning and overall organization of words in the mind. It is said to proceed slowly and not necessarily in a linear path toward adult meaning. Aitchison cites Bowerman's (1982) data from a two-year-old, which showed adult-like knowledge of the verbs 'put' and 'give' at age two and regression at age three, when the meanings of these two words are exchanged. In addition to this U-shaped developmental curve, semantic network building may extend even throughout an entire lifetime.[3] To create some correspondence with the SPPL processing terminology, we could say that labeling, especially the matching of word and object is driven by the imitation mechanism; packaging is clearly related to the notion of variation as it is used here; and network building, as an organizational task, can be assumed to make use of integration and control mechanisms to coordinate labeling and packaging. The declaration of kinship between Aitchison's schema and the SPPL Model is not trivial; it allows us to take valuable insights on the processing aspects of acquisition and use the structure of the SPPL Model to relate then to the entire range of the bilingual experience.

All four processing mechanisms (as well as others) are necessary for the development of bilingualism. Chapter 4 showed that processes involving imitation and variation are widespread in bilingual speech. Implicit in that discussion was the idea that fluency, built up from recognition and identification tasks involving imitation, will contribute to the development of fluency in a second language. Similarly, mental operations involving discrimination, class-ification, and categorization, like those found in codeswitching and translation (see Chapter 5), help in lexical, grammatical, and pragmatic language acquisition. The argument here is that the interplay between imitation and variation may be important in understanding what drives language acquisition. Imitation alone is insufficient to learn even the most basic of cognitive skills, particularly those involving discrimination and classification. Similarly, variation by itself does not permit entry to some of the critical aspects of language learning, especially those involving fluency.

The Chomskyan view, even in its strongest statement on behalf of an innate language acquisition device, always admitted that the child would need a 'trigger' to release the full impact of the genetic program. In the half century since the beginning of the enterprise, precious little has been written about the nature of that 'trigger.' The proposal here is that processing, not structure, is the key to the time-release of the linguistic program available to most infants at birth. More specifically, to go from a finite set of hierarchically-organized structures to a potentially infinite set of linear sentences, the child needs to be able to perceive and make use of contrast. From distinctive features in phonology to form-content mapping in structural linguistics, contrast is the axial construct in linguistics. Among the contrasts relevant for language acquisition is the one between imitation and variation. The imitation mechanism tells the child to move forward, to let speech flow. The variation mechanism tells her to stop, to make finer and finer distinctions, in sounds and eventually in meanings. Together these mechanisms provide an account for the fluency-accuracy contrast in speech production, and may provide a clue to one of the hidden secrets of how a child's innate language acquisition device emerges.

Fluency depends in large part on structural and processing features of a person's lexicon. Structurally, the size and diversity of one's lexicon both contribute to fluency. Processing features include the rate at which words are accessed and retrieved. These features differ across languages, giving some languages the impression of being faster and more automatic, others the reputation of being slower and more deliberate.[4] But lexical knowledge is neither monolithic nor subject to equal access and retrieval. Words come in single, double, and multisyllabic varieties, with initial, final, and penultimate stress, one by one or in collocations. They are used to convey content and as grammatical connectors; some are independent in the mental lexicon, while others are collocated. Words fit sometimes smoothly, sometimes not so effortlessly into a variety of syntactic frames.

One of the key issues for fluency raised in this book is that structural representations of words are not the same across speakers, nor are they the same for an individual speaker across time. This idea comes from bilingualism, and in it lies a bilingual dilemma: How to maintain fluency in the face of incomplete and variant lexical representations, and all this in two languages. A similar dilemma exists in bilingual processing: How to sustain fluency given the need to manage two lexicons. Codeswitching and translation are two phenomena that help a bilingual speaker compensate for disturbances in fluency. As explained in the previous chapter, these phenomena rely on imitation and variation, integration and control. Fluent speech is produced when there is an appropriate and balanced use of the imitation and variation mechanisms.

From a developmental perspective, one might want to examine the plausible hypothesis that imitation processes might be more involved at the initial stages of second language acquisition. When second language resources are limited, and the learner has to rely heavily on what is known about language and language learning in general (from L1) and what little is known about L2, then mimetic processes may be more useful. Variation processes such as discrimination, classification, and categorization, could kick in later. Such would appear to be the case in certain aspects of first language acquisition, as Aitchison says so clearly.

TRANSLATION EQUIVALENTS AND CODESWITCHING IN EARLY BILINGUAL ACQUISITION

Among the perennial issues in bilingual acquisition is the question of representation of two languages in bilingual children, or more specifically, whether, when, and to what extent the two languages of a bilingual child are differentiated. In discussing this question, Genesee (2001) says that "the languages of the bilingual child are represented in underlyingly differentiated ways at least from the beginning of early language production, and possibly earlier" (p. 158). A related, but not identical question, is the extent to which the development of two languages proceeds along an autonomous or interdependent course.[5] Genesee summarizes the evidence on this question as favoring autonomy and that bilingual development is largely parallel to monolingual development (p. 160; White & Genesee, 1996). But the data cited for these generalizations are for the most part based on studies of syntactic and phonological development. Lexical development has only recently entered this discussion.

One of the questions about lexical development asks whether bilingual children show evidence of translation equivalents or synonyms in the early stages of learning another language. Zentella (1997) reports relatively limited overlap in the Spanish and English lexicons transcribed from a one hour language sample recorded at age 2;8, and cites Snow (1993) as further evidence of differentiation. Volterra and Taeschner (1978; Taeschner, 1983) also reported that the two subjects in her study produced "few" equivalents, but Quay (1995) shows that the proportion was actually from 8 to 20 percent in Taeschner's data. Translation equivalents were found in greater numbers (36-41 percent) in Quay's case study of a Spanish-English bilingual child, while Pearson, Fernandez and Oller (1995) reported an average of 30 percent 'doublets' for Spanish-English bilingual children.[6] Notwithstanding the difficulties in data collection and comparability across studies (due to differences in age and context), the empirical question seems to be resolved in favor of the presence of translation equivalents, perhaps to a greater extent for language pairs that are genealogically related.

A theoretical issue raised by these data relates to what Clark (1987, 1990) has called the 'principle of contrast.' This principle, grounded in structural linguistics and linguistic form, states that "Speakers take every difference in form to mark a difference in meaning" (Clark, 1993:69). It follows from the principle of contrast that speakers should not like, perhaps should not even allow, synonymy in language use. First language acquisition research (both observational as well as experimental studies) shows general agreement regarding the implications of the principle (see Clark 1987 for a summary). But, the presence of translation equivalents in bilingual children's lexical development stands as thorn in the side of this consensus. Translation equivalents contradict the assumption that one referent can have two labels in early bilingual development. This is a very restricted, referential view of language. Another interpretation of translation equivalents takes us beyond the confines of the words and beneath the surface of language production, to the context in which the words were uttered and to the child's intentions in uttering them. In the framework of the SPPL Model, then, the bilingual child who uses Spanish 'perro' as well as English 'dog' may do so to mark differences in setting, participants, or sociopragmatic intentions. He might also do so to talk about two different dogs. It is likely that the bilingual child was exposed to the two words in different settings, by different speakers, and/or in connection with different topics. This external contextual information is encoded in the child's representation of the two words. This interpretation of translation equivalents is more consistent with a sociopragmatic view of language acquisition. In fact, the 'principle of contrast,' conceived initially and essentially as a pragmatic principle (Clark, 1987), may be nothing more than the child language researcher's recognition of the importance of sociopragmatic context.

Another phenomenon relevant to bilingual representation and language differentiation is codeswitching in early child language. At the one word stage codeswitching would involve changes in language use across speaking turns, i.e. inter-sententially. In two word speech it could also involve intrasentential switching. Unfortunately, despite more than fifty years of scientific research on codeswitching, folk wisdom prevails outside of academia. And the folkwisdom about codeswitching, even among those who do a lot of it, is that it's bad for the brain, it causes confusion, and it will lead to problems in school. This view implies that codeswitching is a sign of lack of differentiation, and lack of differentiation is bad. But, as Zentella says so forcefully, the pediatrician, school official, or other 'professional' makes this kind of assessment based on scanty data. The child is usually (if not always) assessed in the majority language. The diversity of patterns of bilingualism in the home, on *el bloque*, and even in the schoolyard is ignored. Socialization patterns, and their effect on bilingual language use and acquisition, are disregarded. In this connection, Zentella points out that Puerto Rican families are more situation-centered than the child-centered pattern of middle class white Americans.

Beyond the emotional charges accompanying much of the talk about codeswitching, I offer the following attempt at reconciliation. Structural properties of codeswitching (e.g. its syntactic locus, distributional properties and prevalence) alone cannot tell us unequivocally about whether a child's two languages are represented in like fashion or whether they are differentiated. Neither can structural and distributional features of codeswitching in the child's environment (e.g. how much his parents and siblings codeswitch, the direction of their codeswitching, etc.) tell us much about questions of representation. However, coupled with organized information about identity, context, genre, and intention, this structural information can contribute to a wider picture of the role of codeswitching in child language acquisition. Zentella (1997:96, 254) noted that codeswitched translations/repetitions only amounted to about 14 percent of the instances in her corpus. Moreover, these hundred or so occurrences were spread over five children in a large number of situations. They numbered even fewer in the case study of the mother-daughter pair Isabel-Maria. Despite their limited use, translation/repetition was shown to fulfill a variety of functions, many of which were to promote communication and socialization of the child. This variation, as argued in the previous chapter, is not strictly sociolinguistic, and can have cognitive implications as well. Variation, then, is a common dimension in structural and functional approaches to bilingualism. The principle of contrast and sociopragmatic variation in codeswitching rely on the same underlying processing mechanisms. Thus, at the level of processing it may be possible to find a common language for the child language researcher to talk to the bilingual ethnographer.

Another area of common interest is intentions. Tomasello (2003) and Clark (1990) point to the "recognition of intentions" as an important beginning in the child's overall understanding of rational behavior. Ethnographers like Zentella and Rampton and students of bilingual socialization like Lanza and Schieffelin are also interested in speaker intentions, and in the ways they encode knowledge about the identity, ethnicity, family and discourse. Clark and Clark (1979) talk about speaker intentions in terms of lexical choice, indicating that part of the child's acquisition of lexical knowledge involves learning that different words are chosen for different situations. Language crossing (Rampton, 1995) is grounded in the intentions of the speaker to do the unexpected, to use a language that doesn't 'belong' to him. Thus, variation in lexical choice and language choice as a function of contextual information may be an important contributor to language acquisition and socialization. In the SPPL Model, intentions are derived from speech act information and pragmatic markers; they are an integral of context and illocutionary force. The variation mechanism of the SPPL Model may be useful, then, in informing this aspect of bilingual acquisition.

INVESTIGATING BILINGUAL LOSS AND ATTRITION

Like the previous section, this brief statement is not intended to be representative of the literature on language attrition, nor does it attempt to clarify some of the confusion surrounding terminology such as shift and loss, markedness and simplicity. Myers-Scotton (2002) does this job both precisely and extensively, albeit from the structural perspective of her model (see Chapter 2). Rather, I make this statement as a way of showing another set of problems for which the structural-processing and sociopragmatic-psycholinguistic distinctions in the SPPL Model might be useful. Another purpose here is to foreshadow the discussion of atypical language use in the following section in order to indicate that the same components and processing mechanisms can handle both kinds of phenomena.

LOSS OF LANGUAGE STRUCTURES: WYSINOTWYG (WHAT YOU SEE IS NOT WHAT YOU GET)

The fundamental distinction between structure and process in the SPPL Model may be a useful starting point in looking at language loss. The overall approach to the study of language attrition, in language contact as well as language pathology, has been to focus on *what* has been lost. The conventional research strategy has been to look for missing structures in one or more components of a speaker's knowledge, e.g. a morpheme lost, a lexeme attrited.

Language, however, is more than inventory, and a list of missing parts does not really tell enough about a complex process that is really best analyzed with an integrated framework. For example, we can begin by speculating as to what might be indicative of attrition in the language choice module. Codeswitching, interference, and dysfluencies such as pauses and false starts, have all been considered bona fide evidence of loss and attrition. But, as I attempted to show in Chapter 5, these same phenomena can also be considered evidence of dynamic language contact and language change. Some of the problems in deciding about these phenomena are reflected in studies as to whether a word or phrase is borrowed or codeswitched, and whether codeswitching is flagged or smooth. In that line of work, the question of loss and attrition unfortunately does not generally arise. Déjà vu states, tip-of-the-tongue conditions, and everyday memory lapses about where you put the keys to the house are all temporary states of loss or its recovery. For language, a person might not have lost a certain lexeme–when describing let's say the name of a car part which he usually knows very well in L1. But exposure to an intellectually or emotionally demanding L2-dominated environment like a language lab or a conference podium may make that lexeme appear temporarily attrited even though the person has been dealing intensively in L1 garage language of late.

DISTINGUISHING ATTRITION FROM NON-ACQUISITION

Another problem with the structural, WYSIWYG approach to attrition is deciding whether errors and gaps in a bilingual's speech come from an intact system or are perhaps due to 'incomplete' acquisition. This problem is no less difficult for research on aphasia and children's language disorders, where primordial data on language use rarely exist, than it is for bilingual research, where even long-term, longitudinal studies have no criterion for knowing whether a particular structure has been acquired and lost or whether it was never acquired in the first place. There is no apparent solution to this problem for group studies of attrition at present. Thus, we have no choice but to make edu-cated guesses about prior acquisition based on evidence amassed across a range of studies in the field and frequency data available in word lists and corpora.

Unfortunately, none of the methods used to study of attrition offers insight into individual language use. For example, children who live abroad and travel with professional parents might appear to be perfectly fluent in L1. But after many adult years in an L2 environment, they seem to have lost some of their L1 faculties. Closer examination shows that in the years that other children picked up that L1 faculty, these children were traveling elsewhere. Only deep but focused interviews could reveal why what you see or hear is not necessarily what you get. In lieu of, or until the advent of, extensive recordings and archiving of speech from birth through maturity and exhaustive comparisons with resources as diverse as school curricula and TV scripts, the least objectionable approach for dealing with our lack of knowledge about a priori language ability in bilingualism as well as in language pathology would appear to be longitudinal studies. These studies should aim to gather large quantities of data from individual language users. As such, they are labor intensive, in particular at the stages of data collection, transcription, and digitilization. There are a number of ways to conserve resources without sacrificing focus on the primary research interest. These include limiting the number of speakers/ participants and broadening the time interval between data collection sessions (e.g. de Bot & Clyne, 1994). They also include selective and calculated data collection, transcription, and analysis procedures (e.g. Feldman, 1997) rather than more exhaustive and exhausting methods (DeWaele, 1998, 2001).

A potential research strategy, which conforms to the sociopragmatic biases of this work in general and fits into the *language choice module* in particular, would be to examine the social history of an attriting individual to see the extent to which linguistic phenomena (performance codeswitching, interference, and dysfluencies) are supported by societal patterns of language use and individual changes in identity. Systematic profiling of three sources of information (societal language use, individual identity, and indicators of attrition) would be a first step in this direction. These profiles could be constructed from multiple sources of data based on corpora, questionnaires, interviews, behavioral observations, and experimental probes, each one making a unique contribution to the general picture. One would then look for convergence of evidence across sources of information as well as data collection procedures. Contradictions among data sources ought to be taken seriously and not simply passed off as task-related differences. Too much convergence should be held suspect as hostile to the inherent individuality of bilingual behavior in general and attrition in particular.

Attrition and loss of *speech act* information are somewhat problematic for a discussion of loss and attrition. We would like to imagine illocutionary force to be a more or less universal construct (Fraser, Rintell, & Walters, 1980; but see Wierzbicka, 1991, for a well-placed critique of this claim). In other words, all speakers are presumed to be capable of making requests, promises, dares, offers, refusals, etc. The formulation, or encoding, of these constructs, however, is seen as governed by more particular, sociopragmatic processes and language specific constraints. For example, some cultures discourage oaths, vows, and promises and provide formal means for annulling them (cf., Babylonian Talmud, Tractate Nedarim). In other cultures, refusals are never encoded explicitly, and the interlocutor must be sensitive to a variety of non-verbal cues and conventions in order to detect one. Even a Wernicke's aphasic has intentions, though conventional means for formulating those speech acts may be severely constrained by his medical condition. In general, then, *illocutionary force* cannot be subject to attrition if it is to retain its defined capacities.

Speech acts, on the other hand, are subject to deactivation and modification as a result of language and culture contact, aging, and other social phenomena. For example, a parent, even a young parent, in his or her twenties and thirties, learns quickly to intentionally limit or curb the use of promises in the home as a survival technique for dealing with consumer-oriented children. The illocutionary force of a promise does not undergo attrition through lack of use; nor does its related propositional content. What may be attrited, however, is the range of possibilities for issuing a promise. In attrition, then, we may find evidence of language use restricted to a single form or perhaps even the use of literal, explicit utterances to issue bona fide promises. Constrained variation in use may lead to temporary attrition, whereas changes in social milieu, to a community where promising and committing are more prevalent, can bring about re-acquisition, or at least put the brakes on attrition. The dynamic relationships among acquisition, attrition, and re-acquisition are so far uncharted territory.

The strategy of looking for observable gaps as evidence of attrition ordinarily leads the researcher to the *formulator*, and in particular, to the study of a speaker's lexical knowledge. Usually the focus is on lexemes, the language user's concrete knowledge of words, including both form and meaning. Lemmas, when defined as the abstract syntactic and semantic information about a word, are not considered attrited. But, as argued in earlier chapters, bilingual speakers, like monolinguals in a tip-of-the-tongue state, may have better access to certain aspects of a lemma (e.g. initial sound, number of syllables, synonyms) than to others (e.g. syntactic arguments). We generally do not think of lexical concepts as attrited, but a sociopragmatic view of language attrition implies that lexico-pragmatic concepts are influenced by language contact. And these concepts put the notion of a lemma on wobbly ground, as indicated earlier in this book. Thus, while there may be no hard evidence for attrition at the conceptual level, there is plausible evidence that for bilinguals, conceptual nodes are re-organized, semantic fields are integrated, and pragmatic notions are adapted. Attrition and loss at the level of formulation may be an appropriate beginning for a study of malapropisms and speech errors, but the dynamic nature of language use behooves us to cast a wider net for the data.

One way to integrate sociopragmatic and psycholinguistic concerns is to focus on individual *identity*. To the extent that loss and attrition are reflected in a person's individual identity, they involve both macro- and micro-level information. Macro-level social change can be investigated in language use influenced by the experiences of war, famine, terrorism, immigration, and the like. These changes are accompanied by related shifts in interpersonal experiences, shifts in social networks, or exposure to new languages. Societal and interpersonal shifts can lead to changes in social identity. The individual is not passive in this process. Rather, individual choices take into account both macro and micro level social information. These choices are relevant to a range of phenomena, including the fact that communication among bilinguals is usually monolingual and that L1 to L2 codeswitching is motivated socially by identity considerations or pragmatically by goals to indicate emphasis, focus, and attention. These phenomena need to be examined with experimental research on lexical attrition using techniques such as naming, tip-of-the-tongue tasks, role-playing, etc. A study involving this combination of methods, while focused on the individual, still falls short of an understanding of underlying processes and mechanisms and a fully integrated approach to the complex problems in the study of language attrition.

A ROLE FOR PROCESSING IN LOSS AND ATTRITION

Bilingual loss and attrition research has focused primarily on the lexicon, probably because lexical loss is readily observable and easily measurable, and not necessarily because of theoretical commitment to the 'word' as the primary unit of analysis. However, an approach restricted to observables may mask important aspects of language loss and attrition. Attrition of advanced level syntax, pragmatics, and some of the subtleties underlying phonological processing have not received much research attention.

The literature on language disorders, especially Leonard's (1998) comprehensive review of research on specific language impairment (SLI) in children, may be a useful place to begin consideration of some of the processing questions in bilingual attrition. Leonard distinguishes between general and specific processing limitations. In the former category, he names limitations in memory, energy, and time as characteristic of children with SLI. Among specific processing difficulties, he names deficits in phonological and temporal processing and neuromaturational delay.

Each of the general processing factors discussed by Leonard is also relevant to fluent processing among bilinguals. One of the formidable questions in studying bilingual language loss is how to distinguish real attrition from the everyday bilingual annoyance of retrieving a word not readily accessible. Unfortunately, studies of bilingual vocabulary continue to suffer from methodological flaws, including *between-subjects* experimental designs, which compare bilinguals to monolinguals, often without appropriate controls for intelligence, socio-economic status, input, etc. Exceptions are beginning to appear in the literature (e.g. Leseman, 2000). Throughout this work, I have expressed a strong preference single or multiple case study analyses, where the most important comparison in studies of bilingualism is a *within-subjects* comparison of the individual's performance in both L1 and L2. For immigrant bilingualism, limitations on the cognitive effort available for bilingual processing are likely to result from energy committed to immigrating. In the best of all immigration experiences, a great deal of resources are allocated to daily decisions regarding identity, leaving a more restricted pool of cognitive means to deal with the language-related issues of bilingualism.

One area of language processing which has not yet made its way systematically to studies of bilingualism concerns temporal processing variables (e.g. Merzenich et al., 1996). Among the relevant parameters in this area are duration, density, frequency, redundancy, and salience of sounds, words, or grammatical patterns. When any of these parameters differ across languages, and they invariably do, the bilingual must make a cognitive adjustment. That adjustment takes up space in memory and requires cognitive resources. The few studies of bilingual timing have come more from an interest in second language acquisition and 'foreign accent' than in bilingualism per se, most research being focused at the phonetic and phonemic levels of processing (see Piske, MacKay & Flege, 2001 for a review).

The SPPL Model offers a somewhat different perspective on processing. It allows for loss, attrition and even pathology due to sociopragmatic as well as psycholinguistic factors, investigating all of these phenomena with the same constructs and methods. Language loss or attrition due to impairment of the imitation mechanism should show up in tasks involving recognition, naming, recall, and priming using conventional response measures, e.g. accuracy, reaction time, and errors. Loss due to impairment in the variation mechanism could be assessed in tasks based on discrimination and classification processes, especially those involving codeswitching, paraphrase and translation, and relevant response measures such as linguistic diversity.

Research on processing in loss and attrition is highly constrained and generally restricted to laboratory settings and experimental designs. Generally, there is very little in the way of context. Language is assessed in the framework of traditional input-output models of production, which do not take explicit account of intentions. Intentions can be incorporated into traditional methods, by manipulating instructions in experimental paradigms and by including information about identity and goals within a framework of personal design (Anderson, 1990). This modification would be an important first step toward deriving the methodology from the substantive claims of the Sociopragmatic-Psycholinguistic Information Model and its accompanying mechanisms.

A FURTHER METHODOLOGICAL COMMENT

The sociopragmatic information components and psycholinguistic processing mechanisms mapped out in Chapters 3 and 4 suggest an integrated methodology for studying loss and attrition. Myers-Scotton's (2002) recent effort takes notions of cross-generational shift and social domain into account in her treatment of shift and attrition. But I'm not sure she would see her work as a tight integration of social and psycholinguistic information. Sociological issues in language loss aim for broad scope, investigating patterns across region, nation, ethnolinguistic group, and community. They attempt to explain trends across time and place. Sociolinguistic studies of language loss are designed with large numbers of participants and group comparisons, using interviews, questionnaires, and ethnographic techniques. Interpretive tools include data reduction measures such as factor analysis and regression and qualitative interpretation of interview and ethnographic data such as discourse analysis. Future work will certainly involve the use of large speech corpora and accompanying concordancing and statistical techniques.

The issues in language attrition of interest to psycholinguistics are focused on the individual and on mental processing. Psycholinguistic studies of attrition prefer small numbers of subjects and experimental designs manipulating linguistic stimuli and task parameters. Data are submitted to parametric and non-parametric statistical tests, using response measures such as accuracy, reaction time, and errors. Qualitative analyses tend to be more post-hoc than pre-planned, and they focus on lexical attrition almost to the exclusion of other linguistic domains.

The gap engendered by these methodological differences is more difficult to bridge than substantive divisions. It was because of these difficulties I came up with the SPPL Model and devoted so much effort to methodological issues. One way to begin cross-fertilization between sociolinguistic and psycholinguistic approaches to the study of loss and attrition was to combine methods from the two fields in a single study. In Dittmar, Spolsky and Walters (1997, 1998) we took the initial steps in this direction. These studies began with a set of sociolinguistic interviews of immigrants with a pre-planned set of demographic characteristics and moved to a longitudinal study of a smaller group of immigrants, who were probed for specific lexical, semantic, and pragmatic knowledge in the framework of information about individual identity and social networks. But combining methods is still far from integrating them. The SPPL framework and its processing mechanisms go further, calling for an integrative of sociopragmatic and psycholinguistic information via methods derived from the constructs themselves. Data include actual language behavior as well as attitudinal evidence and metalinguistic judgments. Interpretive tools include qualitative and quantitative techniques, each appropriate to the source of data. This is no mean feat in an academic atmosphere beset by disciplinary entrenchment and and methodological dissent. The section that follows is a modest attempt to chart out such a course for the study of bilingualism and atypical language use.

BILINGUALISM AND LANGUAGE DISTURBANCES[7]

Despite (or perhaps because of) the large numbers of bilinguals and language minorities throughout the world and the widespread migrations of the 1990s, the study of bilingualism in populations with various developmental and adult language disturbances has remained a neglected area of research. One reason for this may be a fear of repeating the mistakes of an earlier era when language minorities and non-standard dialect speakers were over-represented in classrooms and institutions for retarded children. A related reason may be assimilationist government policies and the politically-charged nature of bilingualism and its relation to ethnic identity. A further reason may be the lack of a clear direction as to how to treat, or even to diagnose, a bilingual with a possible language impairment. And still another reason for the dearth of data on bilingualism and language disturbances is the absence of a workable scientific framework and the fact that research on language impairment has been largely based on notions of 'normality' which do not exist for bilinguals. Traditional research designs involving group comparisons make studies of bilinguals with language disturbances a labor intensive enterprise, requiring comparisons with no fewer than five comparison groups (two groups of 'normal' unilinguals, a group of 'normal' bilinguals, and two groups of unilingual language impaired children).[8] Clearly the issues are not simple or one-dimensional. They extend to linguistic, social, and cognitive aspects of spoken as well as written language.

Repeated searches for studies on bilingualism in Down syndrome, PDD/autism, schizophrenia, SLI, stuttering, and Tourette's populations revealed less than a handful of papers, mostly geared to parents and practitioners. As a result of the lack of attention to this subject, folk wisdom reigns—in the schools, in the clinic, and in the minds of policy-makers. Ask a speech and language clinician whether a child with immigrant parents diagnosed as SLI (specific language impairment) should be spoken to at home in the parents' native language or in the school language, and the answer is more than likely to be 'the school language.' If the parents are unable, or unwilling, to act on this advice, perhaps the professional will reconsider. But the alternative advice will almost invariably be a paraphrase of the following recommendation, taken from a "Speech and Language Evaluation" of a prestigious center for developmental disorders: "The parents should expose the child to a single language." The bilingual option is not offered. The same story underlies the philosophy behind those school curricula that rule that a child should not receive reading instruction in two languages at the same time. That story plays itself out daily among clinicians, reading specialists, and program administrators. Even in Montreal, a city which has done perhaps more than any in the world to promote bilingualism, anglophone children who begin in French immersion programs and are diagnosed as SLI/learning disabled are often tracked back to English language schools. Again, the bilingual option is rejected.

The cognitive implication of these decisions is that bilingualism interferes with cognitive processing, that a second language will take up resources that the child needs to compensate for the impairment. In crude terms, that's as if cognitive resources were a gas tank that could power a car wherever one pointed the steering wheel. But the research on bilingualism and cognitive development over the past 35 years tells a different story. This line of studies argues that bilingualism is related to cognitive advantage, to flexibility, to creativity, and to originality, not to mention the fact that the bilingual is able to function in two societies, two cultures. This body of work, which consistently reports positive effects of bilingualism on cognitive development, is also not impervious to criticism. It, too, is politically charged and motivated, methodologically imperfect, and in some cases out and out defective.

Socially, bilingual children with difficulties in language use may be ostracized or excluded for their sociolinguistic differences as members of a language minority community and for their socio-educational differences when they do not conform to the expectations of teachers and peers. These severe social conditions clearly have an influence on social identity and are likely to find at least indirect expression in language choice and affective information as well as in the formulation of intentions, in lexical retrieval, and in bilingual articulation. I hope the SPPL Model will be be a useful tool for understanding some of the complexity of linguistic, cognitive, and social information and underlying processes in language disturbances and bilingualism. Since the issue is inherently complex in terms of definition, design, data collection, and interpretation, one first should spend some time formulating the problem.

THREE SETS OF QUESTIONS FOR THE STUDY OF BILINGUALISM AND LANGUAGE DISTURBANCES

The primary aim of this application of the SPPL Model is to identify critical questions that must be considered for investigating bilingualism and language impairment, and to offer a framework and guidelines for how to begin. This section presents the questions. The following section presents some guidelines about how to use the SPPL framework to begin to address these questions.

Bilingualism and the bilingual phenomena discussed in this volume offer a stage on which differences play themselves out. These differences include social comparisons between natives and non-natives, between monolinguals and bilinguals–what the idiom of research design calls 'between-subject' differences. In bilingualism, there are also 'within-subject' differences–between L1 and L2 and between and among multiple identities–native, immigrant, L2, child, friend, student. The study of language disorders has by and large been the study of deviance, i.e. the comparison of the speech of those assessed as language deviant with the speech of those called 'normals' (today labeled 'typically developing'). This, too, is a between-subjects comparison, with all the difficulty and compromise it entails. I am arguing here that language impairment, like bilingualism, can be looked at as 'difference,' not deviance, where differences are seen as desirable in a society which values diversity and pluralism. To make this argument, one needs to avoid social comparison–between immigrants and natives, between bilinguals and monolinguals–and focus on individual language use. The two fields brought together here, bilingualism and language disorders, offer an exceptional opportunity to examine difference and deviance in a single framework at the individual level of analysis.

Three sets of questions are a good place to start. One set stems from a discrepancy of the assumptions in the fields of bilingualism and language disorders. These issues are more theoretical and may be untestable for ethical as well as empirical reasons. A second set hits at the heart of the bias of the present work that both bilingualism and language disorders are first and foremost social phenomena. A third query asks how to approach the integrated study of bilingualism and language disorders.

The study of bilingualism in language disordered populations, especially children, presents a contradiction between the assumptions and findings of some of the literature in the two fields. Bilingualism is conceptualized in terms of cognitive advantage, language disorders in terms of deficit. Since Peal and Lambert's (1962) study claiming that bilinguals performed better on certain subtests of the Wechsler Adult Intelligence Scale (WAIS), bilingualism is alleged to have a variety of cognitive advantages. These include: flexibility, originality, and imagination (see Genesee, 2001, for a review). In the field of language disorders, clinically diagnosed populations are assumed and reported to have various limitations in processing capacity (e.g. Leonard, 1998). These assumptions lead to the following competing questions:

Would the cognitive advantages of bilingualism stimulate language processing in language disordered individuals and thus help compensate for some of their limitations? Or, alternatively, would bilingualism use up already limited cognitive resources and exacerbate the effects of a language disorder?

If the first question can be answered positively, many new interventive and therapeutic approaches would be opened, perhaps even beyond bilingualism, where the introduction of a new language might be used to stimulate language development in populations not thought to be capable of handling the 'burden' of such a complex cognitive skill. This was the rationale when Marty Albert had his Israeli research assistant teach Hebrew to global aphasics in Boston 25 years ago. If, however, an affirmative answer to the second question seems more plausible, then exposure of a child with language disturbances to a second language may further impair or even block the development of skills necessary to cope with family, school, and other mundane activities, thus raising concerns about ethical propriety. In the absence of solid research evidence about the cognitive advantages of bilingualism, the default approach has been to impose monolingualism on language minority children, and along with it, assume that their cognitive capacity is limited. Much of the thinking behind this perspective comes from a social comparison approach to research and practice, where bilinguals are compared to monolinguals and language disordered children are compared to those assumed to be 'normal.' Group data takes precedence over individual analysis.

A second set of issues is related to social aspects of bilingualism and language disorders, in particular to identity and attitudes. Are we talking about bilinguals with language disorders or language disordered children who happen to be bilingual?

These alternative formulations of the question bring us to the heart of the difference/deviance issue. In the study of bilingualism, especially subtractive bilingualism, the relevant constructs include ethnolinguistic vitality, language status, and attitudes to the second language and its speakers. In the area of language-related learning disabilities, intentions and goals are critical notions along with affective factors, such as self-esteem and self-confidence, as illustrated by Donahue's (2001) description of some classroom social interaction involving a nine-year-old with learning disabilities (Example 6.1).

Example 6.1 *Social interaction with an LD child (from Donahue, 2001)*

… suppose Marco brings cupcakes to celebrate his birthday, and his teacher suggests that he pass one out to each child. Marco goes by Kevin's desk without giving him a cupcake. How will Kevin respond? If he has been bullied or treated rudely by Marco in the past, he is likely to attend to those cues that signal a hostile intent rather than an accident, and to then interpret the causes and Marco's intent as intentionally "mean."…Kevin selects a goal or desired prosocial or antisocial outcome (e.g., getting a cupcake, making a friend, avoiding conflict or embarrassment, retaliating), and then accesses from memory possible responses to meet that goal (e.g., giving up, trying to get Marco's attention, grabbing a cupcake, telling the teacher)…Kevin evaluate[s] his repertoire of possible responses, a process that involves analyzing the appropriateness and the possible consequences of each response, as well as his self-efficacy (beliefs that he has the ability to enact the response). The final decision leads to Kevin's social behavior and Marco's response, which then provides input to start the cycle again. (In the actual incident on which this example is based, Kevin was a child with a history of language delay, and persisting word retrieval problems.) His reputation for angry outbursts and impulsive, aggressive behavior caused most peers to avoid him. Probably in light of these experiences, Kevin incorrectly interpreted the situation as a deliberate omission on Marco's part. Choosing the goal of getting a cupcake, Kevin may have accessed an appropriate set of solutions, but then rejected verbal responses due to his lack of self-efficacy that he could skillfully attract Marco's attention. So Kevin chose the non-verbal strategy of sticking his foot out to trip Marco as he came down the other side of the aisle. Startled, Marco looked down at Kevin's desk, said "Oh sorry," hurriedly gave him a cupcake, and backed off.

Extending this example to bilinguals, if Kevin's real name is Jose or Pierre or Ahmed and he comes from a language minority background, it is not hard to imagine how ethnic relations might get acted out in the interaction between the two boys. In fact, it is not hard to imagine that verbal hostility directed at a bilingual child with learning disabilities will include ethnic epithets as well as malicious comments about his disability.

It is noteworthy that although Donahue (1994, 2001) does not deal with bilingualism explicitly in her work, two of the three profiles she uses to describe social skills in learning disabled children involve reference to social identity among non-natives. In that work she proposes the terms "newcomer," "immigrant," and "imposter" as a way to summarize the principal variables which emerged from a review of the social skills literature (viz., language proficiency, discourse environments, and beliefs about social status). A newcomer is said to show "incomplete or inaccurate derivation of the classroom's discourse rules." An immigrant is described as having received "quantitatively and qualitatively different data for deriving discourse norms" and having experienced "'interference'" from the communicative norms of the special education setting." Only the label "imposters," those who "are well aware of the appropriate rules for social interaction, but feel like imposters among their peers" does not borrow from the idiom of bilingualism.

But analogy and metaphor between bilingualism and language disorders will not necessarily get at the central questions of concern. Nor will they generate a unified framework for investigation. Thus, while I share a bias with Donahue that language is fundamentally a social phenomenon, her implicit acceptance of a social comparison perspective between LD (learning disabilities) children and peers is rejected here in favor of an approach which focuses on the bilingualism and language disorders of individuals and draws on methodologies involving within-subjects designs.[9]

An initial set of questions focused on social aspects of bilingualism and language impairment would include:

a. How are both bilingualism and language impairment expressed in a speaker's social identity?

b. How do positive attitudes to a bilingual's native and/or second language and its speakers contribute to achievement in L2 (additive bilingualism)? How do negative attitudes to L1 and its speakers and positive attitudes to L2 and its speakers contribute to or impede achievement in L2 (subtractive bilingualism)?

c. What are some of the goals and beliefs of bilinguals with language disturbances about their bilingualism and about language disabilities, and how are those goals and beliefs expressed in their perceptions of self, in their notions about language and communication, and in their language behavior? In particular, how do the intentions/speech acts of bilingual language-different individuals reflect their social identities, attitudes, goals, and beliefs?

Another set of questions that could shed light on theoretical issues in bilingualism as well as clinical practice, might begin as follows:

a. Do a bilingual's language disturbances have the same manifestations in both languages?

b. How is it possible to distinguish between language contact phenomena in developing language and what might constitute a language impairment, or in the jargon of the field, between 'typical' second language acquisition and bilingual language disorders?

There are two reasons for the first question. One is the practical need to know what to tell parents, teachers, and speech clinicians about educational planning for the child. The second stems from the research bias that favors individual analysis, personal design, and case studies and rejecting approaches that rely on group means, large samples, and social comparisons. I do not envision a simple, all-or-none, either/or answer to this question, recommending that the child be spoken to in one language only at home or at school. Unfortunately, this is the answer sought–and unfortunately often adopted–by clinicians and educational personnel, whose own monolingualism is often the single most important determinant of policy and practice.

To address this question, I would begin by collecting ethnographic and demographic information about language use and language choice in the home, neighborhood, and school environments in both languages, and then proceed to sociolinguistic interviewing in both languages, sampling a range of topics and, to the extent possible, with a variety of interviewers. Eventually, I would attempt to elicit language samples, again in both languages, using multiple stimuli, tasks, and response measures. Within this mass of data, I would pay special attention to bilingual phenomena such as codeswitching, interference, and translation and how these interact with fluency and psychopragmatic phenomena such as certainty and confidence, insecurity and defensiveness.

The second question is much more difficult to answer, and given the individual bias adopted in this work, of lesser interest, certainly in the short run. I begin by breaking it into two parts: Studies of bilingual language acquisition, and studies of bilingual impairment. The most appropriate methodological decisions in studies of bilingual language acquisition should involve a series of sampling decisions, each of which would account for a large share of experimental variance. These decisions would include: (1) the specific linguistic structures to investigate, (2) the tasks and response measures needed to elicit those structures, and (3) which bilingual speakers should be examined. The question of which linguistic structures to examine poses a problem of whether to aim for depth or breadth. Linguistic studies tend to aim for depth (e.g. Genesee, 2001 for bilingualism; Rice & Wexler, 1996 for SLI), while clinical, psychoeducational studies seek breadth (e.g. Stuart-Smith & Martin, 1999). Assuming we could somehow come up with an appropriate set of structures and functions in two languages, and assuming we could devise appropriate tasks and response measures derived from our theoretical constructs, by the time we get to the second part of the question–a comparison of impaired bilingual language users and 'normals'–we would be introducing yet another major source of variance, this time the between-group variance caused by a comparison of 'typical' bilinguals and language impaired bilinguals. These sources of variance make it vary hard to design and effectively carry out studies that can keep track of all of them. As a result, there is a bias here that bilingual research should favor large amounts of data, gathered in both languages, from relatively small numbers of bilinguals, each individual offering a relatively self-contained basis for analysis and interpretation. In the terminology of design and statistics, each subject in effect serves as his or her own control (Anderson, 2001).

TOWARDS A FRAMEWORK FOR STUDYING BILINGUALISM AND LANGUAGE DISTURBANCES

Some of the same kinds disciplinary fragmentation in the field of bilingualism can be seen across a variety of developmental disorders with language-related indications. Down and Williams Syndromes, which are defined genetically, 'present' primarily as cognitive deficits. Expressive language is one of the differentiating characteristics, Down Syndrome being accompanied by expressive language disorders (e.g. Chapman, Sueng, Schwartz, and Kay-Raining Bird, 1998) and Williams Syndrome by relatively intact language skills.

PDD (Pervasive Developmental Disorder), and two of its sub-classes Autism and Asperger's, is clinically diagnosed to include impaired communication, social interaction, and repetitive or stereotypic motor behaviors (Fine, in press). Here, too, language performance is often used as a clinical marker to distinguish Asperger's from Autism, the former presenting relatively intact syntax, the latter relatively limited interpersonal language skills.

Specific Language Impairment (SLI) is defined sometimes by its linguistic indicators (where the most commonly impaired domain is morphosyntax) but more often by exclusionary criteria, like the lack of a hearing loss, no emotional and behavioral problems, average non-verbal IQ, no neurological problems, and no oral or facial defects (Stark & Tallal, 1981). SLI and its varieties, GSLI (grammatical SLI) and PSLI (pragmatic SLI), have attracted so much interest by linguists (Levy & Schaeffer, 2003) because they are presumed to be centered directly in the so-called language faculty.

To begin untangling bilingualism from language disturbances and address the questions raised above, the two fundamental distinctions pursued throughout this work, one between structure and processing and one between sociopragmatic and psycholinguistic information, are revisited here. Table 6.1 contains an outline of the SPPL Model and its processing mechanisms; it is offered as a first step in developing profiles for the study and assessment of bilinguals with speech and language-related disturbances.

Table 6.1 SPPL framework for assessing bilinguals with special language

Structural components of bilingualism
1. Sociopragmatic profiles
    Social identity: accent, names, greetings
    Bilingual social networks: Focus on settings and participants
    Genre profile: Conversations and Home-school scripts
2. Psycholinguistic profiles with a particular focus on codeswitching
    Speech acts: requests, challenges, clarifications
    Lexical pragmatics: lexical choice, pragmatic markers
    Lexicalization differences and general-purpose verbs
    Morphosyntax: tense markers, infinitives, bare forms
    Phonology and phonotactics
    Prosody and fluency: pitch, duration, intensity, speech rate, pauses

Processing in bilingualism
1. Basic processes
    Attention
    Discrimination
    Recognition
    Identification
    Classification
    Categorization
2. Processing mechanisms
    Imitation
    Variation
    Integration
    Control

The development of an SPPL profile of a bilingual child with a suspected or diagnosed language disturbance requires collecting data in two languages, across a range of sociopragmatic and psycholinguistic information, and tapping a multiplicity of processes and processing mechanisms. The following paragraphs illustrate how this framework can be used to develop such a profile to keep track of some of the complexity in bilingualism as well as language disturbances. The discussion here is illustrative, intending to convey an application of the overall SPPL framework and some general principles. Down Syndrome, PDD, and SLI, three conditions not usually considered in a single framework, are selected for this illustration. They are brought together here to distinguish the relative importance of the different modules, information components, and processing mechanisms. The language choice and affective modules are central to an understanding of bilingualism in Down Syndrome and PDD. The identity component offers a way to look at multiple identities in bilingualism (e.g. language identity, immigrant identity, ethnic, religious, national) as well as a range of less obvious identities related to language disturbances (e.g. protected, sheltered, handicapped, socially isolated, victimized). Information from the identity, contextual, and intentional components coupled with the input from the language choice and affective modules may help differentiate some of the overlapping features of Down Syndrome and PDD. The formulation component, in both its lexical and discourse parts, is the first place to begin an examination of bilingual SLI. Imitation and control processing mechanisms are likely to contribute to an understanding of non-normative repetitive, automatic behavior in Down Syndrome and PDD/Autism; variation and integration may provide explanations of some of the processing dimensions of SLI. In matrix terms, the profile generated from the SPPL Model can be laid out in a four (information components) by four (processing mechanisms) by two (languages) array. The ensuing discussion samples from three information components (social identity, intentions, and formulation) to illustrate some of the similarities and differences in the language and bilingualism of Down, PDD, and SLI.

Social identity. Given the bias in this work favoring the sociopragmatic aspects of language, I would begin data collection for a research program and clinical assessment of a bilingual child by looking at social identity. Information about names, accent, and greetings is assessed through the content and language use elicited from observations and clinical-sociolinguistic interviews. From the point of view of bilingualism, the most important decision in conducting the observations is to elicit data in both languages and from among uniquely bilingual phenomena such as codeswitching, interference, and translation. Sociopragmatically, it is crucial to sample from a variety of settings, interlocutors, and topics in each of the child's languages as well as in situations where bilingual phenomena are likely to occur. For the clinical interviews, the decision about when and how to introduce the two languages is critical. If the interviewer is not herself/himself bilingual, a second interviewer will need to collect the same information in the other, often primary language (for all the difficulty and expense this entails).

Three principle strategies are offered here to guide the interview. One is the need for empathy or reflectivity on the part of the examiner. This is a general feature of clinical professions (sometimes overlooked in research), and not inherently linked to language or bilingualism. There is, however, a corollary to this strategy relevant to bilingualism: the advantage of initiating the interview in the child's preferred language. And it is relevant to the affective module of the SPPL Model. A second strategy is to guide the interview from external topics at the outset to more personal subject matter further into the interview or even in a second session. For example, when collecting social identity information about names and name preferences, one might begin by asking the child to talk about the names and nicknames of friends and classmates, then about other children in the child's family (nuclear as well as extended), and later about parents' and grandparents' names, the child's own name, nicknames, and personal name preferences. These names as well as the affect conveyed along with them (via prosodic features and pragmatic markers) should generate a set of identities related to the child's bilingualism and language behavior. In this light, I recall working with a 12-year-old dyslexic whose multiple identities included: Israeli, religious, Moroccan, English speaking, and sick (the label for his dyslexia apparently acquired from an adult). A third strategy is to speak as little as possible or to leave the child ample opportunity for self expression. This may mean larger pauses between conversational turns than what the interviewer is used to in more conventional social interaction. The purpose of this strategy is to attain large segments of uninterrupted spoken material from the child.

Information related to the child's attitudes and feelings about L1 and L2 is relevant. These data can be obtained by asking the child classical sociolinguistic questions about who speaks which language to whom, where, when, and for what purpose (reported language use). A conversation about accents and dialects should also be part of this segment of the interview, where attitudinal information comes in the content of this conversation and actual use of accents and dialects comes with the child's language behavior. The metalinguistic statements a person makes about a particular language, its prestige, and its utility, may be useful indicators of identity. Nevertheless, they should be interpreted with caution and corroborated, since they may reflect social norms (e.g. parents' opinions or peers' attitudes) rather than the actual feelings of the child. Finally, greetings have been used to assess social identity in two ways: by asking the child to report his/her language use to various participants and in different settings and by role playing in those same settings (Walters & Popko, 1997). Personal design (Anderson, 1996), based on people and places in the child's own social network is another useful way to get this information for clinical and educational purposes.

The multiple identities of a bilingual are formed by their individual experiences as children, siblings, friends, students and their exposure to various languages. No two are alike. Similarly, a Down Syndrome, PDD, or SLI child constructs a set of identities that take into account how he perceives his genetic, social, and linguistic makeup as well as how others perceive him. That complex integral of identities makes each bilingual Down Syndrome child unique, both in terms of bilingualism and with regard to his or her cognitive state. My first memory of contact with a Down Syndrome person came in a bakery when I was about seven. The girl with Down Syndrome must have been at least twice my age, and at that first meeting she greeted me with a warm hug and kiss. This unencumbered affect, labeled impulsiveness in some clinical circles, may have linguistic manifestations. So far, the linguistic correlates of affect in Down Syndrome remain uncharted in psycholinguistics as well as in clinical settings. An examination of pragmatic markers (ya' know, like, really) and prosodic correlates of affect (pitch, duration, intensity) may uncover clues to the linguistic phenomena associated with both Down Syndrome and bilingualism. The SPPL Model identifies the locus of this phenomenon in the circuit encompassing the affective module and the intentional and articulation components.

In terms of processing, the control mechanism is an obvious candidate to explain how these sources of information are directed, regulated, and monitored. Bilingualism offers an opportunity to examine how a child maximizes her cognitive resources in order to accommodate increased demands in terms of sounds, words, and syntactic structures from the two languages. A recent study of codemixing in French-English Down Syndrome bilinguals is an important structural beginning in this direction (Kay-Rainingbird et al., 2002). Future clinical assessment and research should assess social and identity aspects in Down Syndrome by examining children's statements about language and dialect, about names, and about greetings. These data would offer a broad picture of a child's language preferences and choices, based on attitudes (reported language use) as well as (language) behavior. They could provide a direction for the language(s) in which further testing should be conducted and some indication about the language(s) to use for intervention.

Intentions via speech acts and pragmatic markers. The starting point for an evaluation of psycholinguistic aspects of bilingualism is an assessment of intentions. There are several reasons for this. First, in the SPPL Model intentions sit on the border between sociopragmatic and psycholinguistic information, between social identity/context and formulation, offering a bridge from the external social world to the mind. Speech acts and pragmatic markers are the explicit verbal cues to intentions. Second, speech acts do not come alone. They are accompanied by a full range of linguistic information, including syntax, morphology, phonology, and most important, lexis. Third, the intentional aspects of speech acts, i.e. their illocutionary force, may be general enough to allow a certain degree of comparability across cultures.

Following the framework and procedures described in Chapter 3, a range of speech acts relevant to the child's world is identified. The evaluator can make use of the various taxonomies in speech act theory as a starting point (e.g. Austin, 1962; Searle, 1975), but the child's own narratives, requests and responses, invitations and refusals, and dares are likely to be more relevant. The initial aim of the evaluation is to gather a range of speech acts from each of the bilingual child's two languages. Role playing offers a reasonable compromise between language use in natural settings and more traditional clinical tasks such as picture naming. A couple of dozen requests and 'blame avoiding' utterances in L1 and L2 would provide a modest corpus and complement the conversational data of the initial clinical interview. Of the two speech acts cited here, requests in most languages are conveyed by a wide range of syntactic and semantic options (more than 20 in English and Spanish and more than a dozen in Modern Hebrew). Blame avoiding, on the other hand, is more constrained structurally, due perhaps to its emotional origins. Comparing the bilingual child's facility in using a speech act with a wide degree of variation (request) and one with limited variation (avoiding blame) in both languages will help highlight the extent to which the child makes use of variation in language use. Pragmatic markers add an important layer to the verb-based information gathered from such an assessment. Cross-language comparisons would include morphosyntactic and lexical information in addition to the semantic and pragmatic properties of the utterance. In addition, fluency markers such as repetitions, pauses, and false starts are likely to be more revealing in a task of this sort, where the child has been led to express a particular intention and is working on how to formulate it, than in the more open-ended interview where much of the child's cognitive energy is devoted to deciding what to say, consuming resources which might be used to formulate utterances.

To get at the heart of the child's bilingualism, the evaluation must go beyond the fundamentally contrastive approach described above. It can do so in two ways. First, it can endorse or even encourage codeswitching by ensuring that the role playing scripts make liberal use of codeswitching on the part of the examiner. Codeswitching should activate the language choice module of the SPPL Model. Second, the assessment might include tests of paraphrase and translation techniques to probe the breadth and accuracy of the child's linguistic knowledge. Paraphrase, especially multiple attempts to capture meaning, is expected to indicate the scope of a child's knowledge. Translation, when assessed in both languages to examine directionality differences, i.e. from L1 to L2 and from L2 to L1, can be used to gain information about linguistic accuracy as well as language preference. Both of these tasks are rooted in psycholinguistic aspects of bilingual processing (in the formulation component of the SPPL Model). They can, however, yield sociopragmatic relevance by embedding them in role playing activities involving requests for clarification and natural translation where the child is asked to transmit information to a monolingual speaker.

Pervasive Developmental Disorders (PDD) is defined by the DSM-V as an impairment in three areas: social interaction skills, communicative skills, and stereotypic and repetitive behaviors. Fine (in press), in criticizing this clinical definition for not differentiating clearly between social interaction and communicative skills, enumerates the following language features of the social interaction impairment in PDD: a. failure to develop peer relationships; b. lack of spontaneous efforts to share; c. lack of social or emotional reciprocity. All of these can be located in the sociopragmatic components of the SPPL. Communicative impairment in PDD is said to involve: a. delay in the onset of spoken language; b. impairment in initiating or continuing conversations; c. stereotyped, repetitive or idiosyncratic language; d. lack of make-believe and social imitative play. These features are spread across the various components and processing mechanisms of the SPPL Model. For example, they may have to do with the PDD/autistic child's identity; they may be due to disturbances in the affective module or in the channel connecting the affective module to the contextual component (a kind of flip side disturbance to the spontaneity described in the Down Syndrome child above); or they may be due to disturbances in the discourse formulation component (impairment in initiating and continuing conversations).

Both research and clinical assessment of bilingual PDD would examine the distribution of potentially autistic language across different settings, inter-locutors, and topics, making sure that both languages are given an equal opportunity to occur. Among the seven definitional characteristics of autism, two are particularly important for examining its relationship to bilingualism. One of these is related to the sociopragmatics of bilingualism and autism; the second is a disturbance in processing. In order to understand the sociopragmatics of bilingual autism, I would first look carefully at the bilingualism (L1 and L2 use) of all of the major figures in the child's life, including mother, father, siblings, peers, caretaker, teacher, media. I would also look at the languages used by all of the above to refer to and to address pets, toys and other things that might elicit affect. This list includes relatives and strangers, humans and animals, three dimensional as well as two dimensional objects. These are some of the structural elements of social interaction and communication. A key to understanding the interactive, processing aspects of bilingualism and autism is to map the languages, dialects, and varieties produced by and input to all of these figures and objects. The result of such mapping would look like a sociolinguistic network. And lest we think these languages are all dialects with armies (to use Bolinger's definition of a language), the following cat and mouse story indicates the importance of bilingualism:

> A litter of kittens meowed furiously as a mouse scampered by, too quick for the kittens' newborn innate hunger satisfaction device. The mouse made his way safely into his mousehole. The mother cat appears, sniffs around the mousehole and shoos the kittens to the side. Several minutes, some heavy purring and subtle squeaking later, the mouse meanders confidently out of its hole…into the salivating mouths of the kittens. As they lick their proverbial chops, Mother Cat turns to her kittens and preaches: "See how important it is to know languages."

Finally, from a processing perspective, a key to understanding the nature of "stereotyped, repetitive or idiosyncratic language" among autistic bilinguals would be to look at automatic language such as idioms, curses, counting and basic arithmetic. A first pass using the tools of SPPL's processing mechanisms points to an imbalance between imitation and variation. To get at this balance, examination of the distribution of automatic language across the speaker's languages is called for. This could even involve training exercises for teaching idioms, curses, counting and arithmetic in both languages as a way of assessing which language lends itself to automaticity, which language (if any) might stimulate a certain degree of spontaneity, and intentionality.

The intentional aspects of PDD and its relationship to bilingualism are much more complex than can be described in these few paragraphs. In her ethnography of multilingual families with high functioning autistic children, Kremer-Sadlik (2003) captures some of the extreme complexity in the interaction between bilingualism and autism. The following excerpt was recorded during dinner as the family watched a news broadcast of an avalanche. According to the ethnographer, the autistic adolescent (John) had suggested that the avalanche had been caused by a bomb. The parents both disagree, and John asks for an another explanation. In attempting to give one, his father, a native speaker of Mandarin Chinese and an immigrant to Los Angeles, finds himself unable to retrieve an English word for 'gravity,' and turns to Jay, for the translation.

Example 6.2 *Illustration of bilingualism in autism* (from Kremer-Sadlik, 2003)
John:　　((looking at father)) How did they, um, make it go down?
Father:　You know, it's heavy so, that-*Jay, chung li chiao se ma?*
(Jay, How do you say gravity in English?)
Jay:　　　Gravity.
Father:　Gravity! OK? They pour down. Something look like this.
You s-((makes gestures))

The father's intention is clear in his appeal to John's brother, Jay, for an English translation of the word for gravity. His ability to formulate that intention, even when equipped with the translation, is not as clear, as seen in father's last utterance in the quoted excerpt.

Among the many identities enveloped in this excerpt are John's father's immigrant and parental identities and John's distinctiveness as a son, a brother, and a member of a clinical category called high functioning autism. The father's rejection of John's proposition that the avalanche resulted from a bomb, along with the parents' decision to comply with a therapist's recommendation to stop speaking Mandarin with him, despite continued use of their native language with each other and with John's brother, do not bode well either for his bilingualism or for his relationship with his father.

Formulation. The conventional research tools and assessment measures in child language research (e.g. spontaneous conversation between researcher/ clinician and child, elicited imitation, picture naming, and narratives) are likely to be the first place one would start to examine bilingual SLI. Such an approach, not far afield from looking for a lost object under the lamppost, would probably lead to a disorder in morphosyntax, phonology, or lexical retrieval, all disturbances which can be located in the formulation component of the SPPL Model. Such was the approach I took 25 years ago in an investigation of two eight year old 'bilingual' children enrolled in a class for high-risk children with unspecified language problems (Walters, 1981).

Another approach, more grounded in bilingualism, would attempt to characterize the disturbances in bilingual performance. The following is a brief summary of that study. Two children participated: one girl (G) and one boy (B), both age 8;0 at the time of the study from a 'high risk' bilingual (Spanish-English) early elementary class, for which they had been screened and selected on the basis of their performance on a series of psycho-educational tests (e.g. Slingerland, ITPA). G was born in Puerto Rico and had relatively consistent attendance in kindergarten and first grade. B was born in New York and had only sporadic attendance (only 92 days over two years) in kindergarten and first grade. G's mother was monolingual in Spanish; B's mother was bilingual. Unfortunately, no data were available about birth order.

A total of 11 eleven sessions of data collection were conducted, seven in Spanish and four in English. Sessions included spontaneous speech, elicited imitation, and verbal responses to black and white line drawings. Probes of specific morphosyntactic structures, including gender and reflexives in Spanish, articles (a, the) in English, and conjoined sentences in both languages, were developed based on difficulties noted in spontaneous speech.

The data were analyzed for grammaticality and code-mixing in the two languages of each child. Quantitatively, both children showed evidence of grammatical difficulties, a distinguishing feature of SLI. Nearly 50 percent of G's utterances (289/649) and almost two thirds of B's utterances (359/596) were ungrammatical. G exhibited more grammatical diffculties in English; B had more grammatical difficulty in Spanish. With regard to code-mixing, only 24 of G's 649 utterances (3%) involved CS, more in Spanish than in English. B, on the other hand, had 127 instances of CS across his 596 utterances (approximately 20%), with almost five times more in the Spanish sessions than in English.

Qualitatively, three phenomena were examined in the corpus: omissions, substitutions, and word finding problems. Omissions of function words (articles, conjunctions, and prepositions) were more prevalent in Spanish than English for G, but substitutions were more frequent in English than Spanish. The former observation runs counter to the fact that Spanish emerged as G's stronger language in the quantitative analysis. Giving the lack of comparable data for 'typically-developing' bilingual children at the time of the study, G's word retrieval difficulties were perhaps a better indicator of language disturbance. In Spanish there were 10 instances, all in the sentence repetition probes. In English, word finding difficulties were more prevalent (n=32), and they all came in the picture reponse task. For B, the portrait of language performance and disturbance was quite different. Omissions greatly exceeded substitutions in both

Spanish and English. In addition, word finding difficulties were not as frequent. But, by far the most distinguishing characteristic of B's corpus was the frequency of CS. A more qualitative analysis of the nature of CS in the two corpora revealed that G's relatively infrequent examples were all sociopragmatically motivated (as attention-getters, to elaborate, or to mark a switch in topic). B's highly frequent codeswitching, which involved function words as well as content items, was apparently more psycholinguistically motivated, perhaps to compensate for limitations on fluency.

In summary, G and B differed in terms of the locus of grammatical distrubance and the prevalence of code-mixing. G's omissions and substitutions were distributed differently across her two languages, as were her word finding difficulties. Her relatively few instances of codeswitching were sociopragmatic. B's morphosyntactic errors were similar across languages, and his highly frequent codeswitching may have minimized his word retrieval difficulties. Thus, B's CS may have had a compensatory effect for what otherwise may have emerged as word finding difficulties.

With 25 years of hindsight and the SPPL Model, we can now begin to look beyond the morphosyntactic aspects of SLI, at the connections between formulation and sociopragmatic features of identity, context, and intentions. My reinterpretation here of G's codeswitching as sociopragmatic and B's as psycholinguistic were one of the benefits of the SPPL framework. Probing of social identity beyond birthplace, mother tongue, and attendance records would be the kind of information one needs to complement the longitudinal data collection sessions.

In terms of the SPPL Model's processing mechanisms, the disturbances in morphosyntactic processing described here may be attributed to impaired performance in the imitation/variation mechanisms. Morphosyntactic omissions may be due to impaired integration of lexical and morphosyntactic information in the formulation component. And lexical retrieval difficulties may be due to limitations or impairment in the control mechanism. More speculatively, the literature in neurolinguistics in general and bilingualism in particular has begun to point to two areas worthy of further investigation: 1) a role for Brodmann's areas 44 and 45 in storage and retrieval of grammatical knowledge, in sequential/hierarchical processing, and in implicit memory (Ullman, 2001); 2) frontal lobe participation in people with control and fluency issues such as Parkinson's patients, who may have motor trouble getting started but, once moving, can be relatively fluent in speech as well as motor behavior. The former substrates would help provide a neurolinguistic basis for morphosyntactic issues in SLI, the latter for disturbances related to lexical knowledge.

Methodological Note. Unfortunately, the data collection techniques in the study reported here ('spontaneous' conversation with a single bilingual experimenter, description of pictures/toys, and elicited sentence imitation) do not tell us much about the social, interactive aspects of the child's language behavior or about the disturbances in processing that may underlie that behavior. A study just getting under way with English-Hebrew, Russian-Hebrew, and Arabic-Hebrew SLI children attempts to address this particular methodological shortcoming.

Summaries. In this brief introduction to bilingualism and language disturbances, I've tried to give a taste of some of the complexity in trying to untangle the two domains. Both have their own aggregate of identities, which are constructed from social relationships with insiders and outsiders in bilingual and clinical settings. The identities are many and varied; so are the relationships from which the identities are assembled. Those identities and relationships both draw on and contribute to the language and affective choices of a bilingual with language differences. In this section, I have stressed the importance of identity and sociopragmatic aspects of the problem, in part to counter clinical as well as research traditions which have neglected these components of bilingualism and language disorders in designing research and in making real life clinical recommendations. All three language phenomena referred to here (Down Syndrome, PDD, and SLI) can benefit from the broader perspective preached here. This approach is intended to help researchers and clinicians see some of the common affective and social-interactional processes that cut across different forms of bilingualism and different language disturbances.

Lateral thinking, coupled with insight about subtle processes and submerged processing mechanisms, may then generate new tasks and techniques for investigating bilingualism and language disturbances. It is this same quest for the unlikely connection, for the improbable relationship, for the unexpected link that led me to bring together the three topics of this chapter. Language acquisition, language attrition, and language disturbances today are part of a science of fragmentation. The overarching constructs of structure and processing, sociopragmatics and psycholinguistics, are an attempt to step back, to think about overriding issues. But these transcendent constructs need mundane issues like those highlighted in this chapter. These constructs need grounding in order to provide an empirical base for the claims of the SPPL Model and its processing mechanisms and to chart the course of empirical testing. Raising these issues in the context of the SPPL Model is an attempt to provide a framework and tools for the fields of language acquisition, attrition, and language disturbances to look at the particular issues they consider important, how these issues are formulated, and how they are investigated.

A CONCLUDING STATEMENT

One might ask, given the fact that even the most fluent bilinguals spend the better share of their linguistic time in what Grosjean would call 'monolingual mode,' why we should go to the trouble of assessing the bilingual aspects of language processing? The short answer to this question is that monolingual mode may be more of a reaction to external forces, the demands of setting and other speakers. Moreover, monolingual mode may not give a fully honest picture of a bilingual speaker's internal processes, in particular with regard to identity. These internal processes, concealed in pragmatic markers, lexical choices, and fluency phenomena, consume more cognitive energy and are likely to be more involved in bilingualism than in monolingualism. For the longer answer to this question, we need to turn to the distinction made here between sociopragmatic and psycholinguistic concerns. Sociopragmatic matters include equity issues, the role of bilingualism in cultural pluralism, and language policy questions, all of which were beyond the scope of this work. From a psycholinguistic perspective, the questions introduced in Chapter 1 about brain-behavior relations, and whether bilingualism can lead to structural or processing changes in the brain, are also relevant, but answers are beyond the current state of the art. As Paula Menyuk was wont to say: "The task is colossal, and the data are chincey."

WHAT THIS BOOK INTENDED

This book began by arguing that there is a set of phenomena unique to bilingualism which cannot be accounted for fully by current models of bilingual production. Codeswitching, interference and related instances of dysfluency, and translation were contrasted with parallel events in the lives of monolingual speakers. The inquiry was situated on language use and language processing and their relationship to language structure. In this light, this work differs from research in second language acquisition and cross-linguistic studies, where the focus is squarely centered on structure. After presenting biological, processing, phenomenological, and sociolinguistic motivations for the Bilingual Model, I introduced some general issues in cognitive science, which have served as subtexts throughout.

This work could have begun and ended by focusing on bilinguals rather than bilingualism. Then, it may have limited the study to an examination of the small minority of bilingual speakers who grow up with two languages from birth. But the interest here was broader. The distinctions pursued throughout, between structure and processing, between acquisition and use, and between sociopragmatics and psycholinguistics, are intended to contribute to a particular view of language. In that view, linguistic structure can never be more than a window to processing. Acquisition cannot be studied without a deep understanding of language use. And psycholinguistic processing is lifeless without sociopragmatic grounding.

The ten models of bilingual processing reviewed in Chapter 2 were selected for their special contributions in the effort to integrate sociopragmatic and psycholinguistic information in a single research framework and to distinguish representation from processing. Three structural models, despite their biases, address the processing construct, albeit in different ways. Myers-Scotton's wide-ranging research program on codeswitching *combines*, but does not necessarily *integrate*, sociolinguistic and structural aspects of codeswitching. Processing is inferred from product, as derived from generative theory, and is not tapped directly via tasks and procedures. Clyne utilizes processing as an interpretive tool to explain his notion of triggering and to distinguish three possible relationships between L1 and L2 (separation, adaptation, and mixing). Auer's claim that situational factors "underspecify language choice" and Heller's parallel notion of "strategic ambiguity," both from a perspective of functional linguistics, have clear implications for bilingual processing. In reviewing this work, I suggested that these claims at the conversational level might be applied to the lexical level of processing as well. Thus, the bilingual might leave language choice 'underspecified' and open to negotiation, using techniques of strategic ambiguity, lexically as well as conversationally.

The three psychological models reviewed, given their focus on processing and on lexis, were challenged from the sociopragmatic end of the linguistic spectrum. Green's Model of Inhibitory Control, in contrast to de Groot and Kroll's largely lexical model, is explicitly interested in how L1 and L2 find expression in a bilingual speaker's intentions and goals. Green's model, in particular its "supervisory attentional system" and task schemas, provides an architecture for carrying out intentional, non-automatic linguistic acts. The model does this by manipulating the activation levels of L1 and L2 and by inhibiting output. But Green's model, even in its most recent form, is not set up to account for information about social identity, social context, and genre information, to name the uppermost components of the SPPL Model. The data it assembles for support do not include production phenomena such as codeswitching and interlanguage forms. The last of the three psychological models reviewed, Grosjean's BIMOLA, does take social aspects of bilingualism into account (in its imaginative data gathering technique) and does make use of codeswitching data (as its central focus of concern).

Sociolinguistics originally did not try to get inside the minds of the individuals it investigated. Cognitive anthropology, ethnography and discourse analysis have changed that attitude. Rampton's and Zentella's research give us a look at both individual and group processes, grounding claims about societal processes and social roles in micro-sociolinguistic data about code-crossing and codeswitching. They, too, are interested in processing as well as structure. I located Rampton's processing interests in his version of liminality, an explanatory construct for some of his data on language crossing, claimed here to be related to the variation mechanism of the SPPL Model. Zentella makes use of many levels of analysis, including quantification, discourse analysis, and ethnography. She superimposes ethnicity and educational policy issues structurally on her codeswitching data and gets at processing by looking at cross-language parity and directionality of switching.

The last two approaches discussed (Poulisse and De Bot), despite their origins in the science of monolingual lexical production, go far beyond lexis in their modeling of bilingual production, addressing all of the major concerns of the present work.

Chapter 2 ends by summarizing a few of the themes, some major and some minor, addressed in the remainder of the book. These included: (1) the relevance of both sociopragmatic and psycholinguistic information to just about all work in bilingualism, from the most decontextualized, laboratory tasks to the richest, most socially-grounded analyses; (2) the role of intentions in any model of language production; and (3) the facility with which bilinguals are able to produce monolingual speech in two languages, generally undisturbed by the other language, and the skill with which they generate fluent codeswitching, weaving lexis and syntax from two distinct linguistic worlds.

The model of information laid out in Chapter 3 is not an attempt to burden the field with yet another model and another set of terminology. Indeed, a good deal of the architecture of the model should be familiar to students of monolingual language production and investigators of bilingualism. But beyond the surface similarities, especially in the formulator and articulator components of the model, the SPPL Model suggests several essential differences and implies several others. The model builds four components into the architecture which are left out or not fully specified in previous models. These include information about social identity, contextual information, genre, and the discourse component in the formulator. The model also makes speech act information a central component, attempting to incorporate the study of intentions in the study of bilingualism. The language choice information component has two advantages. In terms of codeswitching, it allows a distinction between intentional, sociopragmatic codeswitching and performance codeswitching due to word finding difficulties. In addition, it eliminates the need for language tags buried deeply in the formulator and provides a principled account of a wide range of linguistically-deviant forms, lexical inventions, and the like. Finally, within the formulator, the model distinguishes among lexico-pragmatic concepts, lemmas, and lexemes, attempting to mitigate some of the rancor generated on this topic recently.

Chapter 4 on bilingual processing was first of all an attempt to open channels for future discussions of some of the major constructs relevant to bilingualism and foremost an attempt to make explicit the distinction between representation and processing. Imitation was shown to be currently popular in social psychology, neo-Darwinism, and neuroscience, and claimed to be an essential construct for a processing account of language contact. For variation, the background discussion centered initially on linguistic types of variation, primarily sociolinguistic and pragmatic, ending up with an explanation of how variation and its molecular processes, discrimination and classification, operate in codeswitching.

The two executive mechanisms discussed, integration and control, represent opposite poles in the research program behind the SPPL Model. Integration processes in bilingualism have been documented for both sociopragmatic and lexical tasks. In contrast, work on control processes in bilingualism is only beginning and is highly speculative at present. Beyond the substantive importance of these two processing mechanisms for the study of bilingualism, another, no less important, goal of these sections of the chapter was to introduce two general purpose psychological theories to the bilingual research community. Norman H. Anderson's Information Integration Theory and William Powers' Perceptual Control Theory provide explicit theoretical frameworks, testable claims, and practicable methodologies. As research frameworks in cognitive science, they stand out for their tight fit of theory and method.

Chapter 5 returned to the phenomena identified as central to the study of bilingualism, codeswitching, interference, and translation, and discussed them within the framework of the SPPL Model and its processing mechanisms. The framework was shown to be useful for identifying and accounting for a number of key distinctions in different aspects of bilingualism, among them:

- ❑ Sociopragmatic and psycholinguistic differences across a range of production phenomena
- ❑ Identity, contextual, and discourse functions of sociopragmatic codeswitching
- ❑ Directionality and triggering in psycholinguistic code-switching
- ❑ Differential roles for imitation, variation, integration, and control in codeswitching
- ❑ Fluency, automaticity, and completeness in bilingual processing

In a treatment of translation and interpretation, I selected Wadensjo's interactive, discourse-oriented approach as one of the few attempts in the field to make sociopragmatic issues explicit. Within the psycholinguistic domain, I presented the work of Shlesinger (2000) to illustrate some of the psycholinguistic issues in the field. Then, I discussed how the language choice and affective modules, the six information components, and the four processing mechanisms in the SPPL Model would approach the phenomena of translation and interpretation. The remainder of the chapter was more speculative, examining the interaction of bilingualism with computation and cursing, two skills which are neither unique to bilinguals nor uniquely linguistic. For computation, I outlined a set of hypotheses and the beginnings of a research design to investigate automaticity, the construct presumed to be most central to the study of bilingual computation. Despite the inherent psycholinguistic nature of automaticity in arithmetic, the SPPL Model is offered as a framework in order not to ignore social and pragmatic aspects of mathematics literacy. For cursing, I discussed directionality and triggering (two processing constructs treated in the section on codeswitching) and their relevance to an examination of the affective and psycholinguistic implications of cursing in a non-native language. The chapter ends with a relatively detailed statement of methodological principles and a set of guidelines for conducting research in bilingualism, among them:

- ❑ The value of a tight fit between theory and method
- ❑ The need for a multidimensional framework
- ❑ Implications of analyzing both group and individual data
- ❑ Triangulation of data collection procedures
- ❑ Consideration of the units of analysis, what to count, and how to measure them

This statement drew heavily on the philosophy of science underlying Anderson's Information Integration Theory and Powers' Perceptual Control Theory.

Finally, the present chapter addresses three potential areas of application for the model: acquisition, attrition, and language disorders. Regarding acquisition, after raising relevant questions about identity, language choice, and affect, I focused on lexical acquisition as perhaps the hottest issue in the study of bilingual child language. In particular, the role of the basic processes of discrimination and classification and the variation mechanism are mentioned as critical to a fuller understanding of acquisition in bilingualism. Child bilingualism and the presence of meaningful numbers of translation equivalents in early bilingual lexical acquisition is shown to conform to Clark's pragmatic 'principle of contrast.' For addressing questions in language attrition, two main distinctions are made, one between attrition and non-acquisition and one between attrition of structures and attrition of processes. Attrition in the information components of the SPPL Model is assessed, and more processing oriented research is called for in the investigation of immigrant language attrition. The section of this chapter on bilingualism and language disorders is more thorough than the sections on acquisition and attrition, but it still represents only an entrée to the topic. It lays out some of the problems, scientific as well as political, in conducting research in this area. Then it delineates some of the sociopragmatic and psycholinguistic questions a merger of these two fields ought to address. Finally, it discusses how the SPPL Model, in particular the social identity and speech act components and the variation mechanism, might be used to design research on bilingual language disturbances in children.

WHAT'S NEXT

This inquiry has attempted to find support for some of the basic assumptions in the study of bilingualism and to challenge others. The SPPL Model answers Grosjean's call for a less fragmented, more integrated research orientation in the field of bilingualism. The book identifies some of the key phenomena in need of a unified account, and offers a plausible account for codeswitching, interference, and translation, leaving the issues of bilingual arithmetic and cursing for future research.

A distinction between sociopragmatic and psycholinguistic codeswitching is pursued throughout. Issues such as directionality and triggering are at present not completely resolved in the field of bilingualism, and the state of the art leaves more to be understood than is already known in the study of codeswitching. I have suggested that the distinction between intentional codeswitching (motivated by social identity considerations and contextual factors such as setting, topic, and participants) and codeswitching motivated by fluency and/or disturbances in lexical access is supported by the directionality construct. Directionality of intrasentential codeswitching, while not yet systematically studied in field-based or laboratory studies, may be related to lexical processing issues. I argued that the cross-language connections in Kroll's model may be similar to codeswitching and that conceptually-based processing in Kroll's model may be likened to sociopragmatic, L1-to-L2 codeswitching, while lexically-based processing may be related to performance codeswitching. Future research from a involving more sociopragmatic data gathering and interpretive tools should complement the laboratory work which has already laid out some of the issues in directionality.

In discussing the various components of the SPPL Model, speech acts and pragmatic markers were singled out as crucial to getting at speakers' intentions. The study of bilingual intentions will continue to be an important part of this research program. The methodologies for this work include role playing and retelling approaches for data collection and a combination of qualitative discourse/conversational analysis techniques and metalinguistic judgment tasks for data interpretation. The wider scope of data analysis and interpretation offers rich ways to get at some of the more subtle aspects of bilingual intentions.

The SPPL Model calls for an expansion and more detailed specification of information required in bilingual formulation. A discourse formulation component has been added to current models of bilingual processing. Lemmas were said to be derived from lexico-pragmatic concepts and to be more dynamic, i.e. to vary both within and across individuals, and to have access to both L1 and L2 information via the language choice module. The issues raised by these claims ask experimental psycholinguists to seriously consider the descriptive data produced by taxonomies like those of Clyne (discussed in Chapter 2) and implore structural and sociolinguists come to see a value in laboratory testing of hypotheses about fusion and compromise forms.

Another potentially useful way to take bilingual lexical research beyond questions of representation and storage is to look at processing with various degrees of complexity. Trilingualism would sit at the complex end of that spectrum. Studies carried out by Festman (2004) on German-French-English trilinguals attempt to operationalize processing notions such as activation and control and their role in lexical retrieval. Less complex processes and processing mechanisms can be investigated in children, assuming some of the data elicitation difficulties can be managed effectively. In this regard, cross-linguistic, longitudinal studies of bilingual children from infancy through childhood would provide a useful database. Lexical development and phonological awareness have been targeted as important in this regard. Although vocabulary levels of bilingual children may be lower in each language in a comparison with monolinguals, the overall size of the bilingual lexicon may be large and critical landmarks (e.g. 50-word level, 200-word level) may occur early (when translation equivalents are taken into account). Moreover, precious little has been said about what an enlarged lexicon does to bilingual processing. Translation equivalents, even at the earliest stages of bilingual lexical development, are one way of compensating for increased demands on memory.

A further set of studies (among native Hebrew speaking children, children of Ethiopian immigrants, and Russian-Hebrew bilinguals) is currently underway to examine connections between social perceptions of bilingualism and literacy and fundamental processes of discrimination, recognition, and identification in phonological awareness tasks. These studies, along with work by Saiegh-Haddad (in press) on Arabic diglossia and Arabic-Hebrew bilingualism, examine sociopragmatic and psycholinguistic connections in bilingual processing.

In all of this work, methodology is a major concern, from the fine details in the ways that data are collected to the analytical tools by which they are interpreted and reported. But methodology which is not linked to substantive inquiry has no more value than content without form. The present investigation has focused on language contact, in particular codeswitching, translation, and fluency phenomena. The approach taken here has attempted to go beyond these domain-specific issues, offering a framework which encompasses socio-pragmatic as well as psycholinguistic matter, process as well as structure. It has challenged some of the prevailing approaches to bilingualism, attempting to show a place for integrative, processing-oriented research–not as an alternative to the 'languages in competition' metaphor, but as a complementary notion whose purpose is to account for some of the same phenomena in a somewhat different manner.

NOTES

---

[1] Other recent exceptions to the generative orientation, but less practically focused, can be seen in the line of work where language is viewed as 'activity' from a Vygotskyan perspective (e.g. Lantolf & Appel, 1994) and in the work on conceptual transfer (e.g. Jarvis, 2000).

[2] Swain (1972) coined this phrase in the title of her Ph.D. dissertation.

[3] Recall the data from Sankoff and Lessard (1975) that there was evidence for vocabulary growth until age 50 (see Chapter 4).

[4] A recent revival of Whorf's linguistic relativity hypothesis is relevant here (e.g. Hunt & Agnoli, 1991).

[5] This issue in childhood bilingualism is fundamentally the same as the question debated in bilingual language processing regarding single/shared/interdependent vs. dual/separate/autonomous storage and representation. See Chapter 2 above.

[6] The same authors reported 80-85 translation equivalents in an earlier study (Pearson, Fernandez & Oller, 1993).

[7] The more conventional terms in clinical linguistics and educational frameworks, 'language disorders' or 'language impairment,' carry with them both a sense of abnormality and social stigma. The term "atypical language" also implies social comparison and reeks of political correctness. None of these properly convey my view that we are all atypical language users and that bilingualism and various clinical conditions share a lot of common features. My choice of the term "language disturbances" in part reflects this bias and in part adopts a Perceptual Control Theory view, where intentions are no less important than behavioral data.

[8] Martha Crago (personal communication).

[9] Donahue cites Kavale and Forness' (1996) meta-analysis that "about 75% of students with LD had social skills characteristics that are significantly different from typical peers" and concludes that "no single cognitive, language, or academic measure is as powerful [as social skills characteristics] in differentiating students with LD from typical peers."

References

Abutalevi, J., Cappa, S.F., & Perani, D. 2001. The bilingual brain as revealed by functional neuroimaging. *Bilingualism: Language and Cognition, 4*, 179-190.

Aitchison, J. 1987. *Words in the mind*. Oxford: Blackwell.

Albert, M. & Obler, L.K. 1978. The bilingual brain: Neuropsychological and neurolinguistics aspects of bilingualism. New York: Academic Press.

Altarriba, J. & Bauer, L.M. 1998. Counseling the Hispanic client: Cuban Americans, Mexican Americans, and Puerto Ricans. *Journal of Counseling & Development, 76*, 389-395.

Alvarez, C. 1990. The institutionalization of Galician: Linguistic practices, power, and ideology in public discourse. Ph.D. thesis. University of California at Berkeley.

Anderson, N.H. & Cuneo, D.O. 1978. The height + width rule in children's judgments of quantity. *Journal of Experimental Psychology: General, 107*, 335-378.

Anderson, N.H. 1981. *Foundations of information integration theory*. New York: Academic Press.

Anderson, N.H. 1982. *Methods of information integration theory*. New York: Academic Press.

Anderson, N.H. 1990. Personal design in social cognition. In C. Hendrick & M.S. Clark (eds.) Research Methods in Personality and Social Psychology. *Review of Personality and Social Psychology, 11*, 243-278.

Anderson, N.H. 1996. *A functional theory of cognition*. Mahwah, NJ: Lawrence Erlbaum Associates.

Anderson, N.H. 2001. *Empirical direction in design and analysis*. Mahwah, NJ: Lawrence Erlbaum Associates.

Argyle, M. 1969. *Social interaction*. London: Methuen.

Aristotle. 1954. *The Rhetoric*. Translated by R. Roberts. New York: Modern Library.

Au, K. & Jordan, C. 1981. Teaching reading to Hawaiian children: Finding a culturally appropriate solution. In H. Trueba, G.P. Guthrie, & K. Au (eds.), *Culture and the bilingual classroom: Studies in classroom ethnography*. Rowley, MA: Newbury House, 139-152.

Auer, P. 1984. On the meaning of conversational code-switching. In P. Auer & A. di Lucio (eds) *Interpretative sociolinguistics*. Tubingen: Narr, 87-112.

Auer, P. 1995. The pragmatics of code-switching: a sequential approach. In L. Milroy & P. Muysken (eds.) *One speaker, two languages: Cross-*

disciplinary perspectives on code-switching. Cambridge: Cambridge University.

Auer, P. 1998. Code-switching in conversation: Language, interaction and identity. London, England: Routledge.

Auer, P. 1999. From code-switching via language mixing to fused lects: Toward a dynamic typology of bilingual speech. *International Journal of Bilingualism, 3*, 309-332.

Austin, J.L. 1962. *How to do things with words*. Oxford. Oxford University Press.

Azuma, Sh. 1991 Two-level processing hypothesis in speech production: Evidence from code-switching. *Papers from the 27th Regional Meeting of the Chicago Linguistics*. Chicago: Chicago Linguistics Society.

Baars, B.J. (ed.) 1992. The experimental psychology of human error: Implications for the architecture of voluntary control. NY: Plenum Press.

Bach K. & Harnish, R.M. 1979. *Linguistic communication and speech acts*. Cambridge, MA: MIT Press.

Bakhtin, M.M. 1986. *Speech genres and other late essays*. Austin: University of Texas Press.

Bardovi-Harlig, K. 1999. Exploring the interlanguage of interlanguage pragmatics: A research agenda for acquisitional pragmatics. *Language Learning, 49*, 677-713.

Baumel, S. & Walters, J. ms. Cognates as trigger words in judgments of intra-sentential codeswitched sentences. Ramat Gan: Bar-Ilan University.

Bazerman, C. 1989. Shaping written knowledge: The genre and activity of the experimental article in science. Mahwah, NJ: Lawrence Erlbaum Associates.

Beauregard, M., Chertkow, H., Bub, D., Murtha, S., Dixon, R., Evans, A. (1997) The neural substrate for concrete, abstract, and emotional word lexica: A positron emission tomography study. *Journal of Cognitive Neuroscience, 9, 4*, 441-461.

Bell, A. 1984. Language style as audience design. *Language in Society, 13*, 2, 145-204.

Berkenkotter, C. & Huckin, T. 1994. *Genre knowledge in disciplinary communication: Cognition/culture/power*. Mahwah, NJ: Lawrence Erlbaum Associates.

Berkowits, R. 1984. Recognition memory for input language in nonfluent bilinguals. *Revue Roumaine de Linguistique: Cahiers de Linguistique Theorique et Appliquee, 21*, 119-130.

Bialystok, E. 1978. A theoretical model of second language learning. *Language Learning 28*, 69-84.

Bialystok, E. 1988. Levels of bilingualism and levels of linguistic awareness. *Developmental Psychology 28*, 560-567.

Bialystok, E. 1990. Communication strategies. A psychological analysis of second language use. Oxford: Basil Blackwell.

Bialystok, E. 1994. Analysis and control in the development of second language proficiency. *Studies in Second Language Acquisition*, 157-168.

Bialystok, E. 2001. *Bilingualism in development: Language, literacy, & cognition*. Cambridge: Cambridge University Press.

Biber, D. 1995. *Variation across speech and writing*. Cambridge: Cambridge University Press.

Bierwisch, M. & Schreuder, R. 1992. From concepts to lexical items. *Cognition*, *432*, 23-60.

Birdsong, D. 1999. Second language acquisition and the critical period hypothesis. Mahwah, NJ: Lawrence Erlbaum Associates.

Black, M. 1962. *Models and metaphor: Studies in language and philosophy*. Ithaca, NY: Cornell University Press.

Blakemore, D. 1987. *Semantic constraints on relevance*. London: Blackwell.

Blakemore, D. 1992. Understanding utterances. An introduction to pragmatics. Oxford: Blackwell.

Bloch, M. 1985. Religion and ritual. In A. Kuper & J. Kuper (eds). *The social science encyclopaedia*. London: Routledge, pp. 698-701.

Blom, P. & Gumperz, J. J. 1972. Social meaning in linguistic structures: Code-switching in Norway. In J.J Gumperz & D. Hymes (eds.) *Directions in sociolinguistics. The ethnography of communication*. New York: Holt, Rinehart & Winston, 407-34.

Blommaert, J. 1992. Codeswitching and the exclusivity of social identities: Some data from Camus Kiswahili. *Journal of Multilingual and Multicultural Development*, *13*, 57-70.

Blum-Kulka, Sh. 1997. Dinner Talk: Cultural Patterns of Sociability and Socialisation in Family Discourse. Mahwah, New Jersey: Lawrence Erlbaum Associates.

Blum-Kulka, S., & Olshtain, E. 1986. Too many words: Length of utterance and pragmatic failure. *Studies in Second Language Acquisition*, *8*, 47-61.

Blumstein, S.E., Alexander, M.P., Ryalls, J.H., Katz, W. & Dworetzky, B. (1987). On the nature of foreign accent syndrome: A case study. *Brain and Language*, 31, 215-244.

Bock, J.K. & Kroch, A.S. 1989. The isolability of syntactic processing. In G.N. Carlson (ed.) *Language processing in children*. Dordrecht: Kluwer.

Bohn, O.-S. & Flege, J. E., 1992, The production of new and similar vowels by adult German learners of English. *Studies in Second Language Acquisition*, *14*, 131-158.

Bolinger, D. 1961. *Generality, gradience, and the all-or-none.* The Hague, Mouton, 1961.

Bolinger, D. 1975. *Aspects of language.* New York: Harcourt, Brace, and World

Bourhis, R.Y. 1979. Language in ethnic interaction: A social psychological approach. In H. Giles & B. St.-Jacques (eds.) *Language and ethnic relations.* Oxford: Pergamon Press.

Bourhis, R.Y. 2001. Acculturation, language maintenance, and language shift. In J. Klatter-Folmer & P. Van Avermaet (eds.) *Theories on maintenance and loss of minority languages. Towards a more integrated explanatory framework.* Munster/New York: Waxmann Verlag.

Bower, G., Black, J. & Turner, T. 1979. Scripts in memory for text. *Cognitive Psychology, 11,* 177-220.

Bowerman, M. 1982. Reorganizational processes in lexical development. In E. Wanner & L.R. Gleitman (eds.) *Language acquisition: The state of the art.* Cambridge: Cambridge University Press.

Bradac, J.J. & Wisegarver, R. 1984. Ascribed status, lexical diversity, and accent: Determinants of perceived status, solidarity, and control of speech style. *Journal of Language and Social Psychology, 3,* 239-255.

Bratman, M. 1987. *Intentions, plans, and practical reason.* Cambridge, MA: Harvard University Press.

Bratt-Paulston, C. 1986. Social factors in language maintenance and language shift. In J.A. Fishman, A. Tabouret-Keller, M. Clyne, B. Krishnamurti & M. Abdul-Aziz (eds.) *The Fergusonian Impact. In Honor of Charles A. Ferguson: Volume II: Sociolinguistics and the Sociology of Language.* Berlin: Mouton de Gruyter.

Broeder, P., Extra,G., & Maartens J. 1998. Durban Language Survey. In G. Extra and J. Maartens (eds.) *Multilingualism in a Multilingual Context: Case Studies on South Africa and Western Europe.* Tilburg: Tilburg University Press, 121-138.

Brown, P. & Levinson, S. 1987. *Politeness: Some universals in language use.* Cambridge: Cambridge University Press.

Byrne, R.W. and Russon, A.E. 1997. Learning by imitation: A hierarchical approach. *Brain and Behavioral Sciences, 21,* 667-721.

Campbell, S. 1998, *Translation into the second language.* Essex: Addison Wesley Longman Ltd.

Canale, M. & Swain, M. 1980. Theoretical bases of communicative approaches to second language teaching and testing. *Applied Linguistics, 1,* 1-29.

Caramazza, A. & Brones, I. 1980. Semantic classification by bilinguals. *Canadian Journal of Psychology, 34,* 1, 77-81

Caramazza, A. 1986. On drawing inferences about the structure of normal cognitive systems from the analysis of patterns of impaired performance. The case for single-patient studies. *Brain and Cognition, 5,* 41-66.

Caramazza, A. 1988. Some aspects of language processing revealed through the analysis of acquired aphasia: The lexical system. *Annual Review of Neurosciences, 11,* 395-421.

Caramazza, A. 1990. Cognitive neuropsychology and neurolinguistics: Advances in models of cognitive function and impairment. Hillsdale, NJ: Lawrence Erlbaum Associates.

Caramazza, A. 1997. How many levels of processing are there in lexical access. *Cognitive Neuropsychology, 14,* 177-208.

Caramazza, A. Yeni-Komshian, G. Zurif, E., & Carbone, E. 1973. The acquisition of a new phonological contrast: The case of stop consonants in French-English bilinguals. *Journal of the Acoustical Society of America, 54,* 421-428.

Carrell, P.L. 1984. Evidence of a formal schema in second language comprehension. *Language Learning, 34,* 87-111.

Cernis, M. 2001. Second language readers' sensitivity to language redundancy. PhD. Dissertation. Bar-Ilan University.

Chapman, R.S., Sueng, H-K., Schwartz, S.E. & E. Kay-Raining Bird. 1998. Language skills of children and adolescents with Down Syndrome: II. Production deficits. *Journal of Speech, Language, and Hearing Research, 41,* 861-873.

Chomsky, N. & Halle, M. 1968. *The sound pattern of English.* New York:

Chomsky, N. 1957. *Syntactic structures.* Mouton: The Hague.

Chomsky, N. 1965. *Aspects of the theory of syntax.* Cambridge, MA: MIT Press.

Chomsky, N. 1986. Knowledge of language: Its nature, origin and use. New York: Praeger.

Clark, E.V. 1987. The principle of contrast: a constraint on language acquisition. In B. MacWinney (ed.), *Mechanisms of language acquisition.* Hillsdale, NJ: Lawrence Erlbaum Associates.

Clark, E.V. 1990. On the pragmatics of contrast. *Journal of Child Language, 17,* 417-431.

Clark, E. 1993. *The lexicon in acquisition.* Cambridge, MA: Cambridge University Press.

Clark, H.H. & Clark, E.V. 1979. When nouns surface as verbs. *Language, 55,* 4, 767-811.

Clyne, M. 1967. *Transference and triggering.* The Hague: Marinus Nijhoff.

Clyne, M. 1969. The analogy between first and second language learning. *IRAL, 7,* 207-216.

Clyne, M. 1972. *Perspectives on language contact.* Melbourne: Hawthorne.

Clyne, M. 1980. Triggering and language processing. *Canadian Journal of Psychology, 34,* 400-406.

Clyne, M. (2003) *Dynamics of immigrant language contact*. Cambridge: Cambridge University Press.

Connor, U. 1996 Contrastic rhetoric: Cross-cultural aspects of second-language writing. Cambridge: Cambridge University Press.

Cook, V.J. 1992. Evidence for multicompetence. *Language Learning*, *42*:4, 557-591.

Cook, V.J. 1997 *Inside language*. London: Edward Arnold.

Cooper. R. 1969. How can we measure the roles which a bilingual's languages play in his everyday behavior? In L.Kelly (ed.) *The measurement and description of bilingualism*. Toronto: University of Toronto Press.

Costa, A. & Caramazza, A. 1999. Is lexical selection in bilingual speech production language-specific? Further evidence from Spanish-English and English-Spanish bilinguals. *Bilingualism: Language and Cognition*, *2* (3), 231-244.

Coulmas, F. 1981. Conversational Routine. Explorations in prepatterned speech and standardized communication situations. The Hague 1981. Mouton.

Cucchiarini, C., Strik, H.. & Boves, L. 2000. Quantitative assessment of second language learners' fluency by means of automatic speech recognition technology. *Journal of the Acoustical Society of America*, *107* (2), 989-999.

Cummins, J. 1991. Interdependence of first- and second-language proficiency in bilingual children. In E. Bialystok (ed.). *Language Processes in Bilingual Children*. Cambridge: Cambridge University Press.

Cziko, G. 1995. Without miracles: Universal selection theory and the second Darwinian revolution. Cambridge, MA: MIT Press.

Cziko, G. 2000. The things we do: Using the insights of Bernard and Darwin to understand the what, how and why of behavior. Cambridge, MA: MIT Press.

Damasio, H., Grabowski, T.J. Tranel, D. Hichwa, R.D. & A.R. Damasio. 1996. A neural basis for lexical retrieval. *Nature*, *380*, 504-505.

Darcy, N. J. 1953. A review of the literature on the effects of bilingualism upon the measurement of intelligence. *The Journal of Genetic Psychology*, 82, 21-57.

Dawkins, R. 1989. *The selfish gene*. Oxford: Oxford University Press.

de Bot, K. 1992. A bilingual production model: Levelt's speaking model adapted. *Applied Linguistics*, *13*, 1-24.

de Bot, K. 2000. Language use as an interface between sociolinguistic and psycholinguistic processes in attrition and language shift. In J. Klatter-Folmer & P. Van Avermaet (eds.) *Theories on maintenance and loss of minority languages. Towards a more integrated explanatory framework*. Munster/New York: Waxmann Verlag.

de Bot, K. & Clyne, M. 1994. A 16-year longitudinal study of language attrition in Dutch immigrants in Australia. *Journal of Multilingual and Multicultural Development, 15*, 17-28.

de Bot, K. & Schreuder, R. 1993. Word production and the bilingual lexicon. In R. Schreuder & B. Weltens (eds.) *The bilingual lexicon.* Amsterdam: John Benjamins, 191-214.

de Groot, A.M.B. & Kroll, J. (eds.) 1997. *Tutorials in bilingualism.* Mahwah, NJ: Lawrence Erlbaum Associates.

de Groot, A.M.B. 1992. Determinants of word translation. *Journal of Experimental Psychology, 18* (5), 1001-1018.

de Groot, A.M.B. 2000. On the source and nature of semantic and conceptual knowledge. *Bilingualism: Language & Cognition, 3(1), 7-9.*

de Rooij, V. 2000. French discourse markers in Shaba Swahili conversations. *International Journal of Bilingualism, 4*, 447-467.

Dell, G. (1985) Positive feedback in hierarchical connectionist models: Applications to language production. *Cognitive Science, 9* (1), 3-23.

Dewaele, J.-M. 1998. Lexical inventions: French interlanguage as L2 versus L3. *Applied Linguistics, 19*, 4, 471-490.

DeWaele, J.-M. 2001. Activation or inhibition? The interaction of L1, L2 and L3 on the language mode continuum. In J. Cenoz, B. Hufeisen, & U. Jessner (eds) *Cross-linguistic influence in third language acquisition: Psycholinguistic perspectives.* Clevedon: Multilingual Matters, 69-89.

Dewaele, J.-M. & A. Pavlenko (2002) Emotion vocabulary in interlanguage. *Language Learning, 52, 2.*

Diller, K.C. 1970: "Compound" and "coordinate" bilingualism. A conceptual artifact. *Word, 26*, 254-261.

Dittmar, N., Spolsky, B. & Walters, J. 1997. Grammaticalization and social convergence in second language acquisition. In R. Hickey & S. Puppel (eds.) *Feschschrift for Jacek Fisiak.* Berlin: deGruyter.

Dittmar, N., Spolsky, B. & Walters, J. 1998. Convergence and divergence in second language acquisition and use: Towards an integrated model. In V. Regan (ed.) *Contemporary Approaches to Second Language Acquisition in Social Context.* Dublin: University College Press.

Dittmar, N., Spolsky, B. & Walters, J. 2002. *Convergence and Divergence in Second Language Acquistion and Use: An Examination of Immigrant Identities.* Final Project Report. Jerusalem: German Israel Research Foundation.

Dodds, J. 1999. Friends, false friends and foes or back to basics in L1 and L2 translation. In G. Anderman & M. Rogers (eds.) *Word, text, translation: Liber amicorum for Peter Newmark.* Clevedon, UK: Multilingual Matters Ltd.

Donahue, M. 1994. Differences in classroom discourse styles of students with learning disabilities. In D. Ripich and N. Creaghead (eds.), *School discourse*, San Diego, CA: Singular Press, pp. 229-261.

Donahue, M.L. 2001. Hanging with friends: Making sense of research on peer discourse in children with language and learning disabilities. In K. Butler & E. Silliman (eds.). *Speaking, reading, and writing in students with language learning disabilities.* Mahwah, NJ: Lawrence Erlbaum Associates.

Donitsa-Schmidt, S. 1999. Language maintenance or shift: Determinants of language choice among Soviet immigrants in Israel. Ph.D. dissertation, Ontario Institute for Studies in Education, University of Toronto.

Dopke, S. 1992. One parent—one language: An interactional approach. Amsterdam: Benjamins.

Duchan, J. 1983. Language processing and geodesic domes. In T. Gallagher & C. Prutting (eds.) *Pragmatic issues: Assessment and intervention.* Baltimore, Md.: University Park Press, 83-100.

Duncan, S. 1974. Some signals and rules for taking speaking turns in conversation. In: S. Weitz (ed.) *Nonverbal communication. Readings with a commentary.* New York: Oxford University Press.

Duranti, A. 1993, Intentionality and truth: An ethnographic critique. *Cultural Anthropology, 8*, 214-245.

Duranti, A. 2000. Intentionality. *Journal of Linguistic Anthropology, 9*, 134-136.

Edwards, A. L. 1957. *Techniques of attitude scale construction.* New York: Appleton-Century-Crofts.

Ellis, R. 1994. *Second language acquisition.* Oxford: Oxford University Press.

Ellinger, B. 1997. The relationship between ethnolinguistic identity and English language achievement for native Russian speakers and native Hebrew speakers in Israel. Ph.D. Dissertation, Bar-Ilan University.

Emmorey, K., Borinstein, H.B., & Thompson, R. 2003. Bimodal Bilingualism: Code-blending between spoken English and American Sign Language. Paper presented at ISB4, Tempe, AZ.

Epstein, S.D., Flynn, S., & Martohardjono, G. 1996. Second language acquisition: *Theoretical and experimental issues in contemporary research. Behavioral and Brain Sciences*, 19 (4): 677-758.

Erickson, E. 1968. *Identity, youth and crisis.* New York: Norton.

Erickson, F. & Schultz, J. 1982. The counselor as gatekeeper: *Social interaction interviews.* New York: Free Press.

Ervin, S. & Osgood, C. 1954. Second Language Learning and Bilingualism. *Journal of Abnormal and Social Psychology, Supplement*, 139-146.

Ervin-Tripp, S. 1964. An analysis of the interaction of language, topic and listener. *American Anthropologist, 66*, 86-102

Ervin-Tripp, S. 1974. Is second language learning like the first? *TESOL Quarterly, 8*, 111-27.

Fase, W. & Jaespert, K. 1991. Migrant Languages in Western Europe. Special Issue. *International Journal of the Sociology of Language, 90*.

Feldman, Z. 1997. First language attrition in Russian immigrants: focus on the lexicon. In E. Kellerman & B. Weltens (ed.) *Proceedings of the VIth Annual Meeting of EUROSLA*. Amsterdam: ANELA.

Fellbaum, C. (ed.) 1998. *WordNet: An electronic lexical database.* Cambridge, MA: MIT Press.

Ferguson, C.A. 1959. Diglossia. *Word, 15*, 325-240.

Ferreira, F. & Clifton, C. 1986. The independence of syntactic processing. *Journal of Memory and Language, 25*, 348-368.

Festman, J. 2004. Lexical production phenomena as evidence for activation and control processes in trilingual lexical retrieval. Ph.D. Dissertation, Bar-Ilan University.

Fillmore, C.J. 1979. On fluency. In C.J. Fillmore, D. Kempler & WS-Y. Wang (eds), *Individual differences in language ability and language behavior.* New York: Academic Press.

Fine, J. in press. Language and psychiatry: A handbook for clinical practice. London: Equinox.

Fishman, J.A. 1964. The sociology of language. In T. Sebeok (ed.) *Current trends in linguistics.* The Hague: Mouton.

Fishman, J.A. 1965. Who speaks what language to whom and when? *La Linguistique, 2*, 67-88.

Fishman, J.A. 1972. Domains and the relationship between micro- and macro-sociolinguistics. In J.J. Gumperz & D. Hymes (eds.) *Explorations in Sociolinguistics.* New York: Holt, Rinehart, & Winston.

Fishman, J.A., Cooper, R.L. & Ma, R. 1971. *Bilingualism in the barrio.* Bloomington, IN: Indiana University Press.

Flege, J.E. 1993. Production and perception of a novel, second language phonetic contrast. *Journal of the Acoustical Society of America, 93*, 1589-1608.

Flege, J.E. 1995. Second-language speech learning: Theory, findings, and problems, in W. Strange (ed.) *Speech perception and linguistic experience: Theoretical and methodological issues.* Timonium, MD: York Press, 233-277.

Flynn, S., Martohardjono, G. & O'Neil, W. (eds). 1998. *The generative study of second language acquisition.* Mahwah, NJ: Lawrence Erlbaum Associates.

Fodor, J.A. 1983. *The modularity of mind.* Cambridge, MA: MIT Press.

Ford Meyer, C. 1991. Cognitive networks in conversation. In D.G. Lockwood, P.H. Fries & J.E. Copeland (eds.) *Functional Approaches to Language,*

Culture and Cognition. Papers in honor of Sydney M. Lamb. Amsterdam: John Benjamins.

Francis, W.S., Tokiwicz, N. & J.F. Kroll. 2003. Translation priming as a function of bilingual proficiency and item difficulty. Paper presented at ISB4, Tempe, AZ.

Francis, W.S. 1999. Cognitive integration of language and memory in bilinguals: Semantic representation. *Psychological Bulletin, 125,* 2, 193-222.

Francis, W.S. 2000. Clarifying the cognitive experimental approach to bilingual research. *Bilingualism: Language & Cognition, 3,* 1, 13-15.

Fraser, B. 1979. Interpretation of novel metaphors. In A. Ortony (ed.) *Metaphor and thought.* Cambridge: Cambridge University Press, 329-341.

Fraser, B. 1987. Pragmatic formatives. *The pragmatic perspective.* In J. Verschueren & M. Pertuccellli-Papi (eds.). Amsterdam: Benjamins.

Fraser, B. 1990. Perspectives on politeness. *Pragmatics, 14,* 219-236.

Fraser, B. 1996. Pragmatic markers. *Journal of Pragmatics, 6,* 2 167-190.

Fraser, B., Rintell, E. & Walters, J. 1980. An approach to conducting research on the acquisition of pragmatic competence in a second language. In D. Larsen-Freeman (ed.) *Discourse Analysis in Second Language Acquisition.* Rowley, MA: Newbury House, 75-91.

Freedman, A. 1993. Show and tell? The role of explicit teaching in the learning of new genres. *Research in the Teaching of English, 27,* 222-250.

Frenck-Mestre & Vaid, 1993 Activation of number facts in bilinguals. *Memory and Cognition, 21,* 809–818.

Fridja, N. 1986. *The emotions.* Cambridge: Cambridge University Press.

Fries, C.C. 1945. *Teaching and learning English as a foreign language.* Ann Arbor: University of Michigan Press.

Fromkin, V. 1973. *Speech errors as linguistic evidence.* The Hague: Mouton.

Gabora, L. 1998. Autocatalytic closure in a cognitive system. *Psycholoquy, 9,* 67.http://www.cogsci.soton.ac.uk/cgi/psyc/ newpsy.9.67.

Garrett, M.F. 1975. The analysis of sentence production. In G. Bower (ed.) *The psychology of learning and motivation.* New York: Academic Press, 133-177.

Garrett, M.F.1988. Processes in language production. In F.J. Newmeyer (ed.) *The Cambridge Survey of Linguistics. Volume 3: Biological and Psychological Aspects of Language.* Cambridge, MA: Harvard University.

Gee, J. 1990/1996. Social linguistics and literacies: Ideology in Discourses. London: Falmer.

Geis, M.L. 1995. *Speech acts and conversational interaction.* Cambridge: Cambridge University Press.

Genesee, F. 2001. Bilingual first language acquisition: Exploring the limits of the language faculty. *Annual Review of Applied Linguistics, 21,* 153-168.

Gernsbacher, M. A. & Shlesinger, M. 1997. The proposed role of suppression in simultaneous interpretation. *Interpreting: International Journal of Research and Practice in Interpreting, 2* (1/2), 119-140.

Geva, E. & L. Verhoeven. (eds.) 2001. Basic Processes in Early Second Language Reading. Special Issue of *Scientific Studies of Reading, 4,* 4.

Gibbs, R. 1999. *Intentions in the experience of meaning.* Cambridge: Cambridge University Press.

Giles, H (ed.) 1977. *Language, ethnicity and intergroup relations.* New York: Academic Press.

Giles, H. & Johnson, P. 1987. Ethnolinguistic identity theory: a social psychological approach to language maintenance. *International Journal of the Sociology of Language, 68,* 66-99.

Giles, H., Coupland, J. & Coupland, N. 1991. *Contexts of accommodation: Developments in applied sociolinguistics.* Cambridge: Cambridge University Press.

Goffman, E. 1959. *The presentation of self in everyday life.* Garden City, New York: Doubleday.

Goldman-Eisler, F. 1972. Pauses, clauses, sentences. *Language and Speech, 15,* 103-113.

Goldstein, K. 1948. *Language and language disturbances.* NY: Grune and Stratton.

Gollan, T.H. & Silverberg, N.B. 2001. Tip-of-the-tongue states in Hebrew-English bilinguals. *Bilingualism: Language and Cognition, 4* (1), 63-83.

Grainger, J. & Beauvillain, C. 1987. Language blocking and lexical access in bilinguals. *Quarterly Journal of Experimental Psychology, 39,* 295-319.

Grainger, J. & Dijkstra, T. 1992. On *the Representation and Use of Language Information.* In R.J. Harris (ed.) *Cognitive processing in bilinguals.* Amsterdam: Elsevier, 207-220.

Green, D.W. (ed.) 2001. The cognitive neuroscience of bilingualism. Special issue of *Bilingualism: Language and Cognition, 4* (2).

Green, D.W. 1986. Control, activation, and resource: A framework and a model for the control of speech in bilinguals. *Brain and Language, 27,* 210-233.

Green, D.W. 1993. Towards a model of L2 comprehension and production. In R. Schreuder & B. Weltens (eds.) *The bilingual lexicon.* Amsterdam: John Benjamins, 249-277.

Green, D.W. 1998. Mental control of the bilingual lexico-semantic system. *Bilingualism: Language and Cognition, 1* (2), 67-81.

Green, D.W. 2000. Concepts, experiments and mechanisms. *Bilingualism: Language and Cognition, 3* (1), 16-18.

Grosjean, F. & Frauenfelder, U. (eds.) 1997. *A guide to spoken word recognition paradigms.* Hove, UK: Psychology Press.

Grosjean, F. 1982. *Life with two languages: An introduction to bilingualism.* Cambridge: Harvard University Press.

Grosjean, F. 1988. Exploring the recognition of guest words in bilingual speech. *Language and Cognitive Processes, 3*, 233-274.

Grosjean, F. 1989. Neurolinguists, beware! The bilingual is not two monolinguals in one person. *Brain and Language, 36*, 3-15.

Grosjean, F. 1997. Processing mixed languages. In A.M.B. de Groot & J. Kroll (eds.) *Tutorials in bilingualism.* Mahwah, NJ: Lawrence Erlbaum Associates, 225-254.

Gudykunst, W. & Ting-Toomey, S. 1990. Ethnic identity, language and communication breakdowns. In H. Giles & W.P. Robinson (eds.). *Handbook of language and social psychology.* New York: Wiley.

Gumperz, J. 1982. *Discourse strategies.* Cambridge: Cambridge University.

Gumperz, J. 1992. Further notes on contextualisation. In P. Auer & A. di Luzio (eds.) *Contextualising language.* Amsterdam: Benjamins, 39-53.

Gumperz, J. J. 1967. Linguistic markers of bilingual communication. *Journal of Social Issues, 23*, 137-153.

Gumperz, J.J. & Hernandez-Chavez, E. 1972. Bilingualism, bidialectalism and classroom interaction. In C.B. Cazden, V.P. Johns, & D. Hymes (eds.) *Functions of language in the classroom.* New York: Teachers College Press.

Hakuta, K. 1974. Prefabricated patterns and the emergence of structure in second language acquisition. *Language Learning, 24,* 287-298.

Halliday, M.A.K. & Hasan, R. 1976. *Cohesion in English.* London: Longman.

Halliday, M.A.K. 1994. *An introduction to functional grammar.* London: Edward Arnold.

Hanauer, D. 1995. Literary and poetic text categorization judgments. *Journal of Literary Semantics, 24* (3), 187-210.

Harris, B. 1992. Natural Translation: A Reply to Hans P. Krings. *Target, 4*(1), 97-103.

Hatch, E. 1983. Psycholinguistics: A second language perspective. Rowley, MA: Newbury House.

Haugen, E. 1953. *The Norwegian language in America.* Philadelphia, PA: University of Pennsylvania.

Heller, M. (ed.) 1988. Codeswitching: Anthropological and sociolinguistic perspectives. Berlin: Mouton de Gruyter.

Heller, M. 1982. Negogiations of language choice in Montreal. In J.J. Gumperz (ed.). *Language and social identity*. Cambridge: Cambridge University Press.

Herdina, P. & U. Jessner. 2001. A dynamic model of multilingualism: Perspectives of change in psycholinguistics. Clevedon: Multilingual Matters.

Ho-Dac, T. 1997. Tonal facilitation of code-switching. *Australian Review of Applied Linguistics*, *20*, 129-151.

Hoffman, E. 1989. Lost in translation: A life in a new language. New York: Penguin Books.

Hovy, E.H. 1995 The multifunctionality of discourse markers. In *The proceedings of the workshop on discourse markers*. Egmond-aan.zee, The Netherlands.

Hunt, E. & F. Agnoli. 1991. The Whorfian hypothesis: A cognitive psychology perspective. *Psychological Review*, *98*, 3, 377-389.

Hymes, D. 1981. In vain I tried to tell you: Essays in Native American ethno-poetics. Philadelphia: University of Pennsylvania Press.

Hymes, D. 1974. Models of the interaction of language and social setting. In J.J. Gumperz & D. Hymes (eds.) *Directions in sociolinguistics: The ethnography of communication*. New York: Holt, Rinehart & Winston.

Jackendoff, R. 1983. *Semantics and cognition*. Cambridge, MA: MIT Press.

Jackendoff, R. 2002. *Foundations of language*. Oxford: Oxford University Press.

Jake, J.L. & Myers-Scotton, C. 1997. Codeswitching and compromise strategies: Implications for Lexical Structure. *International Journal of Bilingualism*, *1*, 25-39.

Jake, J. & Myers-Scotton, C. 2000. Explaining aspects of codeswitching and their implications. In J. Nicol (ed.). *One mind, two languages: Bilingual language processing*. New York: Blackwell.

James, W. 1890. *Principles of psychology*. London: MacMillan.

Jarvis, S. 2000. Methodological rigor in the study of transfer: Identifying L1 influence in the interlanguage lexicon. *Language Learning*, *50*, 2, 245-309.

Jaspaert, K. & Kroon, S. 1989. Social determinants of language shift by Italians in the Netherlands and Flanders. *International Journal of the Sociology of Language*, *90*, 77-96.

Johnson, J.S. & Newport, E.L. 1989. Critical period effects in second language learning: The influence of maturational state on the acquisition of English as a second language. *Cognitive Psychology*, *21*, 60-99.

Johnson, P. 1982. Effects of reading comprehension on building background knowledge. *TESOL Quarterly*, *16*, 503-516.

Joos, M. 1961. The five clocks: A linguistic excursion into the five styles of English usage. New York: Harcourt, Brace & World.

Jucker, A.H. & Ziv, Y. (eds.) 1998. *Discourse markers: Descriptions and theory.* Amsterdam: John Benjamins.

Kaplan, R. B. 1966. Cultural thought patterns in inter-cultural education. *Language Learning, 16,* 1-20.

Kasper, G. 2001. Four perspectives on pragmatic development. *Applied Linguistics, 22,* 502-530.

Kavale, K., & Forness, S. 1996. Social skill deficits and learning disabilities: A meta-analysis. *Journal of Learning Disabilities, 29,* 226-237.

Kay-Raining Bird, E, Cleave, P.L., Cupit, J. Demers, L. Randall-Gryz, A. & G. Nowell. 2002. Language mixing in children with Down Syndrome. Poster presented at the Symposium on Research in Child Language Disorders and the International Congress for the Study of Child Language, Madison, WI.

Kilborn, K. & Ito, T. 1989. Sentence Processing Strategies in Adult Bilinguals. In B. MacWhinney & E. Bates. *The crosslinguistic study of sentence processing.* Cambridge: Cambridge University, 257-291.

Klatter-Folmer, J. & Van Avermaet, P. (eds.) 2001. Theories on maintenance and loss of minority languages. Towards a more integrated explanatory framework. Munster/New York: Waxmann Verlag.

Klavans, J.L. & Resnick, P. 1996. The balancing act: Combining symbolic and statistical approaches to language. Cambridge, MA: MIT Press.

Klein, D., Milner, B., Zatorre, R., Evans, A., & Meyer, E. 1994. Functional anatomy of bilingual language processing: A neuroimaging study. *Brain and Language, 47,* 464-466.

Koenig, E. 1991. *The Meaning of Focus Particles.* London: Routledge.

Koster, C. 1987. Word recognition in foreign and native language. Dordrecht: Foris.

Kremer-Sadlik, T. 2003. To be or not to be bilingual: Autistic children from multilingual families. Paper presented at ISB4, Tempe, AZ.

Kroll, J.F. & de Groot, A.M.B. 1997. Lexical and conceptual memory in the bilingual: Mapping form to meaning in two languages. In A.M.B. de Groot & J. Kroll (eds.) *Tutorials in bilingualism.* Mahwah, NJ: Lawrence Erlbaum Associates, 169-199.

Kroll, J.F. & Stewart, E. 1994. Category interference in translation and picture naming: Evidence for asymmetric connections between bilingual memory representation. *Journal of Memory and Language, 33,* 149-174.

Kroll, J.F., Michael, E. & Sankaranarayanan, A. 1998. A model of bilingual representation and its implications for second language acquisition. In A.F. Healy & L.E. Bourne (eds) *Foreign language learning: Psycholinguistic experiments on training and retention.* Mahwah, NJ: Lawrence Erlbaum Associates.

Kucera, H. & Francis, W.N. 1967. *Computational analysis of present-day American English*. Providence, RI: Brown University.

Labov, W. 1972. *Sociolinguistic patterns*. Philadelphia: University of Pennsylvania Press.

Lado, R. 1957. *Linguistics across cultures*. Ann Arbor: University of Michigan Press.

Lambert, W.E. & Tucker, G.R. 1972. *Bilingual education of children: The St. Lambert Experiment*. Rowley, MA: Newbury House.

Lambert, W.E. & Taylor, D.M. 1991. Coping with cultural and racial diversity in urban America. New York: Praeger.

Lambert, W.E. 1977. Effects of bilingualism on the individual: Cognitive and socio-cultural consequences. In P.A. Hornby (ed.) *Bilingualism: Psychological, social and educational implications*. New York: Academic Press, 15-28.

Landry, R. & Bourhis, R.Y. 1997. Linguistic landscape and ethnolinguistic vitality. *Journal of Language and Social Psychology, 16*, 1, 23-49.

Lantolf, J.P. & Appel, G. (eds.) 1994. *Vygotskian approaches to second language research*. Norwood, NJ: Ablex.

Lanza, E. 1997. *Language mixing in infant bilingualism: A sociolinguistic perspective*. Oxford: Oxford University Press.

Laufer, B. & Nation, P. 1995. Vocabulary size and use: Lexical richness in L2 Written Production. *Applied Linguistics, 16*, 307-322.

Lawson, S. & Sachdev, I. 2000. Codeswitching in Tunisia: Attitudinal and behavioural dimensions. *Journal of Pragmatics, 32*, 1343-1361.

Lenneberg, E. 1967. *Biological foundations of language*. New York: Wiley.

Leonard, L. 1998. *Specific language impairment*. Cambridge, MA: MIT Press.

Leseman, P.P.P. 2000. Bilingual vocabulary development in Turkish-Dutch preschoolers. *Journal of Multilingual Multicultural Development, 21*, 2, 93-112.

Levelt, W.J.M. 1989. *Speaking: From intention to articulation*. Cambridge, MA: MIT Press.

Levelt, W.J.M. 1995. The ability to speak: From intentions to spoken words. *European Review, 3*, 13-23.

Levelt, W.J.M., Roelofs, A. & Meyer, A. 1999. A theory of lexical access in speech production. *Behavioral and Brain Sciences, 22*, 1-38.

Levy, Y. & Schaeffer, J. (eds.). 2003. *Language competence across populations: Toward a definition of SLI*. Mahwah, NJ: Lawrence Erlbaum Associates.

Lewy, N. & Grosjean, F. ms. BIMOLA: A computational model of bilingual spoken word recognition.

Li, P. 1996. Spoken word recognition of code-switched words by Chinese-English bilinguals. *Journal of Memory and Language, 35*, 757-774.

Li, P. & Farkas, I. 2002. A self-organizing connectionist model of bilingual processing. In R.O. Heredia & J. Altarriba (eds.) *Bilingual sentence processing. Advances in Psychology 134*, Amerstand: North-Holland Publishing.

Li Wei. 1994. Three generations Two languages One family: Language choice and langugage shift in a Chinese community in Britain. Clevedon: Multilingual Matters.

Li Wei. 2000. *The bilingualism reader*. London: Routledge.

Li Wei & Milroy, L. 1995. Conversational code-switching in a Chinese community in Britain: a sequential analysis. *Journal of Pragmatics, 23*, 281-299.

Li Wei, Milroy, L. & Pong, S.C. 2000. A two-step sociolinguistic analysis of code-switching and language choice. *International Journal of Applied Linguistics, 2*(1), 63-86.

Lieberson, S. 1981. *Language diversity and language contact*. Stanford: Stanford University Press.

Lipski, J.M. 1985. *Linguistic aspects of Spanish-English language switching*. Tempe: Arizona State University Center for Latin American Studies.

Logan, J.S., Lively, S.E. & Pisoni, D.B. 1991. Training Japanese listeners to identify English /r/ and /l/: A first report. *Journal of the Acoustical Society of America, 89*, 2, 874-886.

Ludi, G. 1990. Synthesis. In Code-switching and language contact: Impact and consequences: Broader considerations. Strasbourg: European Science Foundation, pp. 22-24.

Lukes, S. 1975. Political ritual and social integration. *Sociology, 9*, 289-308.

Mack, M. 1990. Phonetic transfer ina French-English bilingual child. In P.H. Nelde (ed.) *Language attitudes and language conflict*. Bonn: Dummler.

MacLeod, C. M. 1991. Half a century of research on the Stroop effect: An integrative review. *Psychological Bulletin, 109*, 163-203.

Macnamara, J. 1976. Comparison between first and second language learning. *Die Neuren Sprachen, 75*, 175-88

Macnamara, J., Krauthammer, M. & Bolgar, M. 1968. Language switching in bilinguals as a function of stimulus and response uncertainty. *Journal of Experimental Psychology, 78*, 208-215.

MacSwan, J. 2000. The architecture of the bilingual language faculty: evidence from intrasentential code switching. *Bilingualism: Language & Cognition, 3*, 37-54.

Magiste, E. 1979. The competing language systems of the multilingual: A developmental study of decoding and encoding processes. *Journal of Verbal Learning and Verbal Behavior, 18*, 79-89.

Magiste, E. 1982. Automaticity and interference in bilinguals. *Psychological Research, 44*, 29-43.

Marian, V. & Neisser, U. 2000. Language-dependent recall of autobiographical memories. *Journal of Experimental Psychology: General, 129*, 3, 361-368.

Marslen-Wilson, W.D. 1975. Sentence perception as an interactive parallel process. *Science, 189*, 226-228.

Maschler, Y. 1994. Metalanguage and discourse markers in bilingual conversation. *Language in Society, 23*, 325-366.

Maschler, Y. 1997. Discourse markers as frame shifts in Israeli Hebrew talk-in-interaction. *Journal of Pragmatics, 7*, 2, 183-211.

Maschler, Y. 1998. *Rotse lishmoa keta*? 'wanna hear something weird/funny [lit. 'a segment']?': The discourse markers segmenting Israeli Hebrew Talk-in-interaction. In A.H. Jucker & Y. Ziv (eds.) *Discourse markers: Descriptions and theory*. Amsterdam: John Benjamins.

Massaro, D.W. & Shlesinger, M. 1997. Information processing and a computational approach to the study of simultaneous interpretation. *Interpreting: of Research and Practice in Interpreting, 2*(1/2), 13-53.

Matras, Y. 2000. Mixed languages: A functional-communicative approach. *Bilingualism, Language and Cognition, 3*, 79-99.

Maugham, W.S. 1938. *The summing up*. London: Heinemann.

McCann, C.D. & Higgins, E.T. 1990. Social cognition and communication. In H. Giles & W.P. Robinson (eds.). *Handbook of language and social psychology*. New York: Wiley.

McClelland, J. L. 1987. The case for interactionism in language processing. In M. Coltheart (Ed.), *Attention and performance XII: The psychology of reading*. Hillsdale, NJ: Lawrence Erlbaum Associates, 3–36.

McClelland, J.L. & Elman, J.L. 1986. The TRACE Model of Speech Perception. *Cognitive Psychology, 18*, 1-86.

McLaughlin, B. 1987. *Theories of second-language learning*. London: Edward

Mead, G.H. 1964. *On social psychology; selected papers*. Edited and with an introduction by Anselm Strauss. Chicago: University of Chicago Press.

Meisel, J. (ed.) 1994. Bilingual first language acquisition: French and German grammatical development. Amsterdam: John Benjamins.

Merzenich, M., Jenkins, W., Johnston, P., Schreiner, C., Miller, S. L. & Tallal, P. 1996. Temporal processing deficits of language-learning impaired children ameliorated by training. *Science, 271*, 77-81.

Meuter, R.F.I. & Allport, A. 1999. Bilingual language switching in naming: Asymmetrical costs of language selection. *Journal of Memory and Language, 40*, 25-40.

Miller, C.R. 1984. Genre as social action. *Quarterly Journal of Speech, 70*, 151-167.

Milroy, L. & Wei, L. 1995. A social network approach to code-switching. In L. Milroy & P. Muysken (eds.) *One speaker, two languages: Cross-*

disciplinary perspectives on code-switching. Cambridge: Cambridge University Press.

Milroy, L. 2001 Bridging the micro-macro gap: social change, social networks and bilingual repertoires. In J. Klatter-Folmer & P. Van Avermaet (eds.) *Theories on maintenance and loss of minority languages. Towards a more integrated explanatory framework.* Munster/New York: Waxmann Verlag.

Mohle, D. 1984. A comparison of the second language speech production of different native speakers. In H.W. Dechert, D. Mohle, M. Raupach (eds.) *Second language production.* Tubingen: Gunter Narr, 26-49.

Morgan, J.L. 1978. Two types of convention indirect speech acts. *Syntax and Semantics, Volume 9: Pragmatics.* New York: Academic Press, 261-280.

Motley, M. 1976. Laboratory induction of verbal slips: A new method for psycholinguistic research. *Communication Quarterly,* 24, 28-34.

Mrosovsky, N. 1990. *Rheostasis: The physiology of change.* New York: Oxford University Press.

Muller, N. & Hulk, A. 2001. Crosslinguistic influence in bilingual acquisition: Italian and French as recipient languages. *Bilingualism: Language and Cognition,* 4(1), 1-21.

Murphy, S.T. & Zajonc, R.B. 1993. Affect, cognition, and awareness: Affective priming with optimal and suboptimal stimulus exposures. *Journal of Personality & Social Psychology,* 64, 723-739.

Muysken, P. 1997. Code-Switching Processes: Alternation, Insertion, Congruent Lexicalization. In M. Putz (ed.) *Language Choices: Conditions, Constraints, and Consequences.* Amsterdam: Benjamins.

Muysken, P. 2000. *Bilingual speech: A typology of code-mixing.* Cambridge: Cambridge University Press.

Myers-Scotton, C. 1990. Intersections between social motivations and structural processing in code-switching. In *Papers for the workshop on constraints, conditions and models.* Strasbourg: European Science Foundation, 57-82.

Myers-Scotton, C. 1992. Constructing the frame in intrasentential codeswitching. *Multilingua, 11*-1,101-127.

Myers-Scotton, C. 1993. Social motivations for codeswitching: Evidence from Africa. Oxford: Oxford University.

Myers-Scotton, C. 1993/1997. *Duelling languages: Grammatical structure in codswitching.* Oxford: Oxford University Press.

Myers-Scotton, C. 1995. A lexically-based model of code-switching. In L. Milroy & P. Muysken (eds) *One speaker, two languages: Cross-disciplinary perspectives on code-switching.* Cambridge: Cambridge University Press, 233-256.

Myers-Scotton, C. 1999. Inside and outside: Structural and social constraints on contact phenomena. Paper presented at the Second International Symposium on Language Policy. Bar-Ilan University.

Myers-Scotton, C. 2002. Contact linguistics: Bilingual encounters and grammatical outcomes. Oxford: Oxford University Press.

Myers-Scotton, C. & Jake, J.L. 1995. Matching lemmas in a bilingual language competence and production model. *Linguistics, 33,* 981-1024.

Myers-Scotton, C. & Jake, J.L. 2000. Testing a model of morpheme classification with language contact data. *International Journal of Bilingualism,* 4, 1, 1-8.

Nemser, W. 1971. The approximative system of foreign language learners, *IRAL, 9,* 115-123.

Ninio, A. 1986. The illocutionary aspect of utterances. *Discourse Processes, 9,* 2, 127-148.

Nooteboom, S.G. & Truin, P.J.M. 1980. The recognition of fragments of spoken words by native and non-native listeners. *IPOAPR, 15,* 42-47.

Norman, D.A. & Shallice, T. 1986. Attention to action: Willed and automatic control of behaviour. In R.J. Davidson, G.E. Schwartz & D. Shapiro (eds.), *Consciousness & self-regulation: Volume 4* (pp. 1-18). New York: Plenum Press.

Novak, J.D. & Gowin, D.B. 1984. *Learning how to learn.* New York: Cambridge University Press.

Novak, J.D. 1998. Learning, creating, and using knowledge: Concept maps as facilitative tools in schools and corporations. Mahwah, NJ: Lawrence Erlbaum Associates.

Obler, L.K. 1982. The parsimonious bilingual. In L.K. Obler & L. Menn (eds.) *Exceptional language and linguistics.* New York: Academic Press.

Ohta, A. 2001. Second language acquisition processes in the classroom: Learning Japanese. Mahwah, NJ: Lawrence Erlbaum Associates.

Ortony A., Clore G.L., & Collins A. 1988. *The cognitive structure of emotions.* Cambridge: Cambridge University Press.

Ortony, A. 1980. Some psycholinguistic aspects of metaphor. In R. Honeck & R. Hoffman (Eds.), *Cognition and figurative language.* Hillsdale, NJ: Lawrence Erlbaum Associates.

Osgood, C. E., Suci, G. J., & Tannebaum, P.H. 1957. *The measurement of meaning.* Urbana: University of Illinois Press.

Paradis, M. 1981. Neurolinguistic organisation of a bilingual's two languages. In J. Copeland (ed.) *The Seventh LACUS Forum:* Columbia, SC: Hornbeam Press.

Paradis, M. 1989. Bilingual and polyglot aphasia. In F. Boller & J. Grafman (eds) *Handbook of Psychology, Vol. 2,* Amsterdam: Elsevier, 117-140.

Paradis, M. 1995. *Aspects of bilingual aphasia.* Oxford: Pergamon.

Paradis, M., Goldblum, M-C., & Abidi, R. 1982. Alternate antagonism with paradoxical translation behavior in two bilingual aphasic patients. *Brain and Language, 15*, 55-69.

Paradis, J., Nicoladis, E. & Genesee, F. 2000. Early emergence of structural constraints on code-mixing: Evidence from French-English bilingual children. *Bingualism: Language & Cognition, 3*, 245-261.

Parsons, T. 1967. *Sociological theory and modern society*. New York: Free Press.

Pavlenko, A. 1999. New approaches to concepts in bilingual memory. *Bilingualism: Language & Cognition, 2*(3), 209-230.

Pavlenko, A. 2000. New approaches to concepts in bilingual memory. *Bilingualism: Language & Cognition, 3(1)*, 1-4.

Peal, E. & W. E. Lambert. 1962. The relation of bilingualism to intelligence. *Psychological Monographs, 76*, 1-23.

Pearson, B.Z., Fernandez, S.C. & Oller, D.K. 1993. Lexical development in bilingual infants and toddlers. *Language Learning, 43*, 93-120.

Pearson, B.Z., Fernandez, S. & Oller, D.K. 1995. Cross-language synonyms in the lexicons of bilingual infants: one language or two? *Journal of Child Language, 22*, 345-368.

Peng, S.H. 1993. Cross-language influence on the production of Mandarin /f/ and /x/ and Taiwanese /h/ by native speakers of Taiwanese Amoy. *Phonetica, 50*, 245-260.

Petty, R.E., Wegener, D.T. & Fabrigar, L.R. 1997. Attitudes and attitude change. *Annual Review of Psychology, 48*, 609-647.

Perrault, C.R. 1990. An application of default logic to speech act theory. In Cohen, P.R, Morgan, J., & Pollack, M.E. (eds.) *Intentions in communication*. Cambridge: MIT Press.

Piaget, J. & Inhelder, B. 1966. *The psychology of the child*. New York: Basic Books.

Pienemann, M. 1998. Language processing and second language development. Amsterdam: Benjamins.

Pinker, S. 1995. *The language instinct*. New York Harper.

Pinker, S. 1998. Words and rules. *Lingua, 106*, 219-242.

Piske, T., MacKay, I.R.A. & Flege, J.E. 2001. Factors affecting degree of foreign accent in an L2: a review. *Journal of Phonetics, 29*, 191-215.

Poplack, S. 1980. Sometimes I'll start a sentence in Spanish y termino espanol: Toward a typology of code-switching. *Linguistics, 18*, 581-618.

Poplack, S. & Meechan, M. (eds) 1997. Instant loans, easy conditions: The productivity of bilingual borrowing. *International Journal of Bilingualism, 2* (2).

Poplack, S. & Meechan, M. 1997. Introduction: How languages fit together in code-switching. *International Journal of Bilingualism, 2* (2), 127-138.

Poplack, S. & Sankoff, D. 1988. Code-switching. In Ammon, U., Dittmar, N., & Mattheier, K.J. (eds.) *Sociolinguistics: An international handbook.* Berlin: Walter de Gruyter.

Poulisse, N. & Bongaerts, T. 1994. First language use in second language production. *Applied Linguistics, 15* (1), 36-57.

Poulisse, N. 1997. Language production in bilinguals. In A.M.B. de Groot & J.F. Kroll (eds) *Tutorials in bilingualism: Psycholinguistic perspectives.* Mahwah, NJ: Lawrence Erlbaum Associates, 201-224.

Poulisse, N. 1999. Slips of the tongue: Speech errors in first and second language production. Amsterdam: Benjamins.

Powers, W.T. 1973. *Behavior: The control of perception.* Chicago: Aldine.

Powers, W.T. 1978. Quantitative analysis of purposive systems: Some spadework at the foundations of scientific psychology. *Psychology Review, 85*(5), 417-435.

Price, C., Green, D., & von Studnitz, R. 1999. A functional imaging study of translation and language switching. *Brain, 122,* 2221-2235.

Quay, S. 1995. The bilingual lexicon: implications for studies of language choice. *Journal of Child Language, 22,* 2, 369-387.

Radford, A. 1992. *Transformational grammar: A first course.* Cambridge: Cambridge University Press.

Rampton, B. 1995. *Crossing: Language and ethnicity among adolescents.* Harlow: Longman.

Rampton, B. 1999. Sociolinguistics and cultural studies: New ethnicities, liminality and interaction. *Social Semiotics, 9,* 353-373.

Ranney, S. 1992. Learning a new script: An exploration of sociolinguistic competence. *Applied Linguistics, 13,* 1, 24-50.

Regev, I. 2004. Socio-pragmatic and psycholinguistic aspects of code-switching in bilingual discourse. Ph.D. Dissertation, Bar-Ilan University.

Reynolds, M. & Akram, M. 1998. The maintenance of Punjabi and Urdu in Sheffield. Paper presented at the 3rd International Conference on Language Maintenance of Minority Languages, Veldhoven.

Rice, M. & Wexler, K. 1996 Toward Tense as a Clinical Marker of Specific Language Impairment in English-speaking Children. *Journal of Speech and Hearing Research, 39,* 1239-1257.

Richards, B. 1987. Type/Token ratios: what do they really tell us? *Journal of Child Language, 14,* 201-209.

Rintell, E. 1981. Sociolinguistic variation and pragmatic ability: a look at learners. *International Journal of the Sociology of Language, 27,* 11-34.

Robertson, Richard J. & Powers, William T. (eds.). 1990. *Introduction to modern psychology: The control theory view.* New Canaan, CT: Benchmark Publications.

Rodriguez, R. 1982. Hunger of Memory: The Education of Richard Rodriguez. New York: Bantam Books.

Roelofs, A. 1992. A spreading activation theory of lemma retrieval in speaking. *Cognition, 42*, 107-142.

Rosansky, E. 1976. Methods and morphemes in second language acquisition research. *Language Learning, 26* (2): 409-25.

Roy, Cynthia B. 1999. *Interpreting as a discourse process*. Oxford: Oxford University Press.

Runkel, P. 1990. Casting Nets and Testing Specimens: Two Grand Methods of Psychology. New York: Praeger.

Sacks, H., Schegloff, Emanuel A., & Jefferson, G. (1974). A simplest systematics for the organization of turn-taking for conversation. *Language, 53,* 361-382.

Saiegh-Haddad, E. 2003. Linguistic distance and initial reading acquisition: The case of Arabic diglossia. *Applied Psycholinguistics, 24*, 431-451.

Sankoff, D. & Labov, W. 1979. On the uses of variable rules. *Language in Society, 8*, 189-222.

Sankoff, D. & Lessard, R. 1975. Vocabulary richness. *Science, 190*, 689-690.

Sankoff, D. 1998. A formal production-based explanation of the facts of code-switching. *Bilingualism: Language and Cognition, 1* (1), 39-50.

Santiago-Rivera & Altarriba, J. in press. The role of language in therapy with bilingual Spanish-speaking clients: Past contributions, contemporary perspectives, and future directions. *Professional Psychology: Research and Practice.*

Schachter, J. 1990. On the issue of completeness in second language acquisition. *Second-Language Research, 6*, 2, 93-124.

Schaerlaekens, A., Zink, I., & Verheyden, L. 1995. Comparative vocabulary development in kindergarten classes with a mixed population of monolinguals, simultaneous and successive bilinguals. *Journal of Multilingual and Multicultural Development, 16*(6), 490-495.

Schank, R. C. & Abelson, R. 1977. *Scripts, goals, plans, and understanding*. Hillsdale, NJ: Lawrence Erlbaum Associates.

Schiffrin, D. 1984. Jewish argument as sociability. *Language in Society, 13*, 311-335.

Schiffrin, D. 1987. *Discourse markers*. Cambridge: Cambridge University Press.

Schmidt, R. 1992. Psychological mechanisms underlying second language fluency. *Studies in Second Language Acquisition, 14*, 357-385.

Schneider, W. & Schiffrin, R. M. (1977) Controlled and automatic human information processing: I. *Psychological Review, 84*, 1-66.

Schoenfeld, W.N. 1974. Notes on a bit of psychological nonsense: Race differences in intelligence. *Psychological Record, 24*, 17-32.

Schrauf, B. & Rubin, D. C. 1998. Bilingual autobiographical memory in older adult immigrants: A test of cognitive explanations of the reminiscence bump. *Journal of Memory and Language, 39*, 437-457.

Schrauf, R.W. & D.C. Rubin. 2003. On the bilingual's two sets of memories. In R. Fivush and C. Haden (eds.). *Autobiographical memory and the construction of a narrative self: Developmental and cultural perspectives* (pp. 121-145). Lawrence Erlbaum Associates.

Schumann, J. 1997. The neurobiology of affect in language. *Language Learning, 48, Supplement 1.*

Scotton, C.M. 1986. Diglossia and code switching. In J.A. Fishman, A. Tabouret-Keller, M. Clyne, B. Krishnamurti & M. Abdul-Aziz (eds.) *The Fergusonian Impact. In Honor of Charles A. Ferguson. Volume II: Sociolinguistics and the Sociology of Language.* Berlin: Mouton de Gruyter, 403-415.

Scotton, C.M. 1988. Self-enhancing codeswitching as interactional power. *Language and Communication, 8*, 3-4, 199-211.

Searle, J.R. 1969. *Speech acts. An essay in the philosophy of language.* Cambridge: Cambridge University Press.

Searle, J.R. 1975 A taxonomy of illocutionary acts. In K. Gunderson (ed.) *Language, mind and knowledge.* Minneapolis, MI: University of Minnesota Press, pp. 344-369.

Segalowitz, N. 1986. Skilled reading in the second language, In J. Vaid (ed.) *Language processing in bilinguals: Psycholinguistic and neuropsychological perspectives.* Hillsdale, NJ: Lawrence Erlbaum Associates.

Segalowitz, N. 1991. Does advanced skill in a second language reduce automaticity in the first language? *Language Learning, 41*, 59–83.

Selinker, L. 1972. Interlanguage, *IRAL, 10*, 209-3.

Shallice, T. 1982. Specific impairments in planning. In D. Broadbent & L. Weiskrantz (eds.) *The neuropsychology of cognitive function.* London: The Royal Society.

Shallice, T. 1988. Specialization within the semantic system. *Cognitive Neuropsychology, 5* (1), 133-142.

Shannon, C.E. & Weaver, W. 1949. *The mathematical theory of communication.* Urbana, IL: University of Illinois Press.

Shlesinger, M. 2000. Strategic Allocation of Working Memory and Other Attentional Resources in Simultaneous Interpreting. Doctoral dissertation, Bar Ilan University, Israel.

Sholl, A. 1995. Animacy effects in picture naming and bilingual translation: Perceptual and semantic contributions to concept mediation. Ph.D. dissertation. University of Massachusetts, Amherst.

Sieratzki, J.S. & Woll, B., 1998. Toddling into language: Precocious language development in motor-impaired children with spinal muscular atrophy. In A. Greenhill, M. Hughes, H. Littlefield, H. Walsh (eds.), *Proceedings of the 22nd Annual Boston University Conference on Language Development, 2*, 684-694. Somerville, MA: Cascadilla Press.

Skoyles, J.R. 1998. Mirror neurons and the motor theory of speech. *Brain and Behavioral Sciences*, 21.

Smith, M.C. 1997. How do bilinguals access lexical information. In M.B. de Groot & J.F. Kroll (eds) *Tutorials in bilingualism: Psycholinguistic perspectives*. Mahwah, NJ: Lawrence Erlbaum Associates, 145-168.

Snow, C.E. 1993. Bilingualism and second language acquisition. In J. Berko-Gleason & N. Bernstein Ratner (eds.) *Psycholinguistics*. Fort Worth, TX: Harcourt, Brace & Jovanovich.

Spolsky, B. 1989. *Conditions for second language learning*. Oxford: Oxford University Press.

Stark, R. & P. Tallal. 1981. Selection of children with specific language deficits. *Journal of Speech and Hearing Disorders, 46*, 114-122.

Steffenson, M.S., Joag-Dev, C. & Anderson, R.C. 1979. A cross-cultural perspective on reading comprehension. *Reading Research Quarterly, 15*, 10-29.

Stein, N., & Glenn, C. 1979. An analysis of story comprehension in elementary school children. In R. Freedle (ed.) *New directions in discourse processing*, Volume 2, 53-120.

Stern, H.H. 1975. What can we learn from the good language learner? *Canadian Modern Language Review, 31*, 304-18.

Stets, J.E. & Burke, P.J. 2000. Identity theory and social identity theory. *Social Psychology Quarterly, 63*, 224-237.

Strange, W. 1992. Learning non-native phoneme contrasts: Interactions among subjects, stimulus, and task variables. In Y. Tohkura, E. Vatikiotis-Bateson, & Y. Sagisaka (eds.) *Speech Perception, Production and Linguistic Structure*. Tokyo: Ohmsha Ltd.

Stroop, J.R., 1935. Studies of interference in serial verbal reactions. *Journal of Experimental Psychology, 18*, 643–662.

Stuart Smith, J. & Martin, D. 1999. Developing assessment procedures for phonological awareness for use with Panjabi-English bilingual children. *International Journal of Bilingualism, 3*, 55-80.

Swain, M. 1972. *Bilingualism as a first language*. Ph.D. dissertation. University of California, Irvine.

Swales, J. 1990. *Genre analysis. English in academic and research settings*. Cambridge: Cambridge University Press.

Tabouret-Keller, A. 1995. Code-switching research as a theoretical challenge. In L. Milroy & P. Muysken, P. *One speaker, two languages: Cross-*

disciplinary perspectives on code-switching. Cambridge: Cambridge University Press.

Taeschner, T. 1983. *The sun is feminine.* Springer: Berlin

Tajfel, H. 1982. *Social identity and intergroup relations.* Cambridge: Cambridge University Press.

Tannen, D. 1989. Talking voices: repetition, dialogue, and imagery in conversational discourse. Cambridge: Cambridge University Press.

Thomason, S. & Kaufman, T. 1988. *Language contact, creolization, and genetic linguistics.* Berkeley, CA: University of California Press.

Tomasello, M. 1992. *First verbs. A case study of early grammatical development.* Cambridge: Cambridge University Press.

Tomasello, M. 2003. *Constructing a language: A usage-based theory of language acquisition.* Cambridge: Cambridge University Press.

Too, Y.L. 1995. The rhetoric of identity in Isocrates: Text, power, pedagogy. Cambridge: Cambridge University Press.

Toury, G. 1995. *Descriptive translation studies and beyond.* Amsterdam: John Benjamins.

Towell, R., Hawkins, R., & Bazergui, N. 1996. The development of fluency in advanced learners of French. *Applied Linguistics, 17,* 1, 84-119.

Turner, V. 1981. From ritual to theatre: The human seriousness of play. New York: PAJ Publications.

Ullman, M.T. 2001. The neural basis of lexicon and grammar in first and second language: the declarative/procedural model. *Bilingualism: Language & Cognition, 4,* 105-122.

Vaid, J. & Menon, R. 2000. Correlates of bilinguals' preferred language for mental computations. *Spanish Applied Linguistics, 4,* 2, 325-342.

Valdes, G. 1981. Code-switching as a deliberate verbal strategy: A microanalysis of direct and indirect requests among Chicano bilingual speakers. In R.P. Duran (ed.) *Latino language and communicative behavior.* Norwood, NJ: Ablex.

Van Heuven, W.J.B., Dijkstra, A., & Grainger, J. 1998. Orthographic neighborhood effects in bilingual word recognition. *Journal of Memory and Language* 39, 458-483.

Volterra, V., & Taeschner, R. 1978. The acquisition and development of language by bilingual children. *Journal of Child Language, 5,* 311-326.

Wadensjo, C. 1998. *Interpreting as interaction.* London: Longman.

Walters, J. 1979a. Strategies for requesting in Spanish and English: Structural similarities and pragmatic differences. *Language Learning, 29,* 113-128.

Walters, J. 1979b. The role of contextual factors in first and second language acquisition. In D.R. Omark & J.G. Erickson (eds.) *Communication*

Assessment of Bilingual Children. College Park, MD: University Park Press.

Walters, J. 1979c. Language variation in assessing bilingual children's communicative competence. In R. Silverstein (ed.) *Proceedings of the Third Annual Conference on Frontiers in Language Proficiency and Dominance Testing*. Carbondale, IL: Southern Illinois University, 293-305.

Walters, J. 1980. Grammar, meaning, and sociocultural appropriateness in second language acquisition. *Canadian Journal of Psychology, 34*, 337-345.

Walters, J. 1981. Variation in the requesting behavior of bilingual children. *International Journal of the Sociology of Language, 27*, 77-92.

Walters, J. 1990. A philosophical note on the nature of applied linguistics. *Issues in Applied Linguistics, 2*, 160-161.

Walters, J. 2001. Sociolinguistic and psycholinguistic considerations in language loss among bilinguals. In J. Klatter-Folmer & P. Van Avermaet (eds.) *Theories on maintenance and loss of minority languages. Towards a more integrated explanatory framework.* Munster/New York: Waxmann Verlag.

Walters, J. 2002. Two ways of studying bilingualism and affect. Paper presented at the Second Symposium on Bilingualism, Vigo, Spain, October 26-29.

Walters, J. ms. Codeswitching and pragmatic markers as indicators of affect in bilingual processing. Submitted for publication.

Walters, J. & Popko, D. 1997. Identity and language use: Case report of a Russian immigrant to Israel. Paper presented at EUROSLA 6, Dublin.

Walters, J. & Wolf, Y. 1986. Language ability, text content and order effects in narrative recall. *Language Learning, 36*, 47-64.

Walters, J. & Wolf, Y. 1988. Integration of first language material in second language comprehension. In J. Fine (ed.), *Second Language Discourse*. Norwood, NJ: Ablex.

Walters, J. & Wolf, Y. 1992. Metalinguistic integration under conditions of uncertainty: second language, metaphor and idiom comprehension. *Quantitative Linguistics, 13*, 1-105.

Walters, J., Kadry, A., Eisenhamer, M., Kramarski, B. & Rosenblum, T. 2003. Language, Mathematics, and Science Literacy among Israeli 15-year-olds. Final Project Report. Jerusalem: Israel Ministry of Education.

Wardaugh, R. 1998. *An introduction to sociolinguistics*. Oxford: Blackwell.

Waters, M.C. 1990. *Ethnic options: Choosing identities in America*. University of California Press.

Waugh, L. 1976. *Roman Jakobson's science of language*. Lisse: Peter de Ridder.

Weiner, N. 1950. The human use of human beings; cybernetics and society. Boston: Houghton Mifflin.

Weinreich, P. 1986. The operationalization of identity theory in racial and ethnic relations. In J. Rex & D. Mason (eds.) *Theory of race and ethnic relations.* Cambridge: Cambridge University Press.

Weinreich, U. 1953/1968. *Languages in contact.* The Hague: Mouton.

Wexler, P. 1991. The schizoid nature of Modern Hebrew. A Slavic language in search of a Semitic past. Wiesbaden: Otto Harrassowitz.

Wheeldon L.R. & Levelt, W.J.M. 1995. Monitoring the time course of phonological encoding. *Journal of Memory and Language, 34,* 3, 311-334.

White, L. & Genesee, F. 1996. How native is near native? The issue of ultimate attainment in adult second language acquisition. *Second Language Research, 12,* 233-265.

Wierzbicka, A. 1991. *Cross-cultural pragmatics.* Berlin: Mouton De Gruyter.

Wierzbicka, A. 1999. *Emotions across languages and cultures: Diversity and universals.* Cambridge, England: University Press.

Wiese, R. 1982. Remarks on modularity in cognitive theories of language. *Linguistische Berichte, 80,* 18-31.

Wiese, R. 1984. Language production in foreign and native languages: Same or different? In H.W. Dechert, D. Mohle, & M. Raupach. *Second Language Productions.* Tuebingen: Narr, 11-25.

Williams, G. 1995. Sociolinguistics: A sociological critique. London: Routledge.

Winford, D. 2002. *An introduction to contact linguistics.* Oxford: Blackwell.

Wolf, Y. 1995. Estimation of Euclidean quantity by 5- and 6-year-old children: Facilitating a multiplication rule. *Journal of Experimental Child Psychology, 59,* 49-75.

Woodworth, R.L. 1938. *Experimental psychology.* New York: Holt.

Wray, A. 2002. *Formulaic language and the lexicon.* Cambridge: Cambridge University Press.

Yngve, V. H. 1970. On getting a word in edgewise. *Papers from the Sixth Regional Meeting of the Chicago Linguistic Society.* Chicago: University of Chicago, Department of Linguistics. pp. 567-578.

Zampini, M.L. & Green, K.P. 2001. The voicing contrast in English and Spanish: The relationship between perception and production. In Janet Nicol (Ed.), *One mind, two languages: Bilingual language processing.* Cambridge, MA: Blackwell.

Zentella, A.C. 1997. Growing up bilingual: Puerto Rican children in New York. Malden, MA: Blackwell.

Zheng, L. 1997. Tonal aspects of code-switching. *Monash University Linguistics Papers, 1,* 53-63.

Author Index

Subject Index

175-176, 183, 186-187, 203, 256, 265, 270
hesitation phenomena/hesitations, 59, 69, 75, 81, 82, 95, 101, 142, 144, 157, 160, 165, 196, 203, 207, 209, 218, 223; see also false starts, pauses
humor, 94, 106, 109-111, 164 ; see also affect

I

identification, 14, 43-45, 144, 150-151, 170, 188, 205-206, 216, 223, 231, 243, 277; see also processes
identity; see social identity
Information Integration Theory/IIT, 32, 150, 184-186, 197, 205, 235, 274-275, 279
illocutionary force/point, 96, 102, 107, 111, 114, 130-137, 211, 216, 225, 247-250, 264; see also speech acts
imitation, viii-x, 14-15, 32, 42, 97, 101, 117, 131, 137, 149-152, 159, 169-177, 183-184, 188-189, 197, 204-208, 218-219, 223-226, 231, 234, 236, 243-244, 252, 266-269, 274; see also copying, mimesis
immigrant/immigration, 1, 14-15, 19, 47, 84-85, 87-88, 98, 103-106, 110-112, 115-116, 118-120, 123-124, 127-128, 135, 140, 146, 152, 154, 163, 173, 185-186, 197, 200-201, 206, 222, 238, 252-256, 258, 262, 267, 275, 277
-immigrant bilingual/s, 84-85, 88, 116, 222, 252

-immigrant identity 118, 163, 262
incompleteness, 13, 18, 34, 78, 81, 88, 138, 147, 199, 207-209
-and lemmas, 13, 18, 81, 138, 147, 208,
-and variability, 138, 147
Information Integration Theory, 32, 150, 184-185, 197, 205, 235, 274-275
inhibition/inhibitory, 20, 40, 61, 67-75, 87, 94, 191-192, 198, 205-206, 236,
integration, 150, 155-156, 159, 163-164, 169, 184-185, 188, 197, 204-205, 219, 261, 274-275; see also Information Integration Theory, processes
-integration mechanism/process, 150, 155-156, 159, 163-164, 169, 175, 186, 188-189, 197, 205, 219,
-and control, 156, 159, 169, 197, 205, 261, 274-275
-and idioms, 185-186, 197
-and metaphor, 185-187, 304
intentionality/intentions, viii-ix, 4-14, 16, 23, 92-96, 98, 101-102, 105, 107, 111-118, 131-138, 146, 148, 272-273, 276, 278
-goals and intentions, 72, 117, 118, 181, 196, 205, 211
-speaker intentions, 4, 7, 13, 39, 41, 59, 94-95, 113, 131, 138, 192, 200-201, 204, 247, 272
-and codeswitching, 200-201, 204-208
-and Green's model, 95, 192, 236, 272
-and language disturbances, 255, 257, 259, 262, 264-265, 267, 269